RIDDLES OF THE GOBI DESERT

RIDDLES OF THE GOBI DESERT

SVEN HEDIN

WITH 24 PLATES AND A MAP

GYAN

Published by

GYAN

Gyan Publishing House
5, Ansari Road
Daryaganj, New Delhi-110002
Phone: 011-47034999, 9811692060
E-mail: books@gyanbooks.com

Distribution Network
gyanbooks.com
India, USA, Canada, UK, Australia, France

ISBN : 978-81-212-3953-0 (PB)
First Published, London, 1933

2nd Impression 2020

Printed at: Gyan Press, Delhi.

Riddles of The Gobi Desert
Author: Sven Hedin

RIDDLES OF THE GOBI DESERT

BY

SVEN HEDIN

WITH 24 PLATES
AND A MAP

LONDON
GEORGE ROUTLEDGE & SONS, LTD.
BROADWAY HOUSE: 68–74 CARTER LANE, E.C.
1933

Lieberenz Photo

Mongol Woman

[front

CONTENTS

LIST OF ILLUSTRATIONS

PREFACE

IT is with both doubt and pride that I send this book to press. I have myself nothing of importance or interest to relate, and the little that I shall tell, for the sake of the continuity of the narrative and in discharge of my responsibility, about my own experiences has little or nothing to do with geographical research.

My part in the expedition has, in fact, been confined to organizing and leading the whole, to negotiating with the Central Government at Nanking and conferring with our friends in the scientific world of Peking, and to fitting out the various caravan parties with their staff, equipment, instruments and money. This, my personal responsibility for the success of the great expedition, has so fully occupied my time during the past two years that I have seen myself with regret compelled again and again to sacrifice my own wishes and to defer my departure for the solution of certain geographical problems.

I am proud to record in popular form the achievements of my comrades, the members of my staff, in natural science and archæology, by which they have brilliantly achieved so honourable a place among the scientific explorers of Central Asia. I hope that those Swedes who are chiefly interested in our year-long struggle to add to the stock of mankind's knowledge of the earth will understand that the material we have gathered is already immense and that the conception I have tried to convey of it cannot be otherwise than faint and meagre. For, to speak honestly, I myself am without a clear and penetrating view of all the conquests that have been made by so many hands and in departments to which I am a complete stranger. But I may also confidently assert that, when once these results have been placed before the world, they will build an imperishable monument to Swedish enterprise, tenacity and knowledge in our time.

At the time when this preface is being written, on the nineteenth anniversary of the declaration of the Republic in China, I sit awaiting a detailed report from Folke Bergman, our archæologist, who not long ago made discoveries in the midst of the Gobi Desert of unexpected magnitude and throwing new light on the old Han emperors' military operations and fortifications against the Turko-Mongolian Huns. I long eagerly for the opportunity to impart to the world the first intelligence of his epoch-making find.

So much for the expedition.

I have also to convey my thanks and those of my comrades to all those who have extended their understanding and sympathy to our work.

Our first duty is to offer our humble thanks to the King and to the Lindman Government for the powerful and liberal support afforded us in 1928 and 1929.

It is also a pleasure to us to present to the Crown Prince our warm thanks for the powerful and enlightened support he unceasingly has been pleased to afford by word and deed to our undertaking.

My sincere thanks to all my comrades for their loyalty and endurance and for the great confidence they have always showed me. I am convinced that they all agree with me when I say that we form a brotherhood united by exceptionally firm ties in our high collective aim.

My especial and cordial thanks are due to our Chinese friends in Peking, who during the past years have continually drawn closer to us and whose one desire is that we should not be harassed.

Several firms and individuals have kindly furnished us with gifts for our equipment. I beg to thank them all.

To Professor Bernhard Karlgren I am indebted for kindly assisting me with the spelling of the Chinese names in the Swedish edition of this book.

And in conclusion I wish to express my hearty thanks to my brother and sisters, who with wisdom, patience and love watched over the interests and affairs of the expedition from one centre, Stockholm, while I had the other, Peking, for my lot.

SVEN HEDIN.

PEKING, *October 10th*, 1930.

RIDDLES OF THE GOBI DESERT

INTRODUCTION

VAST, immeasurable, inmost Asia stretched westward in front of us when, in the summer of 1927, we started on the expedition through the Gobi Desert, the home of howling storms and oppressive silences, with new conquests in the service of exploration for our goal. Enigmatic, shrouded in mist, the horizon stretched its curves around us. Dizzy distances must be conquered by the slow, sure tread of the camels. From Peking in the east to the Caspian Sea in the west, our kingdom extended for 3,000 miles, and for 1,200 from Dzungaria to the Himalayas. We laid one territory after another under our sceptre; we established a system of depots from which neighbouring territories were traversed. The greatest continuous stretch of the earth's surface, whose innermost expanses lie furthest from the ocean, this formed our battleground.

Now, three years of severe struggle against the opposition of man and nature—against revolutionary and subversive political disturbances—lie behind us. We have already made extensive conquests and broken much new ground, but we can see ahead of us years of work upon problems yet unsolved.

Wherever we have turned our steps in this vast realm of deserts and mountains we have met with evidence of its marvellous past. Everywhere on the aged and wrinkled face of the earth it has left its traces. Our eyes rove over the pages of a gigantic book lying beneath our feet, and we seek to interpret its difficult and often obliterated inscriptions. The most ancient indications are interpreted by our geologists, whose task it is to trace the outlines of the earth's history in our chosen territory. The various strata are classified according to their period by our palæontologists who draw, from their hiding-places in the mountains, rich harvests of fossils of the vegetable and animal life which hundreds of millions of years ago lived and throve in what was then sea or marshy ground. Our meteorologists investigate the laws governing the path of the winds, to a height of 20,000 metres above the surface of the earth, and the interchange between the north-polar and equatorial currents. In co-operation with the geologists they investigate the effect of atmospheric movement on the shaping of the earth's solid crust, which suffers constant change, not only through climatically caused disintegration, but also in consequence of the secular undulating motion of its own mass. The picture that the earth's face presents to us in our own time, the result of all its past history, extending over periods of time beyond our comprehension, is reproduced on their maps by our topographers. Like the ruins of walls, fortresses and towers of a bygone age, jagged mountains rise out of the waste, and their snow-capped summits gaze out over the boundless deserts of Central Asia. The geographical features, mountains, lakes, rivers, springs and oases, are set down by our astronomers in their positions in the rectangular co-ordinates, and their height in metres above sea-level is indicated. By the growing speed of the pendulum oscillations our investigators also ascertain the form and mass of the earth, a problem which concerns not Asia alone but the whole of our planet.

We seek to interpret the eternal physical laws which, since the beginning of time, rule over the earth. Our thoughts turn giddy before this immense perspective. The life of man, animals and vegetables, as it appears to us in traversing the Gobi Desert and its adjacent mountains, embraces only a second in eternity. They are transient visitors upon the earth, a picture of impermanence. But they are nevertheless descendants of high ancestry, and their roots disappear in the distant past. Our botanists and geologists collect specimens from the vegetable and animal kingdoms, and we seek also, by anthropological measurements, to obtain the distinguishing marks of the various races.

Our imagination and our curiosity are also vividly appealed to by the origin and the wanderings of primitive man, his development and vicissitudes throughout the ages. The most ancient remains of primitive man were found in the neighbourhood of Peking, *Sinanthropus Pekinensis*, whose antiquity is estimated to be at least half a million and at most a million years. Perhaps future investigators will succeed in finding the remains of his forefathers who wandered on the earth several million years ago; yes, it may be that our own palæontologists will have the good fortune to contribute to the solution of this fascinating problem. Our archæologists have found tools and instruments of *Sinanthropus's* descendants—the neolithic or later stone-age man—who inhabited Gobi five thousand years ago, which can be counted in tens of thousands.

Yet one step, and we come to the legendary obscurity that preceded the dawn of historical times. In the oldest historical traditions of the Chinese, knowledge of the countries to the westward does not extend very far into the heart of the great continent. In the epic poems of the Hindus and their forefathers, the country to the north of India plays a certain part, and cosmographic and religious tradition in these are blended into pictures full of visionary poetry. Between India and Central Asia the Himalayas stand as an insurmountable wall, and beyond the snow-clad mountain masses and the misty draperies of monsoon clouds is concealed a world of sacred places and a pantheon of divine figures. Kailas and Manasarowar, the sacred mountain and the sacred lake, were early known. In the Buddhist cosmogony Meru was the venerable Olympus, which rises from the axis of the earth and constitutes the supporting pillar and centre of the universe. On Meru is Indra's heaven, with the abode of the gods and the home of the spirits. Brahma's city is situated on this mountain, which is sung in the greatest epic in the literature of the world, the Mahābhārata. A hundred years ago there were savants in Europe who believed that this Meru, which haunted the most ancient religious hymns and epic poems, signified the whole of Upper Asia, Tibet and High Tartary, but especially the mountains round the sacred lake and beyond the sources of the Indus and the Ganges. In the seas about Meru lie four world islands, of which the southernmost, Jambūdvīpa, is India with Buddhgayā, and the Bodhi Tree, in its midst.

For the West, that part of the world where our Swedish expedition has been working for three years in co-operation with learned Chinese, has slowly and laboriously emerged from the legendary darkness of the East. Herodotus related that India was the uttermost eastward boundary of the known world, while the northern boundary touched upon the country of the Hyperboreans. Alexander knew that India was bounded on the north by gigantic mountains—indeed he himself twice marched with armies over the Hindu Kush and showed that the Indus proceeds from the mighty range whose name, Himalaya or Abode of Winter, first became known to the people of Europe two thousand years later. Strabo knew that the sources of the Ganges were to be sought in *Emōdi montes*, but Pliny says that they lie in the mountains of Scythia. Basing himself on information derived from Marinus of Tyrus and on conceptions handed down from the geographical system of Eratosthenes and Strabo, Ptolemæus erected a meridional *Imaus mons* that divided Scythia *intra Imaum montem* from Scythia *extra Imaum montem*, as well as a latitudinal *Imaus mons* situated to the south of this, forming a boundary wall between the Scythians in the north and the Aryan Indians in the south. Mela and Pliny knew the Seres, a people who dwelt in secluded peace and plenty by the shores of the eastern sea. Ptolemæus uses the names, Sera, Serice and Sinæ. Sin, Chin, Sinæ and Seres are old names for that engimatic China which in the Middle Ages was called Cathay. It probably derives the name Sin or Chin from the name of the Tsin dynasty. From the legendary land of the Seres in the East the longest caravan route on earth, the Silk Route, carried to the polite world and the imperial court of Rome the noble silk sung by Virgil.

Here we are treading everywhere on classic ground. We

are constantly reminded of historical events and often find their traces. Peoples and tribes of various race and origin have succeeded one another as rulers over kingdoms which have been founded, have flourished, have fallen and have been obliterated. Here influences from China, India, Greece, Persia and the mist-wrapped country of the Scythians have left their mark upon the arts. Hence migrations have set forth, here barbarian hordes have warred against each other, captains have led their hosts through these wastes to force the countries of the west into allegiance to the Son of Heaven. Here conquered races and fleeing armies have drooped from thirst and left their dead behind them. By their caravans, merchants, pilgrims, couriers and travellers with deathless names have maintained the connexion between east and west. And vast as is this territory which is now step by step conquered by our expedition, it forms only a part of the enormous kingdom whose peoples and races, seven hundred years ago, obeyed the slightest whim of the world conqueror, Chingis Khan.

We are walking in the tracks of innumerable fore-runners. Already in the days of the elder Han dynasty, under the great Emperor Wu Ti, 140 to 87 B.C., the Chinese were in alliance with the countries to the west of Bolor. In the year 122, Chang Ch'ien led an expedition to Bactria, and speaks of India. Some sixty years before the birth of Christ, the dominion of the Chinese extended over the whole of Eastern Turkistan where they counted fifty-five states, and they had vassals in Transoxania and Bactriana. In the first century A.D. the Chinese commanders, Pan Ch'ao, Li Kuang-li and Li Ling, marched westward and made war upon the kingdoms of Central Asia, upon Hsiung-nu, the Huns and the people of Yüeh-chih, who were compelled to pay tribute. The General-Protector Pan Ch'ao is commonly said to have marched to the westward of Ts'ung-ling or the Onion Mountain, Pamir; and Ta Ch'in, the Roman Kingdom, is mentioned in the annals of Han. At the time of the later Han dynasty there are accounts of musicians and jugglers from Ta Ch'in who came to Burma. There were then already four routes to the west, namely from Tung-huang by Cherchen and Khotan, from Tung-huang by Kurla, Kucha and Aqsu, from Hami by Turfan and Kucha, and from Hami by Barköl, skirting the northern foot of Tien Shan. In the years 265–290 Wu Ti of Western Chin re-united the previously divided China and sought afresh to lay the Tarim territory under its dominion. As a continuation of the old great wall he built a new wall with watch towers extending to the region beyond Su-chou, as a protection against the barbarians. The great Emperor T'ai Tsung of the T'ang dynasty, in 643, laid innermost Asia under his sceptre and extended his dominion southward around the Hindu Kush and to the Caspian Sea. To him came ambassadors from Byzantium with rubies, emeralds and other treasure. The conquests of the Tibetans and the Arabs, 670–692, made an end of this Chinese dominion of Inner Asia, and China was once more cut off from the countries of the West.

In the last-named year they recovered power over " the four garrisons " of Kashgar, Khotan, Kucha and Qara Shahr. In the year 694, the first harbingers and pilgrims of Manicheeism came to China and had their cave temple near Turfan.

Long ere the West had any notion about the geography of Central Asia, the Chinese were thus well acquainted with the limitless deserts and their oases. A succession of Buddhist pilgrims contributed to this knowledge by their pious pilgrimages westward through Gobi and over the mountains round Pamir to India. One of them, Fa Hsien, made his journey, renowned even in the West, in the years 399–414. Buddhism had reached China in the first half of the third century before Christ. Fa Hsien was a devout Buddhist who made pilgrimage to the Holy places. He says of the Gobi Desert, where we several times crossed his route: " In this desert is a great multitude of evil spirits and also of hot winds; those who meet with them perish to the last man. Here there are fair birds above and beasts below. Gazing in every direction as far as the eye can reach to discover the path, one finds no guidance except from the mouldering bones of the dead that mark the way."

Now, one thousand five hundred years later, it is we who listen to the voices of the evil spirits and, just as little as he, allow ourselves to be hindered by the winds which in the summer sweep hot across "the flying sand," and in winter come driving with icy cold. Like him we visit the country of Shan-shan, where the king of that time had embraced the teaching of Buddha, and where four thousand priests performed the rites of Hīna-yāna in regions where the servants of Islam now call their "Allahu Akbar" from the minarets. Qara Shahr, one of the bases of our journeys in the last three years, was visited by Fa Hsien in order to continue thence his pilgrimage to Khotan, to witness the ceremonial processions in which the image of Buddha was carried on a car decked with gold and precious stones, fluttering streamers and embroidered canopies. He speaks of the King's new cloisters which rose in splendid majesty eight *li* outside the town and whose erection had needed the reigns of three kings. To this period belong several of the antiquities which more than thirty years ago I brought home from Khotan and which are now displayed in the East Asiatic Collections in Stockholm. He visits Kashgar and from Bolor-tagh gives an account of the poisonous dragons which belch forth poisoned winds and of the "people of the snow mountains."

How marvellously enticing the old accounts sound in our ears as we rock across the windswept dunes in the pilgrims' obliterated tracks, imagining that we hear the bells ringing in the caravan of the greatest of all the pilgrims, Hsüan Tsang, as, in the time of T'ang (628–645), he performed his pious journey through the shifting sands of Gobi and over the mountains into India and back to China.

From the West the Arabs, beneath the green banner of the Prophet, penetrated into the heart of Asia. In the ninth century one of the leaders of the holy war conquered Kuteibe, Bokhara, Samarqand, Khwarizm, Ferghana and Kashgar, thus beginning the victorious march of Islam over Inner Asia, where to this day it holds sway over the people of the Oases.

The Christian gospel early made its way into these far off and almost inaccessible parts. It is said that the Word was first preached in China in the second century, Saint Thomas and Bartolomeus being named as the first apostles. In the year 420 a metropolitan appears in Merv. In the ninth century, when the Nestorians came to China, David was their metropolitan, and there were Christians in Hang-chou in 878. On the famous Si-ngan stone, which was discovered in 1625, it is said that the missionary Olupun came to China from Ta Ch'in, in the year 635, with holy books and images. Three years later the Emperor T'ai Tsung took, by edict, the new teaching under his protection. Later the Nestorian torches were extinguished, but were again lighted in the days of the Yüan dynasty.

In the year 1245, Innocent IV summoned a council against Christendom's enemy the Great Khan and the descendants of Chingis Khan, who threatened to conquer the whole world. In the same year the Pope sent the Franciscan monk Plano Carpini to Kuyuk Khan at Kara-korum, and eight years later Rubruck followed to the court of Mangu Khan in the same city. They were the first to send reports to Europe of far Cathay, a name which during the Middle Ages signified China and, under the form Kitai, was employed by many Central Asiatic peoples and is still used by the Russians, Sarts and Kirghiz.

Immediately after Rubruck, Hayton I, King of Lesser Armenia, journeyed to the court of Mangu Khan and was received by the Great Khan Batu at Karakorum. His return journey lay through Dzungaria, Samarqand, Bokhara, Khorasan and Tabrīz. He describes Buddhism, calling Buddha, Shakemonia, and Maidari, Madri. On China he makes some very pertinent comments.

> "The Empire of Cathay is the greatest on the surface of the earth and it has an abundant population and unlimited riches. . . . In this Kingdom of Cathay there are more notable and singular things than in any other kingdom in the world. The people of this country are excessively full of cunning and subtlety and despise the knowledge of other nations in all kinds of art and science."

As we move westward we cross the routes of the old travellers again and again, and often think of the descriptions that they left in their scanty writings. Towering above all the rest rises the figure of Marco Polo. His narratives of travel are the finest that have survived from the Middle Ages, and none of the old travellers can compare with him in keen power of observation, wisdom and humour. His description of Cathay is a masterpiece, and his account of the deserts, which we too crossed six hundred and sixty years after his time, are veracious and apt, even if sometimes adorned with legendary beings.

There were many other Europeans in China in Marco Polo's time, but of them nothing is known. He himself mentions a German engineer who assisted the Emperor Kublai Khan with his artillery.

In the Kingdom of Cascar, Marco Polo visited the capital city, its orchards and vineyards. He also went to Yarcan and Cotan and found these realms and provinces under the dominion of the Great Khan and worshipping Mohammed, and he met everywhere with Nestorian Christians. In the province of Charchan he notes the rivers that produce jasper and chalcedony, which are sold at a great price in China. All around stretches the sandy waste into which the inhabitants take flight when armies invade the country. It is impossible to find the fugitives "for the wind immediately blows sand over their tracks."

In five days he comes to the city of Lop in the province of the same name, a district which our expedition explored more thoroughly than any before us. Marco Polo relates :

> "Lop is a great city on the edge of the desert which is called the Lop Desert, and is situated between east and north-east. It belongs to the Great Khan, and the people worship Mohammed. Such persons as design to cross the desert take a week's rest in this city to refresh themselves and their cattle, and then prepare themselves for the journey, taking with them a month's provision for man and beast. After leaving this city they enter into the desert.
>
> "The length of this desert is so great that it is said to take a year and more to ride from one end of it to the other. And here, where its width is least, it takes a month to cross it. It

is entirely composed of hills and valleys of sand and there is nothing to eat in it. But after having ridden a day and a night one finds fresh water, enough maybe for about fifty or a hundred persons and their beasts, but not for more. And across the whole desert water is to be found in the same manner, that is to say there is good water in about twenty-eight places in all, but not in great quantity, and in four places besides there is brackish water.

"No animals are found there, for there is nothing for them to eat. But a notable thing is told of this desert, which is that, if travellers be on the march by night and any of them chance to fall behind or to fall asleep or the like, then, when he attempts to overtake his company again, he hears spirits speaking and believes them to be his travelling companions. Sometimes the spirits call him by name, and then a traveller often is led astray, so that he never finds his company. And in this manner many have been lost. Even in the daytime these spirits are heard speaking. And sometimes one will hear the sound of a multitude of divers instruments of music and yet oftener the sound of drums. When one undertakes this journey it is therefore customary for the travellers to keep close together. All the beasts also have bells about their necks so that they cannot so easily go astray. And when they encamp they set up a signal to show the direction of the next march.

"Thus it is to cross the desert."

No doubt Marco Polo himself heard the strange sound which arises when the wind soughs across the crests of the dunes, and was willing to believe the legendary tales that were served up to him. In truth something enigmatic lies over the desert, where the silence is broken by strange sounds and where the traveller, gripped by the lifelessness which everywhere prevails and with the help of his aroused imagination, peoples the desert spaces with supernatural beings. None has described this impression more tellingly or more dramatically than Marco Polo. As one follows his tracks through the desert and reads his thoughts and memories, one easily falls to wondering *how* he travelled, how he was equipped and how the caravans were organized at that time. Probably these desert crossings were arranged in the same way as now. What he says himself is that the travellers kept together in a compact string, that the camels, for only such could cross the desert, carried bells, just as they do to-day, and that, probably only when the visibility was poor, they set out marks, as buoys are set in a fairway, so as not to lose the direction. It is evident that visibility was bad, for he never mentions the high mountains to the southward, nor did he ever see or hear tell of the lake of Lop Nor.

For Hami, an oasis which played an important part in our destiny, Marco Polo uses the Mohammedan East-Turkish name Comul and says that this province lies between two deserts.

He speaks, too, of the province of Chingintalas, which is identified as the district around Barköl.

> " After ten days one comes to another province called Sukchur, in the which are numerous towns and villages. The principal town is called Sukchu (Su-chou). The people are in part Christian and in part idolaters, and all are subject to the Great Khan.
>
> " When one leaves the town of Campichu (Kan-chou), one rides twelve days, after which one comes to a town called Etsina, which lies to the north, on the edge of the sand desert; it appertains to the province of Tangut. The people are idolaters and have a multitude of camels and of cattle, and the land produces a number of good hawks. . . . The inhabitants live by their husbandry and their cattle, for they have no commerce. In this town a man must needs furnish himself with provisions for forty days, for when he has left Etsina, he enters upon a desert which stretches forty days' journey to the northward, wherein he meets with no human dwelling or pasturage. In the summer one may, in fact, meet people, but in winter the cold is too severe. Also one meets with wild beasts and wild asses in great numbers. . . ."

Almost all the towns he names in the heart of Asia have been visited by members of our expedition, and most of our young Swedish explorers have copies of Marco Polo's famous book in their travelling libraries. I have myself two in English, one in French and one in German. We have crossed his deserts in many directions and have suffered many of the vicissitudes and adventures that he clothes in so poetic a glamour of romance.

In the beginning of the fourteenth century several

bishops and missionaries were sent out to the Far East. Thus the Franciscan monk John of Monte Corvino became Archbishop of Khanbalik or Cambalu, Peking, and died in 1328.

In the years 1342 to 1346 John Marignolli was Papal Legate at the Court of Peking, a city also described by Odorico de Pordenone.

Between 1325 and 1355 the Moor Ibn Batuta carried out his celebrated travels in Africa and Asia. In his time one travelled more safely in China than in our days. He says:

> "China is the safest as also the most agreeable of all the regions of the earth for a traveller. You can make the whole nine months' journey, which is the extent of the kingdom, without the least occasion for fear, even if you have treasure in your keeping. For at every resting-place there is an inn under the superintendence of an officer, who is stationed there with a detachment of horse and foot. Every evening at sunset, or rather at nightfall, this officer visits the inn accompanied by his secretary; he records the name of every stranger who is to spend the night there, seals the list and locks the inn door. In the morning he returns with his secretary, calls out the names and marks them off one by one. Then he sends with the travellers a person whose duty it is to escort them to the next station and to bring back with him from the officer in command there a written acknowledgment of the arrival of all of them; otherwise this person is held responsible. Such is the custom in China at all stations from Sin-ul-Sin to Khanbaliq (Canton to Peking). In the inns the travellers find all needful provision, particularly fowls and geese. But mutton is scarce."

After 1350 the journeys to China of the missionaries and merchants ceased, and it was not till a century and a half later that the Portuguese and Spaniards steered their course to the Far East. Still later came the Jesuits from Rome, and opened new perspectives for European exploration in China.

The Emir Timur Gurigan, "The Magnificent," Tamerlane, the last conqueror of gigantic dimensions, having laid all Western Asia under his sceptre, turned his gaze upon the eastern half of the continent. He wished to re-open the Silk Route to China and despatched his Tartars to explore the Gobi Desert east of Khotan. They reported that it was two months' march from Khotan to Kambalu or Peking. He had heard in his youth of Gobi and Mongolia, and one of his consorts was the daughter of the Mongolian Khan. Now, in his old age, he dreamed of breaking through the Great Wall that protected Cathay. He was sixty-nine years old. At the palace of Dilkusha in Samarqand he received the Mongolian princes and the envoys of the Emperor of China, and in 1403 gave audience to Ruy Gonzalez de Clavijo, ambassador of Henry III of Castile. At the audience the envoys from China were made to sit below Clavijo because they came from "a thief and a base man." This "base man," however, was the great Ming Emperor, Yung Lo, who built a considerable part of the city wall of Peking and whose splendid tomb may be admired to this day not far from the Nankou pass. Then Tamerlane spoke to the Emirs, saying that he had conquered the whole of Asia excepting China, which now at last would be an easy prey. At the head of an army of 200,000 men, which he considered enough for the conquest of China, he marched across the ice of Sir-darya, intending to use the northern route to Cathay. Otrar was selected for winter quarters, and in the spring the march was to begin against the Emperor of China, a monarch no less magnificent and powerful than that Sultan Bayezid of Turkey whom he had conquered two years earlier. In March, 1405, the great war drums summoned the troops to march. But Timur's white horse bore no rider in its saddle under the victorious banner. He lay dying in his tent. But before his last hour struck, he gave the Emirs orders to continue the march against Cathay and to carry on the campaign.

It was just at the start of this never accomplished campaign that the sage and observant Clavijo brought greetings from his king to the ruler in Samarqand. His journey falls between the years 1403 and 1406.

In Abd-ur-razzak's description of the embassy from Tamerlane's son, Shah Rukh, to the Emperor of China (1419–22), we find mention of many of the places and deserts which our expedition visited and traversed five hundred years later.

The embassy consisted of 510 members. They set out from Herat in Khorasan. On the way to Kamul (Hami), where they found a Buddhist Temple, they were met by the Chinese envoy. It took twenty-five days to cross the great desert. There they saw a wild camel and a wild yak. On the boundary of China proper a new reception took place. Then there was desert again till they reached the fortress of Karaul (guard post) in a mountain pass, where all were counted and recorded before they were allowed to proceed. The first town on the other side of the desert was Sukchan (Su-chou), where they were lodged in the great Yam-Khaan or gatehouse by the town gate.

On the 14th of December, 1420, they reached the gate of Peking before daybreak, and then follows a description of the reception they encountered from the Son of Heaven. On the 18th of May, 1421, the ambassadors left Peking, and on the 1st of September did homage to their lord Shah Rukh and delivered their report to him.

The lettered and learned Mussulmans who were subject to Timur's descendants undoubtedly had a far clearer conception of the Central Asiatic route to China than had contemporary Europe, which was as yet unaware of Marco Polo's wonderful journey. Columbus, however, was seeking a shorter way to Marco Polo's Cathay and the Island of Cipangu (Japan). He discovered America, but supposed himself to have come to the eastern coasts of Asia.

In past centuries not only Europeans but Mohammedans too have trodden our lonely desert ways in great numbers without a word having been preserved about their wanderings. During a thousand years countless caravans have traversed Gobi and Central Asia without a line having been recorded by the travellers who journeyed with them. And why, for example, should the merchants who, both before and after Marco Polo's time, travelled between Peking and Samarqand, pay attention to anything beyond their commerce and their gains? Yet occasionally a chance echo from the depths of the desert penetrates to European ears. Thus, about 1550, the Persian, Hadji Mohammed, relates to Giovanni Battista Ramusio that he has been in Succuir (Su-chou) and in Kampion (Kan-chou), and that he accompanied a trading caravan to these towns. The last named town has so wide a wall that four carriages can drive abreast along its top, and Su-chou is a great town with brick houses and temples; silk, pears, apples, apricots, peaches, melons and grapes are cultivated there, and rhubarb in the adjacent high mountains. He reckons the journey from Su-chou to Hami at fifteen days and that from Hami to Turfan at thirteen.

A very notable and celebrated traveller whose ways our expedition often followed, and in whose headquarters we stayed, is Benedict Goes. He was born in the Azores in 1561, and, in 1594, accompanied the missionaries to India. With the assistance of the great Shah Akbar, he left Lahore in the spring of 1603. He was commissioned by the missionaries in Goa to find out whether China was the same country as Marco Polo's Cathay. He travelled in company with a great caravan, reached Kashgar, Aqsu, Kucha and Qara Shahr, where he made a sojourn of three months and where he came to know that Cathay and China were the same country, and that Cambalu was Peking. He stayed a month in Turfan, and one in Camul or Hami. At the end of 1605 he reached Sucieu (Su-chou), with five servants, two coolies and thirteen animals as well as his travelling companion, the Armenian, Isak. He apprised Father Matteo Ricci in Peking of his arrival. The latter and the other Jesuits in Peking had already received intelligence from India of the approach of Brother Goes and now, in November, 1606, rejoiced to have news from himself. From Su-chou to Peking was counted four months' journey. On the 12th of December, 1606, Father Ricci sent a Christian, Johan Ferdinand, to meet Goes. The latter had two months' travel from Si-nan and arrived at the end of March, 1607. He found Brother Benedict sick unto death. Benedict cried happily: "Nunc dimittis servum tuum Domine!" He read the letter of the Peking Jesuits and held it all night against his heart, thinking that now his pilgrimage was ended. Johan Ferdinand did all in his power to save him and bring him with him to Peking, but eleven days after Johan Ferdinand's arrival, Goes died at Su-chou and was buried there. Immediately after his death the Mohammedans threw themselves upon his property.

> "This they did in the most brutal fashion, but none of the damage they occasioned was so lamentable as the destruction of his journal, which he had kept in the minutest detail. Shortly before his death, he wrote warning our members in Peking never to put trust in the Mohammedans, and also advised decidedly against any future attempts to travel by the way he had come, as being both perilous and unprofitable."

It was only after several months of vexations both from Mohammedans and Chinese that Johan Ferdinand and Isak were able to return to Peking, where they later set down their recollections for Father Matteo, "with the aid of some papers of Benedict's."

What would not the explorers of our time give for the diary of Goes? It was quite certainly burned by the Mohammedans immediately after his death. Doubtless many other journals have met the same unhappy fate. Marco Polo's memoirs were preserved for posterity almost by chance. The journal of Bengt Oxenstierna, which was begun in the year that Goes died, has been traced far back in time, but has never been recovered.

During four and a half centuries the geography of our districts slowly and step by step crept forward on the Europeans' map picture of the greatest continent. On Fra Mauro's map, 1457, we meet for the first time with the name Tebet and on this, too, appear the names Cina and India Terza. In Jacopo Gastaldi, 1561, we recognize Marco Polo's experiences. A double mountain range divides India from Diserto de Camul, the desert of Hami, which we traversed with our great caravan in the autumn and winter of 1927, and to the north of this he has Diserto de Lop, and he has adopted several others of Marco Polo's names, Ciarcian, Cashar, Colan and others. In the Sala della Sardo in the Doge's Palace, Giacomo Gastaldi, in the middle of the seventeenth century, painted a map of Asia in fresco. This was damaged by fire and was restored by Grisellini in 1762. In this we find Camul (Hami), south of the Himalayas, Cataio Provincia (China), Tangut, Diserto de Lop and Thebeth. The great cartographer Gerhard Mercator, Ortelius, Hondius and others do not increase our knowledge in any essential degree. In 1695, in Coronelli, the well-known names from Marco Polo's route recur, as well as Acsu and Tibet or Tobbot. Father Verbiest acquired much knowledge of Eastern Tartary from his travels during 1682 and 1683, and, from his journey through Eastern Mongolia between 1688 and 1698, the wise Father Gerbillon obtained a conception of the extent of Greater Tartary, and he left a good description of the route from Koko-nor to Lhasa, but no maps. In the years 1692 to 1694 Isbrants Ides travelled with the embassy through Siberia to China and located Desertum Lob by the upper reach of the Irtish.

The publication of Guillaume Delisle's map, which appeared in 1723, marks a giant stride forward in Europe's knowledge of Central Asia. We find there the Tanla mountains and Kunlun. In Eastern Turkistan he has no rivers and no Lop Nor, but he has a multitude of other names.

In *Histoire Genealogique des Tartares*, Leyden, 1726, are found maps giving, in our district, the names Aksu, Katsha, Luczin, Turfan, Chamill (Hami) and the Tarim, which falls into a great lake north of Turfan, while the mountains which bound its basin to the south are called Mus Tag.

Without doubt the deepening knowledge of Eastern Turkistan is derived from the Swedish officers in Siberia. When, in his old age, the Emperor K'ang Hsi wrote to the Governor of Siberia, praying him to send a physician to Peking, the Tsar Peter took the opportunity to send the English doctor Garwin as a member of a whole embassy. The leader of this mission was the Swede Lorenz Lange, who had entered the Russian service and, between 1715 and 1737, had made four journeys from Russia to Peking and had essentially contributed to the establishment of Russo-Chinese commerce. He travelled by Tobolsk, Tomsk, Kyakhta, Urga and Kalgan. The years 1721–2 brought him to Peking, where he heard tell of Dalai Lama, who dwelt in Potala in the Kingdom of Tangut, on a high mountain to the south of the Zamo Desert. He also conceived that China's trade with India was prevented by impassable sandy deserts.

One of the most notable maps of Asia produced in the last century was constructed by the Swedish Lieutenant Colonel, Philipp Johan von Strahlenberg. It marks a milestone in Europe's complete knowledge of Northern and Central Asia. Strahlenberg was born in Stralsund in 1676, remained in Siberia for thirteen years after Pultava, returned to Sweden in 1723 and died there in 1747. In Tobolsk, where he spent most of his captivity, he gathered information from the Tatars and also obtained help from his countrymen, Captain Johan Anton Matern and Lieutenant Colonel Petter Schönström. He was never in Central Asia himself. His books, *Das Nord-und-Ostliche Theil von Europa und Asia* and *Historie der Reisen in Russland, Siberien und der grossen Tartarey*, appeared in Stockholm and Leipzig in 1730.

Adolf Nordenskiöld, who had as thorough a knowledge of Siberia as of cartographical history, says of Strahlenberg's map that it is a valuable original work, in which a man with a knowledge of cartography has combined personal observations with all that was known in his time about these regions. The first copy was completed in 1721, before Strahlenberg returned home from captivity. "It was sent to a merchant of Moscow, but when he died soon afterwards, the map chanced to be shown to the Tsar Peter, who did not return it." But Strahlenberg had retained the original sketch and completed it with his own observations, and it was published in the first of the two books I have mentioned.

Among other places in our region, he is aware of Provincia Chamyl (Hami), Provincia Turfan, Lukzin, Urumtza, Musart, Regnum Chotan and all the towns in Eastern Turkistan and several of the rivers, though not Tarim or Lop Nor. He knows Goby or Xamo, Ordus, Mungales, Tumet, the Great Wall, Urga, Koko-Kota (Kuei-hua-ch'êng), Kalgan, Mungalia with its people, Mungalos and so forth.

Another of our Swedish forerunners in the extension of knowledge of Dzungaria and Eastern Turkistan was the lieutenant of artillery, Johan Gustaf Renat, who also was imprisoned by the Tsar Peter after Pultava. On an expedition in 1715 and 1716, he was taken captive by the Kalmuks, taught them to cast cannon and shells, became commander in chief of their troops and, having collected gold, silver and precious stones, returned in 1733 through Siberia and Russia to Sweden.

His surprisingly correct and well-drawn map of Dzungaria and Eastern Turkistan, a territory which is now covered by the name Sinkiang and which constitutes one of our principal fields of labour, was discovered in 1879 by August Strindberg in the diocesan library at Linköping. Two hundred years before, it had aroused keen interest in the Benzelius brothers. Now, when we know so well the geography of these regions and have begun to explore in detail, we are perhaps even more astonished to find so very old a map agreeing in its main features so closely with the reality. Strindberg relates that, in March, 1735, Bishop Eric Benzelius wrote from Linköping to his brother Gustaf Benzelstierna in Stockholm requesting him to remind Lieutenant Renat of his promise to send him a copy of *Charta Geographica Calmachorum*. He adds that he recorded his conversation with Renat at Linköping. "Without interrogating him, one can get nothing out of him, for he has no learning at all. May God give you time, my dear brother, to speak to him."

Perceiving that the map was of the greatest interest to the Russians, Strindberg sent it to the Geographical Society of Petersburg, where it was published by General O. E. von Stubendorff.

This map is admirable. In particular, the hydrographic system of Eastern Turkistan is more correctly indicated than in any earlier map. There is Kashgar with its river, Yerekon (Yarkend) with its river, and Kiria with its. Below the name Kiria is written in Swedish: "Here is gold." He calls the Tarim simply Daria. Acksu, strangely enough, appears with no river, while the towns by Chaidu are missing. Läp, Lop Nor, lies in the northern part of the Lop Desert, just as in the Chinese maps. It is also interesting to observe that he makes a river, Bolansiu, coming from the East, flow into the eastern part of Lop Nor. This river is, of course, Bolundsir-gol, the Sulo-ho of the Chinese, which, now at least, does not reach so far west. In Carangoj, a forest tract north of Lop Nor, Renat has the legend: "In Inur forest are found wild camels." The Russians consider that, in certain respects, Renat's map is better than Klaproth's famous map of 1836, for example in the drawing of Balkash and Issiq-köl. One can sit by the hour staring at this map and marvelling at the patience and acuteness it displays. To us Swedes now working in these regions it is of peculiar interest that a map of Dzungaria, the Tarim basin and Northern Tibet, so admirable for its time, should have been produced two hundred years ago by a Swedish man.

In 1708 the Emperor K'ang Hsi ordered the Jesuits in Peking, who were learned in the mathematical and astronomical sciences and therefore enjoyed the Emperor's admiration and favour, to prepare a general map of the whole of his enormous realm. And, with the help of existing maps of the several provinces, a map of China proper was actually produced. Only the dependency of Tibet, the domain of the Dalai Lama, was wanting. But the Emperor had already sent an embassy to the lamaistic Pope at Lhasa, and the ambassadors, who remained two years in Tibet, had received orders to prepare a map of "all the countries which immediately appertain to the Grand Lama." In 1711 the material was delivered to Father Regis, but he was not satisfied with it, and the Emperor then sent two Chinese Lamas, well skilled in the use of topographical instruments, with instructions to prepare a new map of Tibet from Koko-nor to Lhasa and to the sources of the Ganges, and to bring thence in sealed flasks some of the water of the sacred river.

After the return of the Chinese topographers, the material was elaborated by the Jesuits on the same principles that they had applied to the preparation of the sheets representing China proper. A map of Tibet was completed in three sheets, admirable in many respects and of a certain historical importance, for it includes in correct co-ordinates and under their right Tibetan names both Mount Everest and Gaurisankar.

This gigantic work became known through d'Anville, to whom the Jesuits sent the groundwork.

Our interest in this famous map is confined to the Province of Sinkiang in which Eastern Turkistan is not nearly so well rendered as in that of the Swede Renat. Two great rivers, Hayitou-mouren from west to east and Rivière d'Yerghien from south-west to north-east, unite and immediately thereupon run into Lop Nor. At its termination Hotomni-Solon-mouren bears the legend : "*Cette rivière se perd dans les Sables de ce Desert de même que plusieurs autres.*" On the same river lies Hotom or Khotan, but all places to the east of Khotan are wanting.

Etshine-mouren, our old River Etsin-gol, discharges into two lakes, Soukouc-nor and Sopou-nor, corresponding with Sogho-nor and Gaschun-nor. On the same river we find Maomo, which we commonly call Mamo. Among other well-known names on our route are marked Hami, Pitchan, Tourfan, Marias and Tocsun. The great desert is called Cobi.

It is not strange that this map, published by d'Anville, should be so unlike its contemporary by Renat, since the draughtsmen depended upon different sources.

In 1761, the Jesuits, d'Espinha, d'Aroha and Hallerstein, travelled, by order of the Emperor Ch'ien-lung, to Lop Nor and other parts of Eastern Turkistan to determine astronomically the position of places. After them, more than a century elapsed without trustworthy information from Eastern Turkistan. When, in 1808, the government of India sent an embassy to Kabul under Elphinstone, one of its members, Lieutenant J. Macartney, was able to collect much information about the countries to the northward of the route of the mission.

In Stieler's Hand-Atlas for 1826, Eastern Turkistan bore the name of "*Turfan oder Kleine Bucharey oder Ost-Dsagatai,*" and is far from being as well drawn as Renat's map a hundred years earlier. But Renat's map was not then known ; it lay forgotten in an archive awaiting the eagle eye of August Strindberg. This German map which has since passed through so many editions, and is now the best there is of Asia, has Etsin-gol and its terminal lakes, taken from d'Anville.

A giant stride forward towards system and clarity was marked ten years later by Klaproth's famous map, l'Asie Centrale, 1836.

In no respect could Berghaus's meritorious map of 1843 compete, as regards our regions, with Renat's. He, however, has the Tarim as a continuous river, and his Lop Nor resembles that of the Chinese.

The Lazarists Huc and Gabet travelled through Ordos in 1844, and to Lhasa in 1846, without affording to our maps any serviceable data. Between 1854 and 1858, the brothers Hermann, Adolph and Robert Schlagintweit carried out their celebrated travels in India, and Adolph wandered over the high lands to Kashgar where, in 1857, he was murdered by Valikhan Tura. With them Eastern Turkistan begins to take shape.

Europe's knowledge of inmost Asia has since gradually been widened through the journeys of several English travellers and the information they gathered by inquiry. Of these it suffices to mention the names of Johnson, Shaw, Hayward, Forsyth, Bellew, and Dr. Stoliczka the Czech, who took part in Forsyth's embassy to Yakub Beg.

The most important of all journeys in these latter times was, however, that which during 1876 and 1877 was carried out by Nik. Mich. Prjevalsky, for he improved the whole eastern half of the map of Eastern Turkistan. He moved Lop Nor down a geographical degree to the south from its old position on the Chinese maps, and he moved Kunlun's border range, Altin-tagh, up to the north, so that the famous lake came to lie altogether by the northern foot of the mountains.

Time after time Prjevalsky returned, in the course of his four great expeditions, to the tracts where we are now working, and other travellers also found their way thither, among them the Englishmen Carey and Dalgleish and the Frenchmen Bonvalot and Prince Henry of Orleans. After Prjevalsky's death in 1888, his mantle fell upon his countrymen Pevtsov, Roborovsky, Koslov and Bogdanovich. As years went on and the modern desire for a profounder knowledge of the earth grew more intense, the number of travellers increased in the far countries where our Swedish expedition now feels itself at home. There travelled Ney Elias, Younghusband, Dutreuil de Rhins and Fernand Grenard, while Koslov undertook a whole series of journeys which actually had Eastern Tibet for their goal. After my first visit to Kashgar in 1890, I too several times made Eastern Turkistan and Tibet the object of my geographical explorations, as from 1893 to 1897, 1899 to 1902 and 1905 to 1908. Encouraged by my discovery of three old towns, Dendan-uilik, Kara-dung and Lou-lan, several well-equipped archæologists, of whom the foremost were M. A. Stein, von le Coq, Grünwedel and P. Pelliot, made their way to Eastern Turkistan. Since my last journey in Tibet, only one white man has crossed Transhimalaya, namely Sir Henry Hayden, while another, Dr. Wilhelm Filchner, skirted its northern foot. Among journeys in Western Tibet and Karakoram, the meritorious work of Dr. Filippo de Filippi takes the first place. In Karakoram we specially notice Mr. and Mrs. Visser, and for the road between Ladak and Aksai-chin, Dr. Emil Trinkler's expedition, which also worked in the western part of the Tarim basin. Dr. De Terra took part, as geologist, in this expedition. During the last ten years a series of books about Sinkiang and Gobi have appeared. Most of these are rather of the nature of tourists' journals. The English have usually the common feature of ignoring all other than English predecessors.

We have now briefly reviewed two thousand years' arduous exploration work in the heart of Asia and have cast a glance over the most important expeditions which have been concerned with our present field of activity. After the Asiatic coast-line became known in its main features, centuries elapsed before European exploration contrived to penetrate the interior. In our own day scarcely any great geographical discoveries remain to be made, for the regions of innermost Asia where no traveller has set foot have dwindled more and more in recent centuries and have become so small in area that there is scarcely space for any great geographical discoveries.

Detailed scientific research may be said to have begun

with the opening of the present century. It is now less a question of geographical discovery than of the extension of our knowledge of the earth's surface in these regions, always difficult of access.

Having so long worked as a pioneer in the then still unknown parts of Tibet and Eastern Turkistan, I gradually conceived an irresistible desire to lead an expedition of exceptionally wide scope. How it finally became my fortune to bring such an enterprise into being, I have described in the first part of our chronicle, *Across the Gobi Desert*. This second part contains a preliminary account of the subdivision of the expedition and of the difficulties of various kinds we have had to contend with and to overcome. It has often looked hopeless, but by patience we have yet succeeded in maintaining our positions and in extending them. The difficulties we met did not arise from the inhabitants, nor yet from niggard nature. They have in part been of the political kind in this formerly more or less forbidden continent, which now, like the rest of the world, is swept by the storms of the new era, following the volcanic eruption of the world war. They have also been of an economic nature, for to conduct and maintain an expedition of such dimensions costs considerable sums. In the exploration of Central Asia, Sweden has had traditions, ever since the days of Strahlenberg and Renat, which confer obligations. It is my desire and my dream to build up for the heart of Asia a body of young Swedish explorers such as gave to Swedish geographical exploration its golden age in the polar regions.

For me the difference between this great enterprise and the circumstances under which I travelled in old days has been immense. Formerly I travelled in the unknown parts of Asia and moved unhindered, with small light caravans, in what districts I would. Now I have changed from explorer into a sort of centre at which all the threads converge and from which I supervise and watch over the interests of the various groups working in the field. My own desires, to follow up and solve certain geographical problems upon which I began in my youth and which I therefore embrace with peculiar sympathy, I have been obliged to abandon one after the other. I have been an administrator and organizing authority, having my headquarters located successively in Peking, Etsin-gol, Urumchi, Stockholm, Peking and Nanking, Boston and Stockholm, and now, for the third time, in Peking. My plan and my wish had been to travel hence to Sinkiang, but to this day it has still been impossible for me to get free. Every day I have various urgent matters to attend to in the interest of the expedition; instructions, correspondence, couriers, despatch of instruments and money, applications to the authorities, conferences and innumerable other things. I feel myself a sheep-dog who has to guard his flock against wolves and other threatening dangers, a shepherd who has to lead his sheep to new pastures.

At the moment our expedition consists of eighteen salaried members, of whom nine are Swedish, six Chinese, one German, one Danish and one Russian. The eighteen include thirteen scientists, three assistants, one caravan leader, and one photographer. In addition there are two students from Szechuan and four from Sinkiang, all unpaid, or, more exactly, supported by their provincial authorities. In a separate group are three Swedes resident in Eastern Asia, Mr. Folke Kullgren at the Swedish Legation in Peking, who is accountant for both the Eastern contingents of the expedition and, as such, salaried, Duke Larson, who at the moment is not in service, and Mr. Yngve Laurell, who often assists in the purchase of ethnographic objects.

The expedition is at present divided into five different groups, namely:

1. Dr. Erik Norin and Dr. Nils Ambolt, who are working in Eastern Turkistan, with the young Russian Vorotnikov, as assistant.

2. Folke Bergman and Gerhard Bexell.

3. Dr. Birger Bohlin and Dr. Nils Hörner, with the Chinese geodesist, Chên, as assistant, and the Dane, Friis Johansen, as caravan leader. This group and group 2 are working in Kansu and the Gobi Desert. They work on different lines, but are usually in contact with each other.

4. Dr. David Hummel, with the German, Manfred Bökenkamp, and the student Hao as assistants, and two

Ssŭ-chuan students. Their route has lain through Ssŭ-chuan to Kansu, and their proper field of work is the Choni valley on the borders of Tibet.

5. Dr. Gösta Montell, with Georg Söderbom as assistant. This group has its working territory in Inner Mongolia, Peking and Jehol. On practical and political grounds I have my headquarters with this group, but hope later on to be able to transfer them to Sinkiang.

Next year are further added two groups, namely:

6. Dr. Waldemar Haude, with a German or a Swedish assistant and two Chinese students. Their field will be North-Eastern Tibet and Nan-shan.

7. Dr. T. Arne, with two young Swedish archæologists; field of work, Persian Turkistan.

These two latter groups are already economically assured, 7 through Mr. Albert Appleton's donation, and 6 through a grant from Germany. The cost of group 5 is defrayed by Mr. Vincent Bendix, and that of the first four groups by the Swedish Government. It is only for these four that we have occasion to be anxious, since the grant is now beginning to come to an end.

Among our Chinese members I wish specially to mention three, Dr. P. L. Yüan, professor at the Tsing-hua College in Peking, the historical archæologist Huang, and the palæontologist Ting, a pupil of Dr. A. Grabau. Two of our students, Li and Liu, have, after three years' exemplary service, gone to Berlin to study meteorology and physics at the expense of the National University of Peking. The meteorological stations, at which observations have been carried out for two years and which we established, have now been transferred, under Chinese superintendence, to Urumchi, Singer, Kucha, Turfan and Keriya. These stations, which are intended to be permanent, are thus direct offshoots of our expedition.

The three first-named Chinese form three working groups for themselves which accordingly are not included in the five formerly mentioned. Professor Yüan has during the two last years been active in Tien Shan and Dzungaria; Huang and Ting in the region of Kashgar, in Kucha, and now at last in Turfan. In actual fact we have already eight groups, of which three are purely Chinese, three purely Swedish and two jointly Swedish and Chinese.[1]

In all these groups work is proceeding in the interest of science. China profits by our experiences and the discoveries of the Chinese conduce to our advantage. We work together in confidence and concord without friction or suspicion. Eighty chests full of fossils and archæological objects, collected by our Chinese colleagues, have arrived in Peking. Two fresh consignments of Swedish and Chinese collections are on the way.[2] By means of this harmonious co-operation we strengthen the cultural bond between Sweden and China which is a by-product of the expedition not estimable in money.

As regards the labours of groups 1, 2, 3 and 4, it may be said of them without the least exaggeration, that they constitute the most important breaking of new ground ever undertaken in scientific exploration in the interior of Asia. The geological, palæontological, meteorological and physical researches that are being carried out by my young Swedes and Dr. Haude mark absolutely new conquests for science, and will appear epoch-making in several departments. For post-tertiary and general geological surveys of such thoroughness, palæontological collections of such comprehensiveness, in which Dr. Yüan's dinosaurus find is also of the greatest importance, stone-age finds amounting to nearly a hundred thousand, pendulum observations in the heart of the world's greatest continent and in the deepest torrid depression on earth, the sending up of pilot balloons to a height of 20,000 metres and more—in a word researches of so high a scientific quality as these have never been carried out in the interior of Asia and imply jointly a very notable contribution to the fund of human knowledge. And still I have not even mentioned our acquisitions in botany, zoology, anthropology, enthnography and religious

[1] This grouping still applied last summer. Now, in October, the arrangement is different. Our Chinese colleagues Huang and Ting have returned to Peking, and groups 2 and 3 are divided into four groups, all Swedish, in order to cover as large a territory as possible. For the present the Swedes are working in innermost Asia at various stations.

[2] One of them has recently reached Peking.

research. I have not mentioned the minutely exact astronomical determination of localities, the magnetic inclination and declination, the triangulation and the maps of innermost Asia, which provide a picture of the vast desert spaces and certain of the mountainous tracts whose like has never been seen before, and which furnish a conception of these regions entirely different from that which had formerly been entertained. In this respect, too, the topographical, as with regard to the absolute determination of heights, our expedition can be described as epoch-making.

We have to thank the confidence and complaisance of the Chinese for these magnificent conquests.

The only contribution I myself have been able to make to the acquisition of these rich results has been my time and my forty-five years of experience in the dim ways of Asia.

I

SEMIPALATINSK

NOW begins a new phase of our expedition to the heart of Asia. I have been home to Stockholm for two months in order to write to the King concerning support for new Swedish researches in various branches of science. I have been buying automobiles on behalf of Sinkiang, buying and testing new instruments and completing the equipment, and have added to the scientific staff yet another distinguished force, the young astronomer from Lund, Dr. Nils P. Ambolt.

And now everything is in order. On the 8th of August, 1928, the *von Döbeln* bears us away from the quay and from those we love. It is raining and blowing. Through the haze I cast glances tinged with sadness at the little red cottage at Klippudden where my beloved mother left us three years ago.

A cyclonic storm passes over the Åland Sea. In darkness we land at Helsingfors, in rain and damp we pass the custom house and passport control at Rajajoki and Bjeli Ostrov, and at 1 o'clock on the 10th are met in Leningrad by our consul, Ytterberg, and his factotum Rosenhagen, who take charge of our baggage.

We are conveyed by automobile to number 64 Nabereshnaya Krasnaya Flota, on our door the three crowns of Sweden shine golden and there is a magnificent view over the Neva from our windows. We drive round the islands and through the town which now gives an impression of greater cleanliness and livelier traffic than in 1923. It is said that the population has risen to 1,600,000.

Our two mechanics, Carlson and Lagerbäck, had already left Stockholm on July 20th, and had set out for the East with one locked tent and four open goods waggons for the enormous cases containing the automobiles and all the rest of our belongings. The Consul had most obligingly helped them on their way, and some days earlier I had received a telegram from them saying that they had passed Vyatka without adventure.

Our train for Moscow started at 12.30 that night. After expressing our cordial thanks to Consul Ytterberg for his active assistance, we rolled out into the night.

Next morning we were met by the whole Swedish Legation with the Councillor of Embassy, Johansson, at its head. Here, too, we drove round the Kremlin and the Red Square; I visited Karakhan, and in the evening we installed ourselves in a clean and comfortable coupé on the Siberian express.

A young man joined us, Folke Kullgren, a courier to our Legation at Peking, where he later obtained a permanent appointment. I did not then imagine that he was to become, a year later, an efficient member of our expedition. He speaks Chinese fluently and is the son of a Swedish missionary in whose house I once lived at the end of last century.

We take exercise on the platforms and read aloud during the journey. Professor Karlgren's history of China keeps us awake far into the night by its captivating style.

At 4 o'clock in the morning of the 15th of August we arrive at Novo-Sibirsk. The next train for Semipalatinsk leaves at 9.30. On this one is not pampered. There is only one class with wooden bunks in two tiers, not overclean. The train is full, but we get places by an extra payment. At Altaiskaya we reinforce our commissariat in spite of the crush round the buffet. The train glides slowly through woods and fields where newly cut hay is drying in cocks. In the evening we cross the Ob by a mighty iron bridge, and the train stops for a while at Barnaul, at the foot of a terraced hill.

Early in the morning of the 16th of August the rain was pouring down in streams, as we ran through steppes and groves. By noon we were at Semipalatinsk. Carlson and Lagerbäck were on the platform looking out for us. They had been waiting five days for us, and had not been able to begin the putting together of the automobiles until the freight had been paid.

At Semipalatinsk we took a room at the Hotel Kasakstan, while the two mechanics lived entirely in the goods van in which they had come from Leningrad. Here summer prevailed. It was blazing hot and clouds of suffocating dust were raised by the vehicles and the wind. The streets are wide and straight, but no trees cast their shade over them. A few of the houses have two storeys, but most of them are small wooden erections in the usual Siberian style, with rectangular ground plan and pyramidal roof, not at all disagreeable, often very picturesque, with their galleries, outside stair and porches. The government offices, institutions and schools are located in large two-storeyed houses.

Semipalatinsk is a seat of government. The President of the Gubispolkom or Executive Committee of Government is a Kirgiz named Ataniasov. The Vice-President, Sergievsky, an agreeable and civil fellow, immediately offered to put a special guard on our automobiles for as long as they were being assembled at the goods station. For the district is far from safe. Especially between the railway station and the town one has every possible prospect of being fired upon and plundered to the bare skin. Since we had six tons of goods and could not take the whole on our two lorries we wished to hire an extra automobile. Sergievsky, in a word, fulfilled all our desires and moreover wished to offer us better quarters than the primitive Hotel Kasakstan.

At the goods yard, too, we met with goodwill and helpfulness. Carlson and Lagerbäck did not delay a moment after permission was given. They hewed valiantly into the gigantic packing-cases. Splinters and chips flew around their crowbars and axes, and the well-packed chassis of the first lorry issued forth in all its glory.

One of my first visits was to the Chinese Consul, General Liu, who gave me a new and more detailed story of the atrocious murder of Governor-General Yang. I asked him to inform the latter's successor of our approach, and that we requested exemption from duty at the Chinese boundary. Myself, I telegraphed to headquarters at Urumchi where I knew they were daily expecting us, since I ought to have been back by the middle of August.

On the 18th of August one lorry stood completed on its wheels. While the mechanics worked, we occupied our hours of waiting in reading, writing and the study of Semipalatinsk. We visited Stadion, a public park on an island in the Irtish, approached by a pontoon bridge 270 metres in length, where youth amuses itself, and where, on an open space, merry-go-rounds, football grounds and other diversions provide recreation. Under tall leafy poplars the Kirghiz sit roasting " Shislik " or mutton on skewers, and at the tables of an open-air restaurant couples or groups sit drinking tea or beer.

One evening we visited Letny Teatr or the summer theatre in Gorodskoi Sad, the State Gardens, which are full every evening of strollers listening to the orchestra. In the theatre they performed " The Geisha " with humour and elegance, dazzling oriental costumes, beautiful voices, charming girls and admirable music. I remembered the pretty operetta thirty years ago at the Gaiety in London, and it is no exaggeration to say that it was no worse rendered here in Semipalatinsk. But what air in the hall and how the clothes of the public stood out against the gay-coloured costumes! There was not one lady with a hat; all had white or many-coloured stuffs wound round their heads as turbans, often quite becomingly. Nor were any well-dressed people to be seen. One saw only the simple Russian folk, decent, quiet and good-humoured.

Another evening we were visited by three gentlemen, two of them in Bolshevik blouses and the third in ordinary summer clothes. The former were Matskevich and Chekaninsky, president and secretary of the Geographical Society; the third, Vice-President Hartstein, was a railway engineer. They explained that the society was only a branch of the Geographical Society of Leningrad and had been founded twenty-five years ago on the initiative of old P. P. Semenov. Intimately connected with this association are the library and the museum. The latter, however, is still in its infancy and not to be compared with the museums at Omsk, Irkutsk or Minussinsk.

It is with astonishment that one hears of all the institutions and educational establishments located in Semipalatinsk, and one understands that this town is an intellectual centre for the whole surrounding Government. Of its population of 1,207,000, 60,000 young people under eighteen years of age are receiving education in schools and institutions. In the capital there are several elementary schools, one secondary school with a six-year course, corresponding to the old gymnasium, a technical school, a school of industrial economics, two pedagogic institutes, one Russian and the other Kirghiz, a school of practical medicine where midwives also are trained, a party school for the training of agitators, a chemical and a bacteriological laboratory, a birth-control institute, a meteorological station, a seismographical station, a museum and a library, as well as seven clubs for various callings. Moreover there are three newspapers of which the most widely circulated, *Priirtishskaya Pravda*, has only 4,800 subscribers, and a periodical *Our Agriculture*. The town has five churches, of which Snamensky Sobor, built in 1776, is the largest, and thirteen mosques. There is one Lutheran and one Baptist Chapel and one Synagogue. The town possesses two steam flour mills, an electricity plant, a waterworks, a tannery and a foundry, three hospitals, three dispensaries, a Pasteur and Röntgen Institute, a theatre and four cinemas.

The trade is for the most part co-operative; only in the bazaars and in the open market there is some individual trading. All sorts of iron articles, groceries, paraffin and petrol, cigarette papers and tobacco, matches, tiles and other goods are exported hence to China via Vladivostok, and from China are imported, among other things, wool, cotton, hides, live cattle and fruits.

The steamboat traffic on the Irtish gives to Semipalatinsk easy summer communications with the country round Saisan-nor and with Omsk. Of even greater importance is the railway, which during our visit was in course of construction and will unite Semipalatinsk with Tashkent. Work was proceeding from both terminals simultaneously, and preparations were in progress at Sergiopol. A hundred and eighty-one kilometres have now been completed in the direction of that place. The mighty iron bridge over the Irtish was approaching completion and has cost 2,000,000 roubles. Twenty thousand workmen were employed along the line, which is expected to be finished in 1931.[1] It will carry cotton from Turkistan to Siberia and corn and timber in the reverse direction.

Not less than forty-five different races live in the Government of Semipalatinsk; the most numerous being the Cossacks, the Great Russians and the Ukrainians. There are 11,270 Germans and 7 Swedes.

Obliquely facing our hotel, the Kasakstan, rises a little whitewashed building with the inscription "Museum" above its door. It contains two large halls with show-cases and cupboards. We make the round under expert guidance. The ethnographical section includes household utensils, weapons, folk-drawings, textiles, etc. In other cases are preserved old and more recent Russian coins, while the archæological collection is placed in a large glazed cupboard. There one sees flint arrow-heads, skin scrapers, axes, clubs and knives of stone as well as a number of bronze objects, all derived from the Province, most of them excavated from "kurgans," ancient or more recent royal burial mounds. All the larger kurgans in Kasakstan have at various times been plundered of their treasures, but this does not preclude the possibility of their still containing valuable objects from neolithic or later periods.

"Souvenirs of the Revolution" is a collection of more local interest. On the walls of the Natural Science Room are statistical diagrams; in the show-cases, minerals, kinds of soil, varieties of corn, etc.; and in the cupboards stuffed mammals and birds, and reptiles, fishes and insects in alcohol.

The library is said to contain 17,660 volumes, mostly unbound, and therefore laid in piles, not standing on the shelves. Here and there hang portraits of famous Russians who have been connected with this region. Dostoevsky lived in exile for three years at Semipalatinsk, and a memorial plaque has been placed over the entrance to his house. The celebrated Grigor Nikolaevich Potanin

[1] By the use of forced labour it was finished in the spring of 1930.

also spent some time in this town. Once in his youth and again in his old age he was banished to Siberia, and died in 1920 at the American Red Cross Hospital at Tomsk, at the age of eighty-five. I visited one day a Russian, Belosludov, living in Dostoevsky Street, who had looked after Potanin in his old age.

At Ustkamenny Gorsk a pair of elk antlers of three metres span, skeletons of mammoths and aurochses and several extinct animals have been found. In Saisansky Ujasd there is abundance of vegetable fossils and in the same district there is estimated to be coal amounting to 15 milliards of pud. In Pavlodarsky and Burlinsky Ujasd occurs excellent salt. They export the skins of sheep, lambs, foxes, marmots, hares and weasels; sheep's, camels' and goats' wool, and also sheep's guts and pigs' bristles.

One day we paid a visit to the meteorological station, which is said to be sixty-five years old. The Republic of Kasakstan has control of not less than sixty-six meteorological stations, more or less completely equipped. The station at Semipalatinsk has its own little house with a couple of small rooms. Every other day a pilot balloon is sent up, and the result is telegraphed to Moscow, Leningrad and Vladivostok. The balloons have a diameter of eighty-five centimetres. On the 25th of July, 1928, a record of 22,000 metres was achieved. Otherwise five or six thousand was the usual height. Pilot balloons are also sent up at Kizil-arda and Alma-ata as well as at Sverdlovsk, Tomsk and Irkutsk. For us, with our new meteorological stations in the heart of Asia, and for the investigation of our pilot balloons' courses these Russian experiments simultaneously carried out are of high value.

On the 23rd of August my lecture to the Geographical Society took place in an open-air theatre in the public gardens. The hall had walls but no roof. On the stage sat the governing body at a table. There also was observed the distinguished lecturer in geology in the University of Tomsk, Herr Gornostaiev. After a speech of welcome from the chairman, I spoke of my earlier travels and of the present expedition's significance and aims. The large audience was appreciative and interested, and this also appeared from the fact that after the chairman had announced that everyone was free to ask questions, a whole pile of question slips was collected on the directors' table. These were sorted according to their contents, read aloud by the vice-chairman and afterwards answered by me. Finally there were fine speeches by several members of the governing body.

On one of our last days Hartstein, the railway engineer, gave a little farewell feast for Ambolt and me. He informed us that the railway to Tashkent is to be 1,440 kilometres in length and to cost 203,400,000 roubles. The new bridge over the Irtish is 740 metres long.

The last evening we sat in the dining-hall of the Hotel Kasakstan among all kinds of strange figures, listening to the excellent music which the last White Governor's widow made on the piano. She entertained the guests and attracted customers, and received for her work a monthly salary of eighty-five roubles. She was elegant and agreeable, and her French was truly Parisian.

II

TO THE CHINESE FRONTIER

ON the 28th of August everything was ready for our departure from Semipalatinsk. The two lorries between them carry three tons of our baggage, and the packing cases are secured by strong ropes. The rest, almost as much, has been committed to a Renault lorry which we have hired from "Autotranstorg." It may seem surprising that we should take the whole 6,000 kilogrammes of baggage with us, but it is explainable when the lion's share consists of spare parts for the four automobiles, and a whole small mechanical workshop of tools of all kinds. The automobiles, which I brought to Sinkiang and which had been ordered by Governor-General Yang, were of the make of Dodge Brothers and Graham Brothers of Detroit. Of course we would have preferred to take cars of Swedish make, but since all the cars that were already in Urumchi were of the American makes mentioned, and since the Chinese had equipped the repair shops and laid in their stock of spare parts accordingly, I thought it wiser not to introduce any new types. When old Yang asked this service of me I could not refuse his request. I certainly got no pleasure out of the commission, which only involved time and trouble both in Stockholm and on the way to Urumchi. But I was ably assisted both by Dr. Ambolt and by the two mechanics Carlson and Lagerbäck; and the purveyors, the firms of Philipson, Löwener and B. A. Hjorth and Co., facilitated the complicated business in every way.

Our cases moreover contained many unusual articles for the people at Urumchi, such as a separator, a L. M. Ericsson telephone apparatus, a "Facit" calculating machine, a Siewer's cooking apparatus, lamps, radiators and Primus stoves from B. A. Hjorth & Co., a cinematograph exhibiting apparatus with a number of films, a Klepper boat and much besides, most of which were presented free of cost to the expedition.

The most valuable articles in our baggage were Dr. Ambolt's astronomical and geodetic instruments, well stowed in padded cases. The photographic equipment also weighed heavily.

It was 4 o'clock when we set out. The first day's journey of the 750 miles we had to drive to Urumchi was to be short. But only to have succeeded in crossing the Irtish was so much gained. We had assured ourselves that the ferry-boats could carry the lorries. They were able to take fifteen carts with their loads, each attached to one or more horses, at one crossing, as well as some fifty people. It looked as if the poor Russian or Kirghiz country people, who had come over to Semipalatinsk from the left bank to sell watermelons and other produce, might have to wait half a day or a day for their turn to drive on to the ferry. They were now standing on our side in a queue several hundred metres in length.

We drove down to the ferry, and the queue was told to wait. A pier about seventy-five metres long stretches out into the river to a point at which the water is deep enough to allow the laden ferry to lie alongside.

Lagerbäck drove out with his lorry. The pier creaked, a couple of planks snapped, and I trembled for the Renault machine which was twice as heavy. Then I drove down in my Dodge with the hired chauffeur Davidov at the wheel. Next it was Carlson's turn, and last of all came Ambolt. Although all four cars stood together on the ferry-boat, it had still space and carrying capacity for several carts and a whole lot of people.

The ferry-boat swings pendulumwise on a cable anchored a bit upstream and supported by several small boats which take part in the oscillation. It took seven minutes to cross this arm of the river, which at the ferry is divided by an island, Ostrov Krugly or the Round Island. At its shore we lay to and the ferry-boat was made fast to the pier rail with hawsers. The queue of carts which filled the pier and the road backed outward and made room for us.

On the island we waited for the Renault which was in charge of two young Russians. "Now he's driving out on to the pier," cried Carlson. Half a minute later we heard a mighty crash of shattering timbers. A roar of voices reached us from the right bank. "He's going into the river," someone shouted. I could see through the field glasses the heavy hulk heeling over to the right, and the topmost of the heavy cases sliding overboard and plunging into the river. Was the whole lorry with its three-ton load going to follow it?

No, he is holding his ground, but yet another couple of planks break under him, so that his plight is desperate. The pier men got help from peasants and farmers who had the strongest possible motives for coming to the assistance of the stranded lorry, which has been holding up all traffic for a good hour. Some courageous youths went out into the river and succeeded in bringing the drowned packing-case on to dry land.

Carlson and I returned by the ferry to the right bank. The lorry had such a list on it that it was a wonder it did not overturn. By combined effort the cases were taken out of the lorry, placed one by one on the carts and carried on to the ferry-boat. One of these simple conveyances was crushed beneath the weight of an 800-kilogramme packing-case. The pier was strengthened with new planks, and finally the lorry was able to make its way on to the ferry-boat.

After a drive of some minutes across the island we are confronted with the second ferry and pass in twelve minutes from one of its short solid piers to the other. Night had now fallen after a blood-red sunset, and the moon was shining upon the rugged road that brought us up to Djani Semi, the part of Semipalatinsk which lies on the left bank. Here we got quarters at the house of Bulgakov, a decent farmer, who had been four years in France and remembered a few words of the language. His wife put a simple supper on the table and, tired after the day's labours, we went to bed.

In the morning of the 29th of August our column of five lorries was ready to start in earnest. Our way lies to the southward and in a short while we are out upon the unbroken levels of the stern wilderness. We cross the new railway at Tashkent. If the road all the way to Urumchi were such as it is here we should be able to do the 750 miles in three or four days. It was a pleasure to drive. The weather was divine, the temperature being 24·1° at 10.30 a.m. As we sped across the waste, it was good to feel ourselves penetrating ever deeper into the heart of the great continent. But unhappily we had a travelling companion named Renault who, owing to first one defect and then another, constantly lagged behind. When we had been running at full speed for some miles, there would be no sign of it on the northern horizon, and we had to wait. Once Carlson and my driver, Davidov, drove back to see what had happened. A water tube had burst. Carlson repaired it. Meanwhile I lay dreaming in the shade of one of the lorries. In the distance is heard a shout, a barking of dogs. The crickets sing. There is a rumble of wheels. It comes nearer. Eight carts, drawn by oxen, drive past. Otherwise all is silent.

Then Renault comes up puffing, and we proceed in a united troop to Ulugus, an outpost or guard-house with " dorozhnydom " or a roadhouse where travellers may pass the night in a quite clean room. The second outpost is called Burli. There one drives over a bridge across a stream, among sparse dry herbage. The afternoon sun burns. A train of fifty-two ox-carts goes creaking by. In the middle of the long procession walks a camel drawing its cart. We meet more trains. They are bringing wool and cotton from China to Russia, and some of them timber from the forests.

We drive across a salt marsh which is now dried up, but in autumn and winter is almost impassable. Among the hills to the south-south-west the Kirghiz graze their flocks of sheep and camels, horses and cattle. Certain of them are rich and own as many as 10,000 sheep.

Beyond the tent village of Arkalik we go over a little pass. After this the ground falls slowly towards the south. The sun sinks in flaming red, and violet clouds float across the horizon. The moon rises, the crimson colours fade and pass into grey blue. A more poetic twilight cannot be imagined. At Achi-köl, or outpost number three, we halt for the night at the guest-house. Still, at 9 o'clock, the temperature is 15·4°.

On the following morning Renault was despatched in advance at 4 o'clock, and we set off three hours later. On our left we passed a whole string of extensive lakes, Achi-kul, the Bitter Lakes, by whose shores cattle, horses and sheep were grazing and fourteen Kirghiz blanket tents or "yurts" clustered. Endless lines of ox-carts with wool, cotton and hides. Those going southward carry tea, tobacco, cigarettes, matches, groceries and other goods.

At Dchartavsky outpost we meet a motor-cyclist from Sergiopol, the only one we saw on the whole road. We ascend among low hills to a shallow pass. Kizil-mula, like all the other outposts, consists of an inn and a cluster of cottages, built of sun-dried bricks, from which dogs rush out to attack us. The road shows as a winding pale greyish yellow ribbon on the grey-green plain. The railway is far to the left of us. We are constantly passing or meeting new strings of carts drawn now by oxen, now by horses.

To the right rises the little group of hills of Arkat. The outpost of the same name has a post and telegraph station. A long narrow valley leads to the little pass and to the station of Aldshanadinsky. The dustclouds stirred up by carts and beasts of burden lie like a yellowish-grey veil over the land and often interrupt the view. At 2 o'clock the temperature is 27·9°.

Beyond Usun-bulak we again cross a belt of dried-up salt marsh, and at Inrekysky outpost a bridge crosses a still watercourse. At Altin-kolak we are quite close to the railway embankment and time after time pass whole colonies of white tents and little airy huts where the railway workers have their quarters. We are approaching Sergiopol. In this district they are engaged in excavation, embankment building and the laying of sleepers. The rails have not yet reached so far. The road is worse than hitherto. One is rocked as on bolsters of soft fine dust. It whirls round the lorries like a smoke cloud at a conflagration.

Sergiopol is no town, only a so-called stanitsa which is believed to have 1,500 inhabitants. There we went to the Turksibs Hotel which has at its disposal two rooms for travelling engineers and officials in the service of the Turkistan-Siberia railway. We met the aviator Sotov who has come here from Verni (Alma-ata) to investigate and report on the flying route Tashkent-Semipalatinsk-Novo-Sibirsk. There is already a regular flying service between Tashkent and Verni which is to be extended in the near future to Novo-Sibirsk, where it will meet the great air-route across Siberia. It is Dobrovolny Vosdusny or the Volunteer Air Fleet which lays out the new immense air-ways. At Sergiopol there is an excellent landing-place four versts north-east of the stanitsa, and it is there too that the railway station is being built.

Next day, after we had filled up with petrol, our imposing column of lorries drove on towards the south, across the River Ajag-us and over dried-up salt marshes, now between distant hills, now over rugged steppes. In a short space of time we met 214 ox-carts laden with hides, wool and cotton. Only occasionally are the oxen disturbed when we go whirling past them. Outside the outpost of Aj we camped for the night in the open. It was still summer, and the temperature at 9 o'clock was 16·1° and next morning at seven, 24·9°.

But now it blew hard from the south-east. Light streamers of dust whirled up from the road even without help from our wheels. The air grew thick and murky, but in the zenith the sky shone blue. Time and again we pass little villages of mud cabins and yurts, and here and there flocks of sheep grazing. The Russian goods, going to the south, are usually conveyed in waggons drawn by horses.

The road is thick with dust, which is a strain on our stock of petrol. Near the outpost and village of Kara-köl we cross a wide dry river bed. To our left rises the inconsiderable mountain range of Tarbagatai, and to our right, at a great distance, are low hills. Between these stretches a level grass steppe, and here we pass the villages of Tesbakan and Kaska. Beyond the River

Ingensu, the dusty road descends slowly among scattered yurts. A few deeply cut water furrows are crossed by bridges.

Udchar is a large and lively stanitsa, the population of which is said to reach 3,000. The road goes straight across its market-place where there is much life and movement and where we could count 400 resting ox-carts. The place seems for the most part to be peopled by Russians. Their houses are small, white and fairly clean. When we stopped for a moment, we were surrounded by hundreds of inquisitive folk, men, women and children on foot and riders on camels and horses.

A little beyond Udchar an irrigation canal had overflowed the road which had thus become so soft that the wheels sank a foot into the mud. We made a detour which, however, was little better, but by the aid of jacks, faggots and planks we got clear at last.

At the spring of Malak we camped early in the open air. At 5 o'clock the thermometer stood at 23·7°, while the divine, crystal-clear spring water had a temperature of 11·5°. Our four lorries were formed into a square in which we laid out our evening meal and lighted the Primus stove. In the clear evening Ambolt delivered a little astronomical lecture.

But at 1 o'clock in the morning it was quite another matter. Then we were awakened by a gale that raged and howled round the lorries. At 3 o'clock it began to rain. We tucked ourselves in and went to sleep again. In the morning my whole bed was soaking wet and I moved under a lorry while Ambolt and Lagerbäck stretched tarpaulins as a roof between two more. I had to change every stitch and afterwards sat in a driver's cabin and read. The Renault had not been heard of all night. Carlson and Davidov had therefore driven back to trace the brute. Late in the day they came back with the information that the lorry was a wreck and would have to be towed into Udchar by oxen. In the stanitsa there was fortunately a branch of " Autotranstorg " which undertook to convey our three tons of packing-cases into Bachti with horses and carts in two days. But what a difference with our own cars and our Swedish chauffeurs! It was after three when we started again.

The sun was shining and dried our things. We had not gone far, however, before one of the lorries sank into the ground, which had been softened by the overflowing of a stream. It took us two hours to get clear, and the Kirghiz living in the neighbourhood were called in to put their shoulders to the wheel. The River Navala, now insignificant, is greatly swollen in early summer. One has to drive carefully. A young Kirghiz rider kept up with us for a long time. I feared he would founder his horse before he at last fell behind. In the twilight we passed the little two-headed hill Mokantjinskaya Gora, where, according to Davidov, it is always windy. In the village of Mokantya we found quarters in a simple Russian farmhouse. The whole family, husband and wife and their brothers and sisters and children, were a fine-looking lot.

In the morning of the 3rd of September we had a journey of two hours and a half to Bachti, where we stopped at the custom house and submitted to an exceedingly mild and friendly examination. Nothing was opened; they only counted the number of our packages and endorsed our passports. In the little bank at Bachti I changed 300 United States dollars for 1,603 Sinkiang taels or "liang." We had much to do at the Russian frontier post, especially to send letters and telegrams home. It was the last time we had a regular and well-managed telegraph station at our disposal, and I had had painful experience of how that business was managed on the Chinese side.

From Bachti it is not far to the Russian frontier bar, but we took all of half an hour, for Carlson broke down the last Russian bridge, and the back wheels of his lorry hung for a while between its rotten planks.

The Chinese have no frontier bar. The road runs between two small houses where we stop while the customs people step forward and ask to see our passports. The baggage would be examined in Chuguchak.

On the outskirts of this little town Carlson promptly slaughtered the first Chinese bridge with his heavily laden lorry, but he got safely across it without overturning. In the town we were met by the acting Russian Consul, Baravoi. We set our course for the house of Ivan Michailovich Hochriekov, where his sister Panya Michailovna set out an evening meal while he himself entertained us with his accordion. Late in the evening the Governor's interpreter arrived with a customs officer to fetch our passports and take a number of notes.

III

WE ARE HELD UP AT CHUGUCHAK

ON the morning of September 4th, that is to say the day after our arrival in Chuguchak, the Governor's interpreter, Hong Loye, in fluent Russian, formally introduced himself and a revenue officer to examine our baggage. They only counted the number of packages and took a lot of notes, and we found them as kindly and good-natured as the Russians on the other side of the frontier.

After they had gone we drove in our Dodge, we four Swedes and our host Ivan Michailovich, to the Governor's " yamên " in the Chinese part of the town. The Mohammedans' quarters and the Russian concession lie outside this. The Governor's name is Li Shao-ch'in, but he is commonly called by his title, Li Tao-yin. I had made his acquaintance the previous spring. Now, too, he received us courteously and hospitably. He is a man of honour, full of humour and droll sallies, who would not hurt a fly. Moreover, he speaks Russian, not very well, but so much the more comically, and quite intelligibly—he has been employed in his time in the Russian Consulate at Kuldja. Li Tao-yin has not only children and grandchildren in Chuguchak, but his mother as well. The old woman lives in a house not far from her son's yamên, and he spends several hours with her daily. The tenderness with which he treated her was touching.

We sat down at a small table in his reception-room and were offered cigarettes, tea and melon seeds. And it went off well. But afterwards salted gherkins were served and arrack *ad infinitum*, and even if one detests this drink, common politeness demands that one should drink " kan-pei " or to the bottom, when one is called upon to do so by the host, and when he sets a good example. And this Li did. Laughing with his infectious, cooing laugh, he declared that he was the greatest drunkard in all Sinkiang.

When we got down to serious business, I told Li Tao-yin that we intended to continue our journey on the following day, the 5th of September. But the matter was not so simple. "If it only depended on me, you could start at once," he assured me. "In Yang's time you were free to come and go wherever you wished; but now Yang is dead. The conditions in Sinkiang are entirely changed. Without permission from Urumchi no-one may travel thither. If I let you go without permission, I shall lose my job or, in any case, be severely reprimanded. Perhaps you have not heard what has happened about your seven cases of goods. Yang had given me orders to send them to Urumchi without examining the contents. The cases were a long time on the way and did not arrive until after Yang's death. They were examined in Urumchi, and ammunition was found in one of them. And it was I who got into trouble for allowing such dangerous things to pass unnoticed."

Li Tao-yin offered to send a telegram to the new Governor immediately, asking permission for us and our lorries to proceed. He spoke of despatches on that route as camel-telegrams, for it has happened that camels have covered the distance between Chuguchak and Urumchi more speedily than telegrams. However, he dictated a despatch to a secretary, and it was sent off at once.

Later he gave us an account of the murder of Yang, which he regarded as a misfortune both for Sinkiang and for China.

He described with rapture a motor journey he made seven years ago from China to Urumchi with the Russian bank director Suvorov. They had started with seven cars and travelled through Southern Mongolia. Only one of the cars had got through, a Packard, which Yang went on using until his death. All the others had been wrecked on the way. Li declared that it was only through his cunning that they ultimately came through with their lives. When Mongolian brigands and highwaymen arose out of the desert, he only needed to adopt a threatening attitude with his gigantic tobacco pipe to make them vanish like chaff before the wind. On a later occasion he showed me with pride the wonderful pipe that had saved both him and Suvorov as well as the car.

At the house of the acting-Consul Baravoi we found the first intelligence of the new Dungan rebellion which had broken out in Kansu and involved, among others, the towns of Ning-hsia and Liangchow. We did not pay particular attention to this and did not foresee what an influence this new seat of unrest would come to exercise upon our winter plans.

We were beginning to grow impatient, and after a couple of days I went again to the Governor and implored him to release us from captivity. He knew well that Yang had extended the greatest favour to our expedition, and he could not desire that I, who carried the responsibility for it, should be kept apart from my people. The least I could ask was to be allowed to travel alone in advance with one of the lorries to look after our interests at Urumchi.

No, that was impossible. He deeply regretted that he could do nothing. After Yang's death he had already received from the new Governor-General, or, as his title now was, the President of the Provincial Council, definite instructions to let no-one, no matter whom, not even the Chinese, go on to Urumchi without special permission, and this order had since been repeated—categorically. " But wait another day or two," he suggested. " The chief of the telegraph service has been travelling down the line for two weeks to inspect it and repair its defects. We are daily expecting him back, and the moment I get an answer to my telegram I will inform you. No," he added, " neither I nor anyone else can help your being held up; only Yang's death is to blame for it, and you may be sure that I am not the only one in the Province who laments his departure."

Two more days passed and then I received a message from Li Tao-yin that the line was clear and that the answer might come at any moment. On the 10th of September it became evident that something had been heard, since the interpreter Hong Loye and the exciseman Wang appeared and demanded to open all our forty-three packing-cases.

"You might have told us so at least a week ago, when you were here looking round. It takes two days to unpack all our baggage and pack it again."

"It is not our fault," they answered. "We have received orders to examine your effects."

So the inspection began. Ambolt, Carlson and Lagerbäck were kept busy for nearly two days. We understood only too well that a special order had arrived from Urumchi and that they wished above all to ascertain whether we were carrying arms or ammunition in our cases. Feeling in the provincial capital was nervous and uncertain, everyone had noticed that. Why should they suppose that we would import six tons of arms and ammunition into Sinkiang? Well, why not? Stranger things had happened in this world. A violent coup had quite lately taken place in Urumchi, and new men were now occupying almost all the higher posts. They did not know us and had not the same qualifications as Yang to judge us and our intentions. The Chinese on my staff were all of the Kuomintang party, but Sinkiang stood entirely outside this, the victorious party in China. In any event one could not be too careful. It did us no harm to unpack our cases; it was merely troublesome. They found no ammunition to speak of. Only a couple of hundred cartridges for a sporting gun which a Mongol prince had asked me for, and a thousand cartridges in all for our own weapons. Yang had asked me to buy him a pair of small pistols with ammunition. To facilitate the exciseman's work we ourselves pulled out all these dangerous things, and they made precise notes about them. The arsenal was put on one side and packed in a separate case which was to be sent to Urumchi and returned to us later. At my request Li Tao-yin allowed us to keep the pistols, since it is not customary to travel entirely weaponless from the Russian frontier to the capital of the province.

Thus there was no doubt that a telegram had arrived with orders to make a thorough search. But why had Li Tao-yin had no answer to his question as to whether we might set out? For the simple reason that it was impossible to give us permission to travel until they were assured that we were not carrying arms to Urumchi. This became so much the more evident in that Li Tao-yin did not communicate with us until his two subordinates had made an exhaustive report upon their examination. But then he did come, in the evening of the 11th, and was entertained, according to custom, with tea, cigarettes and sweetmeats. He was not in the best of humours. He was probably ashamed of having issued an order of a nature insulting to us. He knew us and our intentions, and was aware that, when we had been searched, at the beginning of the year, at the eastern frontier of Sinkiang, the only weapons found on us had been sporting guns and revolvers, necessary for practical purposes and for defence in a country in which civil war, robbery and banditry were rife. He must therefore have regarded a new examination as entirely unnecessary and absurd.

Li Tao-yin sat down and lit a cigar.

"You may start now," he said. "I have just had a telegram."

"Then we'll be off in the morning," I replied.

"No," he said. "You are dining with me to-morrow."

"Impossible. We have lost time enough already, and I don't want to lose another day."

As he continued to invite and I to decline, Ambolt, who is more polite than I, begged me not to wound him by a refusal, especially as Li could not help the muddle that had its origin at Urumchi. Finally I promised that we would come, and we wrote our names on the big red paper on which all those invited were inscribed.

"We must fill up our petrol tanks in the morning," I said, "and also have a pass authorizing us to obtain more at the stations on the way."

"I have nothing to do with that. Speak to the Sart, Hassan Abdullah Birisheff, head of the garage."

After the Governor had gone, I accordingly betook myself to Hassan Abdullah's house. He is a strongly built little old man with a white beard and, besides his own language, speaks Russian and Chinese. His manner was dictatorial and cocksure. He answered my request briefly and to the point, saying:

"I cannot give out any petrol without special orders from Urumchi."

"Listen, Hassan Abdullah, don't you understand that one can't drive cars without petrol?"

"I can't help the orders being what they are. I will telegraph to-morrow for permission."

Next morning the old man came, in a more pliable mood, to say that the Governor had given orders that we were to have all the petrol we required. In Chuguchak one ran one's head into the wall whichever way one turned. We had four cars. Ambolt, Carlson and Lagerbäck would each drive one, but I am no chauffeur. Thus we were obliged to have a driver for the fourth car. There was a Russian driver in the employ of the Governor whom we should be able to borrow, since Li never drove in his decrepit cars. No, it may possibly happen that he will need him, and he must then be available.

Maksud Hadji was a venerable merchant who had occasion to go to Urumchi on important business. He had heard that we had a spare place and asked if he might go with us.

"Yes, willingly," I replied, "but only on condition that you, who are on such friendly terms with the Governor, will get us Fornin as driver, since otherwise we must leave the fourth car behind."

He thought the prospect was gloomy, but would try.

IV

AMBOLT'S ILLNESS

ALL these adversities were, however, insignificant compared with an occurrence which at this juncture upset all our plans. We were to start on the 13th of September, and Li Tao-yin's dinner, to which Ambolt and I were invited, was on the 12th. But on the night of the 12th Ambolt was taken ill; his stomach had risen in the wildest revolt, and he stayed in bed all day. I had to go alone to the dinner, at which the other guests were seven Chinese officials, Consul Baravoi and the Consul at Shara-Sume in Altai. At Chinese feasts the sole object is to drink. One is incessantly urged to drink. All kinds of drinking games promote the consumption. Thus, for example, a match is set firmly in a box and lighted. One passes the box with the lighted match to one's neighbour and thus it goes round the table to one after another. He in whose hand the match goes out has to drink kan-pei or to the bottom. I drank not a drop more than I wanted to, and was certainly regarded as a poor "kumpan," a circumstance which the other heroes were free to reflect upon when they awoke next morning with hot coppers.

When I got home at midnight, I found Ambolt with a temperature of 38·9° and feeling prostrate. Carlson is an excellent sick nurse. I now relieved him and took the night watch till 6 o'clock, when I woke Carlson. The invalid needed constant attention. We had supposed that he was suffering from a chill and would soon be about again, but on the 13th one could tell, without being a doctor, that he was in for a severe attack of dysentery. We then sent at once for the town's one barber-surgeon, the White Russian, Kalinkin, an uncommonly skilful, honest and humane man. He made a thorough examination and supplied all the necessary medicine.

The lorries were now all filled up with petrol, and the Governor had promised me Fornin. All was ready for the start. The weather was glorious, the temperature between 23° and 24° in the shade at 2 p.m., and the road was dry and in good condition. And we were more immovably stuck than ever. On the 14th Ambolt was clearly worse. I sent an urgent telegram to our Swedish surgeon, Dr. Hummel, to come at once by car, since Ambolt's condition appeared to be very grave. This telegram arrived at Urumchi on the 24th of September, having been ten days on the way.

On the 15th a raging westerly gale passed over the district, Tarbagatai was blotted out, and the poplars were bent almost double. In the evening it rained smartly. Now the roads would be ruined, now we could not cross the salt marshes with our lorries. It was all the same to us; indeed we could not stir out of the place. Ambolt was growing worse, and I could not think of leaving him. It would be no use to send the two mechanics on in advance with the lorries, since not only does Carlson watch over the invalid by day, but also they could not accomplish anything in Urumchi in my absence.

On the same day our friend the Tater, Burkhan, came from Urumchi. He is chief of garages, motor-cars and motor drivers in that town, and had now come to Chuguchak with twenty chauffeurs to take back fifteen new lorries which have arrived at Bachti from Semipalatinsk. Burkhan was able to inform me that my telegrams from Stockholm, Semipalatinsk and Chuguchak had not reached headquarters. Thus our people did not know we were so near. Since, however, they were able to calculate that we were approaching, they had on three separate occasions requested the new Governor-General that the way to Urumchi should be kept open for us. He had granted their request and had telegraphed orders to Li Tao-yin. This had happened more than three weeks ago. How this business had been muddled we could not exactly know. Probably they had forgotten to telegraph. In any event the road had not been opened until the 11th of September, and then on Li's express request.

Since the sick man's condition constantly grew worse, I determined on the 16th to send Lagerbäck with the one passenger car to Urumchi to fetch Hummel. I wrote him a detailed account of the invalid's symptoms and begged him to come as quickly as was humanly possible. Most of the day was taken up in putting all the necessary papers in order. Burkhan wrote road passes and petrol passes, and the Governor made out special orders. I got leave to employ the German driver, Ansorge, who had been the murdered Yang's favourite chauffeur and who was now living in Chuguchak. He and Lagerbäck took provisions for two days only and each his blanket and overcoat. The car was too lightly laden, so I allowed Maksud Hadji to go as ballast.

It was not till evening that everything was ready. The departure was fixed for 5 o'clock on the following morning, since the gates of the town did not open before that hour, and every outgoing car had to be inspected and registered. Ansorge slept with us, and I undertook to wake them, since I always had the night watch by the invalid.

It rained in the night, and when I woke the drivers at 4.30, it was coming down in sheets. Ansorge suggested waiting an hour or two. Only at 8, when the rain stopped, did they get away. Lagerbäck took money in case they should be obliged to employ waggoners and haulage. I reminded the two messengers that the saving of a human life perhaps depended on their efforts.

Later in the day the weather became fair, and we hoped the road would dry up, even though our yard looked like an inland sea. Ambolt's condition was so grave that I had to telegraph home to warn his family. His temperature had risen to 39·9° and his pulse was 114 to 120. On Kalinkin's advice I gave him a hot bath which did more harm than good. The heart's action became irregular and the pulse fluttering. He fell into the most violent ague fits and afterwards was prostrated with fatigue.

Oh, those horrible nights! It was silent in Chuguchak; all others slept, and I sat alone at the sick man's bedside. He was delirious; he would throw off the bedclothes and spring up right against the wall, shouting: "This is

Marketplace at Chuguchak

Haude Photo

[*face p.* 54

all going wrong. We have forgotten the ammunition." Another time he stared out into the night and cried: "What sort of a fellow is that? Is he going with us?" He did not sleep; he got no rest. He needed constant attention, and his bowels bled continuously.

The next day we got hold of a nurse, the midwife Maria Alexeievna, who helped me with the night watch and was a pattern of efficiency and faithfulness. It rained again and again, and the sky looked ominous. Our thoughts were fixed on the car that had gone to fetch Hummel. Would this rain block the road through the salt marshes for Lagerbäck and Ansorge? How far have they gone, now they have been on the way for thirty hours? Are they approaching Urumchi, a distance of over 370 miles? The days crept on. The condition, however, did not grow worse, and Maria Alexeievna told us there was hope. Both she and Kalinkin had seen cases of dysentery, even more severe than this, recover. On the 20th he was no longer delirious. Perhaps Hummel would yet arrive.

But why do we hear nothing of them? It is the 22nd to-day; that is seven days. Carlson and I discussed all the possibilities with Burkhan. The car may indeed have gone to pieces on the way, or it may have stuck in a salt marsh, and it takes time to haul it out with horses or oxen. Perhaps it has rained far worse in the south than here. Who knew, for the matter of that, whether Dr. Hummel is in Urumchi just now? He has, in fact, spent a large part of the summer at Bogdo-ula, and if he is there it will take at least three days and nights to bring him to the town.

We fancied, in any case, that the condition showed a tendency to improve, and on the night of September the 23rd, I considered that I might send home a reassuring telegram. I had the despatch ready and was going to send it next morning by the Consul's courier to the station at Bachti. It was silent as the grave. Then I heard a strange humming, and a syren sounded outside the window. I sprang up from the writing table, woke Carlson and Hochriekov and hurried out into the yard, just as our noble Dodge came into view through the darkness. Brisk and limber, the doctor jumped out and hurried towards me.

"Is he alive, tell me, is he alive?"

"Yes, the worst is over."

"God be praised!"

While the chauffeurs brought in the baggage and the heavy medicine chest, Hummel went straight in to Ambolt, made a preliminary examination and gave the nurse instructions for the night. I added further details to the telegram I had written a few moments earlier.

Panya Michailovna and her mother produced a proper meal for the travellers, who were hungry, chilled and tired. They had had difficult road conditions on the way to Urumchi and had been held up there the whole of the 20th by exaggeratedly cautious ordinances concerning the customs, their passports and other things. On the morning of the 21st they were ready, but had to undergo a further examination at the yamên. When they finally got away they lost no time. They reached Manas in the darkness, and had to apply to the authorities to get a competent Kirghiz to guide them across the river. They drove all night without stopping and all the next day, and when they reached our yard they had been on the road for thirty-nine hours and, in spite of the rain, had come pretty near breaking a record. They had taken turns at the wheel and had slept and eaten as best they could. Hummel had not slept for forty-eight hours, nor did he get any rest in Chuguchak. After the others had gone to lie down and after the patient had received a last visit for the night, we two veterans from Peking sat talking until 6 o'clock.

On the following day those who so desired were inoculated against dysentery. The doctor found our hygienic arrangements barbaric, to say the least. I had my bed on the floor of the sickroom, which was probably crawling with bacilli; the patient's bed was of the camp type, and we had no sheets for him. But now all was changed. All unnecessary lumber was thrown out, the sickroom was thoroughly scrubbed and three wash-basins of sublimate set out. Flypapers were hung in the window and captured over a thousand the first day—literally, for we counted them—of these infection-carrying little vermin, sheets and pillows were constantly changed and the greatest caution observed at meals. Now there was system, order and discipline, and now the war against the bacilli was waged in earnest.

I went with the doctor to visit our friend, Li Tao-yin; we opened several cases containing medicines and other things for Hummel and got out Ambolt's winter clothing, for the doctor considered that the patient would not be able to move to Urumchi for at least a month. On the 26th I paid my farewell visit to Li, for I was to depart the next day. When there, I received the edifying intelligence that he had fresh telegraphic orders from the highest quarters in the province. These required detailed statements as to who was in my company, how many automobiles we had and what our cases contained. I asked Li what it meant.

" Well," he said smiling, " it is expressly stated in the telegram that you are not to proceed until detailed statements have been delivered and permission telegraphed back from Urumchi."

I answered nothing. It was pouring with rain, and we could not, in any event, drive the heavy lorries. Li sat dictating a new telegram. All at once he leaned towards me and whispered:

" You can go when you like. I take the responsibility."

" Splendid! "

All night the rain poured down, and the streets were turned into mud baths, defying all description. But on the 28th the weather was fine again. It was summer again, with a temperature of 17·2° at 2 o'clock. In the evening we sat writing in the outer room. Then was heard a mighty roar and a rapping on the window shutters of the sick-room. The yard gate was opened, a Russian carriage drove in, and out of it tottered two dead-drunk Russians. Hummel, I and Hochriekov hurried out. The last named tried to head them off but they resisted, and there was a struggle. Finally we got them up into the carriage, and the doctor took the horse by the bridle and would have led the carriage out. Then one of them, a great coarse fellow whom we knew, drew his Browning and threatened to shoot. By a clever trick Hochriekov struck the lethal weapon out of the drunkard's hand, whereupon we drove the rabble out and barred the gate. Then they continued making a noise outside. Ambolt shouted from his sickbed: "Throw ice-water over them from the roof."

He was evidently better! Hochriekov told us that, since the murder of Yang, the carrying of firearms had been forbidden on pain of death. If anyone was caught with them he was brought before a court martial and shot. This seemed to me rather too severe for our disturber of the peace, but I left the lethal weapon next day with the Russian Consul, who would deal with the delinquents.

At last dawned the day, the last of September, when I and the two Swedish mechanics were able to leave our captivity in Chuguchak of sorrowful memory. As usual one is never ready on the day of departure. Innumerable small matters have been put off till the last minute. We must buy six heavy planks to aid us if we stick in a salt marsh; secure all the ropes, check the petrol supply, stow our personal baggage in the passenger car, which is driven by the German, Ansorge. Finally, just as we hoped everything was ready, the Russian Consul arrived on a farewell visit, then Burkhan and after him Hassan Abdullah.

"Are we ready now?"

"Yes, at last."

We take a cordial farewell of Ambolt and his faithful doctor, who are doomed to remain in captivity for perhaps a month yet; we thank our kindly hosts and the two sick nurses. Carlson and Lagerbäck have taken their places in the drivers' cabins, and Ansorge and I climb into the Dodge which goes first with a little Swedish flag in front.

The weather has been fine for two days, but in the town the mud lies a foot deep. It is after half past three. We work our way through the bazaars and have eight small boys hanging on behind. We drive into the Chinese town and are stopped between two posts to undergo, yet once more, examination of passports and inspection. After they have satisfied themselves that we have no extra passengers and no suspected arms chests, we roll out at last over free expanses with Tarbagatai to the left and the steppes to the right.

We were four days on the way. All went well, except

for some small mishaps caused by the wretched road. We spent the last night at Manas with our old friend, the Dutchman, Father Veldman. He accompanied us to Urumchi.

At 4.30 on October the 4th we draw up at our own big yard at the disused Russian Bank which is always our headquarters.

They evidently did not expect us. No one was out to receive us. We came unannounced and unexpected. My letter and telegram had not yet arrived. A servant informed us that Major Hempel, my deputy during my journey to Europe, was at Bogdo-ula, but that the other gentlemen were at home. And now they came out from their dens and studies.

They were Norin, Hsü Ping-chang, Haslund and Dettmann. They were all tanned after the summer's excursions. They welcomed me back cordially, and their first question concerned Ambolt and whether Hummel got there in time. For the Swedes in particular it was pleasant to make the acquaintance of their two countrymen Carlson and Lagerbäck, our mechanics, who, although they did not really belong to our expedition, yet formed a reinforcement of the Swedish colony in Urumchi.

After I had also greeted our servants and the young Russian Vorotnikov, Hummel's assistant, as well as our dogs, among whom Senta was a veteran from Shande-miao, I was conducted to my new room, which was comfortable and was separated from all the others by the inner yard where the meteorological observatory has its place. After supper I talked till 1 o'clock to Professor Hsü and till 4 o'clock to Norin and Haslund. And now begins a new chapter of our saga.

V

THE MURDER OF GOVERNOR-GENERAL YANG

IN my book *Across the Gobi Desert* I described the expedition's intercourse with the celebrated old Governor-General of Sinkiang, Yang Tsêng-hsin—how he treated us with suspicion and mobilized 3,000 Mongols and Mohammedans; how the various contingents on the Eastern frontier of the province were surrounded by 800 mounted troops, interned and later escorted as prisoners to the capital city of Urumchi; how our arms and ammunition were confiscated, our baggage searched and our Mongols sent back; how he wished personally to see us before coming to a further decision; how we at once won his confidence after the first occular inspection and how he then gave us liberty for pretty well any undertakings and travels we pleased. He called us his teachers who came to teach him and the people of Sinkiang to make use of the province's possibilities of production. He became, in a word, our friend and our confidant. We knew that in him we had an extraordinarily powerful backer. After the renowned General Tso Tsung-tang, it was Yang Tsêng-hsin who had created the greatness of Sinkiang and had given the province its present boundaries. Since the revolution of 1911 he had held the reins of power in his hand, not as viceroy or proconsul, but as dictator with full sovereign power. In actual fact one may say that his power was greater than that of Yakub Beg Bedaulet who conquered Alti-shahr in 1865. He governed " The New Province " (Sinkiang) as an autocrat. What Peking or Nanking were pleased to command was to him a matter of complete indifference. He never had any intention of cutting himself loose from China and forming an independent kingdom, greater in area than all the states of Europe outside Russia. But he wished to manage his own affairs, and he took orders from no-one. With China proper he lived in peace and good understanding, and he was loyal and patriotic in the old-time imperialistic meaning of those words. He held the generals carrying on civil war in China in sovereign contempt and expressed himself with extreme severity upon their selfish strife which only led to the impoverishment of the people and the detriment of the country. Just as his province lay far removed from China proper, so he kept himself and his territory apart from every kind of participation in the perpetual civil wars. If China was to be brought to complete ruin by these wars, his province at least should be saved out of the wreck.

Yang Tsêng-hsin, whose title of honour was Tsi-Chou, was born at Mengtsz in Yünnan in 1862, and early gained the highest literary degree, Chin-shih. In 1889 he went to Kansu, where in a short time he became head of a district, or "hsien." On the recommendation of the Manchu military governor of Ning-hsia he was transferred to the staff of the Chêng Shêng army, as one of the army corps stationed in Kansu was called. Subsequently he held higher and higher civil offices in Honan and Chihli. In 1900 he was appointed secretary to Wei Kuang-tao, Governor-General of Shensi and Kansu. He also served as director of the college and military academy of Kansu and conducted the relief works for the starving in that province. On the recommendation of Lien Kuei, the Governor of Sinkiang, he was promoted in 1907 to be Taotai of Aqsu. In April, 1911, he was transferred, still as Taotai, to Tihwa or Urumchi. Two months later he was also appointed Commissioner for Judicial Affairs. In the first year of the republic, 1912, he was appointed acting Lieutenant Governor and Finance Commissioner and, later, Governor of Sinkiang, at the same time serving as Chief of the bureau of civil affairs. In October of the same year he received the rank of Marshal and the second class of the order of Chia-he. In October, 1913, he was specially decorated with the third Order of Merit. Right up to his death he was Sinkiang's military and civil head.

Such are the facts one finds in Chinese handbooks about

one of China's most remarkable men of our time. But it would be a simple matter to write a bulky book on his life work, for during the time that he was the chief ruler of Sinkiang he kept a diary, whose thirty volumes have been printed and which constitutes an important guide to his wise administration and firm policy.

An untoward fate willed that his brilliant career should come to an end little more than four months after our arrival in Urumchi. We often met the Marshal at banquets, either at his house or at ours, and once or twice at that of the Russian Consul-General. I have given some account of these feasts in the first part of the chronicle of the expedition. And I have told of my last parting from Marshal Yang and of my grief at receiving the news of his death, which reached me in Stockholm, by telegram from Shanghai, on July the 17th.

Two months and a half after the murder, I met Dr. Hummel in Chuguchak, as I have already related in the last chapter, and he gave me the account of the distressing affair which follows:

After my departure in May, 1928, Hummel remained in Urumchi for a month, or till June 6th, after which he went to the sacred mountain, Bogdo-ula, to collect plants. On June the 27th he received a summons from the Marshal to hurry down to Urumchi, because Yang's brother-in-law, Liu, the newly appointed Governor of Aqsu, whom Hummel had earlier been attending, had grown worse again. On the following day the doctor was with his patient, and the Marshal was there too.

After Kuomintang or the National People's Party was victorious in China, the new regime was, by the Marshal's orders, introduced in his province also. This took place on the 1st of July. On all the streets and houses of the town waved the flag of the victorious party, the white sun in a blue field. An official ceremony was performed in the morning at the Governor-General's festally decorated yamên, to which all functionaries and officers, Chinese and East Turki, had been summoned. Speeches were made in honour of the historic event, and homage was paid to Sun Yat-sên's portrait.

At a subsequent meeting a Council was appointed for the Kuomintang Party in the province. Opinions and convictions played no part in the selection, for the Marshal himself decided who should be members of the Party and the Council. He changed his own title, as had been done in the other provinces of China, from Governor-General to "President of the Provincial Council."

Then followed a great banquet in the pavilion in the park, where the great hall was adorned with Yang's portrait, like the image of a saint hanging before an altar, and in its courtyard his gilded statue rose beneath a roof supported by columns. The place of honour had been allotted to the Russian Consul-General, Samiatin, and on the Marshal's right sat Fan Yao-nan, the Commissioner for Foreign Affairs. Among the multitude of Chinese officials there were, for the rest, only two foreigners, the Postmaster, the Englishman—or rather Scotsman—McLorn, and Dr. Hummel. Professor Hsü Ping-chang and Major Hempel were away at Bogdo-ula at our meteorological station.

It was said afterwards that the murder was intended to take place at this banquet, but the perpetrator hesitated, for the park was well protected by guards, and at the last moment the day was changed to July the 7th. The Marshal was in the best of spirits and delivered, as usual, a perfectly turned speech, which was responded to by Fan Yao-nan and the Russian Consul. What the aged, wise and crafty Yang thought in his heart of hearts about the new political course of China, history does not relate, but it is probable that he smiled at it, thinking: "Weighty words and gaudy flags, but I govern my province on the same course and by the same principles that I have followed for eighteen years. Here no political boundary marks are removed. I command here."

How many of the mandarins of the province or of the other Chinese in prominent positions were in favour of Kuomintang? How many had adopted the development of the new era and understood the new ideas which were to save China, to unite the vast republic and lead its 400,000,000 of inhabitants into the eternal paradise of peace? I have been told by responsible Chinese that the party in Sinkiang could boast of *one* trustworthy party man. And that was the one who murdered the Marshal.

The old Yang, at the age of sixty-six, tall and stately, was full of the joy of living and activity. He wished to escape for a while the frightful heat and confided in Hummel that he intended to invite himself up to Bogdo-ula to enjoy the coolness from the snow fields and glaciers. Accordingly he asked Hummel for information concerning the way up to the mountain above the village of Fukan, and when, some days later, the doctor returned there, he took a car to try how far it was possible to drive. The Marshal would travel by litter after that.

The new motor road to Turfan had just been completed, and the Marshal had decided to inaugurate it on July the 8th. But he wished to have a report on it first, and on the 6th sent his trusted agent, the Tatar, Burkhan, by car to Turfan.

On the same day Hummel, accompanied by one of our friends, Pan Tsi-lo, went to Bogdo-ula. It was lovely to come from 38° in the shade to the fresh summer breezes in the pinewoods round Fu Shu-hsi's picturesquely situated temple by the shore of a little lake. Yang had asked the doctor to take soundings of the depth of the lake. He had given orders that one of the pavilions of the temple should be his last resting-place. He was a Taoist, and Fu Shu-hsi's Taoist monks and priests would keep watch about his grave.

On July the 10th, in the evening, two of Pan Tsi-lo's friends came up to the station of the "Mountain of God." They were agitated and had the air rather of fugitives. Their disturbing report was not clear, but this much seemed certain, that Fan Yao-nan had shot the Marshal. At the murder fifteen or sixteen others had been killed or wounded. It appeared also that Chin Shu-jên, the chief of the Marshal's chancellery, had taken the red seal of power into his hands and proclaimed himself Governor-General of Sinkiang or President of the Provincial Council.

There was no time for delay. Both Hummel and Pan Tsi-lo considered it their duty to hasten down to Urumchi,

Hempel Photo

Chien Ho Ting, 'Pavilion of the Mirror Lake', at Urumchi

[*face p.* 64

Group photographed just before the murder of Yang

Sitting, from left to right: Hsü, Finance Minister; Li, Governor of Urumchi; Yang, Governor-General; a guest from Nanking; Fan Ta Jen, the murderer; Yen, Industrial Commissioner; Chin, the present Governor-General of Sinkiang

[*face p.* 65

the doctor with the idea that he might be of use to the wounded, the Chinese official to report himself to Chin. At 1 in the morning the horses were saddled, and the two men rode without stopping to Urumchi, where they arrived at 4 p.m. on the 11th.

Hummel went straight to our headquarters at the former Russo-Asiatic Bank, where he met Professor Hsü and was informed that there were hardly any wounded to attend to. Hsü also related what he had learnt about the course of the ghastly festival. A day or two before the murder, Fan Yao-nan paid a visit to our headquarters and afterwards stayed a couple of hours with Professor Hsü. He had then been calm and gentle and had spoken of the new era in China, but, for the rest, of indifferent matters. Professor Hsü could never have surmised that anything so frightful was at hand. It was said that two days before the day of the murder the Marshal had received anonymous letters warning him to beware of Fan and of the conspiracy which this man had prepared against his life. But Yang, who was hardened to this sort of thing, had laughed and had not believed them.

Hummel also learned something from the Russian teacher, Medvyediev, who was present at the banquet.

There is in Urumchi a juridical seminary where the examination was held on the 7th of July. The pupils were examined in various subjects including Russian, and for this reason the personnel of the Russian Consulate were invited. No other Europeans were there, nor any of our Chinese; for that matter only Professor Hsü was in the town. The seminary is situated exactly opposite the Marshal's yamên. Year after year he had honoured this examination with his presence. This year, 1928, he had been in a radiant humour and had delivered an encouraging and brilliant address.

After the examination was completed, those present were photographed in several groups. There one sees in the centre the old Governor-General, serene and confident, in the last half hour of his illustrious life. He sits there like a venerable patriarch among his people. There one also sees the murderer, Fan Yao-nan, smiling and deferential as on numberless occasions before. There is the Governor of Urumchi, the Industrial Commissioner Yen Ting-shan, and the other members of Yang's and Sinkiang's government. And at the end of the row sits Chin, the Chief of the Chancellery who, although his rank was lower than that of several of the other mandarins, was yet a few hours later to hold the reins of supreme power in his hands.

The superintendent of the seminary was one of the conspirators. To begin with he had had the dining-table laid in the great hall whose windows open on the street. But the day before the festival he had given orders that only tea and refreshments should be taken in that hall and that the dinner should be served in an inner room, less easily accessible and out of sight and hearing of the guard. Here the destined victim could obtain no help, and it has been stated that, if he tried to escape into the open, there were also murderers posted in the room through which he must pass. He was to die at all costs.

Three round tables were laid in the small inner hall. At the smallest the Marshal sat with his ministers and two secretaries. Behind Yang's place stood, as usual, his bodyguard, Colonel Kao, who always watched over his personal safety. He was a large-limbed giant of martial aspect, always courteous and jovial, and our particular friend. As a rule the Russians were placed at the Marshal's table, but this time they were at one of the side tables with Fan. At the third table sat the teaching staff, among others Medvyediev, teacher of the Russian language. Pupils, officers and others sat in a side room. The Marshal's escort which always accompanied him was regaled in a more distant room, so that they should not hear the shot and come to his aid.

Chin had been at the examination and the photographing, but shortly before the dinner had gone home to attend to his official duties.

Only ten minutes had passed, the first course had been brought in and the chopsticks were in play. Then Medvyediev heard several shots just behind him. He thought it was a joke with "Russian crackers." But next moment everyone sprang from his chair and he realized that it was real shooting in bloody earnest. He saw ten men dressed as servants surrounding the Marshal's table. Old Yang at once saw his danger and was on the point of rising, when several pistol muzzles were pointed at him and the shots blazed out almost simultaneously. He received three bullets in the head and two in the heart. He crumpled up and slipped to the floor. The faithful Colonel Kao tried to cover him with his mighty body, but was immediately shot. He died in his dead master's arms. Yen got one bullet in the elbow and two in the thigh. He too fell on the floor and remained motionless, pretending to be dead. The two secretaries at the Marshal's table were murdered. General Tou was shot dead or stabbed. Several shots were fired into the roof to scare away all superfluous spectators. The pupils and teachers fled head over heels. The Russians hurried into a side room and hid themselves, and only came out when all was quiet. When Yen supposed that he was the only living man left in the room, he got up and perceived two pistols aimed at his forehead and ready to go off. He held up his hands, begged to be spared and was allowed to go.

The murderers were said to be disguised soldiers of Fan's bodyguard. It is said that the first signal was given by Fan. When he loudly toasted some one of the guests, the murderers were to get to work. Immediately after the first mortal shot, he had hurried out, escorted by some of his men. He steered his course, with his troop, to the Governor-General's yamên and burst into his private room to seize the red seal of power. He who has that seal in his hands is the supreme authority in Sinkiang and must be obeyed by all. But there were two soldiers posted at the entrance who refused him admittance without specific orders from the Marshal. He then ordered his men to shoot them. They fell at their post.

His next proceeding was to write a proclamation to the people, an exhortation to all to remain quiet and obedient. But his hand was trembling, and he made one of his men write from his dictation. He then sent a summons to the Chief of the Chancellery, Chin. But when the latter refused to come, it is said that Fan understood that the game was up.

Chin, who by this time had been informed of what had occurred and suspected Fan, hastily collected such troops as were available and surrounded the yamên. His troops are said to have refused at first to attack, saying that Fan had made himself master of the yamên, but after a repeated order, they obeyed. Fan's men had barricaded themselves in the courtyard, to defend the office buildings and their master. But there were only twenty of them and they were short of ammunition. When they would have used the machine guns that were always mounted in the courtyard, they were unable to do so since they did not understand the mechanism.

Meanwhile Chin's soldiers halted and climbed up on to the walls and roof of the yamên. Some of the conspirators were killed, and the rest surrendered. Then they rushed in and took Fan to prison. His troop was likewise imprisoned.

At the same time, Lu, the engineer at the radio station, came to the yamên and inquired for Fan. Someone had warned him, but he had already been observed and was suspected. Two days after the murder he was arrested and was shot at the same time as the superintendent of the seminary. Lu was accused of having given Fan secret telegraphic communications, which, however, seems unlikely in view of the strict censorship of telegrams of which we had so trying an experience.

Chin acted promptly and energetically. He immediately had the city gates closed and sent out military patrols for the preservation of order.

Several of the murderers were shot the same evening. As to Fan's fate many rumours were current. Late in the evening and at night he was interrogated and urged to betray his accomplices. When he refused, he was put to torture, but still stood firm. It was said that they cut off his upper lip, his nose and his ears and put out his eyes. At night he was strangled by two men each pulling on one end of a rope thrown in a noose round his neck. The corpse was flung over the wall and was lying in front of the yamên on the following day. It was afterwards buried down by the radio station. All the remaining accomplices were executed during the night. This was the lesson that the conspirators and the soldiers got, who believed in fair promises of advancement and reward.

All next day the gates were kept shut and were only opened to holders of valid passports. Proclamations, warnings and orders were posted up everywhere.

In Fan's yamên, his servants had barricaded themselves and were besieged. An old and faithful servant had, however, opened the gate, and the inmates were pardoned. Fan's little daughter and her "ama" fled into the town, and it was not known where they had gone. Some had wished that the girl should be killed beside Yang's coffin, but this was not done. Lu's wife pleaded in vain for her husband and that she might go with her three small children to the coast. But this too was refused. She lived afterwards in penury. If a Governor-General dies in the execution of his duty outside the walls of his yamên, his body is not brought back to the official building. So it was now. Old Yang was borne in his coffin straight from the seminary to a Taoist temple and laid before the high altar. The ritual at the solemn burial service was Taoistic. The whole temple was filled with the long hanging breadths of linen with their black letters of condolence. The usual paper figures and the rest of the time-honoured ceremonies were observed. The wish of the dead to be buried at Fu Shusan was not observed, for his family wished to have him in Peking, and there, later, he was buried.

For some time great tension prevailed in Urumchi, where a state of siege was declared, and no-one might go out after 9 o'clock. At our headquarters, where Hempel, Hsü Ping-chang, Hummel and two of our new meteorological students were then living, they were prepared for the worst. There might be rioting and pillage at any moment. Precious collections and records were buried in the cellar under that part of the Bank which had been burned. But by degrees it became calmer, and when I reached Urumchi on October the 4th, three months after the murder, although the military patrols were still out and the gates were closed early, everything was quiet.

I have already mentioned the trouble that the Governor of Chuguchak had had about our packages, which had been sent us in the summer and which contained articles of equipment, instruments, twelve hundred cartridges for our rifles and six hundred which the prince of the Torguts had asked us to bring him, a saloon rifle and a number of other things. When, on the 30th of June, Hummel asked the Marshal that these cases should be delivered to us unmolested he had at once answered, yes.

Three weeks later the cases arrived and were immediately taken possession of by the President of the Provincial Council. When he found the ammunition he was furious. A rumour spread through the town that we had supplied the murderers with arms and ammunition. They were all confiscated, including the saloon rifle which was to have served the collectors to shoot birds with.

We came, in the course of the autumn, to have experience of the change which had come over our position in relation to the authorities of the province. I shall have something to say of this in the next chapter. To us and the scientific researches that we were engaged in and had planned, the death of Yang was a calamity.

The new President of the Provincial Council from the first day showed himself equal to the occasion. He maintained exemplary order in Sinkiang, and the strictest discipline. It never came to rioting or disturbances, pillage or violence. He possessed presence of mind and energy, and, like Yang, wished to manage the affairs of the province entirely on his own account.

But Sinkiang had lost the finest ruler it had had since the days of its first Governor-General, Lin Chin-tuan, and China one of its best sons. And we had lost a powerful friend, and deeply deplored that we had only for a few months been able to work under his wise and enlightened protection.

VI

LAST DAYS IN URUMCHI

AS the autumn wore on the attitude of the new Governor-General, Chin, became less and less accommodating. In form, he, like the whole provincial government, was courteous and obliging, and all written communications were couched in an engaging and ostensibly amiable tone. But in reality the obstacles in the way of our freedom remained, hampered and delayed our work and increased its cost. The permission already given for our members' travels was revoked. Those who were out in the field were recalled.

On November the 17th we were invited to a gala dinner at the Governor-General's, together with all the high mandarins of the town, the Postmaster, Mr. McLorn and three gentlemen from the Russian Consulate General, twenty-six persons in all. The host received us affably and smiling. As in Yang's time the dinner was prepared by Russian cooks, the wines flowed, and Chin made a speech in favour of neighbourly relations with Russia as well as in favour of our expedition. Fourteen armed soldiers were on guard in the room.

The acting Russian Consul-General, Semiatin, returned thanks on behalf of Russia, and I for the expedition. I observed that we had begun under the Chinese Government's protection and in co-operation with Chinese science, which was richly represented on our staff. When we had encountered difficulties in Kansu our situation had been saved by a single word from Marshal Fêng Yü-hsiang. In Sinkiang we had been received with splendid hospitality by Governor-General Yang, who was our constant friend and powerful protector. We rejoiced in the assurance that that day's brilliant entertainment implied a demonstration that our position had not been changed in the slightest degree by his death.

Then Professor Hsü Ping-chang made a brilliant speech in which he sketched with fluent eloquence the outlines of our journey and our plans. He spoke of the inception of the new era in China and of its demand for freedom, of the scientific importance of the thorough exploration of Asia, of our aims and desires and of the interest Sinkiang ought to take in our work and its success. We had many and powerful friends in China, Chiang Kai-shek and his government, the whole scientific world of China which expected great results from our work both for their own country and for the rest of humanity, Marshal Fêng, who had helped us in a critical situation, and the Universities, which were represented by the students in our company. We on our side expected here in Sinkiang all the understanding and the support which were necessary to a successful issue of our enterprise.

Professor Hsü spoke in a friendly and conciliatory tone, but the content of his speech carried weight. It was amusing to watch the faces of the mandarins. Their attention was strained to the uttermost. They smiled, their faces shone with satisfaction, they looked significantly at one another and nodded, and from time to time were unable to restrain quite noisy shouts of applause.

The Professor concluded. The Governor spoke again. His new speech was very short. The position in Sinkiang was critical, and great difficulties had lately arisen. But he hoped still to be able to be of use to our expedition, and that the various members would attain their objects.

By now it was 4 o'clock, and in an hour the city gates would be closed. We rose, were conducted across the courtyards, took our leave and drove home.

A couple of days later Hsü and I visited the Governor-General. He now appeared unusually accommodating. Norin, Haude and Bergman might get to work in the field if they would keep away from the war zone. As regarded our proposed desert journey, we were to hand in a written application.

Dr. Haude returned to transfer his field of operations to Bogdo-ula and afterwards to Pitshan east of Turfan.

On November the 22nd Major Hempel and the mechanic Lagerbäck started for home. It grieved us all deeply to lose Major Hempel. Everyone loved him, Chinese, Turks and Mongols as well as Europeans. He had been an ideal comrade. As headquarters chief and chief of staff he had maintained the highest order and discipline. In this capacity, which is a full man's job, he worked hard, but he still found time to copy all the maps we had so far produced, since it gives a feeling of security to have two copies of them. We all felt deep regret when Hempel's room stood empty.

Lagerbäck had to be sent home for reasons of health. He and Hempel travelled by cart to Semipalatinsk, and their desire to reach home for Christmas was not fulfilled.

On the 24th Professor Yüan returned from his successful investigations at the northern foot of Tien Shan. He brought with him, in several cases, fragments of the fossil Dinosaurus of the Jurassic period which he called Tien Shan-saurus.[1] We drank his health at dinner in special recognition of his fine and important discovery. During the following days he arranged a little exhibition of his find, to which the mandarins were also invited.

A day later we gave a dinner for the mandarins. We had invited the Governor-General, but he had declined. Nevertheless, we had an entertainment very uncommon in Urumchi to offer our guests, namely a film show. With a view to better lighting we borrowed the apartment of Wu, the chief of the electricity works, and there the handy Carlson set the film in motion. In the spring I had often talked to old Yang about films in general, and had promised him to bring with me from Stockholm an exhibiting apparatus and a series of suitable and instructive pictures. He had been especially interested in military pictures, landscapes, industrial establishments, flying machines and the like, which he had never seen. In Stockholm Captain Gunnar Dyhlén had, most kindly and free of cost, furnished me with all the necessary equipment.

[1] The question of name is undecided.

And now the exhibition was to be launched. The Governor of Urumchi, the Mayor, the Commissioner for Foreign Affairs Chên, the Industrial Commissioner Yen and several other high mandarins sat in tense expectation before the screen.

All went splendidly. Before the worthy gentlemen, Swedish soldiers marched in army manœuvres, ships of war rolled on the high seas, flying machines sailed over Swedish soil, the waterfall of Harspränget tumbled foaming into its abyss, farm girls tended their cows in Jämtland and sugar was boiled in a factory.

After the exhibition a Chinese dinner was served, and the party broke up before the shutting of the city gates.

On November the 26th I received telegraphic information from home that my application for a grant for our expedition had been granted by the King.

You can imagine what joy this message awoke among us. The couriers who were presently sent out to those working in the field conveyed the glad tidings. All were grateful for the active interest that the King and the Government have been pleased to show in our undertaking.

Professor Hsü had requested audience of Chin. The latter answered that he should instead apply to the Commissioner of the Interior, Wang. Three questions were involved. We asked that Chin should telegraph to the Governor at Qara Shahr to the effect that Norin should be left in peace to work; that Yüan should have permission to form a topographical corps for mapping the unknown parts of Dzungaria; and that Hsü, Hummel, Chên and I should receive permission to make our journey through Kansu to Peking. The two first wishes were granted, but the journey through Kansu was refused.

We had lost precious time in negotiations, November was past. My plans for returning to the desert had been thwarted, and there was no knowing how it would go with the other members' plans and work. We were living in an unbearable state of uncertainty.

Finally Professor Hsü Ping-chang and I determined to go to Peking and Nanking and speak to our committee and to the central government. If we got their permission to continue our scientific work, the Governor-General ought not to be able to hinder us.

Our last days in Urumchi were devoted to farewell visits and banquets, and to packing. At our visit to the great yamên the Governor-General did not appear himself, but was represented by Wang. The Foreign and Finance Commissioner received us. The farewell dinner was given by all the Commissioners jointly, and the supreme authority was represented by his big, red, old-fashioned visiting card.

McLorn, the Postmaster, gave a dinner, and so did his subordinates Ting and Chên, and finally we were also invited by Father Hilbrenner, Mr. and Mrs. Gmirkin and the deceased Fan's interpreter for Russian, Chou, who in his time had shared in General Gustaf Mannerheim's travels in Eastern Tibet.

A week before our departure our Tatar friend, Burkhan, who with the Russian Gmirkin is chief of the garage and motor-car service, informed us that a motor-bus and a lorry were at our disposal on December the 17th for the journey to Chuguchak. Together the charge for these was 1,170 crowns, which is pretty stiff for scarcely 380 miles.

Two days before the start we were informed that the Governor-General had had a notice put up in the garage to the effect that until May of next year all automobile traffic to Chuguchak was suspended, on the ground that the local authorities of that route had reported the road impassable. We could only suppose that this was a new blow struck against us, and that the intention was to prevent our journey [1] to Nanking. We discussed the possibility of such a situation. If we were kept in mild captivity, we should still be able to work, if only at half speed. We could always establish communication with the outer world. However, the matter was not so desperate, and we received the assurance that the two conveyances were always at our disposal.

[1] Which must be made via Chuguchak–Siberia–Peking.

VII

FROM URUMCHI TO PEKING

AMBOLT'S recovery had been delayed by complications affecting his heart and lungs. On October the 15th Dr. Hummel writes:

> "Yes, the improvement can now only advance slowly. To-morrow the sixth week of illness begins. This tendency to chronicity is distressing, for in many cases it makes an invalid of the patient for months and years. I *hope* that all will go well, but should the course of the disease be long drawn out, I dare not take the responsibility of his staying out here. I have not wished to raise this question with Nisse for fear of discouraging him."

Only four days later the doctor telegraphs: "Ambolt improving last week. Hope danger past."

After a further ten days, the doctor came to the bold decision to bring his patient, well wrapped up, in an omnibus to Urumchi. The journey took six days and was successfully performed, though not without narrow escapes from accident. A stop was made at a Chinese inn. The doctor helped in the patient and, having made him comfortable on a chair by the fire, went out to make his bed. He heard his name called and rushed in just in time to catch Ambolt, who would otherwise have fallen in dangerous proximity to the fire.

It is superfluous to say that they were welcome at headquarters in Urumchi. Ambolt convalesced slowly and surely, and in the middle of December we ventured to leave him. The Russian physician, Pedeschenko, is an experienced man and promised to look after the convalescent. The mechanic Carlson was continued in his appointment as sick nurse.

The 17th of December dawned. On this day a new phase of our saga began for me and my fellow-travellers. Early in the morning the two conveyances were standing ready at the garage whence our departure was to take place. But I knew by experience what "the morning" meant in such cases, and we did not hurry ourselves. Many of our friends called, and at noon we had luncheon. I gave my last orders to Ambolt and Carlson, who now took over responsibility for headquarters and for the accounts. Professor Yüan was still to remain for a time at Urumchi before returning to his field of work, and Dr. Haude would be riding to Bogdo-ula after Christmas and later to Pichan. Haslund was to proceed to Qara Shahr and then to join Norin. Carlson was given my keys and would be responsible for my possessions. We took the botanical and zoological collections with us. These were to be conveyed to Stockholm by Bergman. We were taking the original maps prepared by Norin, Hempel, Chên, von Massenbach and myself to Peking, while all the geological, palæontological, and archæological collections were left at Urumchi. Hummel's and Haslund's anthropometric results were transmitted to Peking for revision by Dr. Stevenson.

Our finances were pretty satisfactory. The four cars with spare parts and the almost complete equipment for a repairing shop which I had bought in Stockholm, the freight charges on the Russian railways, the wages and travelling expenses of the two mechanics and other charges represented a sum of about 45,000 Mexican dollars, or in round figures 90,000 crowns. Most of this sum I had provided from my own means out of the royalties on the Swedish and German editions of my book *Back to Asia*,[1] together with a generous contribution from Mr. Versteegh. The amount had been repaid by Governor-General Chin to the extent that 20,000 Mexican dollars had been paid in Sinkiang liangs (Urumchi taels), and taken over by Ambolt and Carlson. We got about two and a half liangs for a dollar. Twenty thousand liangs had been deposited at the post office, where we had already 2,000 Mexican dollars

[1] Published in England under the title *Across the Gobi Desert*.

on deposit. Finance Commissioner Hsü had 20,000 dollars to transfer to our account at our bank in Peking, and this had been done. The remaining 5,000 Mexican dollars due to us from Chin remain with Hsü. We had besides something over 4,000 liang due to us from old Yang's estate. In a word, our position was such that we could get along for several months before we need have recourse to the grant voted to us by the Swedish state.

On our way to the garage we looked in on the Russian acting Consul-General Semiatin, who most obligingly provided us with all the papers, visas and recommendations we required and gave us besides a cheque on the Russian bank at Chuguchak. The currency of Sinkiang consists solely of one-liang banknotes, and some thousands of such represent a considerable weight.

Several of our friends had gathered at the garage for a last farewell. The Foreign Commissioner, Chên, was there, a kindly and agreeable man who often complained that he was compelled to issue edicts which he personally disapproved. And Ting from the post office was there with his charming wife, admired by both Europeans and Chinese; Burkhan and Gmirkin and several more. Of our own people there were Professor Yüan, Dr. Haude and Lieutenant Haslund as well as the young collector Pai.

The travelling party consisted of three Swedes and three Chinese, Hummel, Bergman and I, Professor Hsü Ping-chang, the topographer Chan and Hsü's servant Wang. Father Veldman of the Catholic mission station at Manas was going to Holland on a year's leave and was a pleasant and entertaining companion for as long as we had him with us. Our motor omnibus was comfortable. A few Sarts accompanied us, one of them being Hassan Abdullah Birisheff of Chuguchak. Our baggage only just found room in the lorry. The driver of the motor-bus was the capable Svestonov who managed admirably.

"It is 2 o'clock, aren't we ready yet?"

"No, certainly not. All our baggage has to be examined by the customs officer."

"Yes, if you please!"

Everything is opened. Meanwhile, we are invited to tea.

Not till 3 o'clock are we ready. A last farewell. The engines begin to hum, and the cars roll out of the garage. At the eastern gate of the town, which is a double one, we are held up by a military post between two arches. Our passports and permits have to be inspected. It is a matter of routine.

At last we are on our way in earnest. We pass the public gardens with Yang's memorial hall and statue. The city walls disappear behind us, the outermost houses are left behind and we are out in the countryside. We meet camel caravans in winter garb and rows of carts creaking across the white fields. Some loads of hay block the narrow road, but we squeeze past them.

In four days we are in Chuguchak. We drove on to the house of the White Russian merchant Hochriekov. It was here that last autumn Ambolt lay fighting for his life. Now, too, we were hospitably received and stayed in our old quarters.

We were kept three days in Chuguchak, for it always takes a good time to obtain sleighs, horses and coachmen for the journey to Sergiopol. There are plenty of them, and they come and make their offers, but they are exorbitantly dear, and one must bargain with them and let them underbid one another. Finally, we agreed with the same proprietor who took my German friends and me to Saisan-nor in May. We required six sleighs for ourselves and our baggage. They cost 150 roubles each to Sergiopol, 190 miles away. The sleighs are capacious and furnished with side runners which prevent them from upsetting. Each sleigh is drawn by three horses. But 900 roubles for a miserable 190 miles is a bit stiff all the same. They put the blame on the dearness of the times, and it is true that the prices of the necessities of life, corn, fodder and coal, have risen considerably since last year.

The last day in Chuguchak all our affairs were arranged, and we exchanged visits with the Governor, the Mayor and the Chief of Police. Baravoi, the Russian Consul, gave us all necessary papers and permits and greatly simplified our journey on the other side of the frontier. It was not the first time he had given us his assistance.

In the evening Governor Li gave a farewell dinner. It was stiff going, and after each toast sounded his persuasive kan-pei, to the dregs. There were many toasts, and he did not cease his persuasion till we had followed his example.

On the morning of Christmas Eve we were called early, packed and received visits from Chinese and Russian friends, among the latter from the surgeon Kalinkin and the Orthodox priest. To help us through the customs, Consul Baravoi was so kind as to accompany us in person to Bachti. He and I drove in the small, light sleigh belonging to the Consulate, drawn by two excellent horses. We swung out through the yard gates and away from Chuguchak.

We sped away over the snow-covered steppe. The horse between the shafts trotted, carrying its head majestically high, while the other galloped with its head stretched out and downward. A freezing and biting north-wester drove clouds of drifting snow against us, and laid a white armour over us, our fur coats and rugs. It stung the skin; one could hardly open one's eyes, as one sat there keeping one's balance precariously in the ruts and over the drifts, for the sleigh had no support for the back, and unless one was careful one might be thrown out at any moment.

The distance to Bachti is only twenty-three kilometres. The first nineteen are in the territory of Sinkiang. It was really a relief to stop for a quarter of an hour in the Chinese custom house where my handbag and photographic apparatus escaped the notice of the guard. At the Russian frontier bar we were not stopped at all—the consul was in the sleigh. We took the last verst at flying speed and finally drove in through the houses of Bachti to the customs house.

Hummel, Bergman and our Chinese travelling companions did not get in till 4 o'clock. They had been held up for an hour at the customs on account of some new formality.

At the Russian customs all our through baggage was registered under seal, part to Bjeli Ostrov on the Finnish frontier and part to Manchuria on the Manchurian frontier.

The kindly and hospitable bank director, Nikolaieff, had pressed us three Swedes to dine at his house. He had not much to offer us, since his wife had only just arrived from Moscow, but we should none the less be welcome to all the house could provide. " Shchi " (cabbage soup), stewed beef, pudding and tea, thanks and good-bye, and a walk back in the falling Christmas twilight to our quarters for the night in a comfortable Tatar house.

The hours of Christmas Eve wore on. We sat on a mat around a foot-high table in the Tatar's house, Hummel, Bergman, Hsü and I, and talked of the future of the expedition and of the great tasks that awaited us. This Christmas, too, the table was laid by Hummel and decked with a seven-branched candlestick with red candles and two small Swedish flags. In the late evening there appeared Christmas ham, butter, cheese, hardbread, jam, cakes and sparkling wine. We drank a toast to Christmas, to our country and to all our dear ones at home. The last hour of this day of tender memories had struck when we climbed into our bunks in the silent winter night.

On the morning of Christmas Day we should have made an early start, but neither horses nor sleighs put in an appearance. Now, too, Baravoi came to our assistance. The six " troikas " soon drove up to our yard. Our baggage was stowed in three of them, and three accommodated us three Swedes and the three Chinese. The former were open, and the latter covered with rounded tilts of felt and straw matting. A thick layer of hay was spread on the bottom of the sleigh and over it were laid rugs, pelts and cushions, so that we sat, or rather lay, softly and in comfort. We were thoroughly tucked in with rugs and skins and did not feel the biting cold at all.

At noon we took leave of the friendly Consul and drove away from Bachti with bells jingling. The long line of sleighs looked imposing against the white snow. It took us two hours and a half to drive the first twenty-seven versts to Ata-gai. At this post the horses were changed, while we drank tea and ate sandwiches in the well-warmed room of the little station, where the samovar was boiling and an old Russian peasant woman attended on us.

After a couple of hours' rest we crept back into our fur-lined lairs and lay on our backs during the four hours which passed in driving the thirty-three versts to the large village of Makantji. Towards evening it grew very cold, −28°, but the air was still and the sky clear, and the moon shone brightly over the snow. Our coachman, Kurban Gali, who sits on a straw sack in front of us, begins to feel frozen and runs for a while beside the sleigh to keep himself warm. Hour after hour we glide over the crackling snow, the horses steam, we talk and smoke, Bergman and I, but we grow drowsy with the monotonous jingling of the bells, the conversation is more and more frequently broken off and finally ceases altogether, while our procession moves northward through the boundless expanses of Kasakstan, the Kirghiz Republic which is subject to Moscow.

When at length we arrived at a farmhouse at Makantji, we were pretty sleepy, but woke up on meeting with certain quarrelsome, drunken fellows, who had staggered out into the yard after a lively party and were falling into their waiting sleighs. The room was tidied up after the drunkards, and, having eaten a meal, we retired to rest.

Next day we were to have been called at 3 o'clock, but, whether because the coachmen were sleepy or the horses hungry, there was no awakening until 7 o'clock, when the temperature was −14° and it was blowing freshly. The weather was fine, and it was glorious going over the snow. We passed the posts of Barakbai and Kosak-su and met an endless line of sleighs laden with red petrol-tins and drawn by stately camels. We took our afternoon rest at Urdshar and reached Igen-su at 8 o'clock in the evening. Between 11 p.m. and 3 a.m. we covered the distance to Ters-bakan. Here we met rows and rows of camels drawing sleighs. They looked magnificent in the moonlight.

At Ters-bakan we had to make the best of a wretched Kirghiz hovel where an old woman sat feeding a smoky fire with cattle-droppings and where, after a simple meal, we rolled ourselves up on our felt mats and slept in our clothes. Next morning the doctor was called upon to visit a patient.

At 10 a.m. it was only −10·5°; the temperature, instead of falling, was rising as we went towards Siberia.

At Kara-köl we put up in the same pleasant rooms in

which Ambolt, the chauffeurs and I stayed in the autumn. Thence we drove to Tesek-tus and Aj, a village in which we had difficulty in finding quarters. Hummel, however, inquired at a Kirghiz hut whose host made no objection to granting us the use of a corner of it. But his pretty young wife was furious at this unexpected intrusion at midnight and scolded her inoffensive husband uninterruptedly. After we had invited the couple and their daughter to share our late tea and had honourably paid the rent in advance, the young woman melted and became perfectly amiable. On December the 28th our party pressed on by the light of the full moon, and we saw the winter day dawn and fade before we reached the stanitsa of Sergiopol at 6.30 p.m., to which place the railway from Semipalatinsk had been completed since our visit in the autumn. They had worked well, for, in September, they had still seventy miles of rails to lay. We drove on to the " sovtorgflot's " house to which we brought a letter from Consul Baravoi. Two of the employees received us with the greatest friendliness, begging us to put up with the limited space available. In a smallish room we slept nine men deep, together with squalling children, a cat and a dog. The hostess prepared an excellent evening meal and gave us tea and bread, and we had a really pleasant evening.

We had also learned by experience that in winter it is pleasanter and safer to travel by sleigh than by motor-car in these rugged and half-wild regions.

As we were sitting, on the morning of December 29th, 1928, drinking tea and eating " pirogues," three gentlemen called and asked if they could be of any service to us. One of them, Statkevich, was " samestitel " (deputy), or " pomoschnik " (assistant), to the chief of the railway and the senior engineer for its construction. He told us a number of things about the construction of this new line which unites Tashkent to Novo-Sibirsk—Western Turkistan to Siberia. We also came to know that the train for Semipalatinsk would start at 1 o'clock and that a special part of a coach had been reserved for us. And finally we were told that we were the first passengers on this line, which had hitherto only been used for workmen, engineers and railway material. In fact we were thus inaugurating an entirely new track in Russian Asia.

The railway station lies six versts to the south-east of the stanitsa of Sergiopol. A lorry carried our baggage thither, and the three gentlemen then accompanied us over the snow-bound road to the train, which stood ready on the brand-new track. They put us into our reserved compartment, in which all the heavy baggage was heaved up on to the upper shelves. We made ourselves comfortable on the seats with blankets and fur rugs. A stove was glowing in a recess and it was more than warm enough. When all looked like being in order, it was said that the train would start at 1 o'clock. But hour followed hour and the train stood quietly by the platform. A couple of men in uniform stepped up to us and asked civilly to see our passports.

At last at 5.38 the train began to move northward. It was then already dark, and we lighted the candles which we had bought in passing at the co-operative store belonging to the railway.

Next morning we had our sleep out. There was still no sign of the Siberian cold. The day passed quickly in reading and talk and in watching the white monotony of the landscape, the snow-covered steppe, with here and there a little clump of trees, a village or a farm. No long stay was made at the stations, but the pace is slow; they drive cautiously on the new track. With the help of the stove and the doctor we get hot food and enjoy coffee and cigarettes. Our civil conductor gives us the joyful tidings that we shall arrive by 10 o'clock in the evening.

And sure enough, on the stroke of ten the train drew up at Semi Dchana. We packed up our things, and the conductor advised us to keep our revolvers handy during our journey into the town, since night attacks were not uncommon. Before we were yet quite ready he informed us, however, that the sleighs we had engaged by telephone from the town had already gone off, probably appropriated by others wishing to cross the river. Since we could not get our precious baggage across the Irtish without horses and sleighs we had no choice but to go to bed again and spend yet another night on the train. On the following day, the last of the year, we drove in big sleighs over the ice of the Irtish above the new bridge and engaged three rooms at the Hotel Kasakstan. The doctor and I went on to the railway station where all our baggage was registered to Novo-Sibirsk, an affair which was put through by a pleasant young girl, just as sturdy and competent as a railway porter.

The day we spent in Semipalatinsk was used to the best advantage. We visited the museum, where Bergman photographed Pedaschenko's neolithic collection, we fetched welcome letters from the post and spent a couple of hours with that admirable and experienced archæologist Alexei Nikolaievich Bielosludov, from whom we bought two of the albums of his brother Viktor, who died in 1916, one of neolithic finds executed in colour and one of pencil sketches of Siberian architecture, both very skilfully done.

At dinner we toasted the past year, which had brought us so many memorable experiences, and expressed our hope that the new year might be even more fortunate for us. And then we drove to the station, took possession of our compartments, made the hard seats as soft as possible with fur rugs and blankets and resumed the long journey to the trans-Siberian railway.

We started soon after midnight. The first of January, 1929, passed in perfect peace. We read, wrote, chatted and smoked, but saw very little of the country, for the window was covered with dense frost flowers. One more night passed, and at 5 a.m. on January 2nd we alighted at Novo-Sibirsk, that stirring and rapidly-growing town whose Tsentralnaya Gostinitsa (Central Hotel) is fairly modern in its arrangements.

Novo-Sibirsk has also a museum for natural science, Siberian products and ethnography. It is not large but is always a good beginning, and it is managed with care and devotion by a friendly lady. The archæological objects belonging to the museum were not yet displayed. The library, containing 40,000 volumes of scientific works, is also under feminine management. Unfortunately we did not now meet the German Consul, Herr Grosskopf, who later on helped us and other members of the expedition in every conceivable way and, with never failing kindness, took upon himself the trouble of sending many valuable and important instruments to Sinkiang on our account.

At Novo-Sibirsk we took farewell of Folke Bergman, who was going home for a short holiday, and ourselves drove in large sleighs to the station in the darkness of the small hours of January 4th. According to the timetable the east-going express should have left at 4.13 a.m., but it was very late and only got away at 6.38. Hummel and I got a compartment to ourselves. Hsü Ping-chang and Chan got another, and Hsü's cook, Wang, his own seat in the third class. With the moon shining brightly on the snow, we recovered most of our lost night's sleep.

On the Siberian train the days pass quietly and monotonously. One reads and chats and pays visits to newly-acquired acquaintances. Among others we fell in with three Austrian gentlemen who were returning to their work at Shanghai. When the train has passed Krasnoyarsk and Yenisei much of the night is over. After three days and nights we leave Russian territory.

At 9 p.m. on the 7th we are at Manchuria, the frontier station, where all the baggage is carried to the custom house. The Russian inspectors scarcely looked at our things; the Chinese were more punctilious, but made no comment. Then we installed ourselves in a clean and pleasant carriage on the Chinese Eastern Railway.

Next morning at 7.15 we are at Chang-chun, where the Chinese Eastern Railway ends and the Japanese Railway takes over. We threw ourselves down in comfortable armchairs in a very elegant observation car, all glass windows, the last coach in the train. Everything is well kept and polished, and the stations are cosy and neat. Unending fields of kao-liang stretch out on both sides, and the ground is lightly powdered with snow, against which the roads worn by carts drawn by four horses or oxen show up as dark bands.

By 1.30 p.m. we are in Mukden, and the Peking express leaves an hour later. Here the order and system we met with on the Japanese section from Chang-chun is lacking. They did not know at the ticket office whether there were any sleeping berths; only the station-master could supply information about that. He explained that they had all been engaged, but that first-class tickets would entitle us to sit all night in the restaurant car. Yes, that would do very well, and the tickets were bought. But then it was found that our registered baggage was not on the train from Chang-chun, and we certainly could not on this account wait two days for the next express. Hummel arranged to wait to clear the baggage and then take the train to Dairen and from thence the boat to Taku, while I and the three Chinese went on from Mukden—with the risk of having to sit nodding all night in a cold restaurant car. But luckily we got hold of a smart and alert conductor who procured us proper sleeping berths before the train started. How, for the tip he expected, he evicted the other travellers, we never knew.

The lightly snow-covered country takes on more and more the northern Chinese character. Here and there we pass small villages with groves of trees. Only occasionally a few travellers are seen, or a cart or two. The dusk falls and it is night again.

January the 10th was our last day on the way to Peking, and our first spring day—it felt almost warm after the Siberian cold. At Tientsin, where we arrived two hours late, we took farewell of the topographer, Chan, who was now leaving our expedition and returning to his relatives. The ground is everywhere bare. We make the great curve and glide in along the monumental city wall of Peking, and at 3.30 arrive at the Chien-mên station. Herr Kullgren from the Swedish Legation is there to meet us with our mail from Sweden.

At the Hotel Wagons Lits I took a comfortable double room for the doctor and myself, while Professor Hsü drove to his home. The personnel of the hotel was the same as two years ago. The "boys" in the rooms, in the dining-hall, at the telephone booth and at the desk were our old friends and were touching in their delight at seeing us again.

In twenty-five days, of which five had been days of rest, we had accomplished the long journey from Urumchi—a positive record—and now we should soon know our fate.

VIII

NEW YEAR IN PEKING

IT is always a pleasure to me to return to Peking. Over this city there hovers a glamour of departed greatness, a flavour of native nobility and a strangely captivating charm. Peking is one of my favourite cities. The others are Samarqand and Bokhara, Jerusalem and Damascus, Benares, Rome and Moscow. Stockholm and Visby are in a class by themselves. When I first visited Peking in March, 1897, the torches of the last dynasty still burned brilliantly, and, in the midst of the Tatar city, the wall still stood which concealed a world of secrets and treasures around the Imperial court. Three years later much was destroyed of the glamour that surrounded the "Son of Heaven." At the time of his death and that of the Empress Dowager I was in Japan. My intention of going to Peking was frustrated by the court mourning. Then followed the rule of Yüan Shih-kai, and the Republic (1911). When I revisited the proud city in 1923, all its externals had undergone a striking change. No walls rose any longer as an insuperable rampart around alluring secrets. One wandered undisturbed about the forbidden city, inspected the imperial palace and drove in motor-cars on new wide streets. Civil war was raging in China, and in Peking there was a shadow President and a Government whose power scarcely extended beyond the city walls.

Three more years passed, and in November, 1926, I returned to the stately old metropolis. At that time Marshal Chang Tso-lin was the most powerful man in Northern China, and the civil war raged incessantly between the various Generals. The power of Dr. Wellington Koo's Government was so circumscribed that he and his ministers, yes, even the Marshal himself, had to bow to the Federation of Learned Societies and Corporations, when the latter laid down its nationalistic conditions for our great scientific expedition to the interior of China.

On January the 10th, 1929, I entered for the fourth time the capital city of Yung Lo, K'ang Hsi and Ch'ien Lung. Scarcely two years had passed since I last left it. And again a radical change had taken place. The republican central power had removed to Nanking. Peking was no longer the capital of China but only the seat of the authorities and Governor of the Province of Ho-pei, the ancient Chihli, whose name, reminiscent of imperial times, had been abolished like that of the city. It was to *Peiping*, " the northern peace," that I had come. It was only too obvious that something had happened. True, life went its wonted way in the streets and public places, but more thinly and sparsely than before, and the Government buildings stood abandoned. It was stated that 2,000 shops had been closed for lack of customers. All the legations were still there in their inviolable quarter, and when the envoys had important discussions with the Government they travelled down to Nanking, a journey that was not always convenient.

But none of the foreign ministers had travelled such long roads as we to negotiate with those in authority. We had come from the capital of Sinkiang, and our first stage was Peking, where we had to consult with the representatives of the scientific world and with the Committee which had been formed two years earlier to watch over the interests of the expedition. And, as I shall presently relate, the thing was mere child's-play. But Peking is a perilous city. Before one knows where one is, one becomes the helpless victim of a boundless hospitality both from the Chinese and the Westerners.

Time after time we were invited to the houses of our Chinese friends, not least by Professors Hsü Ping-chang and Fu Liu of the National University and Dr. Yüan, a brother of Professor Yüan of the Tsing-hua College, the member of our expedition and discoverer of Tien-shan-saurus not far from Urumchi. I paid a number of official visits with Professor Hsü and sent cards to all the members of our Committee. The first meeting of this took place on

January the 16th in a building appertaining to a temple at Pei-hai or "the north sea," where a jade Buddha is majestically enthroned. Eight members of the Committee were present besides a secretary, Hsü Ping-chang and myself.

They all greeted us affably, and it was easy to perceive that the atmosphere was different, was warmer and more sympathetic, than two years earlier. But during these two years the Europeans and Chinese in the expedition had worked together in the greatest harmony and concord, and no friction had disturbed our relations; we had been friends striving for a common goal.

We sat at a long table at which tea and cigarettes were served, and the former Governor of Honan, old Chow, rose and bade us welcome to Peking. Afterwards Professor Fu Liu acted as chairman. He asked me to give a brief report of the expedition's progress and most important results, and afterwards to put forward my desires for the future. I submitted that Professor Hsü Ping-chang ought to reply in Chinese to the first question, after which I would pass on to the twelve proposals, of which I had already made a list in advance. Hsü's speech only took half an hour, and then came my turn. I only state here the most important points. I considered it superfluous to touch upon the articles of the agreement of April 26th, 1927, since I knew already that the mood of the Chinese was in the highest degree generous and well disposed. Only *one* clause in the agreement was of vital importance, and if this were not altered all further negotiations would have been superfluous. In the agreement it had been laid down that the expedition was not to continue for more than two years. I now requested an extension.

"Until what time?" asked Professor Fu Liu.

"Until May the 9th, 1930, or three years from our first departure from Peking," I answered.

"Let us say May the 9th, 1931," suggested Professor Fu Liu, and they all agreed. In this respect I had thus got more than I asked.

I further asked to be allowed to extend the expedition by the addition of three Swedish geologists and palæontologists and three young Chinese scientists, the more so that the

Hartung Photo

A Corner Tower in the City Wall of Peking

Hartung Photo

The Temple of Heaven, Peking

[face p. 91

student Tsui had been sent home, the topographer Chan had asked to resign and the photographer Kung could, on Professor Hsü's suggestion, be dispensed with.

These proposals were approved without discussion.

The new Governor-General of Sinkiang, Chin Shu-yen, had caused us difficulties during the past autumn. We had obtained permission from the old government to travel in Sinkiang and were besides protected by the agreement of April the 26th, 1927. We considered it strange that the Chinese participants in the expedition should be refused permission to travel and to work in their own country. I now, therefore, requested the Committee's support and recommendation when Professor Hsü and I should presently apply for the new government's protection.

This point too was agreed. At first it was suggested that a deputation of the members of the Committee should accompany us to Nanking, but since the Committee knew already that the Government intended to approve all our requests, it was decided to address an exhaustive official communication to President Chiang Kai-shek and the ministers, and to send it in advance to Nanking. I understood now that we had the highest support to be obtained in China, that of the Government and of the strongly nationalist scientific world. The policy we had observed towards the Chinese in respect of harmonious co-operation and mutual confidence would, sooner or later, assuredly bear fruit.

The next proposal concerned the permission to employ flying machines for geographical and archæological reconnaissances. To this the Committee answered: We are not experts on this question but we suggest that the Committee request the Government that two Chinese flying machines be put at the expedition's disposal free of cost.

Finally the Committee promised its strenuous support for my application to the Government that the expedition might have permission to issue its own postage stamps. The revenue which might be counted on from this service should, I suggested, go uncurtailed to defraying the travelling expenses of the Chinese members and to the maintenance of the meteorological stations founded by us and now under Chinese control. Any surplus could be applied towards the cost of the journal which the Committee intended to publish and which was to be exclusively devoted to the affairs and research results of the expedition. The idea of this source of revenue had been suggested to me by the English expedition to Mount Everest, which had its own postage stamps, and which, according to an oral communication from its geologist, Odell, derived a not inconsiderable income from this source.

After I had stated all the twelve points in my list of requirements, the Committee held a private discussion, which did not take five minutes and which resulted in its approval of all my proposals, though final sanction could only be given by the Government at Nanking. The representation to the Government was to be drawn up from the minutes of the meeting. Some days later I was informed that, since the Committee could guarantee the Government's answer, it was unnecessary for Professor Hsü and me to visit Nanking. It was, however, thought proper that we should wait personally upon the President, Chiang Kai-shek and the ministers directly concerned with our interests, especially upon the head of the Control Yüan, Ts'ai Yüan-p'ei and the Minister of Education, Chiang Mon-lin. A personal meeting with these could not but strengthen our position.

It is impossible to conceive a more cordial and honourable reception than that accorded to us by the Chinese in Peking. The Prefect, the Presidents and the Rectors of the Universities and other scientific institutions, museums and libraries seemed eager to outdo one another in hospitality. We were tossed from one banquet to another and scarcely had breathing space between the brilliant engagements. I would much rather have gone to Nanking, so that I might get back to my staff in Sinkiang. But new reasons for delay constantly arose, now it would be dinners, now official receptions and visits, now lectures to students. Thus precious time was lost, and we had to arm ourselves with patience. And, strictly speaking, the time was not thrown away. We formed many ties of friendship among the learned, and we had, too, certain obligations to the students, three of whom were working at our stations. I was frequently interviewed by the Chinese newspapers, whose interest in our expedition was increasing. The principal papers published portraits and photographs which we placed at their disposal. Time after time, young Chinese came begging to accompany us in any capacity, and it was always painful to refuse their requests.

Some days before the meeting I have described, twenty-four scientists, among whom were the members of our Committee, had given a great banquet for us at a Chinese restaurant, all in authentic Chinese style.

This banquet surpassed anything of the kind that I had attended. The hosts were the Governor of the Province of Hopei, General Chang Chên, the Mayor of Peking, Ho Ki-kong, the Rector of the National University and Chang Ki, President of the Kuomintang Party in Northern China. Among those present were twenty-eight heads of learned societies and rectors of universities, and the guests of honour were Professor Hsü Ping-chang, "Duke" Larson, Dr. Hummel and myself. From the drawing-room, furnished in European style, of the Wai Chiao Pu or Foreign Office we were conducted by our hosts to the banqueting hall, where the table was adorned with three immense crystal bowls filled with red roses, and the cloth was strewn with flowers in the colours of the national flag. Lackeys in Chinese liveries stood as lighted candles behind the chairs, the electric lights shone upon glittering glass, and a festive mood prevailed in the room. When the champagne had been served, President Chang Ki rose and made a very fine speech in French and Chinese, proposing the health of the guests. After observing that he had been present at my lecture twenty years ago in the great hall of the Sorbonne, he congratulated the expedition on its work and on the results it had already gained. Among other things he said: "The co-operation which has taken place in your expedition has given us evidence that Chinese and Europeans can very well work together in harmony and good comradeship, and it has also strengthened the bond between Sweden and China." Finally he expressed his best wishes for the continued activity of the expedition.

After his speech he asked me to give my reply the form

of a lecture, and my oration accordingly occupied over an hour. It was all very well for me, but not so well for Dr. Wong, the head of the Geological Survey of China, who had to act as interpreter. I concluded my speech with an assurance that I and my comrades would be happy if we could contribute in any measure to the understanding between Europeans and Chinese and that our hosts and friends might rest assured that the hospitality and goodwill which had been shown us by the supreme authorities of Peking and by the leaders of the scientific world would be regarded by our countrymen as an act of friendship and sympathy for Sweden.

On one of the following days we were taken by Professor Fu Liu to the first lecture, which took place in the great hall of the Parliament building, and for audience we had the professors and students of the National University. All the 1,200 seats were occupied and there were students standing in the gangways. Just as, duly escorted by learned men, we came on to the platform, a deafening noise broke loose in the hall, the students rose from their places, shrieked, yelled and bellowed like wild beasts and adopted an attitude which seemed to grow more and more threatening. I asked my nearest neighbour if all speakers were received in this vociferous fashion, but he explained that the row was nothing to do with us, but was directed against certain Japanese journalists who were there in pursuance of their calling. The feeling against Japan ran very high in January, 1929, and the students were now demanding in this demonstrative manner that the uninvited guests should be thrown out. It looked like becoming a regular riot when the youths began to rush forward towards the place where the Japanese were standing. One of the authorities mounted the rostrum and demanded silence, but no-one heeded and the hubbub increased. Finally, the Japanese escaped by a back way, but not until the Professor had solemnly assured them that not a single Japanese was left in the hall did the storm subside and the young patriots resume their places.

After this dramatic prelude, old Chou mounted the rostrum and bade us welcome to the meeting and said a few eloquent words about the importance of science.

Then came the turn of Dr. Fu Liu. He spoke of our expedition, of the co-operation between Europeans and Chinese and, in graceful periods, of his and the Committee's appreciation of the successful manner in which we had unravelled the problems we had set ourselves, and wished us success and rich harvests during the two new years yet to come.

Professor Hsü Ping-chang spoke for an hour on the general progress of the expedition and I for an hour and a half on the scientific results. With perfect ease Dr. Li Chi interpreted my English lecture. Each speaker was greeted with tremendous applause.

By way of conclusion the film taken by Mr. Lieberenz was exhibited to an audience more eagerly attentive than ever. Unfortunately there were as yet no English or Chinese captions, and Professor Hsü had constantly to explain what the pictures represented. The film was a decided success, and is to be shown later on in the great towns of China.

When the meeting came to an end half an hour after midnight, it had lasted fully five hours, and, in spite of our furs, we were pretty well frozen. For the place was unheated and the temperature stood at freezing-point or not much higher in the open air.

With the Doctors Berglund, Bohlin and Andersson and their wives, Hummel and Kullgren, I drove to our hotel, where we warmed ourselves with suitable drinks such as tea and bouillon.

Equally warm and friendly was our reception at the ice-cold places where, towards the end of the month, we lectured to the Franco-Chinese University, the Tsing-hua College and the Military Academy. The meeting was always preceded by a banquet with toasts and speeches, and one thus got more or less warmed up before the freezing began.

Our meetings lasted their full five hours, and although on our journey through Kasakstan we had had a taste of pretty biting cold, it proved in the end too much for me, for it is one thing to lie well tucked up in a sleigh and quite another to sit in a hall as cold as a cellar.

On February the 1st a roaring dust storm passed over

Peking, and I sat at the writing table by a draughty window writing a chapter of this book. I felt seedy and took a hot bath, returning afterwards into the draught. Later in the night I was awakened by an excruciating pain in the region under my right shoulder blade. Hummel examined me and diagnosed intercostal neuralgia. And so I was tied to my bed. The pain was so abominable that I could only occasionally manage to read. But on the other hand I received visits and friendly gifts of flowers. On February the 10th Hummel called in Dr. Willner from the Peking Union Medical College, and he advised us to move to that College's hospital for radical examination and treatment. They began with blood pressure, blood tests, pulse, temperature, Röntgen photography, baths and the rest, and I was tended by small, pretty, roguish Chinese nurses who cleaned the room, made the bed and washed my body.

I received visits every day. Once the Professor from Greifswald came, Dr. Jaekel, palæontologist and connoisseur of ancient Chinese bronzes. I had known him in Stockholm, where he had lectured. Now he relieved my loneliness, and we talked of things which interested us both, not least of his bold theories about the age of the Chinese bronzes, which he made out to be considerably less than other investigators held them. Some weeks later he, like me, caught a chill, but his power of resistance was insufficient; he died and was buried in the foreign cemetery at Peking. He was an exceptionally fine and lovable man and enjoyed the highest reputation as a scientist.

Others among my visitors were the American doctors Granger and Stevenson and the Canadian Dr. Davidson Black, Herr Wihelm Schmidt the representative in China of Luft Hansa, Professor Eric Nyström, an engineer from Stockholm named Karlbeck and the Swedish missionary Kullgren in whose house I lived in 1897. I was treated with diathermy for a week without, however, any appreciable amelioration. My old brother in arms Hsü Ping-chang was one of my constant visitors so long as I lay sick.

By February the 23rd I was so far recovered as to be able to return to the hotel. On the way we called upon Professor Hsü who presented to us several beautiful gifts, vases, pictures and books. Ill news reached us from Sinkiang, Ambolt informing us that the Governor-General had forbidden the sending up of pilot balloons, and all kinds of excavation in the earth. Haude, Norin and three of our Chinese members had thus been materially obstructed in their work.

Meanwhile there was ferment among the students, and the red waves rose high. Youth did not approve of all its teachers and went on strike against instruction. Our friend Chang Ki, the most eminent political leader of the Kuomintang party in Peking and Northern China, was especially an object of indignation and, going one evening to his house, I found the street blocked by soldiers and his courtyard looking like a military encampment. However, I got in on showing my passport and found the genial statesman calm and unmoved by the storm raging round the house.

Professor Hsü was one of the few who found favour in the eyes of youth, and he was thus constantly occupied with lectures and classes. He had already lost a month owing to my illness, and when, on February the 25th, Dr. Hummel and I started for Nanking, he was not able to accompany us, but was to follow us in a day or two.

IX

NANKING

ON February the 25th the train rolled softly and warily out of Peking, and the yellow, apparently desolate country unfolded itself around us. There was not much to be seen from the carriage window. Occasionally one sees people, here and there a farmstead, a village, a few trees. The train is packed with Chinese. The coaches have been in use during the unending civil war and are therefore sadly knocked about, and the carriages are worn and shabby. But we had nothing to complain of, especially as we were able to divide our time between travelling companions so distinguished as the American Minister, MacMurray, and Dr. Hu Shi, the simplifier of the Chinese written language, well known as an author in *belles lettres* and philosophy and perhaps the keenest and most critical brain in the new China.

MacMurray's secretary, Mr. Bucknell, had made extensive journeys in Yünnan and Szechuan; the young physician and botanist, Dr. Chên, had been nominated to take part in our expedition, and Tai, the professor of pedagogics, initiated us into the mysteries of Nanking.

We passed Pao-ting-fu and, next morning, stopped an hour and a half for some unknown reason at the station of Kai-fêng. Here the country was once more lying under snow, and dark burial groves stood out against the white covering. One more night and morning. Again the country is bare and the rain is pouring down on rice fields and bamboo thickets. Early in the afternoon we arrive at Pukou and go aboard the crowded ferry boat to cross the Yangtze. The day is oppressive and gloomy. There are liners, junks, merchant craft and gunboats lying in the mighty river. At the quay of Nanking we take a car to the Yangtze Hotel, where we make ourselves at home in two very pleasant rooms. In the new—but also old—capital city of the vast republic there is only one European hotel. The Chinese inns are much more numerous, but the rooms in them are small and fireless, and the Westerner misses the cleanliness and comfort necessary to his well-being. Nanking is in all respects unlike Peking. It is scarcely possible to imagine greater contrasts between two towns in the same country. In Peking one finds everything one can desire, including wide, regular streets and short distances to travel when visiting one's friends, whether European or Chinese. Nanking is a jumble, a number of vast villages separated one from another by open unoccupied fields. From Hsia-kuan, the quarter by the harbour, where our balcony provided a noble view over the river, it is a drive of twenty or thirty minutes by car to that part of the city in which the government buildings and scientific institutions are situated. Every visit is an excursion, and cars are expensive. The road that leads to the heart of the city is narrow and runs now between close rows of houses, now like a country lane across open fields. But the city is being improved, new buildings are in course of erection and wide straight streets are laid out in every direction. The most important of these is the arterial road which has just been laid out between the harbour and Sun Yat-sên's mausoleum at the foot of the Purple Hill.

Our first day in Nanking was quite eventful, and it was easier than we had supposed to make our way into authoritative circles. We went direct to the chief of the Central Meteorological Institute of China, Dr. Ko Ching-chu, whom I had known in Peking and who was himself very eager to meet us. He is a slender young man with polished manners, who completed his studies in America, and a perfect master both of his science and of the English language. He has, moreover, published learned works of the highest value on meteorological subjects. Dr. Ko Ching-chu embraced our plans for the investigation of the climate of Central Asia with the greatest interest. We could not have found a better ally in our struggle. He saw at once that we had done China a great service by establishing the four permanent meteorological stations at Etsin-gol, Urumchi, Charkhlik and Kucha, besides the three mountain stations, and he was quite prepared to assume responsibility for them, their staffing, expenses and maintenance in other respects. Our own students were shortly to leave their posts, and Dr. Ko Ching-chu now proposed to train a staff of ten new observers to take the place of the old. He also expressed a wish to consult with Dr. Haude about the establishment of a complete system of meteorological stations scattered over the whole of China proper, a project which I promised to support in every way. We rejoiced in the hope that the services we could do to China and to science by extending the network of observation points over the earth's greatest continent would be one of the indirect results of the expedition.

Accompanied by Dr. Ko Ching-chu we later visited one of the most influential ministers in the Central Government, old Ts'ai Yüan-p'ei, who was formerly Rector of the National University at Peking and who is now director of the Research Institute at Nanking. He is moreover a celebrated and highly esteemed author. The Government consists of sixteen departments which are grouped in four "yüan" or divisions. Ts'ai is the chief of the Control Yüan, Tan of the Executive, Huang of the Judicial, Hu of the Legislative and Tai of the Examinations. The chief of the Executive Yüan, Tan Yen-kai, is also President of the Council or Prime Minister.

Ts'ai Yüan-p'ei was living in a very simple and unpretentious house in European style. Smiling affably and bowing, he met us with outstretched hands and, in German, bade us welcome to Nanking. We sat down in a small reception-room, where tea and cigarettes were handed round according to Chinese custom, and the courteous and engaging statesman then asked us a multitude of questions concerning the expedition, its work and future plans. He thanked us for our successful co-operation with the Chinese and expressed his pleasure at the advantages that both parties would reap from it. On my side I thanked him for having saved our station at Etsin-gol, at the beginning of the year before, by his telegram to Feng Yü-hsiang, when it was threatened by the authorities of the Province of Kansu. He assured me that he would always plead our cause and asked us now to bring forward all our wishes unreservedly.

I seized the opportunity to tell him that we desired first and foremost to obtain full and undisturbed freedom for scientific work.

To this Ts'ai Yüan-p'ei answered that I and my comrades had no cause at all for anxiety; the Government would send telegraphic orders to the Governor-General.

"Yes, but supposing he does not obey them? It is a long way to Sinkiang, and Yang governed the Province in his own way. His successor may be expected to follow the same methods."

"The Government has means in its hands to enforce its will."

But at this point luncheon was served, and the Minister invited us to join him at the meal. To the accompaniment of Chinese dishes, chopsticks in hand, we continued the conversation until the rice-cups announced that the meal was at an end. But Ts'ai Yüan-p'ei did not content himself with inviting us to luncheon, but also asked us to dinner at half past six on the same day. On this latter occasion we also made the acquaintance of Feng Yü-hsiang's deputy as Minister of War, General Lu Chung-lin, a virile figure, with strong features of the occidental type.

We devoted the following days to paying and receiving visits, and we had now the company of our friend Professor Hsü who had meanwhile arrived in Nanking. Among those who called upon us was Vice-Rector Liu of the University, which is said to have 180 professors and 1,900 students, and consists of eight colleges, two of which are at Shanghai. We also made a number of shorter excursions and saw the Ming tombs, which were used until the year 1405, when the dynasty transferred its capital to Peking. Professor Kai and several other learned gentlemen accompanied us to the Science Society of China, where we inspected the library, the zoological museum and the biological laboratory. This society, which is said to be the largest in China and has 700 members, stands in intimate co-operation with the Research Institute, which is under the direct control of the government and whose President is T'sai Yüan-p'ei.

We visited the Minister for Education, Chiang Mon-lin, a tall, spare, serious man of Western education, with elegant and urbane manners. He evinced the liveliest interest in our plans and promised to do everything to forward them. On the evening of March the 5th the Scientific Society gave a banquet for us, and at this, too, Chiang Mon-lin was present. Ko Ching-chu made a speech, and I replied with an account of our expedition, which was amplified by Professor Hsü.

Just at this time a storm was again brewing in China, and the civil war threatened to grow to greater dimensions than before. The occasion was a decisive trial of strength between Chiang Kai-shek and Nanking on the one side and, on the other, Li Tsung-jên, the Governor-General of Hunan and Hupei, who in conjunction with Wu Han (Wuchang and Hankou) formed what was known as the Kuanghsi group. Li Tsung-jên had, against the wishes of the Central Government, deposed and driven out the former Governor of Hupei, Lu Ti-ping, who was cherished by Chiang Kai-shek and who was now in Nanking. Li Tsung-jên, who was in Shanghai, was supposed to have at his disposal over thirty divisions of 12,000 men each. Chiang Kai-shek was supposed to have 200,000 men with his colours. There was a rumour that an engagement had already taken place at Kiukiang, and the excitement was unprecedented. War hung upon a hair. At any moment the fire might burst into a blaze. The unknown quantity was Fêng Yü-hsiang, the Christian Marshal. His troops were reckoned at 250,000 men, and he himself was sitting on the fence. No-one knew what attitude he might be going to adopt, and in actual fact he was inimical to both the other contending groups. The interior political situation in China affected us in the very highest degree. If the Government's position were weakened, the Governor-General of Sinkiang would no longer observe its orders, but would deal with us at his own discretion. It hailed rumours, and we followed the course of events with increasing attention. In the streets of Nanking nothing unusual was perceptible, except that the gates of Hsia-kuan were shut at 9 o'clock and that one was stopped for inquiry by the police when one drove out through them. But the police soon came to know us and let us pass unchallenged.

On March the 8th we were received by the President of China, General Chiang Kai-shek. On our way Hummel and I picked up Professor Hsü Ping-chang, who was living at the Drum Tower inn not far from the Drum Tower which raises its solid mass over the City Hall, and from which several streets radiate to various parts of Nanking. Thence we steered our course to our friend the Minister, Ts'ai Yüan-p'ei, who had promised to accompany us to the Great Council Hall and present us to the great man. In the middle of the hall there is a long table around which the deliberations of the Ministry take place. An important meeting was presently to be held concerning the war against Wu Han and the Kuanghsi group. The tension of internal politics had reached its culmination, and it particularly surprised us that the responsible leaders spared the time to receive us and to listen to matters so far removed from the impending war. If this were to go against him, if Fêng Yü-hsiang were to join his enemies, then both Chiang Kai-shek and his government were out of the reckoning.

Thus it was not surprising that the President was looking grave when, accompanied by Sun Fo and several other Ministers, he stepped into the hall. Tall and straight, with stiff military bearing, Chiang Kai-shek came forward to the table and invited us to be seated. He wore a simple field-grey uniform of European cut, with nothing to indicate his exalted rank. His manner was courteous but reserved, and he did not waste time in ceremonial bowings or traditional phrases. With Sun Yat-sên's son, Sun Fo, Minister of Railways, as interpreter, he turned directly to me and put some questions as to the expedition, its field of labour and its plans. He asked to be informed of our wishes and undertook to issue his orders in conformity with them. Then he conversed for a while with Professor Hsü Ping-chang, who described in greater detail the progress of the expedition and its hopes for the future. Finally the President expressed his regret that at the moment he had so little time to spare and his hope that on some later occasion he might have us as his guests. We rose and took our leave, and the Council meeting could begin. Three of the five Yüan chiefs were present at the audience, namely Ts'ai Yüan-p'ei, Tan Yen-kai and Huang Chung-hsüeh.

Later in the day we paid a visit of courtesy to General Lu, who received us in a small unpretentious room where we were invited to take tea at a round table. If, he said, it was our intention now or later to travel to Kansu, we might quite well do so, but we must be prepared for attacks by bandits and must therefore be well armed. Since Kansu was one of Fêng Yü-hsiang's provinces, the Marshal would no doubt provide us with an escort and give all necessary orders for our safety.

Finally I had promised to lecture to the Ching-ling College, an American seminary for young girls. A couple of days earlier I had been speaking at the Y.M.C.A., and during the exhibition of the film, had been gallantly attacked by two sweet little Chinese girls, who begged me to tell them, too, about my adventures. Naturally it had been impossible to refuse their request, and there I was in their school and before a public consisting entirely of Chinese girls and their American mistresses, but for three or four men, of whom one was the old Minister, Ts'ai Yüan-p'ei.

Although it was only the 9th of March, it was full summer in Nanking, and warm breezes played about my sunny balcony. The climate here is far softer and milder than that of Peking. There was not much evidence of the tension of internal politics. The people of Nanking took all rumours calmly. Presumably they were used to war and rumours of war. There had been hot work in Nanking. The English proprietor of the Yangtze Hotel, where we were staying, told us that everything he possessed, including all the furniture of the hotel, had been plundered and burnt and that he was compelled at the point of a revolver to hand a considerable sum of money to his assailants. He was now expecting similar evil times and contemplated moving to Shanghai with all his valuables and his wife, a Chinese from Formosa, leaving his hotel in charge of his servants. The moment a black flag was hoisted on the gunboat lying in the river, all British subjects were to go aboard, for it would then be a question of saving their lives. And now the black flag might be expected any time. To avert a repetition of the bloody events of 1927, the British and American consuls in Nanking had advised their nationals to remove to Shanghai. Order and security were maintained in the new capital by a couple of thousand of the Peking police force who had been transferred to Nanking, the streets of which city they were now patrolling in their dark uniforms and silver-edged caps, with revolvers in their belts, and were acting as traffic police at all street crossings.

Scarcely a day passed without speeches or banquets. Usually Professor Hsü and I both spoke, and we always divided the material so as not to deal with the same points. If he dwelt upon the general progress and vicissitudes of the expedition, I gave an account of its scientific labours and results, and if I described the geography of Central Asia and the discoveries I had made in the interior of the continent, he would confine himself to the political and ethnographical aspects, and at such times he always insisted on the importance to the new united China of exploring and intimately attaching to the mother country the great provinces in the far west, Kansu and Sinkiang.

A hundred young men, officers and students, were at this time being trained in Nanking as apostles in the service of the new progressive national policy. Their task was to organize propaganda in Sinkiang and Mongolia and spread the knowledge of the Kuomintang's modern ideas. One of these youths, Lo To-chi, who in six months' time would be sent out with his companions to the Turki and Mongolian countries, sought our Professor Hsü and me to ask us for a lecture. We had just been in those distant tracts and had certainly much to tell which might be of service to these young apostles.

The whole corps was collected in the gymnasium of the military academy against the cold walls of which our message echoed, to the accompaniment of a raging gale which howled and wailed over Nanking. The air was thick with dust, and the streets were empty; even the Peking police had gone home. Professor Hsü dealt generally with geographical points, and I gave the young men a lot of practical advice about equipment and details of the roads, means of transport, inns, camping arrangements and provisioning. My interpreter, the sympathetic Colonel Huang, afterwards invited us to a meal at the officers' mess, where spirits and smoking are forbidden.

On March the 11th we dined with Chiang Mon-lin, the Minister of Education, to meet several of his colleagues. At a later entertainment on the same day given by the Counsellor of the German Legation, Dr. W. Wagner, I met the brothers Hoo Che-shy and Hoo Chi-tsai, both of the Foreign Department, good linguists, intellectual and educated in the West. The latter was Secretary to the Foreign Minister, Dr. C. T. Wang, whom, in spite of several attempts, I never met. When we were in Nanking he was at Shanghai, and when we went to Shanghai he had returned to the capital.

The 12th of March is the anniversary of Sun Yat-sên's death, and is kept as a holiday throughout China. All the official world assembled at his still empty mausoleum for a festivity of mourning and commemoration, and a number of high-flown speeches were made. All work was suspended and the office buildings stood empty. In June the body was to be brought in its sarcophagus from its temporary resting-place in the western hills by Peking to the grave at Nanking.

On March the 13th the Government's telegraphic orders were sent to the Governor-General of Sinkiang. According to Chinese custom these orders were expressed in moderate and courteous terms, although they left no doubt as to their final intention. According to Professor Hsü's French translation, the telegram was as follows:

"To the President of the Provincial Council in Tihwa (Urumchi), Chin.—The Minister for Education, Chiang, certifies that the scientific research expedition composed of Chinese and Swedish scientists has carried on its research work in Kansu and Sinkiang and has attained good results. Now its directors, Hsü and Hedin, desire to increase the number of its members and to extend its sphere of work. The Swedish investigators, Bohlin, Hörner, Bergman and Bexell, will soon enter Chinese territory at Chuguchak. Hedin and the other members are going to Sinkiang by the great road through Kansu. For this reason we beg you to issue orders to the authorities in your province to confirm the expedition's passports during their travels and to give protection to its members and further, within the limits of the expedition's scientific labours, such for example as excavations and the sending up of pilot balloons, in all ways to facilitate their endeavours and in nowise to throw obstacles in their way.

"The scientific development and still more momentous ideas in the new era and the responsibility it entails makes it the duty of the Government to afford them, the members of the expedition, all possible help. We accordingly send you this telegram, and it is your duty to act in accordance with what has been said above.

"EXECUTIVE YÜAN."

13th March.

The particular mention of the two branches of our work, excavation for archæological, geological and palæontological purposes and the sending up of pilot balloons, was the result of a wish expressed by us after we had learned from a telegram received from Urumchi that the Governor-General had forbidden such activities. He regarded excavations as likely to cause unrest among the inhabitants, who might suppose that we would disturb those who slept in their graves, and pilot balloons were entirely outside his horizon. A similar telegram was sent at the same time to Liu, the President of the Kansu Provincial Council at Lanchou. From the latter the Government received an immediate answer in which Liu assured them that he would support the expedition in all ways and would issue orders in the same spirit to all the authorities in Kansu. But Sinkiang lies much farther off, and, ever since the revolution of 1911, its ruler, Yang, had been in the habit of obeying no orders whether from Peking or from any other government in China. To my question whether we need wait for an answer from Urumchi the Ministers replied that an order from the central government required no answer since in practice it *must* be obeyed. The Minister for

Education considered, however, that we ought to wait until it was ascertained that the telegram had arrived, and since the working of the telegraph in the interior of Asia is highly irregular, this might take a long time. He suggested, therefore, that we should, in the meanwhile, visit Hangchou, a town which would arouse our enthusiasm as it had aroused Marco Polo's.

We travelled to Hangchou, Su-chou and Shanghai, but, since our return to Nanking on March the 23rd, we received no confirmation of the receipt by Chin of the Government's orders, we determined to wait no longer. And in this we were wise, for when I reached Stockholm I received a letter from Ambolt, dated July the 16th, in which he said that Chin had still denied in the middle of June that he had received any orders from Nanking. And yet the signature of the telegram, "Executive Yüan," indicates that the whole Government, including General Chiang Kai-shek, stands behind the order.

X

THE EXPEDITION'S HEADQUARTERS ARE TRANSFERRED TO BOSTON

I COME now to a very curious phase in the history of the expedition. But I cannot just drop out half a year. The occurrences during these six months had very little to do with geographical exploration, but they none the less belong to the chronicle. I fear they will give a somewhat motley impression of a hasty journey round the world.

We are still in Shanghai, and at 1 o'clock the guests we have invited to a farewell luncheon before our return to Peking are arriving. Among them are Chu Chang-nien, the new Minister in Stockholm and Oslo, the Swedish Consul, Wisén, and Dr. Wagner, the German Ambassador, all with their wives, Dr. Hu Shih and Professors Lee and Hsü Ping-chang.

Then I visited the office of the Hamburg-America line, where Herr Boolsen informed me that the steamer *Resolute*, sailing round the world with tourists, had arrived and that three cabins were at our disposal, in which I had the honour to be the guest of the Company. At 5 o'clock I was fetched by Herr Wiedmann to give a lecture at the "Garten Klub," on Sinkiang, to 300 Germans. In the evening we drove to the Customs Jetty where the tender was lying, which at 10.15 conveyed the *Resolute's* passengers out to the steamer. In an hour and a half we were there. We had seen from afar the magnificent liner gleaming like a castle of romance out of the darkness, and, courteously greeted by the officers, the travellers filed up the accommodation ladder. Professor Hsü, Dr. Hummel and I made ourselves at home in our comfortable cabins and afterwards stood on deck till the steamer was well out at sea. We spent two pleasant days and nights aboard the *Resolute*. On the morning of the 5th we paid our respects to the excellent and jovial captain, Fritz Kruse of Stettin, who carried us off to luncheon in the grillroom and afterwards showed us the ship, from the impressive engine-room, through magnificent saloons and halls, the gymnasium, the swimming bath and shops, right up to the topmost deck with the navigating bridge and the lifeboats.

On a cruise round the world, the passengers, of whom ninety per cent. were Americans, have to be amused, and this evening was allotted to a fancy dress ball. I sat for an hour among the spectators to watch the ladies and gentlemen in fantastic Oriental costumes, the most successful of which by general vote were awarded prizes after the ball.

On the following day we and the German Consul-General at Batavia, Mr. Kessler, again lunched with Captain Kruse, who treated us to genuine Swedish fare, the menu in Swedish and with a Rättvik girl on the cover, hors d'œuvres, soup and beer, hard bread, pickled herring and potatoes, and finally Swedish punch. The Chief Engineer, Pedersen, gave us a thorough lesson in running the engine, and at 5 o'clock I lectured in the saloon on my desert travels. The boat was swarming with millionaires. Among these we met the brothers Bishop from New York and Mr. Epstein of Chicago, where he builds railway coaches—even for China.

The *Resolute* had, of course, its doctor and two sick nurses. One of these, a charming young German, had long dreamed of seeing Peking, but could not leave the steamer. When on the morning of the 7th we went to say good-bye to our good friend, Captain Kruse, we put in a word for her, and she got permission from his supreme authority to join the party of tourists to the old imperial city. We dropped anchor in the roadstead of Tsin-wang-tao, saw the celebrated summer bathing-place of Peking, Peitaho, and took nearly eleven hours to reach Peking, where our young protégée was hospitably received in Mr. and Mrs. Wilhelm Schmidt's Chinese house.

There is not much to say about our stay in Peking. I

often met my old friends Baron and Baroness Leijonhuvud, Professors Amadeus Grabau and Fu Liu, Roy Chapman Andrews who had abandoned his usual explorations in Mongolia owing to difficulties with the Chinese, the head of the National Library Dr. Tung Li-yüan, Father Teilhard de Chardin, Dr. Paul Stevenson and many others. One day I was delighted to be rung up by Lieutenant-Colonel F. M. Bailey of the Indian Army, who spent some twenty-five years in Sikkim and at Gyangtse in Tibet and with whose thorough and valuable work I was well acquainted. He had taken part in the British mission to Lhasa and had been with Colonel Ryder's expedition up the Tsangpo to Gartok and Simla. But I had never met him. Unfortunately I was engaged that evening and Bailey was starting for home by way of America the next morning. But we had the night before us and sat talking for several hours. He told me about the state of affairs in Tibet and about the Mount Everest expedition, whose request to open a fourth campaign against the world's highest mountain had been refused. Thirty years ago I spent a couple of days in Newcastle with Bailey's father, who was then Secretary of the Geographical Society of that place, while the Chairman, at least for the evening on which I lectured, was Sir Edward Grey, who was Foreign Secretary at the time of the great war.

Among our closest intimates were Professor Osvald Sirén and Dr. Birger Bohlin and his wife. Dr. Bohlin was now a member of my expedition and was preparing for his journey to Sinkiang. I had several conferences with our committee, represented by Fu Liu and Tung Li-yüan.

My plan was to travel back to Sinkiang at the end of April. To escape the tedious Siberian railway, I determined to travel if possible by car from Kalgan by way of Urga, Uliassutai and Kobdo to Chuguchak and Urumchi. But this required permission and passports from the Government of the Mongolian Republic at Urga. I sent thither a detailed telegram, but the days went by and no answer came. The projected journey was put off on other grounds, and I then telegraphed cancelling my application. Just six months later I heard at the Mongolian Mission in Moscow that my request had been granted but that, owing to my cancellation, the answer had never been sent. Now, a year later, the way through Kalgan and Urga is hermetically closed. The unrest on the Manchurian border and the civil war in China, together perhaps with certain political commotions among the republican Mongols, have interrupted all communications. It is impossible for the present to make any definite plans for travel in Eastern Asia. The position is constantly changing, and one never knows where one can get through.

I have related in a previous chapter how in February I caught a chill which kept me tied to my bed for a month. Now on the 21st of April this illness returned and cancelled all our plans for Sinkiang. On the 23rd I was, however, able to dine with Wang Yin-tai, who was Foreign Minister in Chang Tso-lin's and Wellington Koo's administration. On that occasion I renewed acquaintance with two old friends. One of them was Mr. Klemm with whom I stayed for ten days at Bokhara in 1890, when he was Secretary of Legation to the learned Mr. Lessar. Thirty-nine years had passed since that time. The other was General Horvard, who had been commandant at Harbin when I passed through that town on my way home shortly after the Christmas of 1908. I had come from Mukden and was to join the train from Vladivostok to Harbin. There were two hours to wait. Accompanied by a dozen officers the General met me at the station and entertained me sumptuously in the waiting-room. I was on my way from the mild winter of Japan straight into the Siberian cold. Being without a fur cap, I asked the General if it was possible to send a messenger into the town to buy one. No, it was too late; all the shops were shut. Thereupon the General took off his own mighty fur papasch with the blue and silver badge of his rank, and pressed it on to my head. In this warm and ornamental headgear I travelled all the way to Petersburg, and when I promenaded the platforms in Siberia, the gendarmes gave me the military salute, which I condescendingly returned. It was really strange that all went fortunately and that I was never caught. And now I met the white-bearded General again at the house of

Mr. and Mrs. Wang Tin-tai. He had left Siberia at the outbreak of the revolution and had settled with his family in Peking.

I had promised to lecture on the 25th in the auditorium of the Peking Union Medical College, and here I lay in bed with intolerable neuralgic pains in my back. But the lecture had been announced a fortnight earlier, and it would be very disagreeable to disappoint the public. With difficulty I got up, my medical attendant gave me an injection of morphine, and accompanied by him and Professor Sirén I drove to the lecture, which to me seemed more like a penance. The hall was filled with a highly distinguished public. Among others there were most of the legations, headed by the Swedish and the American. I was led to an easy chair on the platform and told the audience that if I, who was feeling dizzy after the morphine injection, said anything idiotic, they were not to believe a word. But everything went successfully, and by 11.30 that affliction was over.

The end of April and the beginning of May were for me a time of severe trials. The pain persisted, and I was once more taken to the Medical College Hospital where a series of examinations was made, conducted by Professor Hilding Berglund and the neurologist, Dr. Schaltenbrand. I had a whole staff of doctors. Besides the two former and Dr. Hummel, I had the oculist Dr. Pillart, Dr. de Vries and Dr. Andersson. On April the 29th Professor Berglund sat at my bedside and read my sentence. The examinations which had been made indicated that I had a tumour on my spinal cord, and this must be removed. After careful consideration it was decided that I should travel to Boston to Dr. Harvey Cushing, the foremost surgeon of our time for diseases of the brain and spinal cord. A telegram was sent to him, and he replied that I would be welcome. On May the 3rd the doctors held a new conference. Dr. Dipper, head of the German hospital, had been called in consultation. The others standing round my bed, while Dipper, after a thorough examination of Babinski's reflex and other nerve reactions, expressed his opinion, were Berglund, Schaltenbrand, Willner, de Vries and Hummel. Dipper did not feel convinced that there actually was a tumour, but he agreed with the others in advising me to go to Boston as soon as possible and entrust myself to Cushing.

Hummel and I sent a telegram to my home requesting my sister, Alma, to meet me in Boston. Berglund and Hummel telegraphed to Professor Jacobæus. Professor Key and Dr. Floderus of Stockholm were consulted. I was well aware that it was a question of a very serious operation. The laminæ of at least six cervical and thoracic vertebræ would be sawn off and the spinal cord exposed, so that it might be relieved of the tumour. Dr. Cushing was said to prefer local anæsthetics so as to be able to talk to the patient during the operation. A convalescence of three or four months would be necessary at the seaside or in the mountains.

But to me the hardest trial was leaving the expedition. Norin and Bergman were on their way back to Sinkiang from their leave of absence, and Hörner and Bexell were to join them. Dr. Bohlin had orders to wait in Peking until the Foreign Minister, Dr. C. T. Wang, sent up passports for the three new members. And now I must leave everything and cross the Pacific Ocean to an operation whose outcome was uncertain. I selected Dr. Erik Norin as my deputy, but still always retained in my own hands the supreme control of the expedition, which was accomplished by the aid of the telegraph and several hundred dollars. To a greater extent than ever the expedition would be dispersed over the centre of Asia, while its headquarters were transferred to — Eastern North America, an arrangement which was original to say the least. Strangely enough this was a success, thanks to the distinguished manner in which Norin carried out his duties. When none of our people were in residence at Urumchi, the headquarters there were in charge of the Anglo-Russian veterinary surgeon, Dr. Etches, who had been appointed to the expedition and is always an excellent stand-by to us. During my absence from Peking, all incoming telegrams were to be opened by Baron Leijonhuvud, who throughout the summer supported Dr. Bohlin in word and deed.

On May the 9th new storm clouds were gathering over

the expedition. Professor Hsü Ping-chang called to inform me that the "Society for the Preservation of Antiquities" at Urumchi had sent three identical telegrams to the Government at Nanking, the Governor-General at Kansu and the Society in Peking which is known among Europeans by the same name as that above mentioned.

It was said in the telegram that our expedition is mischievous and dangerous, that the Chinese members are our accomplices and that they are in the service of a certain foreign power for espionage of the defences of Sinkiang, that we are using a scientific cloak to conceal our political and military espionage, that we have smuggled arms and ammunition into the province, that by excavating ancient Mohammedan tombs we have upset and incensed the Sart population and that revolts and upheavals are therefore to be feared, unless the expedition is compelled to leave the territory of the province. Besides, we were robbing the province of the valuable antiquities which we found in the course of our excavations and exported.

Professor Hsü had just as little as we heard tell of any society of the above name. Quite simply it did not exist. But very likely it had been founded after the Government's categorical order to the ruler of the province, granting us full liberty in all respects, had been despatched on March the 13th. The mysterious telegram came as a reply to the Government's order. It contained an intimation that this order would not be obeyed.

After a conference between Professors Fu Liu, the Chairman of our Committee, and Hsü they sent very strongly protesting telegrams, one to General Chiang Kai-shek in which the telegram was answered point by point, and one to the Governor-General of Sinkiang. To the latter Professor Hsü telegraphed personally and asked in very courteous terms to be informed what gentlemen constituted the governing body of the Urumchi Society for the Protection of Antiquities.

We could calculate on the attitude of the then Governor-General of Kansu to the calumny, since his relations with Sinkiang were strained and since he had already replied to the Government's order of March the 13th by an assurance that we would be welcome in his province and that the local authorities in Kansu had received orders to help us in every way.

The rumour had also emanated from obscure sources in Urumchi that the Chinese members of the expedition were in some way connected with the murder of the old Governor-General Yang. We had thus obviously enemies in Urumchi. The heaviest blow that had fallen on us, Chinese as well as Swedes, in Sinkiang was just the death of old Yang, for he understood our aims and purpose; and the difficulties we encountered began after his death.

Meanwhile the pain in my back loosed its grip, and I was able to get up and return to the hotel. On the last two days in Peking I paid a few farewell visits to Baron Leijonhuvud, Professor Grabau, Roy Chapman Andrews and Professor Stevenson. On the last evening, as we were leaving Stevenson's compound, Professor Berglund, who was there too, came running after my ricksha, shouting:

"If Cushing says you haven't any tumour you mustn't be angry with us."

"No, I promise *that* solemnly."

After a series of telegrams to Stockholm, Boston, Nanking, Bachti, Moscow, Su-chou and other places, I sent the following message to my home on the morning of May the 13th:

> "Fresh intrigues from Urumchi. Committee here requested Government to send special delegation to Urumchi to investigate and support us. Norin and Bohlin can probably get into Sinkiang. If difficulties Norin telegraphs Fu Liu Swedish Legation. If necessary headquarters transfers Western Kansu for present. Kansu authorities very friendly. Pleased with Haslund's collection. Less pain now. Au revoir Boston 18th June. Cordial greetings."

It was not easy to hold all these threads in my hand, but my medical attendant was an excellent secretary and thought of everything.

The final telegram to Georg Söderbom, who was then at Su-chou in Western Kansu, while Major Zimmermann and, as we supposed, Mr. Ma were still at the meteorological station at Etsin-gol, contained some important points of organization.

> "Plans changed. You remain in Kansu awaiting further instructions. Your suggestion of botanical excursion in Richthofen mountains is excellent. Retain our camels. Zimmermann must return to Peking via Lan-chou. We send further 3,000 dollars to post office at Su-chou. Letter follows. Greetings."

Similar telegrams were despatched daily, sometimes several on one day. They concerned fields of labour, routes, personnel, conveyance of money, mails and instruments, relations with the authorities and much besides.

And now I was to leave it all behind. But the cables pass like spiders' webs around the world. At 8.30 on the morning of May the 13th we left Peking. Several of our friends were there, Baron Leijonhuvud and his charming wife with a huge bunch of red roses, Erdmannsdorff and Fischer from the German Legation, Dr. and Mrs. Bohlin, the gentlemen from the Medical College and the Andrews expedition, Professor and Mrs. Hsü Ping-chang and others. By noon we were at Tientsin and an hour later at Tanku, where we went straight on board the fine Japanese steamer *Chojo Maru*, which at 4.30 slipped her moorings and bore us out down the pea-soup coloured Pei-ho between ships carrying all the flags of the world and junks, under sail or oars, conveying goods up and down the river. An hour brings us out into the quiet mirror-bright waters of the bay of Chihli, where here and there a sail lies idle, waiting for the wind. I am still an invalid and sit listlessly in a wicker chair on the upper deck, well tucked up by the doctor.

Next day the sky is overcast, but the sea is as calm as ever and the junks still spread their picturesque sails in vain; the reflections in the Yellow Sea are as clear as the objects themselves. To starboard lies the Shantung coast with the towns of Têng-chou and Ch'i-fu and the island of Weihaiwei and many other islands, and to larboard Port Arthur and Dairen. The day was hazy, during the night the fog thickened and at 6.30 next morning we hove to. The Captain would not venture into the narrow channel by Korea. We lay at anchor all day. The persistent milk-white fog rested heavily on the sea and drove athwart the ship so that her forepart was scarcely visible from the bridge. An amusing couple of travellers with whom we foregathered were a M. and Mme. Torcat, who were travelling round with their circus of 160 cocks of every strain in the world. These were kept in cages, knew certain tricks and were as proud and self-important as the rest of their race.

At 7 in the evening we weighed anchor, but went ahead dead slow with siren blowing and incessant heaving of the lead. At times we heard the warning call of other vessels at various distances.

On May the 16th, islands to port, one of them shaped like a loaf. An hour later we have land on either side, numerous sailing boats and here and there a steamer. The sea is blue and clear under a cool breeze. We anchor off Moji, which is the quarantine station, and there the doctor comes aboard, and passports are examined. We are surrounded by launches and lighters which take off bales from China. There is a swarm of sailing boats. Alas ! we pass through the lovely sound into the Inland Sea after the darkness has descended on the earth, but we shall see this glorious place again before the year is out. It sparkles with hundreds of lights ashore and on the shipping.

Next day we lay to at the quay of Kobe, where the *Suffolk*, the Duke of Gloucester's ship, was already lying. We went to the Oriental Hotel. The usual interviews were not omitted. The *Japan Advertiser*, the *Osaka Mainichi* and several others called on us, all provided with cameras. The Swedish Consul, Ouchterlony, courteously offered us his services. While Hummel was absent on a three days' visit to Kyōtō, I lay in peace and quietness and wrote letters and also tested my returning strength by a motor journey to Ōsaka.

At 4 p.m. on the 21st we left on the *President Taft*, and by 3 on the following afternoon were in Yokohama, where Messrs. Gadelius and Martin Månsson met us. Later we drove with them into Tōkyō and went straight to the Swedish Legation, where the Minister, Mr. Hultman, was just about to furnish his new home. With him and Mr. Månsson we went to a pleasant dinner at the house of my old friend of 1908, Mr. Gertz. On the morning of the 23rd I was fetched by motor-car and carried an endless distance in pouring rain through the new city, rebuilt after the earthquake of 1923, to the house of Mr. Okura where Rabindranath Tagore was living. I spent an agreeable hour with the great poet and philosopher. But the hour was soon past, and I must go back to Yokohama and the *President Taft*.

We hauled out just before 4 o'clock. It was blowing hard and was cold, raw and gloomy. When we had left Tōkyō Bay behind us and were out at sea, a heavy sea was running. A wireless from Bohlin informed me that he had received passports for the newly arrived members, but that Bergman, Hörner and Bexell had been stopped at Chuguchak on the frontier of Sinkiang.

During the following days we had calm seas and frequent fog, with the siren sounding once a minute. On the 26th we received wireless intelligence from the *Empress of Austria* that she was a hundred miles ahead of us in impenetrable fog and heavy seas. When, some hours later, we reached the same spot, the fog was still dense, but the sea not so dangerous.

The *President Taft* is not a particularly attractive boat and can in no respect compare with the Swedish and German ocean liners. Among the passengers on board was Captain Karl Ahlin of Öland, in whose cabin we spent a couple of hours daily listening to excellent gramophone music. On certain evenings there was a cinema show on deck, always of the usual cheaply sensational kind. I generally lay reading in my excellent berth till 4 in the morning, by which time it was already light at this time of year and in this high latitude, just south of the Aleutian Islands.

The temperature remained round about 15°, and we sat well wrapped up in our deck-chairs and read for several hours every afternoon. On the 27th the fog cleared off, the sky was clear and the sea calm. We were 1,498 miles from Yokohama and 2,702 from Victoria. We usually put about 390 miles behind us in the twenty-four hours. A little newspaper comes out daily with radio news. To-day we learned that the Nationalist army in Nanking has declared Marshal Fêng Yü-hsiang a rebel and ordered his arrest.

It is feeling cold with an air temperature of 7° and with the water at 4°. We get no benefit from the warm current of Kuroshiwo.

Tuesday, May the 28th, was counted twice over, for then we passed the date boundary. On the night of the meridian day we had come half-way between Yokohama and Victoria. The sun broke through at times, but the weather was hazy; with the air at 5·5° it felt chilly. The sea was 4·5°. An unpleasant swell made the ship roll. I sent greetings over sea and land to my people in Stockholm and to my sister Alma at Kungsholm. On the 29th we only made 310 miles, owing to the current, head wind, rough sea and fog. We were now 1,701 miles from Victoria. The weather was rainy and disagreeable. We passed the 2,750-metre cone of the Aleutian volcano, Shishaldin, out of sight on the port bow, as were the Island of Unalaska, and the Alaskan Peninsula.

On May the 30th "Memorial Day" was observed by a sermon and the singing of hymns. In the evening I gave a lecture, introduced by Captain Ahlin. Among our circle of acquaintances were the French airman Vicomte de Sibour and his charming English wife.

On the last day of May it rained all day, but the sea was quiet. The pain in my back had now completely disappeared, but I was still carefully looked after by Dr. Hummel. When I was not reading I wrote letters to my lads in Asia, although in fact I knew very little about where they were since we left Peking. Headquarters was moving eastward and was only 950 miles from Victoria.

On the 1st of June the "Captain's dinner" took place, and the inevitable fancy dress ball. On the 2nd we at last enjoyed a glorious day of sunshine. I had a radiogram from my sister Alma to say that Professor Einar Key of Stockholm would arrive on June the 8th at Buffalo where he had gone for a congress. The monotonous life on the open sea is over, and new interests seize our attention. On the port side, to the northward, we make out the lofty coastline of Vancouver. In the course of the day the contours of snow mountains grow clearer and clearer. The sea is calm. We see seals and sea birds through glasses. We are only 193 miles from Victoria. The newspaper announces from Nanking that the Chinese diplomatic and consular representatives have been recalled from Moscow. The ferment in Asia seems to be worse than ever. Civil war in China, unrest in India and the Labour Party in power in England, and in the midst of the political confusion I am responsible for a great expedition in the heart of the great continent and am just about to establish my headquarters in Boston. But there is nothing for me to do but to be calm. I only hope my lads will defend their positions until I get back after the operation.

In the evening we pass Cape Flattery and enter the straits of Juan de Fuca between Canada and the United States. Lightships and shore lights shine forth on both sides. The *President Taft* is running at half-speed so as not to get in too early. A last cinema show on deck offers the usual rubbish, devoid of art, taste and intelligence.

On June the 3rd we go ashore on the west coast of America. We take an early drive through the delightful town of Victoria and later have four hours' journey to Seattle, where Consul Brattström receives us. He had expected to see an invalid who would have to be taken to hospital on a stretcher or in an ambulance, and was much astonished when I walked ashore with buoyant step.

Next afternoon the good Consul conducted us to our train, "The Olympian," which starts from Tacoma with Chicago for its goal. The way up through the narrow gorges of the Cascade Mountains is quite magnificent, and one stands the whole time enjoying it from an open window. At the bottom of the valley we pass a stream running among boulders. Forest grows on the slopes, where the vegetation is often luxuriant, and snow is still lying on the high peaks. In wild winding curves the train toils up a watershed. Later the country grows flatter, more desolate, more monotonous.

We have an elegant and spacious compartment. There is a "Parlour Car" and an "Observation Car." In the former there are magazines and newspapers, radio music and a writing table. The latter is open and is only coupled on when beautiful landscape is being passed. On June the 5th we go through the Rocky Mountains with snowclad peaks, the Butte mining district and, in the afternoon, Montana Canyon, a narrow picturesque valley. We roll over endless expanses and pass the Yellowstone National Park at Three Forks. The country then becomes quite deserted, one sees no people, seldom any dwellings. We are in Montana the whole day.

Dusk, dinner, social life in the saloon, music, the night's rest, and the following day "The Olympian" is rushing through South Dakota. The land is fertile. Wheat is cultivated here, and limitless green fields stretch out on either side.

Disquieting rumours again from our region. The *Chicago Tribune* confirms that all Russian Consuls in the Chinese districts on the borders of Soviet Russia have been ordered to leave. What then has happened to all the letters and telegrams I sent to Norin's group and which were addressed to the Russian Consul at Chuguchak? We are in the new world, but our expedition is in the old. A day seldom passes without my getting tidings of my staff, direct or indirect.

On June the 7th "The Olympian" reaches Chicago. My nephew, Sven Sundström, and Mr. and Mrs. Martin Westerlin are at the station to meet us. It was a pretty busy day, not very suitable for a convalescent, but I had my medical attendant, and all went well. We first saw, in the Field Museum, Dr. Berthold Laufer's fine collections from Tibet. I was especially attracted by the "cult" exhibits. It was such a collection from Tibet or Mongolia that I had wished to acquire for Stockholm, though my request for a grant towards it had been refused. After a visit to Westerlin's house, there was luncheon at the Drake Hotel with Consul and Mrs. von Dardel. Call upon Mrs. Rockefeller McCormick, visit to my nephew's works where, with his Swedish partners, he manufactured surgical lamps, tea at Mrs. Blair's with Mrs. Rockefeller and the French mystic M. Richard, dinner at the Westerlins' and finally a visit to the good old doctor, Otto Schmidt. The train went at 9 o'clock and then at last there was peace.

In twelve hours we are in Buffalo. Now began a fabulous time. Only a day and a night separated me from that horrible Boston which for four months was to be my headquarters and where I was to undergo a dangerous operation.

It was at 9 a.m. on the 8th of June that we reached Buffalo. There I had the pleasure of meeting my sister Alma and my brother Carl, who held an appointment in Detroit and now joined our family gathering. After luncheon at the Hotel Niagara we went for a little drive to the falls. In the evening I received, by telegram from home, the sad news that our Chinese student Ma, who had been engaged since 1927 at our meteorological station at Etsin-gol, had committed suicide. I sent a telegram of condolence to our Committee in Peking with messages of sympathy to his parents.

On the 9th Professor Einar Key arrived with his wife and Dr. Helmer Key's daughter Thyra. They had come with the whole congress to visit Niagara Falls, where we too went for the second time. In the afternoon Professor Key, assisted by Dr. Hummel, made a thorough examination of my body. The great surgeon said not a word of the result, but, when I questioned him directly, he smiled sceptically and answered: " We may as well hear what Cushing has to say." And I clearly understood that he did not believe in any tumour. Dr. Cushing had in any case asked Key to be present at the operation. But Key could not be in Boston before June the 22nd and was to sail home thence on the 27th.

We returned to Buffalo by car and took the night train to Boston. At 11 a.m. on the 10th we arrived and went to the Hotel Copley Plaza. Now remained only the last short stage to Peter Bent Brigham's Hospital where the world-famous Dr. Harvey Cushing performs his wonderful operations on the brain and spinal cord. Dr. Scarff, one of his assistant surgeons, received us. I was assigned a room and was subjected to an hour's general examination, at which the doctor took notes which would be laid before Cushing.

On the following day I was to hear my doom. My sister and Hummel had just come, we had finished our breakfast and sat waiting in an easily explicable state of tension. What would he say, this great judge, who humanly speaking had my fate in his hands? How would it go with the expedition and with all my comrades who were waiting in uncertainty over there on the other side of the world in the heart of the vast continent?

Dr. Scarff had warned us of Cushing's arrival. What did he look like? What sort of fellow was he? Did he treat his patients as numbers in an endless drove whom for a decade he had daily been trepanning and cutting up? Was it just a matter of routine? No, certainly not. In Peking and now again from Dr. Scarff we had had the most charming description of Dr. Cushing. He was a great personality and a lovable man. He always talked long and kindly to his patients and won their confidence and friendship before beginning, with imperturbable calm and admirable sureness, to operate. The disquiet one had perhaps felt disappeared after one had seen and spoken to him.

That morning the hours passed more slowly than usual. But, suddenly the door of my room opened, and in came a small, thin, but strongly built and muscular man with short grey hair, light brown, lively, intelligent and kindly eyes and a fine aquiline nose. With a slight smile, he bowed and sat down without mentioning his name. But we understood that it was he. And instantly it was as if we had known one another for ages.

Harvey Cushing had with him the journal that had been kept of the course of my illness at the Medical College Hospital in Peking and now made on his own account a number of inquiries and notes. And then came the decisive moment. With Hummel as his assistant he made a thorough examination, and then followed the verdict:

" There is no occasion here to operate; I find no indication of a tumour, and it would be absurd to cut you open."

Hummel went out to inform my sister at once. Her surprise and delight was indescribable. It was too much, and we needed a little time to realize that it was true. Dr. Cushing began to talk of other things, of our journey, of Peking, of my sister's voyage to Boston. Finally I asked what I was to do.

"You must stay ten days in Boston."

"For observation?"

"No, to give me the opportunity to show you the city and to make you acquainted with a number of interesting Bostonians."

"And then?"

"Then you shall go back to your expedition in Sinkiang."

Thus sentence was pronounced. The direct way to Sinkiang was to continue my eastward course by way of Stockholm, Russia and Siberia. A complete journey round the world to learn that I was perfectly well and had no tumour! But who would not gladly encircle the world several times to get such a verdict. And to learn to know Dr. Cushing and to win his friendship, that also was worth a journey round the world, for such people as he are rare visitants to the earth.

He advised us for a beginning to pay a visit to Mrs. Gardener's famous house with its marvellous collection of pictures by Rembrandt, Rubens, Valasquez, Sargent, Zorn and other great painters. We scrupulously observed all his prescriptions and went straight to Mrs. Gardener's house. It was all part of the treatment. The next prescription was to go to see "Show Boat" at the Colonial Theatre. Then followed the Art Museum where, thanks to Dr. Cushing's introduction, we had distinguished ciceroni, who showed us the Bigelow collection, the largest Sino-Japanese collection in existence. It comprises over 60,000 items.

We also had the pleasure, at the hospital, of meeting the eminent French surgeon, Dr. Leriche of Strasbourg, who was Cushing's guest for a fortnight. One day Leriche and we went with Cushing to his charming house in the country, where we made the acquaintance of his wife and children. We drove in two cars at furious speed to Henry Ford's Wayside Inn, a hostelry of the old-fashioned cosy kind, where the motor king has assembled old furniture, household utensils, books and other articles which were in use in the United States in old days.

On June the 14th Cushing made a second examination, having on this occasion both Dr. Scarff and Dr. Hummel as assistants. He was then able to send the following telegram to my doctors at the Peking Union Medical College:

> " Practical absence of physical symptoms makes me hesitate to accept diagnosis.
>
> " CUSHING."

Next we visited the Arnold Arboretum whose director, Mr. Wilson, has himself travelled in China, the Athletic Club and the Engineers' Club, and made motor tours in Boston and its surroundings with our fellow countryman Mr. Konrad A. Johnson, my friend since my first visit to America in 1923.

More bad news from Asia reached us on this day in the shape of a telegram from Lieutenant Haslund to the effect that Governor-General Chin was allowing no foreigners to enter Sinkiang and that all the members of the expedition, including the Chinese, were to be expelled. Accordingly I telegraphed to Professors Hsü Ping-chang and Fu Liu asking what the Government had done to protect the expedition, its members and work. We had thus obtained fresh evidence that the telegraphic orders despatched by the Government to Chin on March the 13th had been received by him with complete disregard and that the Government's authority in Sinkiang was illusory. Our whole journey to Nanking, the five weeks and the 3,000 Mexican dollars it cost had been thrown away. The President of the Provincial Council of Sinkiang was autocrat of his province and took no orders from Nanking.

Seldom has a cure been more agreeable or easier to follow than that which Dr. Cushing prescribed for me. It included, as I have already mentioned, making the acquaintance of interesting personalities. And for this I had abundant opportunity when, on June the 15th, the amiable doctor introduced me to Boston's most distinguished club, " The

Saturday." Only a small number of members was present. I sat between Dr. Lowell, the President of Harvard University, and Mr. Jeremiah Smith, who had just returned from the Young Conference in Paris. There were also Bishop Lawrence, the former Governor of the Philippines, Dr. Leriche and two more gentlemen. Smith told us about Schacht and the Conference and among other things expressed the opinion that Germany was the European country that would first recover its economic strength and in ten years would be the richest country in Europe. It was this Mr. Smith who, after the war, was summoned to Budapest to assist Hungary in adjusting its finances. He was offered 2,000,000 dollars for his services, but refused to accept payment. A princely suite was provided for him at the best hotel in the city, but he rented a simple room at his own cost. He was an unusual character and a sympathetic man.

After luncheon Cushing, Leriche and I drove to the Copley Plaza to pick up my sister and my doctor, and we went on to Manchester-by-the-Sea, a pleasant little town, the scene of Kipling's "Captains Courageous." Outside this town is the charming estate of Mr. and Mrs. Hooper, where we were received with splendid hospitality and spent an unforgettable evening before at last driving back to Boston.

We went straight to Peter Bent Brigham. Late as it was, Dr. Cushing wished to visit a patient on whom he had operated the day before, June Johnson, a girl of sixteen who had had a tumour the size of a child's hand on her little brain. The operation had taken several hours. As usual Cushing had done everything himself, including shaving and washing the patient. He had removed the tumour and filled the cavity with a solution of common salt and then replaced the "lid" and sewn up the wound. June Johnson had been very brave. She had not been afraid of the operation. Now she had a high temperature. Dr. Cushing was as solicitous for her as though she had been his own child. She grew better and better and was out of danger before we left.

Cushing invited Hummel to witness the operations that

he performed during these days, and he afterwards described to us what he had seen. They had generally been such bold and profound incursions into the most vital regions of the human body that one would have supposed them absolutely impossible. But Cushing had performed them calmly, slowly and elegantly, and they had all been successful.

Some months earlier Cushing, on his sixtieth birthday, had received, as a gift from his disciples and admirers, a huge volume filled with the precepts a multitude of younger surgeons had acquired from the great master at Peter Bent Brigham.

Not a day passed without some interesting excursion or visit to museums or institutions. One day we spent with Mr. Basil Gavin and his charming Swedish wife at Millis, another at Commencement Day at Harvard, a third with Mrs. Hooper at Sleeper's Museum, a highly original and amusing collection of old furniture and household gear from various bygone periods in the United States. Mr. Sleeper himself was our guide. His museum comprises sixty-five rooms, each representing a certain period, and harmoniously furnished in the minutest detail. There were rooms from the earliest time of the colonization of New England and so on down the ages. We were informed that old furniture now commands fabulous prices, high in proportion to the age of the object, and that such relics were extremely rare.

On another day Mr. Konrad Johnson took us by car to Cape Cod, passing Plymouth and the Pilgrims' Stone of 1620, where the Mayflower company first landed. We were afterwards entertained by Mr. and Mrs. Scheffer at their magnificent place by the sea.

On June the 22nd Professor Einar Key arrived in Boston, and the third examination took place. The Röntgen plates showed nothing suspicious. Dr. Cushing attached great importance to the fact that the pain in the right shoulder had come suddenly and not progressively and that, after both attacks, it had disappeared, leaving no trace.

After a visit to the Swedish Home for the Aged and to Dr. Follin, we supped with Dr. Scarff, and said good-bye to Dr. Hummel, who was going to New York where two of his brothers lived. We did not see him again until after our return to Sweden.

Sunday, June the 23rd, was our last day in Boston. We lunched with Dr. Cushing, who afterwards drove us round the lovely surroundings of the city and its immense, luxuriant, verdant parks. The parting from this illustrious man who has become our friend for life was made easier by his promise to come and visit us in Stockholm—he was to deliver an address to a congress in Amsterdam and would then be quite near to our country.

Dr. Cushing is not only a surgeon. His biography of his teacher, Sir William Osler, in two bulky volumes, is considered to be, from all standpoints, not least that of pure literature, a masterpiece of the highest rank. He is also a connoisseur and collector of ancient medical literature of different lands and times, and he showed us many of these curious works. His greatness lies in his new, delicate and bold methods of operating on the brain and spinal cord, and many surgeons have turned their steps to Peter Bent Brigham to learn from the greatest master of our time.

Harvey Cushing is moreover in the best sense of the word a human being. He enters with the warmest sympathy and interest into the lives of his patients, understands them, calms and consoles them and delivers them from their frightful suffering. He has saved innumerable people by his operations. He can say with reason: "Nil humani a me alienum puto." Everything interests him—we were to find this some months later on his visit to Stockholm. Cushing is also a great humorist. Amusing and witty, he possesses an inexhaustible store of droll stories. He has played an important part in my life. He only had to see me and lay his hands on me for a threatening illness to disappear.

But now I must make haste. I am indeed on my way to Asia again and that way leads through Stockholm. But we could not forego a brief visit to Chicago, the greatest city of the Swedes in America.

XI

VINCENT BENDIX

ON Midsummer Day my sister, my brother and I reached Chicago and put up at Stevens' Hotel, "the biggest in the world," with 3,000 rooms and a staff of 2,500. On the following day I paid a visit to the office of my American fellow-countryman, Vincent Bendix, and was announced by his Swedish friend, Mr. Herbert Linden. The whole office was full of people, secretaries, typists and men of business. After waiting a little I obtained admission, and there was a long conversation about travels in Asia and new plans.

Mr. Bendix is an alert man of wide interests, and it was easy and pleasant to talk to him. One saw from the first that he was a man of large ideas, for he did not so much as blink at vast enterprises. For him there were no such things as difficulties, rather it seemed to excite his ambition to overcome them. He took everything lightly and playfully. There was in him none of the haughty superciliousness which so often makes it unpleasant to lay great plans before purse-proud patrons. We had not been talking a quarter of an hour when Vincent Bendix exclaimed:

"Well, I have money, and I have long been thinking I ought to do something for my parents' native country and for Swedish exploration. But we must have some more talk about your plans. Will you and your sister and brother breakfast with me and my wife to-morrow at 8.30, so that we may have time for a talk?"

At the appointed hour we were at Bendix's magnificent apartment, and he gave us his full attention. The negotiations were not over before 1 o'clock. But he wished to think the matter over for a few days before deciding.

In the interval we met many well-known Swedes. From

Consul von Dardel and his wife and from Mr. and Mrs. Westerlin we received the same ample hospitality as on our previous visit. Mr. Berggren, the engineer, showed us his invention for exhibiting cinematograph pictures stereoscopically, an invention which probably, when it is completely developed, will bring about a complete revolution in the cinema world. For then depth and perspective will become authentic and the figures will stand out clearly on the screen.

We also met Dr. Julius Lincoln, Mr. Seeburg, Mr. Charles S. Peterson and masses of fellow-countrymen and women at the Swedish Club, the Swedish Glee Club and the Swedish Engineers' Club. At the Field Museum we were shown round by Mr. Henry Field, and we were hospitably received at his home. One day we made an excursion with Mr. Linden to Lake Forest, by the beautiful road which partly runs along Lake Michigan and partly winds through towns, residential districts and parks without end. Another day I lunched with Bendix at—I think—the Union League Club, which he showed me from cellar to roof, from the library to the swimming bath. On a carpeted stair on the top storey he stopped suddenly and exclaimed:

"I'm going to subscribe to your plans for temples and ethnographical collections a similar sum to that which you received from the Swedish Government. There's no trouble about that."

The next evening he had a talk with Herbert Linden, who vigorously supported my plans, and the latter was charged to inform me that the business was settled and that the money was at my disposal.

Vincent Bendix is a man of his word. One felt one could depend on this man and his promise. His magnificent donation was to be made over in due form with all legal precautions, and he accordingly instructed his lawyer, Mr. Edwin H. Cassels, to draw up a contract between the donor and myself. No time was lost. Herbert Linden and I went next morning to Mr. Cassels' office, and I gave him all the information he required as to both the composition of the expedition and the new ethnographical plans. Two Lamaistic temples were to be acquired or reproduced, one for Stockholm and one for Chicago, each completely equipped with everything pertaining to their interior and exterior decorations, in the way of images, textiles, costumes, musical instruments, altar vessels and other things. If anything were over of the sum provided, it was to be applied to the purchase of ethnographical objects to be divided equally between the museums of the two cities. By the afternoon the document had been fair copied, and I signed it. Some days later Bendix handed me one copy signed by himself, keeping the other with my signature.

One day we went by car 104 miles to Michigan City and Niles, where our distinguished fellow-countryman Mr. Francis Plym and his wife have a country house in a forest tract where the old trails of the Indians still wind among the trees.

On another day Bendix had invited me to come out to South Bend to see the Bendix Brake Company's works. South Bend is a little town in Indiana, two and half hours' journey by rail from Chicago. Bendix owns great stretches of land in its neighbourhood, and there he has his factory and his palatial new house of seventy-five rooms. He has also provided workmen's dwellings in the form of comfortable cottages, and his factory buildings are being extended on a very large scale. New engine-rooms and warehouses were in process of construction, the largest 1,200 feet long. Owing to these developments the little town is growing, and the land, which Bendix bought at a bargain, is rising enormously in value. In the afternoon Bendix and I drove back to the train for Chicago. It was easy to see how much the Swedish-American was everywhere esteemed. In South Bend he is regarded almost as a prince. The staff at the station and the train greeted him with respect, and aboard the train acquaintances were continually coming forward to press his hand. One could very well see that he was a rising star of the first magnitude.

On July the 6th there were trotting races at Arlington Park outside Chicago. Bendix asked me to go with him in his Cadillac. The trip was a quite thrilling experience. Two police sergeants on motor-cycles preceded our car, one about twenty and the other about forty metres ahead of us.

When these gentry sounded their penetrating sirens, everyone had to get out of the way. Those coming from crossroads had to stop. The traffic was held up everywhere. We drove at a mad speed through one of the most crowded cities in the world. The sergeants rushed along the roads like madmen yelling wildly all the time. As if by magic all vehicles and all pedestrians stopped and stared. One sat with one's heart in one's mouth and one's attention strained to the uttermost. But it was fun having all that swarming traffic stopped for us. Bendix enjoyed it. Again and again he dug me in the ribs, saying:

"Isn't it lovely?"

"Yes, splendid, but it seems to me they might drive a little faster."

Actually we were driving at such a pace that the car was running on two wheels at the turns. The trotting races themselves were like all other entertainments of the kind. It was amusing to see the smart set of Chicago, its aristocracy of wealth, betting on the horses and winning and losing very considerable sums. Everyone knew Bendix, and he was genial and hearty to all. But he treated everyone in the same way. He was as pleasant to the negro waiters as to the priests of mammon. To him they were all human beings like himself.

Sunday, July the 7th, was our last day in Chicago. On my previous visit in 1923 I had taken a certain dislike to this city with its celebrated slaughter-house, its lawlessness and its constant motor accidents. Now I found that Chicago also has its charm. A row of really imposing skyscrapers had grown up along the magnificent lake frontage of Michigan Avenue, and the view from our windows at The Stevens was one of the most impressive any city can offer. The Field Museum, too, is a jewel. And the openhanded way in which Vincent Bendix supported our Swedish expedition materially increased my sympathies for his adopted city. We were now invited by him to lunch with his mother and his sister Esther.

Bendix's mother still gave an impression of youthfulness. She was born in modest circumstances at a farm in Östergötland and was simple and almost shy in manner. She seemed to find it difficult to accommodate herself to the elegant home that her son had provided for her. She had been even less spoilt than he by his unusual success in life. The father, a native of Småland, had been dead for some years. He emigrated early, became a Methodist minister and changed his name from Bengtson to Bendix. Thus Vincent Bendix has unmixed Swedish blood in his veins. But he has only paid a single brief visit to the land of his fathers. As a boy Vincent did not at all appreciate the strict upbringing he received at home. At the age of sixteen he simply ran away to New York, where he became lift boy at a hospital. But to whatever height he rose he was not long content with this profession. He had talent, a clear and alert intelligence and marked financial aptitude. On economic questions he is now considered to be a genius. After luncheon he told us about his wonderful fortune and how he threw himself into the battle for existence and went from one triumph to another. And now he was one of the richest men in America and enjoyed life to the full. "I like the great game," he said.

On July the 8th we left Chicago. Vincent Bendix boarded the train at South Bend. He had his secretary, Mr. Gossner, with him and worked almost all the time. His compartment looked like an office, with piles of letters, telegrams and gigantic portfolios. Everything was well arranged and each task systematically performed. It went at flying speed. One could not help observing that Mr. Gossner had an exacting post.

News came from Asia to my headquarters in Chicago again and again. One day I had a telegram from Professor Fu Liu announcing that the Government in Nanking had given a new and more forcible order to the Governor-General of Sinkiang concerning the treatment of our expedition. This order had left Nanking on June the 17th. But it had clearly made no impression on the Governor-General, who rules his province as an autocrat.

Two days later I had a telegram from Norin that Hörner and Bexell, who, like Norin, were waiting at Bachti for permission to cross the Chinese frontier into Sinkiang, had at last got their answer refusing them admission to the

Province. By this time Bohlin had joined the others and suffered the same fate. Only Norin and Bergman were graciously permitted to return to their old field of labour where only Ambolt, Haude and the Chinese members were employed at that time. Norin had decided, after consultation with Bohlin, Hörner and Bexell, to let them travel to Peking so as to penetrate the interior from the eastward. Bergman joined them later, and only Norin went to Urumchi and Kuruk-tagh, where he met Ambolt.

On July the 2nd again there was bad news from Asia. Mr. Buettner, one of Bendix's secretaries, told me he had had a telegram from Bendix saying that the *Chicago Tribune* that day contained a message from Peking that Dr. Sven Hedin's expedition had been forbidden by the Nanking Government to continue its work and was therefore to be dissolved. Bendix, who had just promised his large donation, was naturally astonished and wished for information. Accordingly I telegraphed to Baron Leijonhuvud and asked him what the telegram in the *Chicago Tribune* meant. It might well be that, for reasons unknown to me, the Government could no longer answer for our safety. Baron Leijonhuvud replied promptly: "Rumours false." And both Bendix and I were reassured.

New York! Excuse me if I do not speak of that densely packed world of skyscrapers, people, swarming streets, pleasure, seething business life and that never resting hunt for dollars. As usual one has to endure the purgatory of interviews, one received visits from managers anxious to arrange lecture tours, one is assailed by literary agents who wish to place one's books, one is taken to Paramount Pictures to appear in a talking film and one encounters a number of pleasant and helpful fellow-countrymen, Olof Lamm, Sten Hammarskjöld, Gustaf Sundelius, Ragnar Hummel, a brother of our doctor, Mr. Seeburg, who later made me acquainted with a new Mæcenas, Mr. Albert Appleton. At the National Museum of Natural History, which sent out my friend Roy Chapman Andrews on his valuable expedition to Mongolia, I met two of his fellow-workers, Messrs. Nelson and Olsen.

New clouds were rising on our Asiatic horizon. There

were disquieting items in the newspaper telegrams from the northern boundaries of Manchuria. The Chinese had seized the East Chinese Railway and imprisoned or expelled the Russian personnel as well as expelling the Consuls from the border districts of China. It was no longer possible to travel by Manchuli and Harbin. In the ensuing days the tension increased, and war seemed inevitable.

Vincent Bendix was just then engaged in fitting up his new offices. We chanced to witness the process. Tables, chairs, records, typewriters—all were moved in and put in place in the course of an hour, and meanwhile young women had begun to tap out the current correspondence. It was done with true American speed. The Bendix Aviation Corporation's New York office was in full swing, and the chief himself was receiving the stream of callers that had already put in an appearance. Two days later we took farewell of Bendix, who dashed back to Chicago with his secretary and his office on the train. There were handsome things about him in one of the newspapers. He was hailed as the great industrialist of Indiana. He enjoyed the highest esteem in the business world, and was honoured by societies, churches and clubs. But he himself was free from pretension, and he always desired that his assistants should receive an ample share of his success and his credit.

The crossing to Cuxhaven was made in the most glorious weather on board the *Albert Ballin*, and Captain Wiehr was the most charming of hosts. Among the passengers was the famous American singer, Madame Schumann Heink, a native of Vienna.

In Berlin we met my sister Clara and my old friend von Blücher, the ambassador. I visited President von Hindenburg, but was compelled for lack of time to decline an invitation from Dr. Stresemann. I saw my friends Milch, Koch, Merkel and von Schröder of Luft Hansa and also Herr Brandenburg, the chief of German aviation, and my publisher Herr Fritz Brockhaus of Leipzig, as well as my old comrades of Richthofen days, Baschin, Ebeling and Tiessen. And I had also the pleasure of meeting again my splendid travelling companions of 1927 and 1928, Major

Hempel and Herr von Kaul. Another friend, whom I met unexpectedly in Berlin, was the German Minister in Stockholm, Herr von Rosenburg.

On August the 2nd the King arrived on his way to Rome where the Queen was lying ill. I had the pleasure of a hasty meeting with the King, in company with the Legation, at Stettiner Bahnhof.

An hour later our train left for Sweden. Herr von Blücher and Herr von Schröder came down to bid us farewell. I little thought as the train glided out that I had spoken for the last time to the excellent and able Herr von Schröder, son of the Admiral, and one of Germany's foremost aviators. A couple of days before Christmas he crashed with his flying machine outside Berlin, on the return journey from Teneriffe.

At Lund, Ambolt's parents came down and received greetings from their accomplished son, at Småland Dr. Hummel boarded our train, and in Stockholm we were met by a host of friends. The same evening I had a long conference with the Crown Prince, who always shows the warmest interest in our expedition and our fate.

I now spent two unforgettable months in my dear old home. When a man has for years been making Viking cruises by land, he needs sometimes to come home and breathe the sweet air of Sweden.

My first visit, as usual, was to the grave of my parents in Adolf Fredrik's churchyard and my second to my kinsfolk at Värmdön, Djursholm and Drottningholm. A description of this time is hardly in place here. I had a thousand things to do, papers to put in order, letters and telegrams to send—headquarters had now been moved to Stockholm, and it was thence that I gave instructions to the various sections of the expedition.

At the Chinese Legation, the Chargé d'affaires, Mr. Lai Ping-yang, did us many services. He telegraphed my requests to Nanking and Peking. On August the 29th the Government answered our inquiry to the effect that the road to Sinkiang was open to us and that the Governor-General had received orders to let us cross the frontier without hindrance. Baron Leijonhuvud informed me by letter that the powerful Ma Fu-hsiang bade us welcome to Kansu. Our path seemed to be clearing up again.

Three new members were added to the expedition. Since, through the friendly intervention of Mr. Seeburg, Mr. Appleton of Chicago had placed a sum of 25,000 dollars at my disposal, we were able to send a separate archæological expedition to Russian Turkistan. The Crown Prince was particularly interested in a continuous chain of neolithic researches throughout the whole of Asia between the Caspian Sea and Honan, and kindly offered to help me with this new undertaking, the chief of which was to be the antiquary, Dr. T. Arne.

Professor Gerhard Lindblom was selected to lead the ethnographic expedition in Eastern Asia. Since however he was still, on the 18th of September, forbidden by his doctors to travel, I was obliged, in consultation with him and Professor Baron Erland Nordenskiöld, to look for another expert. Although it involved a very appreciable sacrifice to Nordenskiöld to lose his own assistant, Dr. Gösta Montell, he surrendered him in the interests of the work.

On August the 16th I sent a very unfortunate telegram through the Swedish Legation in Peking to Georg Söderbom at Su-chou in Kansu with orders to await Dr. Hummel and me and to hold our old camels, forty of them, in readiness. Our plans were, later on, completely altered, and he was needed, not in Su-chou, but in Peking. Thus he came to us too late and was unable to take part in Dr. Hummel's expedition to Ssŭ-chuan and Kansu.

Our new equipment was a chapter in itself. Ambolt and Norin had asked for a large Wild theodolite. It had to be procured and cost 3,000 crowns. They needed complete new photographic equipment. It was all procured. We ourselves needed a very first-class set of cameras and plates for ethnographical purposes, besides all the usual meteorological instruments. It involves innumerable cares to lead an expedition so large and so many-sided. In all these preparations Dr. Hummel was an invaluable help to me.

The Manchurian difficulty continued and forced us to

take the roundabout way by Vladivostok and Japan. Mr. Kopp and Mr. Dmitrievsky of the Russian Legation gave us every assistance in the matter of passports, customs and transport. Professor Kling inoculated us. We got ourselves a new outfit of clothes and travelling trunks. We were in a hurry from morning till night.

And all the other things! Our Mongolian and Chinese servants ought to be honoured with gold and silver medals, which it would certainly be to our advantage to give them and which would redound to the credit of the expedition. To bear the image of a king on the breast is a singular honour. The King readily granted these distinctions, and the Lord High Steward Printzköld sent me the medals engraved with the names of the recipients.

Some time before us Lieutenant Haslund had come home with a temple "yurt" which the Torgut Chief, Sinchin Gegen Khan, had sent to the Swedish King. On September the 8th it was delivered to the King, who decided that the gift should be placed in the ethnographic museum.

And then all the friends I encountered. I was again examined by Professors Einar Key and Jacobaeus with Dr. Hummel as their assistant. The man who knew most about my body was Dr. Björn Floderus, our family doctor for thirty years.

Verner von Heidenstam had, as he did last year, come up from Övralid, and we had a couple of glorious days together. We drove out one day to see our old friend Oscar Björck. He was taken ill soon after, and I was often with him at the hospital, Sophiahemmet. Before the year was out, his bright and fortunate career was ended.

Carl Milles was on the point of starting for America. We were able to tell him that he was impatiently awaited there. Captain Peter Möller, the African, the slayer of elephants and lions, that youth of seventy years, listened eagerly to our accounts. Our Minister in Moscow, Carl von Heidenstam, had on numberless occasions helped us in our journeys to and from our field of work. Professor Erik Nyström of Tai Yüan-fu was one of our brothers in arms in China, whither he returned before us. Emanuel

Nobel was still the oldest of my friends from Assia, and it is always a pleasure to me to see him again. Superintendent Axel Lagrelius and Professor J. G. Andersson were also two old friends of mine. And Professor Wilhelm Nordenson, like his able father, took care of my eyes.

I was also visited by Sir Charles Bell, who maintained himself in Lhasa longer than any European in recent times. Mr. Haardt, who has travelled all over Africa in Citroën cars, sent Major Bertrand and Mr. Goercher to Stockholm to obtain information about the roads through Asia, and it was a very great pleasure to me to give them all I could.

One day my old travelling companion Consul Larson from Jerusalem came on a visit. I also met on two occasions Marquis Tokugawa in whose ancestral home I had been so well received in 1908. To the Prime Minister, Lindman, I was now able orally to express my warm thanks and those of the expedition for the powerful support he had given us in the procuring of the liberal State subsidy.

At the Academy of Science I renewed the acquaintance of my learned colleagues and had several discussions with Professors Gerard De Geer and Söderbaum in the interests of the expedition. From them and from many others of the Academy we had the most powerful support. Dr. Hummel obtained good advice from Professors Robert Fries and Samuelsson and Dr. Hulthén for the coming botanical collections, and from Professor Sjöstedt for the collection of insects.

On September the 5th Dr. Harvey Cushing came to Stockholm, and it was an indescribable pleasure to see our American friend again and to take him round for four days to Gripsholm and Skokloster as well as to Uppsala, where he saw the cathedral, Carolina,[1] with Ulfila's Bible, the Academic Hospital with Gunnar Nyström, the castle and the Governor and Mrs. Hammarskjöld.

At the end of the month Herbert Linden arrived in Stockholm, and shortly afterwards Vincent Bendix. Each was accompanied by his charming wife. Our great Mæcenas arrived on September the 25th and stayed, like Dr.

[1] The University Library, known as Carolina Rediviva, from having been rebuilt in the reign of Charles XI.

Cushing, four days. Now, too, the time passed among proud historic memories. It pleased the stout republican to pay his respects to a King and to have a long conversation with our Crown Prince. On both these occasions he expressed with conviction his intention of giving our expedition his support in the future also. Once when we sat talking in my workroom, there was a ring at the telephone. "Hullo—Chicago. Is Mr. Bendix there?" And then there was a hail of orders and instructions to the head office in Chicago, lasting for forty minutes. The conversation cost 2,400 crowns. Not even while he was visiting Stockholm was he left in peace.

His journey was extended to Paris, and everywhere Herbert Linden was his right hand. And now, as I sit writing in Peking and Bendix sits in his office in Chicago, South Bend or New York, it is still Linden who attends to all negotiations between us. For when one has so many irons in the fire as this restlessly active man one does not penetrate very deeply into Asiatic affairs.

All too quickly fled the short time that we could stay in Stockholm, my native city, my childhood's home and the place where my parents sleep in the churchyard. Once more we must cut all the precious ties and moorings that hold us and return to Asia, the vast and enigmatic.

XII

BACK TO PEKING

I AM now, in December, 1929, at Kalgan, watching the moonlight on the hills of this little town which the Chinese call Chang-Chia-k'ou, but the Mongols and the Russians "The Gate" to Mongolia, and which was formerly the starting-point for the vast caravans which, by way of Urga and Kyakhta, carried tea to Siberia and Russia.

Little more than two months has passed since I left Stockholm. Now I am alone and go over in my thoughts all the wonderful occurrences which have happened in that brief space of time.

It was on September the 30th that we set out for the Far East, Dr. David Hummel, Dr. Gösta Montell and I. Our friends came down to the Skeppsholm quay to bid us farewell. There was a perfect lightning of magnesium—they were immortalizing us on photographic plates. We stood with flowers in our hands, trying to look our best. But that is not so easy at the moment when strong bonds are to be severed for—God knows how long. The gangway is hauled in. With pitiless indifference to our feelings the "Bore" backs away from the quay. The distance grows. The beloved groups are blotted out in the darkness, but over them and all around us twinkle the lights of the city, and over us burn the stars, the only lights that will constantly accompany us even into the depths of Asia. We remain standing by the rail until the city disappears from our view.

We go to our much-needed rest and do not awake till we are running into Åbo. We hurry through the cathedral and the castle before the train takes us to Helsingfors and, the next night, on by Rajajoki, Bjeli Ostrov and Systerbäck to Leningrad.

Sahlin, Attaché at the Legation, meets us and the invaluable Mihail Rosenhagen from the Consulate takes charge of our baggage. We buy a map of the whole of Inner Asia at Gosudarstvennaya Kartographia. In Kasansk Sobor we are sensible of the magic atmosphere of bygone worship and see the wax candles flickering, more sparsely than formerly, in front of the sacred icons. We make an excursion by car to the islands and enjoy the hospitality of Mr. and Mrs. Sahlin before it is time for our train.

Another night and we are in Moscow. I put up as usual with my old friend, the Envoy, Carl von Heidenstam. I pay a visit to the German Ambassador, von Dirksen, where I hear of the death that night of Stresemann; to Mr. Karakhan, who assures me that Russia does not want war with China, and to Bubnov, the Commissar for Education, who promises to support our plans in every way.

My journey to the Far East was necessitated by a curious train of causes. It had been my intention to travel to Sinkiang where I had great geographical plans of my own.

I had thought to travel by the new railway through the Kirghiz steppes from Orenburg to Tashkent and thence by the line under construction to Alma-ata or Verni, and then by car to Bachti, Chuguchak and Urumchi.

All was ready, and the Russians had granted my request for permission to make the journey by that route. But, while I was still in Stockholm, disquieting news had come from Peking. The large contingent of our expedition which had been fitted out there in the autumn had tried in vain to get passports. The weeks went by, and the Foreign Minister, Dr. C. T. Wang, answered nothing from Nanking. Many other obligations drew me eastward and I was obliged to abandon my plan of travel. Sinkiang and its alluring problems must wait, and I took the old familiar route through Siberia.

On this route we had many contacts with the great expedition. Even in Moscow we encountered the antiquary, Dr. Arne, who was soon to belong to our brotherhood.

He was on his way to Russian Turkistan to get his

bearings in the Museums at Tchimkent, Samarqand, Tashkent and Askhabad in preparation for his excavations next year. We were at Mr. Bubov's together and were able to clear the ground for Arne's expedition. He was to start in earnest with two more Swedish archæologists in February, 1931.

In Moscow I also met one of the two Swedish mechanics whom I had taken out to Sinkiang at the old Governor General Yang's request in the summer of 1928, Mr. Aron Carlsson. He had been serving as Dr. Ambolt's assistant and was now on his way home. He is travelling in the company of the Tatar, Mr. Burkhan, who has been sent by Chin, the new Governor-General, to Sweden, Germany and France to form industrial and commercial connexions. This Burkhan was a friend to the expedition and had done us great services in difficult times.

We also met in Moscow the wife of Professor Osvald Sirén, who is travelling to join her husband in Peking. We thus had agreeable company on the train, where we also made the acquaintance of a young Dane from Canton and a Finnish engineer on his way to the great Congress at Tōkyō.

At a charming dinner with our Envoy, von Heidenstam, we met the Japanese Ambassador, Tanaka, the Norwegian, Danish and Finnish Ministers and Mr. Sokolin who kindly assisted us with important despatches to Urumchi.

At 4.30. p.m. on October the 4th the Siberian express carried us off northwards towards Jaroslav. We would willingly have made a stay of some hours in this town, where the Swedish General Electric Company has a factory and to which we had been ceremoniously invited by the engineers, Sander and Lindgren. We had a journey of ten days and nights before us without once changing carriages. It may perhaps be thought that this is a wearisome journey. By no means. I find it pleasant and restful—especially after the hectic time that lay behind me in America and Europe. One throws off all one's worries for a time. One talks to one's travelling companions, Mrs. Sirén, Neckelman the Dane from Canton, The Finn Hjalmar Pettersson and Mr. Sugimura who is returning home from Geneva with his family. He holds a prominent position in the League of Nations and has strange things to tell. One reads and writes letters and gets out for a walk on the platform at the stations. The compartments are clean and well-kept "Wagons Lits," which have been retained in Russia after the Revolution. The Russian cookery is excellent. One is at home on the train—it is like living in a moving hotel.

Here is Vyatka, here Perm, here Sverdlovsk of unhappy memory. We pass Chumen. The days slip by. In the evening of October the 7th we are in Novo-Sibirsk. Our friend the German Consul Grosskopf, whom I had known since the days of the war, met us on the platform. He knew we were passing through the town where he had spent six long years and had now come down with one of his assistants to offer his services. It is from Novo-Sibirsk that the southern line to Semipalatinsk and Sergiopol branches off. We had brought equipment for Norin and Ambolt who were on the point of starting on an expedition to the country round Lop Nor, and Consul Grosskopf undertook the forwarding of this consignment. Of the four packages, one contained the King's portrait, besides a gift for the Torgut Prince, Sinchin Gegen Khan; the second, Wild's large theodolite, and the others, the tripod and photographic plates. We also left in the Consul's hands whole packets of letters for our friends in Urumchi. The following members of our expedition were at this time in Sinkiang: Dr. Eric Norin, Dr. Nils Ambolt, Dr. Waldemar Haude, Professor Yüan and Messrs. Huang, Ting, Kung, Li and Liu. The Anglo-Russian veterinary surgeon Dr. Etches and the young Russian Vorotnikov were also on our staff. Norin was leader of the whole contingent working in Sinkiang. There were soon to be certain changes in his staff, but the nucleus, the Swedes, remained always the same.

The engine whistles the signal for departure, severing the bond we have been able to form with our people in Sinkiang. We run through Krasnoyarsk and Kansk. I make the acquaintance of Mr. Tagichi of Ōsaka who had been present at one of my lectures in Tōkyō in 1908. In the evening of the 9th we are at Irkutsk and, during the night, the train carries us along the southern shore of

Baikal—it is a pity that one always passes the galleries and tunnels in the darkness.

Next day we leave Verkhne Udinsk behind us, whence the road and the air-way start for Urga, and go on to Chita. Not far east of Chita the railway branches. The right or southern branch goes south-eastward to Manshuli and continues through Manchuria, by Harbin and Mukden to Peking. It was by this line that we travelled in January of this year. The left branch goes towards the north-east and runs at some distance to the north of the great River Amur.

The former route has now been closed since the beginning of July, when the Chinese took possession of the Eastern Chinese Railway and imprisoned its Russian officials. Travellers to the Far East are therefore obliged to take the much longer route, by the Ussuri line, which nowhere touches Chinese territory.

This stretch was new to me. And it is rather monotonous. One sees nothing of the Amur before reaching Habarovsk. One only crosses a number of its tributaries running down from the Yablonoi mountains. The temperature was — 0·2° at Mogatscha at noon. It was cloudy. Round Jerofei Pavlovich there was a little snowstorm, and the landscape became wintry. At the stations we amused ourselves with snowball fights. The country is flatter again, and the snow covering is thinning.

The Amur at Habarovsk is a gigantic river. The town is the Russian headquarters during the prevailing disturbances, since Vladivostok may be cut off. Our long journey came to an end at the latter town on the morning of October the 14th.

Once more it is a Russian Consul who takes care of us. I had known Mr. Balser in Stockholm and Peking and, with my travelling companions, found a real home for two days in the bosom of his family. We put up, however, at the Hotel Versailles, a pretty miserable establishment. At the Balsers we met Mr. Ahlbom who has been in business in Vladivostok for fifteen years. Mrs. Krühl, a Swede, has been living here for twenty. We also made there the acquaintance of two well-known travellers, Professor Arseniev, who wrote a brilliant book about Eastern Siberia, and Mr. Stötzer, who has travelled in Ssŭ-chuan, on the borders of Tibet and in Manchuria. We received telegrams from home and from our Envoy in Tōkyō, Hultman, who has just been in Nanking to present his credentials and at the same time has obtained passports for the large group of our expedition that is shortly to start for the Gobi Desert.

Vladivostok is beautifully situated on rugged promontories and peninsulas. But the town strikes one as dead, poverty-stricken and chill. Hotels, cars and *isvostschiks* fleece their foreign customers after the approved fashion. The place swarms with Chinese and Koreans. There are as many as 30,000 of the former and 6,000 of the latter. The diversion of the Eastern Asiatic traffic through Vladivostok has indeed brought some measure of fortuitous prosperity to the town which, after the settlement of the Manchurian difficulty, will resume its slumbers. The proud name, "Ruler of the East," no longer applies.

We have a passage of two days and nights across the Sea of Japan. The steamer *Amakusa Maru* is some thirty years old and is now full to the last berth. The weather was autumnal and chilly, a heavy sea was running and many were seasick. Most of the passengers are Japanese, and next to them in number come the Germans. The sea is dead and deserted; not a sail is in sight.

In Tsuruga: journalists, examination of passports, medical inspection, customs. Telegram from Envoy Hultman with invitation to Tōkyō. Four hours' journey to Kyōto, where Hummel and Montell stay to show Mrs. Sirén the town, while I take the night train to Tōkyō.

There I spent almost two days with the Swedish Minister and his charming wife and daughter, and was told of all the difficulties that Bergman's and Bohlin's group had encountered and how Envoy Hultman, thanks to his old friendship with the Foreign Minister, C. T. Wang, had at once succeeded in obtaining passports for Kansu and Sinkiang. At the Swedish Legation I had the pleasure of meeting some twenty Swedes, including my old friend Gerts, as well as Mr. Kusakabe, the first Japanese Minister to Stockholm.

A night train carries me to Kobe where Professor Sirén and his wife meet me. With my two travelling companions

I go aboard the *Chojo Maru*, which puts out from the quay on the stroke of twelve. Hummel and I travelled on this excellent boat in May. Only a few passengers. We have plenty of room and enjoy the enchanting voyage across the Inland Sea of Japan with its rocky, wooded coast, its picturesque seaport towns and villages and its gay sailing boats, in changing effects of light and colour. At Moji my two young companions go ashore and climb a hill by the harbour.

In the most glorious summer weather we pass out into the Yellow Sea. It is like a mirror, and scarcely a ripple stirs its surface. To the northward the Korean islands can be dimly seen, and on October the 15th, to port, the rocky contours of Shantung. We drop anchor in the roadstead of Taku and, at noon on the following day, are at Tientsin, where our friend Henning Haslund met us. Here we bought a Ford car, which might be needed during the impending travels in Mongolia, and in the afternoon went on to Peking, where we met Larson and put up in our familiar old rooms at the Hotel Wagons Lits. In spite of the long detour by the Ussuri route and through Japan, and in spite of five off days, we had made the journey in twenty-five days. We had made better speed than the mail usually makes between Stockholm and Peking.

On my arrival in Peking, the stately and noble capital of the Ming and Manchu dynasties, the "Imperial City of the North," whose name is now changed to Peiping, or "The Northern Freedom," I heard from Larson that the great eastern contingent of our expedition had started for Inner Mongolia, where it had established its headquarters at the Monastery of Beli-miao (Pe-ling-miao). There the members had been held up, having found that their sixty camels were not enough for their heavy baggage. They required twenty-five more, and these Larson was commissioned to buy.

So soon as I came to know that they were within reach, I determined to travel quickly up to Beli-miao to meet them, to give them necessary instructions and to be present at their final departure for inmost Asia. We had brought from Stockholm various instruments, photographic plates and other things intended for them. I knew, too, that they needed a caravan leader, who could look after their servants and camels and be responsible for the order of march, camping places, pasture, the care of the camels and other of the more tiresome routine duties.

Accordingly we only stayed four days in Peking, and these, to the last night, were filled with a thousand cares. While Larson and Hummel were on the search for the caravan leader and Montell was putting his photographic outfit in order, I visited the leading members of our Committee, Professor Fu Liu and the head of the National Library, Dr. Yüan, as well as my old friend Professor Hsü Ping-chang. All were friendly and charming, and there was no word of any misunderstanding or friction. The Committee could not help it that the Governor-General of Sinkiang was hostile and that Dr. C. T. Wang had kept us waiting an unconscionable time for our passports; it had done all it could to support us. Baron Carl Leijonhuvud gave me a clear survey of the happenings in recent times. He had been a tower of strength to our people in all difficult situations.

We had no time for visiting Europeans and Americans. The only ones I called on were the German Minister, von Borch, and my old friend the celebrated American traveller in Mongolia, Roy Chapman Andrews, by whom my young comrades and I were received with his customary hospitality. Andrews lives in a magnificent palace built by a Manchu prince. The courtesy and kindness displayed by Andrews to my expedition from its first beginning reached its culmination this autumn. The new expedition to Mongolia which he had contemplated for the year 1929 had been abandoned owing to the excessive demands made upon him and his collections by the Chinese. He accordingly placed his camels, tents, saddles, packs, arms, ammunition and the like at our disposal, and we thus obtained a first-class outfit at a moderate price, not to speak of all the trouble and loss of time that we were spared. We had certainly found a good friend and brother in arms in Andrews. To the "jalousie de métier," otherwise so common, he was as much a stranger as we. All the rest of the equipment of the new great caravan was under the supervision of Larson, who placed himself at our people's disposal, and helped them with all purchases, negotiations, engaging of servants and all the other preparations for a long and hard campaign.

We hoped to get the missionary Boberg, who with magnificent courage and gallantry extricated himself from pirates on the Yellow River, as caravan leader to the new expedition. Yes, he would willingly, but duty called him home to Sweden. Then Larson presented the Norwegian, Mamen, an experienced and courageous man who had ridden out many a storm. He too was willing, but he must be back in Peking by March, so this scheme also fell through. Finally we tracked down the Dane, Bent Friis Johansen, who has travelled much as a merchant in Urga, Uliassutai and Kobdo and has had great experience in the care of caravans. He was just disengaged and accepted the post with delight. We signed a contract, and the new member of the expedition was made heartily welcome.

XIII

THE TASHI LAMA'S VISIT TO MONGOLIA

THE region through which we were now about to travel is divided into several territories, provinces, kingdoms or whatever these parts of Inner Mongolia should be called which are still subject to the Chinese Republic, now that Northern or Outer Mongolia has emancipated itself from Chinese dominion and has formed a Republic under powerful Russian influences. The Republic is called, in Mongolian, Gattane Mongol, while Dottor Mongol denotes Inner Mongolia. In the summer of 1929 the Chinese attempted to attach Inner Mongolia to China proper by stronger administrative bonds than hitherto and, to this end, divided the whole country into provinces on the Chinese pattern each with its Governor-General or, as he is now called, President of the Provincial Council. But the Wangs or vassal Kings in the Mongolian countries set themselves against this scheme, and so far it has not been possible to carry it out. In Chang Tso-lin's time the Mongol Wangs felt themselves more drawn to Mukden which was regarded as more conservative and was believed to be able to preserve the freedom of the Mongols. On a visit to the Marshal, the Wang of Barun Sunit received as a gift considerable quantities of arms, machine guns and ammunition.

In the earlier part of 1929 there were still active trade relations between the Mongolian Republic and Inner Mongolia. But after the dispute over the East Chinese Railway became acute in the beginning of July between China and Soviet Russia, the traffic between the Mongolian countries was also stopped.

I ought perhaps to say a few words about the general geographical features of the country through which we were now to travel. Beli-miao lies in Darkhan-bel which, to the westward, borders on Mingan-djassak. West of the last-named territory stretches Dondur-gun, a duchy which we traversed with the first great caravan in the summer of 1927. Eastward of Darkhan-bel lies the kingdom of Durbet, where Durbet Wang holds sway over the Durbet Mongols, and whose greatest monastery, Shara-muren or the Yellow River, was the first goal of our pilgrimage. Eastward of Durbet we come to Barun Sunit, where Sunit Wang is sovereign lord of the Sunit Mongols. All these realms have their greater length from north to south and, to the northward, border on the Mongolian Republic. To the southward Darkhan-bel marches with Mingan and Tumet, while Durbet and Barun border on Chakhar. The last-named territory stretches a couple of hundred "li" northward to Dolon-nor and has to the eastward the province of Jehol, in Mongolian Roho, in whose capital town of the same name the powerful General Tang Yü-lin resides. Jehol extends right up to the Manchurian boundary in districts inhabited by the Harchin Mongols.

These small Mongolian kingdoms were the scene, in the summer of 1929, of a highly distinguished visit, when the Great Lama of Tashi-lunpo, Tashi Lama, made a religious royal progress and gave his blessing to the orthodox Mongol people, fettered in the yellow chains of Lamaism. The Mongols call him Panchen Bogdo, the Tibetans Panchen Rinpoche or "the precious teacher." In the year 1907 I was his guest for forty-seven days in his cloistral city of Tashi-lunpo. In 1924 he became embroiled with the Dalai Lama, whose policy includes an understanding with British India, while the Tashi Lama remains attached to China and has the great monasteries, the monks and the people on his side. But the Dalai Lama, who has at his disposal the army, organized on the English model, and the aristocracy, and who traditionally has in his hands the temporal power over all Tibet except Tsang, where Tashi-lunpo and Shigatse are situated, was stronger than the Tashi Lama. The latter accordingly found himself obliged to flee, and came, in 1924, by way of Koko-nor to Su-chou, intending to proceed to Urga, where Gegen Hutuktu was Grand Lama and was regarded as standing third in the lamaistic hierarchy. However the military Governor of Su-chou prevented the realization of these plans and conveyed the Chinese Government's "invitation" to the Tashi Lama to betake himself to Peking. He was received with royal honours in the republican capital and was assigned a dwelling in the palace of the deceased Emperor Kuang-Hsü at Nan Hai in the forbidden city. I visited him there twice in December, 1926, and received by way of memento a gold ring engraved with his name and a pair of cloisonné vases.

After a while the Tashi Lama set out on his travels through Manchuria and the Mongolian countries. And in the summer of 1929 he made his progress through those parts of Inner Mongolia in which we were on the point of visiting a whole series of lamaistic temples. The Swedish medical missionary Mr. Joel Eriksson's station is at Hattin-sume in the country of the Chakhar Mongols. About 1,000 li to the east of Hattin-sume there is a monastery, Bante Gegene Chit, where the Tashi Lama had his headquarters for two or three months. In the month of June the Mongols held great festivities at the monastery in honour of the Grand Lama. It is estimated that 30,000 Mongols came there, on horseback, on camels or in carts, to worship and receive his blessing. From Barun Sunit alone came 2,000 pilgrims and probably at least as many from Djun Sunit eastward of that place. Around the great temple of Bante Gegene Chit a whole town of yurts arose out of the ground and the most picturesque and bustling scenes were displayed on all sides. There were to be seen Wangs, princes and noblemen in gorgeous, richly coloured robes on the noble horses of the steppes, there nomads from far and near swarmed round the temple city, and none had hesitated to leave his flocks and his possessions behind in the hope of getting a glimpse of the holy one, of winning his blessing and, from the sanctity which emanated from his person, acquiring merit and illumination to light the dim ways to salvation.

The Grand Lama himself dwelt in a yurt. For three days he shut himself up in it, secluded from the world and occupied in " nom tabbena " or reading the sacred writings. He sat upon his papal throne in the yurt, and below him sat the Wangs and Kings of the Mongols, they too absorbed in the reading of the holy books. Outside the yurt of the holy one a countless congregation had cast itself down in breathless silence to listen to the reading, though not a sound penetrated the mats of the yurt, unless possibly a faint murmur was apprehended by the nearest groups. When the three days were at an end, all those present got red fillets, and on the fourth day the congregation were free to come and worship the Grand Lama and receive his blessing.

A Kampo Lama of the highest rank sat in a separate yurt, the treasury, and received the offerings of the faithful in silver, with which one sack after another was filled. For eighteen Mexican dollars it was possible to buy a card containing blessings for ten persons. Such a card entitled the holder to a private visit to the Grand Lama and a private blessing. Those who had not the means to buy so costly a card had to content themselves with being blessed in the lump. There are Peter's pence here, just as in Rome. One quite simply buys forgiveness of sins and eternal life for money which one has perhaps acquired by dubious speculations. But it is a businesslike method, convenient for the sinners and profitable to the monks.

The honour of entertaining the Tashi Lama is said to be a costly affair. The Wang in whose headquarters he is pleased to set up his tent is said to be put to an expense of some 2,000 Mexican dollars a day for the maintenance of the peripatetic ecclesiastical state, its monks of various degrees, its servants and its animals. The Grand Lama derived a revenue of several hundred thousand dollars from his summer tour. And one does not grudge him this income. After all he is a fugitive from his own country, a stranger in China and Mongolia. And he himself is, in contrast with many monks of lower degree, simple and unpretentious in the extreme. He possesses a peculiar charm and is a delightful personality. When he blesses the pilgrims with bare hand or with the yellow silk wrapped staff, he believes in his mission and in his supernatural powers, and he wishes all living beings peace, blessing and eternal salvation in the long rest in Nirvāna.

In July and the beginning of August the Tashi Lama spent a month in Barun Sunit, living at the Wang's headquarters, "Wangin Ortu" or "the King's Camp," where the palace was smartened up and repainted, and where the prince himself had to be satisfied with a more modest lodging. Ten thousand pilgrims had pitched their yurts about the camp. The great well might be used by none but the Tashi Lama; other mortals must get water as best they could. Here too a festival was held in honour of the Grand Lama. The holy one watched the racing from a separate felt tent. The way to the place where the wrestling competitions were to be held was 300 metres long, and along this the Tashi Lama walked on outspread lengths of yellow cloth so as not to soil his shoes with the dust of the field.

Finally he went on to Uchumchi, north of Jehol, thence to set out upon the journey to Mukden, always accompanied by Sunit Wang and several other Mongols of importance. From Mukden he was presently to return to Peking.

XIV

OUR FAREWELL TO THE GREAT DESERT CARAVAN

WHEN, on the morning of October the 30th, Hummel, Montell and I set out by car for the Hsi Chi-mên railway station at the north-west corner of the Tatar city, we were able to look back with satisfaction on the month that had elapsed since we left Stockholm. Then everything had looked muddled and obscure, but now our way lay clear and plain before us, and all the difficulties had been swept out of our path; the Chinese, both the scientists and the Government, were well disposed, and the new great caravan was ready to start. The two Danish members, Haslund and Johansen, had orders to take our cars and a quantity of baggage by Kalgan to Hattin-sume, where they were to pick up the medical missionary, Mr. Joel Eriksson, and his car and then to join us at the camp at Beli-miao.

Besides ourselves there was only one white man aboard the train, Mr. Edwards, an American in the employ of the Famine Relief Fund at the Hwang Ho irrigation works.

Larson joined our train at Kalgan. Several people came down to greet us: Mrs. Larson, Larson's secretary Miss Ruhne, the missionary Mr. Söderbom and Särdje, the Mongol who distinguished himself during the Gobi campaign of 1927.

In the evening of the following day we reached Kuei-hua-ch'êng, which the Mongols call Koko-khoto, or "the Blue City," where Mr. Gustaf Söderbom came down to meet us. We were all four accommodated at his house in one large room warmed by a roaring stove.

At Kuei-hua-ch'êng, one day was allotted to preparations. There was the usual trouble about cars, and we had no choice. But the day was by no means wasted. We had a look at the celebrated Lama Temple, very beautiful though much ruined. Montell bought a number of ethnographic objects and began a systematic labelling, with notes of corresponding legends in his first notebook. It was thus in the Blue City that he began his activity in the service of the expedition. For the large sum of money that Mr. Vincent Bendix had placed at our disposal we were to purchase or have copied a Buddhist Temple for Stockholm and one for Chicago, and also to procure two collections of ethnographic objects. This work was now in full swing and it was not long before the number of objects reached respectable dimensions.

In the course of our wanderings we also went to the "New Town," where we visited the Swedish missionary, Miss Nikolaison, who has been living alone at her station for eight years. She is a marvel. With no guard and without weapons, she defends her station against brigands and thieves, and has with her own hands turned out many rogues who tried to force an entry into her house. It is said that now there are not many men who dare molest this lone woman. She manages her station admirably and had just erected a pretty little chapel with accommodation for 200 people. The German missionary, Dreier and two Swedish female evangelists were of the party and we spent a pleasant hour in Miss Nikolaison's house.

Before describing our meeting with and our parting from the new expedition, I must say a few words about the exasperating hindrances to which they had been subjected. Owing to these they had lost several months of work and time, not to speak of what these everlasting delays cost us in money.

In the spring of 1929 Dr. Nils Hörner, the geologist, and Dr. Gerhard Bexell, the palæobotanist, of the Academy of Science, had been selected as participants in my expedition, while I, in Peking, appointed the palæontologist, Dr. Birger Bohlin, who during the two past years had distinguished himself in the service of the Geological Surveys of China. On April the 10th Hörner and Bexell left Stockholm, accompanied by our archæologist Folke Bergman, who had been home on leave, and travelled by Berlin and Semipalatinsk to Bachti, where they arrived on May the 7th. After a couple of days they drove into Chuguchak on the Chinese side, but were expelled by decree of the Governor-General of Sinkiang, Chin Shu-jên, who, ever since he succeeded our old friend Yang in July, 1928, had been unfriendly to our expedition. Thus they had to return to Bachti and wait while fresh negotiations proceeded.

On June the 19th Norin arrived in Bachti from Stockholm and Bohlin from Peking, the latter accompanied by our new Chinese comrade, the young geodesist, Chên. They proceeded to the Chinese frontier but were turned back. On June the 24th Bohlin, Hörner, Bexell and Mr. Chên left Bachti and reached Peking on July the 9th.

Norin and Bergman remained waiting at Bachti. Not till July the 8th did a message come from Governor-General Chin that all the gentlemen might come to Urumchi—he had presumably heard that four of them had already started for Peking! Only Norin could accept this tardy invitation, for Bergman had to wait for Bohlin's baggage and take it back via Vladivostok to Peking. Thus he could not get away until July the 14th, and arrived in Peking on August the 25th. It may be imagined what these unnecessary journeys to and fro cost in time and money. Money indeed could be replaced, but time and the neglected work!

As though there had not been annoyance enough on the Sinkiang frontier, these interminable delays continued after our travellers reached Peking. On September the 4th Bergman and Bexell went to Kalgan, where they spent a part of the autumn in the house of Mr. and Mrs. Larson, and Bohlin on September the 24th betook himself to Nanking where, with tact and energy, he carried on negotiations with the supreme authorities. By the 13th of October he was back in Peking. It was, however, as I have already indicated, the powerful intervention of our Envoy, Hultman, that saved the situation. At an interview which the Envoy had with the Foreign Minister, C. T. Wang, at Nanking on the first of October, the latter promised to have the passports issued for which we had so long waited in vain. What is more they came immediately and were particularly liberal, in that both Kansu and Sinkiang were included among the provinces thrown open to the expedition. For the happy solution of this difficult and tiresome question we thus owe a very great debt of gratitude to our Envoy and to Dr. C. T. Wang.

On October the 13th Hörner went to Kuei-hua-ch'êng whither Bohlin followed him on the 20th. There sixty-five camels were hired which conveyed the whole of the baggage to Beli-miao, arriving on October the 26th. Bergman and Bexell left Kalgan on October the 1st and went to Hattin-sume to fetch the newly bought camels. They reached Beli-miao on October the 19th, and there the whole new caravan was gradually assembled.

And now we were to drive up to Beli-miao and inspect this Swedish community which had been encamped for some days ready for the start.

At nine in the morning of November the 2nd, Hummel and I took our places in Gustaf Söderbom's Dodge car. He himself was at the wheel, and the rest of the car was crammed with baggage and petrol tins. The road is not bad, and we soon came to the entrance to a valley between the hills. Its bottom is occupied by a little frozen water-course. We meet Mongols on their way down to Kuei-hua to sell horses, and others returning northward with goods that they have bought. Fuel is brought to the town by ox-carts. From the village of Pati the gradient becomes more and more perceptible. The last bit up to the pass is quite steep, but here the road is carefully laid and furnished with parapets. At the top of the ridge we found the height to be 1,480 metres above sea-level. The temperature had fallen to $-6{\cdot}2°$.

On the northern side the descent is steeper. Only here and there remain traces of snow. The traffic is quite lively. We pass a little village of clay houses. Beyond the village of Pai-lo-kuan we climb to another pass, where we read 1,640 metres above sea-level. At the village of Kecheng or Koko-irgen we stopped for luncheon and were regaled with tea and "mien-t'iao-tzŭ," a comestible not unlike macaroni.

After an hour the view opens out to the northward over

endless expanses. It is as though we had reached a coast and saw the ocean in front of us. Here and there we drive past little Chinese villages surrounded by tilled fields. It is the colonists who are pressing on to the north and squeezing out the Mongolian nomads. Chao-ho is a little watercourse by a temple. We are again in a ravine, and the road is rough and bad. Small camel caravans are on their way to the north with cloth, tea, cigarettes, matches, soap, kerosene and other goods.

It is past 5 o'clock when the Temple City of Beli-miao rises before us. By that time we have driven 130 miles. We drive round the market place and its shops, looking for our people's encampment. Finally we are shown the way by some Mongols and see, in the twilight, at the foot of a hill, seven blue tents and rows of provision boxes. The Swedish flag floats above two of the tents. At a signal from our Klaxon, masters and servants hurry out of their airy dwellings without any suspicion who these travellers may be who are visiting them. Here is Bergman, here Hörner and Bexell and Mr. Chên. We saw the three latter now for the first time. Folke Bergman is one of the veterans, having been with us from the beginning, since Peking in 1927. I bade the new members heartily welcome to our fellowship and embraced our old friend Bergman. They all looked well and sunburnt in their practical and becoming garb. It was refreshing to me to feel, from the first moment, the sanguine and resolute mood which prevailed among them and the good comradeship, which also included Mr. Chên, the new Chinese member of our expedition.

"But where is Bohlin?"

"He is out on the ground, working, as we all do all day long. He does not usually come home until it is pitch-dark."

Hörner and Bohlin were living in one tent, Bergman and Bexell in another. Mr. Chên had his own. The remaining tents belonged to the nine Mongols who looked after the camels, and the four Chinese employed in various capacities with the caravan. The camels were just now coming in to their sleeping-place. There were eighty-five, uncommonly fine, large, strong animals. Their wool was thick and hung in mighty tufts from their necks, and their humps were firm and substantial and stood straight up, full of fat. They would stand the winter in Gobi and Kansu, be it never so severe.

It all reminded me of our camp at Huchertu, from which we started out two and a half years ago. Several of the Mongols had been there too. Battur, Jamian Sürun, Banche, Matte Lama, Bimba Jergal, Sarang Geröll and San Bylyk were veterans, but San Gurup and the cook, Bugin Jergal, were new. Battur was headman of the Mongols and was primarily responsible for the care of the camels. He was a particularly capable and trustworthy man and had already distinguished himself. Matte Lama, as we remember, had with Serat caught up and captured the camel thief on the way to Etsin-gol. Banche had been Mr. Mühlenweg's faithful servant when the latter, in the desert to the east of Hami, came upon a band of doubtful customers, probably robbers; and it was Serang Geröll who, in the same region, had brought me the disheartening message that the Governor of Sinkiang would not permit us to cross the boundary of his province.

Among the Chinese there was Chang, a highly skilled taxidermist, trained in Andrews' caravans. Wang served as collector of archæological finds. Yen was cook, and another Wang waiter.

We were frozen after our drive and were glad to sit down round the table in one of the tents and warm ourselves with a mug of hot tea, while the "argal" crackled in the stove. It was already dark when Bohlin came home from the desert and joined us. It was a cheerful evening, and we were all in high spirits. They related their adventures during the past months, and we ours. Dinner was served and did credit to the two cooks. We had coffee and a glass of rum per man, while the west wind howled outside. All rejoiced that the difficulties and anxieties had been overcome for the time and that we could look forward to the future with bright hopes. We were all standing on the threshold of a new phase, of whose outcome we knew nothing. Yet this much was certain, that all would do their best with courage and determination, and that the little band on the point of starting westward would return with rich harvests and new scientific material. It was an historic evening in our saga and we did not separate until 1 o'clock. And ever the west wind sang its old familiar song, while trading caravans filed past with throbbing bells on their way to Sinkiang, Kuei-hua and Kalgan. It was long since Hummel and I had lain in sleeping-bags upon the ground, and we enjoyed the cool pleasure of tent life. It was a bit chilly to creep into the sleeping-bag with seven degrees of frost and still worse to creep out again in the morning.

When I got up next morning all our new scientists were out in their respective fields of labour, and Hummel was gathering plant seeds which he afterwards labelled. I stayed in, read, wrote and received Lamas from Beli-miao, who walked in quite familiarly, peeped at and fingered everything and asked for our empty tins and other rubbish. They told me that the monastery has about 1,000 enrolled Lamas of whom, however, only a couple of hundred are now in residence, the rest being on tour among the nomads, as spiritual guides and beggars. The stately old prior, who on the last occasion showed hospitality to some of our members, had died a year ago, and those who were now in power at Beli-miao were less hospitable towards strangers.

That evening Larson and Montell arrived from Kuei-hua, and dinner was a veritable banquet, with wine and the gramophone and songs by Bergman. The Mongol cook has learnt among the Swedish missionaries to make rissoles and pancakes, and since the expedition is provisioned for at least a year, we had no need to worry about its immediate future.

Next day there was a dust storm. The whole country was wrapped in whirling clouds, yellow, sombre, dismal and cold. No-one could work in the open air. In the midst of the gale, wrapped about with flying sand and dust, we performed, between tents and flapping Swedish flags, a solemn ceremony. Four of the veterans among the Mongols had, in the course of a former expedition, so highly distinguished themselves that Swedish Service Medals had been conferred on them by the King of Sweden—Matte Lama in gold and the rest in silver. The Mongols were called forward, and I made a speech to them and fastened the medals on their broad breasts. Battur stepped in front of the others and returned thanks on behalf of the medallists. He said they had only done their duty, but that they were proud and grateful for the honour that had been done them by a king.

In the evening the Mongols entertained us with their country songs and stringed instruments. Later we read aloud the passages about the Lop Nor problem in Stein's *Innermost Asia* and the letters I had recently received from Norin, Ambolt and Yüan. By this means the members of the new expedition got a notion of the kind of country they had a prospect of encountering next summer in Norin's part of Innermost Asia. We had thus served as lines of communication between the two groups.

We also discussed as thoroughly as possible the new expedition's field of labour. Their passports gave the members unusually extended freedom, including the provinces of Shansi, Suiyuan, Ning-hsia, Kansu and Sinkiang. The Governor of the last-named province had recently refused them admittance, but had since withdrawn his prohibition. They had now moreover their passports from the Government at Nanking. Envoy Hultman had promised the Foreign Minister, C. T. Wang, a list of the chief points that were to be touched upon. We now agreed upon Kuei-hua-ch'êng, Wu-la-te-chung-chi, Bieh-li-po-na, Su-chou, Hami and Tihwa or Urumchi. Whether it would be possible to visit all these places time alone would show. In the internal political conditions now prevailing in China it is by no means easy to lay down a definite route in advance. One may come to hear that a given road is blocked by bands of brigands or that civil war is raging in a district to which one intended to travel, and in others there may be famine or revolt. For this reason one must usually accommodate oneself to the circumstances. In any event it was highly probable that the expedition would fall in with Norin's division in Su-chou. After my return to Kalgan I wrote explicitly to Norin and Ambolt to give them their bearings, and I telegraphed to Envoy Hultman to put him in a position to satisfy Dr. C. T. Wang.

The new expedition was to travel in two separate columns. Bohlin and Hörner were to seek out the tracts in which Norin had not been, while still maintaining connexion with his map of 1927. Bergman and Bexell, with a smaller part of the caravan, were to follow another line, touching on our former route at several points where Bergman, in 1927, had not had time to make several important archæological investigations. This group, too, was to extend Norin's map which, once completed, ought to become a unique survey of a part of Asia which had never been the subject of so profound a topographical treatment.

Bergman and Bexell had already begun their work from Hattin-sume where the missionary Joel Eriksson has his station. The camp at Beli-miao accordingly bore the number XII on Bergman's map, but the number I on Hörner's. The monastery, called by the Mongols Batte Hallak-sume, is situated on the brook Aibek which is the lower reach of our old Huchertu-gol where we spent two months in 1927. The distance thither amounts to two days' march.

Our young investigators regard the region around Beli-miao as in all respects unique and interesting, and none of them complained that we were held up day after day waiting for Haslund, who had orders to bring our cars and various things to headquarters, calling on the way to fetch Mr. Eriksson and his car. Everyone had plenty to do from morning to night and afterwards sat by the lamplight entering up his notes or working out his maps. Bergman had besides undertaken the meteorological journal and in this had the very valuable assistance of Mr. Chên. They took readings from six Paulin's altimeters, Assmann's ventilated psychrometers, whirled thermometers, maximum and minimum thermometers, boiling thermometers, the force and direction of the wind, the frequency and form of clouds and other things, a pretty exacting task, but particularly valuable, especially in connexion with the two and a half years' series of observations already carried out by Dr. Haude and his assistants at our stations.

During the days when the camp was pitched at Beli-miao, our people had been exploring in the neighbourhood and had to go daily at least a Swedish mile to and fro between the camp and their work. Inner Mongolia, which elsewhere is pretty monotonous, has in this particular district a complex and marked conformation, a jumble of ridges, hillocks and glens intersected by little streams. The geology of the district is equally complex, and a thorough investigation of its structure would need months. During various epochs the granite has penetrated through the limestone, and it is not always easy to determine their relative periods.

In certain neighbouring valleys there are elm woods, and in these are many idyllic places where our people would rather have camped than on the plateau by the monastery. In several places there are Mongol yurts. From all sides the caravan roads converged on Beli-miao. Trading caravans went by in the evenings and at night, numbering several hundred camels. One got the impression that the traffic is very brisk.

The district round the temple is holy. For this reason the splendid and powerful argali that graze among the hills are inviolable as are also the great herds of dsere antelopes. Steppe hens and rock pigeons were shot by our sportsmen for the pot. Magpies, ravens, eagles and vultures are often seen.

It was a pleasure to see how this troop of six young Swedes worked each at his job and how their results and their experience grew from day to day.

Hörner had many objects in view. Besides his concern with the general geology of the tracts he was to visit, he had an irresistible longing for a real sand desert where he wished to study the origin of the sandhills and the laws of their migration. I believed myself able to promise him that by and by he would get his fill of that.

Bexell roamed around the district with a confidence and competence as if he had been doing nothing else all his life but wandering through the deserts of Asia. He expected great things in his line of research, palæobotany. But he seemed, despite his youth, to be equally at home in stratigraphy and general geology.

Bohlin was an acknowledged master of palæontology and had served two years with distinction in the Geological Survey of China. It was Professor J. G. Andersson who, in 1921, had begun the investigations at Chou Kou Tien, about twenty-four miles south-west of Peking, which led to the discovery of two human teeth. Holes and caves in the limestone beds had been filled up with various materials, including among other things miscellaneous bone remains. Since Professor Andersson expected important discoveries at that place, Dr. O. Zdansky was sent there to make a more particular investigation. The latter took his material to Professor C. Wiman's institution at Uppsala. Fragments of pottery found at Chou Kou Tien led Professor Andersson to surmise that they might be extremely primitive utensils used by mankind at a very early stage of development. Two teeth were found by Zdansky, of which one was that of an adult and the other that of a child. After exhaustive comparisons it was thought highly probable that the owners of these teeth were contemporary with the Piltdown man discovered in England in 1912 and with Pithecanthropus erectus found in Java by Dr. Dubois in 1891.

The first communication of this epoch-making discovery was made by Professor Andersson at a meeting in Peking on October the 22nd, 1926, of several scientific societies, in the presence of the Crown Prince of Sweden.

The Geological Survey of China now determined to pursue this promising investigation, and this was done in co-operation with the Rockefeller Foundation in Peking. The task was entrusted to Dr. C. Li and Dr. Birger Bohlin, who was summoned to China from Sweden. The material found was to be investigated by Dr. Davidson Black of Canada, a member of the scientific staff of the Rockefeller Institute.

After some time Dr. Bohlin found the molar of a nine-year-old child. Dr. Black examined it and pronounced it to be of anthropoid form, either human or simian, but nearer to the man than to the ape.

Professor Amadeus Grabau of the National University of Peking considers that this find is of extraordinary importance and forms a milestone in the researches into the history of the development of mankind.

Professor Grabau relates to a correspondent how Dr. Bohlin had carried on his excavations alone for six months without finding a trace of the human remains he was seeking. The civil war was raging in the neighbourhood, and the roar of the artillery drowned the ringing of the picks. Soldiers ranged the countryside in search of plunder, and Dr. Bohlin was urged by the management of the Geological Survey to abandon his work and return to his base at Peking. But the young Swedish investigator was not to be deterred. He continued his labours, and on October the 16th, 1927, his persistence was rewarded by the discovery of a tooth which at once made him famous in the scientific world. On his twenty-five-mile ricksha journey to Peking he was several times stopped by suspicious soldiers who inquired what property he had with him, but he got through with his precious find and delivered it with his own hands to Dr. Davidson Black at the Rockefeller Foundation.

During the autumn of 1928 Dr. Bohlin was working at Chou Kou Tien and searched long without finding anything. The cold, too, put obstacles in his way. He was once more recalled to Peking. But on the very last day he found, among the debris he was sorting, half a human lower jaw with all the teeth in position. He continued and found portions of skulls and other skeleton fragments. He now hoped to find a complete skeleton of palæolithic man, that is to say of the man who lived during the elder stone age.

He had thus found an indubitable form of primitive man. For the "Peking man" is more primitive than any found previously and yet ranking as human. The brainpan is moderately large and the teeth quite human.

Professor Grabau considers that this is the most important discovery of prehistoric man yet made. It is a being that justifies in a greater degree than any found before the description of "the missing link." It is of importance that the precious fragments were found together with bones of animals whose geological antiquity is known. These fragments belong to some half-dozen different individuals and are nearer to man than to the ape. Professor Grabau assigns them an antiquity of at most a million and at least half a million years. It is not known where the original home of these people was situated, but it is surmised to have been in Central Asia. Professor Grabau himself believes that the Sinkiang basin is the tract which may with most probability be supposed to be the cradle of the human race.

It was therefore an acquisition of extraordinary value for me to obtain Dr. Bohlin as a member of our expedition. He was just the man to extend the researches he had begun at Chou Kou Tien into the heart of Asia whither he was now on his way. He knew in which formations of the limestone beds he had on the whole a prospect of making similar discoveries, and during the days we spent together at Beli-miao, we often spoke of our hopes and expectations of finding more complete and older fragments of human skeletons. Fortunately Dr. Bohlin's contract with the Geological Survey expired on March the 1st, 1929, and he was thus free to accept my invitation to join my scientific staff. He did so willingly and rejoiced in the wide perspective that now opened out for him.

Scarcely a month after we parted at Beli-miao, Bohlin's assistant, the attractive young W. C. Pei, who continued the excavations at Chou Kou Tien, had the luck to find an almost entire cranium of Sinanthropus Pekinensis. Professor Grabau, Père Teilhard and Dr. Black were, naturally enough, delighted at this discovery, which they regarded as more important than the finding of the Neanderthal man and the ape-man discovered in other places. I only regret that it was not vouchsafed to Bohlin himself to make this find, but, as I have said, we hope he will succeed during his present journey in making equally important discoveries.

As for Bergman, he is now working at three different sciences. He was the archæologist of the expedition, but besides worked out a route map and took readings from the meteorological instruments. In the course of his researches he had already solved several large problems and found the answer to many obscure questions about the life and migrations of the later stone age people.

On November the 7th Larson and I were ceremonially invited to a feast in the Mongols' tent. Bohlin and Bergman, who had work in camp while the others were out in different directions, had also been bidden to this barbarically picturesque desert feast. The reason for the feast was the distribution of medals on the previous day. The Mongols wished to give expression to their gratitude for the honour that had been shown them, and it was the King of Sweden who, though absent, was regarded as being the guest of the evening and who was to be honoured in the customary fashion of the nomads. In the middle of the tent the purple flames of the argal fire blazed under a mighty pot in which large pieces of the sheep the Mongols had slain in our honour were boiling. On the top of it was enthroned the head of the sacrificial beast. The smoke from the fire mingled with the curling steam cloud which ascended from the boiling pot, and through the haze the weather-bitten Mongols could be discerned in their dark brown or blue mantles and their soot and dust begrimed sheepskin coats.

When the meat was done the sheep's head was carried round to the guests, each of whom was expected to pull off a piece of the forelock with the meat attached, and eat it. Then everyone got a mighty mass of flesh and a knife, and the meal began. The Mongols sat still, waiting, and only at my express desire partook of the food at the same time as we. One is amazed at the enormous quantity of meat that they can stuff into themselves. They squat on their knees, leaning forward, and eat with knife and fingers. It is done rather conscientiously than rapidly, and not a word is spoken so long as the meal is in progress. It is considered unmannerly to talk while one is eating. Finally tea is served in wooden bowls, and with that the queer feast comes to an end.

The taxidermist, Chang, who had been with Andrews and had learnt his craft in the latter's caravans, had been taken into our service and exhibited some of the work he had already done. He had caught six different kinds of ground rats in snares and traps, of which he had very skilfully prepared a number of specimens, provisionally stuffed and neatly arranged in wadded boxes. He had prepared the skeletons separately. He had also collected birds and one could not but marvel at the devotion, accuracy and neatness of his work. No European taxidermist could have shown finer results. One could see that young Chang was life and soul in his task. He had also been helpful to Bergman in searching for neolithic remains.

In the night of November the 7th, the temperature fell to — 15°, and it was horribly cold creeping out of one's sleeping-bag in the morning. If only one could have had a decent fire! There was plenty of argal in the district, but it was also gathered by the monks and by the caravans camping at Beli-miao.

The day was brilliantly fine, without a cloud or a breath of wind. The camp presented a pretty sight with its seven blue tents ornamented with Chinese emblems in white. And in the splendour of the setting sun the brown columns of the camels came swaying in to their tethering-places. I am living in Bohlin's and Hörner's tent. A picturesque disorder prevails. Hörner has a table, a camp bed and chairs. Round the edges lie instruments, specimens, maps, clothes, boots and other things. When we assemble in the evening in Bergman's tent the Primus lamp from B. A. Hjorth & Co. is lighted, which gives a splendid light, as well as the Sievert radiator of which, thanks to Sten Scholander, we have several with us.

Our doctor had been fishing in the neighbouring brook and prepared his catch according to all the rules of art. He treated us also to steppe hens and pigeons admirably roasted by the same master-cook. Larson produced hard rye-bread from Sweden. We read Heidenstam's poems aloud, and there was music, talk and jesting in the still, clear night.

Thus one day followed another. We were certainly enjoying ourselves, but the great caravan was ready to start and we ourselves to set out on a long motor tour through Inner Mongolia for the purpose of studying a number of lamaistic temples. Still we were obliged to wait for Haslund and the missionary Eriksson. But nothing had been heard of them, and we could not stir without cars.

A Lama from the monastery prophesied that the cars would arrive before noon on November the 8th, or we might drown him in the brook. When 12 o'clock came and no cars were to be seen I mercifully granted him one more hour of life, to the amusement of the Mongols and the unfeigned gratitude of the Lama.

At 8 o'clock we were sitting as usual at supper in Bergman's tent. Then the dogs began to bark, we heard the hum of motors, and horns sounded in the distance. We hurry out. A dazzling beam from the headlamps lights up the steppe. In a minute two cars run in between the tents. Out jumps Haslund, followed by Johansen, Eriksson, Serat and our Chinese chauffeur. The two cars are loaded down with cases, boxes and rolled-up sleeping-bags. Haslund reported that he had taken two days from Tientsin to Kalgan, where he had stayed two days. From Kalgan to Hattin-sume he had taken one day and from thence to Beli-miao one more. The road had only been bad in the Nankou pass, otherwise excellent. He had had to pay 150 Mexican dollars in customs duties. On this last day they had driven 190 miles from Hattin-sume, which lies 140 li or forty-two miles to the north of Eriksson's old mission station at Hallong-ussu and about 130 miles from Kalgan.

We sat packed like herrings in a barrel in Bergman's tent, nine Swedes, two Danes and a Chinaman. But the party was harmonious and in high spirits. The newcomers related their experiences, and plans were arranged. The instruments and other things that Haslund had with him from Sweden were handed over to Bergman and his comrades, who now were able to set out fully equipped on their long journey through inmost Asia.

Nine Swedes gathered in a tent in Mongolia—that had surely never happened before. It looked like a Swedish invasion of the ancient land of Chingis Khan. Larson, Hummel, Bergman, Bohlin, Hörner, Bexell, Montell, Eriksson and I—marvellous to be all talking Swedish. Formerly I had travelled in Asia for years at a time without speaking a word of my own language. Now it was as though we were at home in Sweden, and Swedish dominated the other tongues, Danish, English, Chinese or Mongolian.

On the night of the 9th we had a temperature of − 19·2°; the real winter cold was impending. We had at last received an invitation to come and see the Temple of Beli-miao, the monks having heard that I was a good friend of the Tashi Lama. Ten deep we took our places in the Ford car, mostly standing on the running board. At the main entrance we were surrounded by a troop of monks, red-robed and bareheaded, and conducted to a great temple hall with close-set red lacquered columns and splendidly painted walls. It is all new and all the colours shriekingly bright, for the temple had been sacked and burnt in 1913 during the war between the Chinese and the Mongols and has been rebuilt since then. In the temple hall of Maitreya stands a ten-foot image of the expected Messiah of Lamaism surrounded by other gods and saints, and whole batteries of sacrificial vessels on the altar. In the library was preserved a copy of the sacred writing, the Kanjur, in 108 volumes, carefully preserved between their hard wooden covers and arranged on shelves. Finally we peeped into a pavilion in which were images of preternatural size of the four spirit kings, who, forbidding to behold and armed with all sorts of weapons, defend the entrance to the sanctuary.

The prelate who showed us round was an indescribably ugly, old, irascible, churlish and fat Lama who grudgingly bestowed on us an hour's hospitality. It was only the part of the monastery in his charge that was shown us. For his pains he got a portrait of the Tashi Lama and me taken in Peking in 1926, and then he brightened up. But by that time we had had enough of Beli-miao, and returned to camp.

Our geologists required yet another day to finish their map-work in that region. Otherwise the packing was done, the loads weighed and placed in couples ready to be hoisted with a single handling on to the packsaddles of their bearers, and these latter were, in the course of the day, adjusted to the camels' backs.

On November the 11th I was awakened at 8 o'clock. A brilliant day. A last breakfast together. The loading up begins. One string of camels after another stands

Montell Photo

Tethered Camels of the Gobi Expedition's Caravan at Beli-miao

[*face p.* 172

Montell Photo

Folke Bergman on his riding camel at the start on November 11th, 1929

[*face p.* 173

ready with their loads. The tents are struck, rolled up and loaded. They have six camels too few. Accordingly the loads are rearranged. All the masters go on foot. The Mongols ride so as to keep watch on the long column. I assemble the departing ones for farewell and make a short speech.

"The eastward marching contingent of our great expedition wishes its westward bound comrades a fortunate journey across the storm-lashed land waves of the desert sea. May a brilliant sun attend your steps, may sand storms and blizzards not too highly try your strength, and may your nightly rest be calm and peaceful in the twinkling starlight. I hope it may be vouchsafed to Bergman, the veteran of your troop, to solve the great archæological problems he has set himself to investigate. I hope that Bohlin may awaken from their million-year sleep in the bosom of the rocks whole hordes of prehistoric people. I hope Hörner may unravel the great post-tertiary riddles bound up with Han-hai or the Asiatic Inland Sea, and that Bexell may obtain from the strata of the sedimentary rocks a vast flora hitherto unknown. And I wish Mr. Chên all possible success on this long journey, hoping that his scientific work may be a great honour to himself and to his native country. And finally I hope that the youngest member of our expedition, Johansen, may conduct the caravan that has been entrusted to him through all the perils and hardships that await it. For myself I hope for the pleasure and good fortune of seeing you all again, in the fulness of time, in health and strength, whether it be in Su-chou, by the coast or in Stockholm. May you all be able one day to look back upon an important pioneering work which has brought honour to your country and yourselves, and service to the cause of science. Blessings on your journey! Farewell, farewell."

Hörner at once stepped forward and made on his own and his comrades' behalf a speech, accomplished in form and content, wishing our eastward bound contingent all fortune and success. He thanked me for having, since my age began to put obstacles in the way of my continuing the adventurous travels of my youth in Asia, given to young

Swedish explorers the opportunity of going farther upon the unknown ways. He bade me be confident that the group now beginning its hard campaign would exert its powers to the utmost not to disappoint my expectations.

A fourfold cheer, a hearty handshake, and our comrades went on foot in the track of the caravan towards the ford over the stream. Soon they had disappeared like small dots among the folds of the land.

But on the other side of the stream, moving towards the low threshold of the hills, we could see the long dark lines of the caravan. Owing to the great distance they seemed to move with appalling slowness. How long a time would be needed for the hundreds of miles before them? But yet they moved, they reached the little plateau. I stood with the glasses to my eyes, as long as I could see the black column. "But my glance was dim with tears, and I saw them soon no more."

XV

A MOTOR TOUR THROUGH INNER MONGOLIA

THERE we stood among the knolls on the plateau at Beli-miao, having watched our comrades' departure towards the Gobi Desert. Meanwhile, our cars had been loaded. One of them was an open Ford of the new type. Mr. Joel Eriksson, who knew all these numberless intersecting roads and could find his way even at night, drove first with Larson and Montell. I sat by my Chinese chauffeur, while Hummel and Haslund occupied the back seat. The cars were methodically loaded with our baggage, our sleeping-bags and blankets and our supply of petrol in metal tanks firmly secured in wooden cases, and we ourselves were wrapped up like polar travellers in ordinary coats and great capacious sheepskin coats, as well as having wolfskin or sheepskin coverings over our knees. Driving through Mongolia in winter in an open car is a pretty bracing experience, especially when it blows, and it generally does blow.

It was almost 2 o'clock before we left our memorable camping ground and drove over the brook, past the monastery and the shop, where we left Serat. He was to go, with the collections already made by Bergman's and Bohlin's expedition, to Kuei-hua, and thence by train to Kalgan.

Thus began our journey of 680 miles over gently undulating country between low hills. The road is pretty good. Now and then one meets a rider or a pedestrian. A herd of dseren antelopes is grazing on the steppe. Uneasily, with ears pricked up, they turn to look at us. With every appearance of alarm they set off, but not immediately away from the danger. They first cross the road right in front of the cars. They always do this, and so, too, did the roe deer at the northern edge of the Grand Canyon in Arizona.

Sometimes we drive past a well. Here is a Mongol camp of nine yurts, here one of four, and farther off a third, of eight. At the monastery of Khotton-goluin-sume we stop for an hour and then continue by an excellent road over more level country. In the twilight we cross a stream where a nomad community has pitched its tent, and in the darkness we come to the river Shara-muren, where Eriksson gets out to reconnoitre. He finds a suitable place and gets across with his own car, but ours breaks through the ice and we stick fast as in a vice. After an hour's toil we succeed in getting the car up on to the ice again. Meanwhile a crowd of Lamas, attracted by the gleam of the lamps, has collected from the neighbouring monastery to enjoy this unusual and interesting spectacle. We drive up to Shara-muren-sume, "The Yellow River Monastery," where a yurt is placed at our disposal and where our doctor prepares a long-desired supper.

On the morning of November the 12th we learned that our visit was pretty useless, for the Gegen or re-incarnate abbot was away, and only he could give strangers permission to cross the threshold of the temple. We had therefore to content ourselves with viewing the temple, the dormitories and the various buildings appertaining to the monastery from the outside. Shara-muren is an ancient, fine and well-kept cloister. It had just been cleaned and whitewashed, and all the buildings and walls gleamed white like milk or snow. The white town is in the form of an amphitheatre with an extensive view to the south-east, and across the plain, between low hills, curves the frozen silver ribbon of the Shara-muren. There are supposed to be 1,200 Lamas—certainly an exaggerated estimate.

Gaped at by a multitude of Lamas we resumed our seats in the cars and went on south-east and east-south-east over insignificant hills, where isolated snow patches remained from the first fall of the winter. It is sparsely peopled, this land whose tribes conquered half the world seven hundred years ago. Very rarely we meet travellers in ox-carts, on camels or on horseback. A little village of thatched mud huts surrounded by cultivated fields bore witness to the northward penetration of the industrious Chinese colonists, a menace to the Mongols, who are thus compelled to give way to the Chinese and to retreat northward step by step.

After five miles' journeying we came to Durbet Wang's capital which is also called simply Durbet Wang. We stopped before his palace, handed in our Chinese visiting cards and were at once courteously received by an obese and genial gentleman of forty-five. He was the Wang or King of the Durbet Mongols. In his great hall of audience, appointed in the Chinese style, he entertained us with tea, cakes, nuts and fruit. Then he showed us his two temples, quite small, but not ill appointed. At parting he gave me a small prayer mat, and I him an alarm-clock. And so we parted with mutual esteem and goodwill.

After I had had the honour to be photographed at the King's side, we drove on north-east and east-north-east through Chinese clearings and tilled fields and, at twilight, reached Baishin, where Deba Gun resides. He is "dosselakchi" or counsellor to Durbet Wang, and is a very rich and powerful lord. He owns tens of thousands of sheep and thousands of horses and camels and is besides a trader on a large scale. He has been twice married, but has no child. His present wife is a really charming little Mongol, and she and her maids giggled and laughed at us when we entered their gigantic yurt, sat down on the mat by the fire and partook heartily of the tea and pastry that were offered us. The dosselakchi himself is an imperturbably good-humoured and self-complacent man, a free-born Mongol of old family, boasting his descent from Chingis Khan He told us that the conqueror's younger brother, Habbet Hasser, had a grandson, Ombo, of whose four sons one became Wang of Durbet, and that his descendants in direct succession have sat ever since—from the fourteenth century to this day—upon the throne of Durbet.

It pleased our host to entertain us with an account of his adventures with the roving bands of robbers who had attacked Baishin in search of plunder, and of how, usually by cunning, he had succeeded in getting the better of them.

The guest yurt quite close to his own was allotted to us, and we spread our sleeping-bags round the fire in its midst. The dosselakchi himself kept us company and shared the sumptuous meal that was served. The stars looked down on us through the open smoke vent after the fire had died down, and one after another we slept after the day's toils.

Next morning, the 13th, we were regaled with porridge and tea, and were afterwards conducted by the dosselakchi himself fourteen minutes run to the east-north-east, to his hereditary family temple, Gapchilin-sume, which has stood in its own grounds for seven generations and which was erected in its original state by his forefathers two hundred years ago. The graceful little temple takes its name from the neighbouring well, Gapchilin-usu. The sanctuary consists of several pavilions and pagodas with a courtyard between, and has 200 Lamas under a "chörch" or prior.

A joint meeting, festival and praying hall bears the name of Choksum-dugun, and there is enthroned an image of Śākyamuni, the eternally dreaming Buddha. The hall of the spirit servants is called Sakhosne-dugun and Chura-dugun is adorned with an image of Maitreya or Maidari, the expected Messiah. The monks had just been engaged in the reading of the sacred writings and their robes were thus still lying on the couches. Here was found a copy of the Tanjur, the commentary on the Kanjur. Abita-dugun is a smaller chapel built by the dosselakchi himself. There there is an image of Abit, the god of boundless light, called by the Tibetans "Ottbagamit," eight feet high, made at Dolon-nor of gilded brass and worth 1,000 taels, or with its gilded wooden aureole, 1,800 taels. The whole chapel had cost him close upon 5,000 taels.

After the round of the temple we were again regaled with food, minced mutton and macaroni, not at all bad, as well as the inevitable tea in bowls of Chinese porcelain.

When we had finished with Gapchilin-sume, we drove back to the dosselakchi's residence, where a photograph of his young wife was added to Montell's pictorial archives and where we were invited to view the two temple yurts of the place. One of them was highly impressive in its substantial and tasteful appointments, its beautiful images and ancient icons, its sacrificial vessels of silver and its lamaistic symbols ranged on the artistically sculptured and painted altar. Round the walls of the yurt were hung "tankas" or bannerlike paintings on cloth representing the Buddha and saints from the iconography of lamaism. The temple yurt was undoubtedly a jewel of the lamaistic cult, for, like Gapchilin-sume, it had been handed down from father to son through many generations. Time after time the felts of the yurt and even its wooden framework had been renewed, and perhaps the altar, too, had been repaired. But the cult objects that stood upon it were of metal and could defy the tooth of time. Each new owner had increased this equipment of cult objects and, as a tribute to Buddha and a memorial of himself, had extended the number of the icons or the sacrificial vessels with some new costly jewel. Accordingly this temple yurt had its own history and was a pearl of its kind. At my request Eriksson asked whether we could buy the temple yurt, to which the dosselakchi answered:

"If you have a coat for the winter, do you sell it?"

"Yes, perhaps, if I have two."

"Well, if you have ten children, do you sell one of them?"

He meant that hereditary sanctuaries are not for sale.

By the side of this yurt was another, in which two Lamas dwelt and, to the strains of spiral horns, drums and handbells, were wont to perform their daily service. When the dosselakchi is on a journey he takes these two yurts along so that he may always be able to satisfy the demands of religion and may never neglect the care of his eternal welfare.

Well on in the afternoon we took to our cars again and went on towards the north and north-east across gently undulating country past a small lake, where we met four horse-drawn carts and six drawn by oxen—Chinese colonists moving or immigrating. In the distance very low hills rise, and the country is tinged with yellow tones and grows flatter and flatter. It grows dark over us and is beginning to blow, and snowflakes float through the air. We pass a string of twenty carts, nothing but migrant Chinese. Our road leads into a valley among hills. At its opening lies a tent village of several yurts. Then the landscape opens out again into vast expanses, where great herds of antelopes are seen on both sides of the road. We reckon 800 or 1,000 in all. They are white and pale grey, enchanting in their noble forms and their elegant and elastic bounds. They regard us inquisitively and slyly for a moment and then scamper, swift and light as a cloud shadow, across the road, sometimes between the two cars though these are running pretty close together.

By half past four we are at Wangin-ortu, Sunit Wang's headquarters or capital, where his palace, built in Chinese style, stands and where he has his private temple and sanctuary. We were deprived of the privilege of seeing his majesty who was on his way to Mukden in the train of the Tashi Lama. He is said to be very religious, and thus does not neglect the precious opportunity of sunning himself in the holy radiance emanating from the pope of Southern Tibet.

Sunit Wang's army numbers a thousand, whereas Durbet Wang has only 300 men. He possesses three motor cars and maintains a quite expensive establishment. Accordingly the taxes he exacts from his people are heavy. At the present time there are two queens-dowager in Sunit, of whom one is his mother. Sunit Wang's father had, in fact, a number of wives. His own queen had quite recently given birth to a child and would therefore not be receiving any strangers for at least a year. She had previously lost four children and must now take extreme precautions to guard the new-born heir against all harmful influences from without.

Thus the King of Sunit was not at home, but the queens would be pleased to see us if we could wait an hour or so while they made their toilet. And we were welcome to stay the night at the palace.

But we preferred to drive on, although it was 6 o'clock, and, after tea and other refreshments, got back into our cars and steered our course eastward on an excellent road,

Montell Photo

Interior of Durbet Wang's Temple

[*face p.* 180

Montell Photo

Sunit Wang's Temple

[face p. 181

with glorious moonlight shining on the silent steppe. But one does not see much of the country ; only now and then the barking of dogs indicates that we are passing a Mongol tent village. A couple of hours' driving brought us to Hattin-sume.

At the foot of a hill stands the little ruined and abandoned temple of Hattin-sume as a monument to the religion which Mr. Eriksson combats by wise and tactful methods. He built his station in the Mongolian wilderness with his own hands. The small white house is a Christian and Swedish outpost in the land of the nomads. There is a dwelling house for Eriksson, his wife and their three children and a nursing sister, Miss Almkvist, sister of Mrs. Eriksson. Some months after our visit the station was reinforced by a young missionary, Mr. Martinsson, from Sweden.

Another building contains the hospital and dispensary and a guest-room. There are also the school, the mission room and the servants' quarters. Mr. Eriksson has his hands full. He is architect, mason, painter, blacksmith, motor mechanic, head gardener, chauffeur, botanist, archæologist, teacher of languages, physician and missionary. There is nothing he cannot do ; he is always cheerful, willing and kindly, and the Mongols love him. They constantly bring their sick to him, and he helps them all. The most widespread ailment is syphilis which decimates this once so vigorous people. Mr. Eriksson travels by car round distant tent villages and cares for his patients with never-failing patience. Through his care of the sick he comes into much closer touch with the Mongols than the missionaries who only preach. He is held in such high esteem throughout the district that even the bandits leave him and his family in peace. Many a time in the course of his journeys he has been attacked by highwaymen ready to plunder him down to the bare skin. But so soon as they have recognized him, he has been allowed to pass unmolested. It was a great advantage to us to have him with us ; he was a protection to us throughout our travels in Mongolia. It had, however, happened not long since that a young woman had been shot dead in Eriksson's car by bandits, who were in despair when they found they had offended against the man who so often had cared for and cured members of their own band. The bandits sometimes visit Eriksson's station, where they are kindly received and invited to tea and therefore, of course, do not lay hands on any of the family's possessions. I know no Swede who has conferred more honour on the Swedish name in Eastern Asia than Mr. Joel Eriksson.

In this home we spent a peaceful night on Swedish soil, in comfortable beds and warm rooms. Next day at 1 o'clock we set out towards the south-east. As usual the excellent road lay over undulating steppe among low hills, past nomads' tent villages, herds of horses and sheep, and here and there a well. One village contained as many as twelve yurts. In one part the country was intersected by canyon-like ravines, and sometimes the hills rose to a considerable height. In the aul of Bongshen-gol we stopped for an hour and bought a fiddle, a harp, a sacrificial vessel, a ring and some other pieces for the ethnographic collection. We also came across a few sets of chessmen with figures amusingly carved. Our way lies on always to the south-east and east-south-east. The road is like a number of shallow parallel furrows made by the cartwheels and the tramping of the flocks. At the foot of a ridge lie a couple of small lakes. Attikin-bulak is an aul of twelve yurts. Here the Norwegian Mongolian Mission Ebenezer has been established since May, 1929. Mr. and Mrs. Karl B. Olsen, Norwegian Americans, conduct its activities. He gave the impression of being a very capable and enterprising man and greeted us as brothers. As always when one calls upon missionaries, here too we were treated to coffee and cakes.

Hence our direction was north-easterly. It was blowing pretty hard from the north-west and one needed to be well wrapped up to escape freezing. At half past eight we arrived at the Swedish station of Gull-chaggan. Here we met a whole Swedish colony, Mr. and Mrs. Skallsjö and their three small children, Dr. Ollén and Miss Dagny Hansen, whom I met in Urga in November 1923 and who had been my father's sick nurse in Stockholm in 1916. We had a pleasant and interesting evening with the missionaries

Montell Photo

Mongol Women at Hattin-sume, Eriksson's Mission Station

[*face p.* 182

and were sumptuously entertained at their table. Finally we were planted out in various guest-rooms. Dr. Ollén resigned his two studies, whose walls were hidden behind medical works, the stove crackled, and the moon shone in through the window.

In the morning we looked over the hospital, the dispensary, the operating room with its table, not quite modern but good enough for thick-skinned Mongols, and pretty good to have been produced so far from civilization. We peeped into Dr. Ollén's photographic dark room, into the hospital ward of six beds and into the schoolroom which serves also as a mission room. In all, the mission station of Gull-chaggan consists of six small houses. For 100 dollars Dr. Montell bought twelve Mongolian dresses which Dr. Ollén had received in place of cash remuneration. The missionaries were glad to dispose of them, and we needed them for our ethnographic collections.

In brilliant winter weather and under a cloudless turquoise blue sky we began our day's journey to the north-east and east-north-east. As usual we drive through a country of gentle undulations, low hills and tent villages beside wells, and pass flocks of white sheep or herds of spirited horses that accompany us at a gallop until they tire. Horned cattle, too, are grazing here and there ; camels are less common. At a village of small mud huts a savage dog chanced to get under my car, but he escaped by a miracle and stood on all fours gazing after us in astonishment.

Through a waterless gorge 100 metres wide we came over sandy ground to the little temple of Arben-tabbene-sume which has fifty Lamas of whom only twenty were in residence; the rest are out among the surrounding tent villages, where they read prayers over the dead and give suitable names to new-born children, as well as supplying wise counsel to the nomads concerning their spiritual and bodily welfare.

The little temple is built in the Chinese style, has a bell and three large praying wheels as well as a quite characteristic pagoda, supported on carved and painted columns. On its parti-coloured altar sat images of gilded brass. Similar ornaments decorated the side walls, which were otherwise occupied by bookshelves and sacred writings. Arben-tabbene was well supplied with all the proper appurtenances of a temple. Numerous tankas or banner-like paintings representing various gods hung upon the walls and columns. Cushions with small praying mats were laid on the floor for the monks, two stately chairs were provided for ecclesiastical dignitaries, the church music was furnished by drums, trombones and flutes, and " haddiks " or long thin silk scarves or veils bore witness to the open-handedness of the pilgrims.

The Lama who showed us the temple and was its veritable Cerberus was of more than usually uncouth appearance in his big white moustaches, and when, smiling genially, he accepted the silver coins we gave him for his trouble, he looked like one of Repin's laughing Cossacks.

After an exhaustive inspection of the building and the usual photographing, we go, still to the north-east, past a couple of small villages with the indispensable stacks of dried cow and camel dung for winter fuel, and stop in front of the main entrance to the temple cloister of Boro-tologain-sume, " The Temple of the Grey Head," where a dozen Lamas receive us and conduct us through the sacred chambers of the gods. To the right and left of the main temple there are smaller side pavilions with medium-sized images of gods. In the middle of the main temple lies a small pavilion with the usual four spirit kings or guardians of the gate who, with terrifying weapons in their hands, defend the holy place from evil spirits of the air and other perils. One of the gods, Gongrok, in the left side-pavilion has bestowed his name on a neighbouring stream which we crossed, Gongrokin-gol. The four buildings thus enclose a little stone-paved courtyard, from the level of which one mounts a few steps to the platforms on which the temple buildings stand. Almost all the temples in this part of Mongolia are laid out on this plan.

Boro-tologain-sume is built in the Manchu style with the gracefully curved tile roof and with the symbolic signs on the roof ridge, the wheel of life and two antelopes. The principal hall, Choksum-dugun, is splendid with forty-eight mighty round columns, tastefully and elegantly carved with sinuous dragons, lacquered and painted, mostly in red. Between them lie eight rows of couches, covered with beautiful little square mats on which the Lamas sit during divine service. Each row provided twenty seats.

Behind and in front of the altar hang numerous ancient draperies of silk in long, narrow, many-coloured breadths and pennons, and at the sides were seen the picturesque and decorative instruments of Church music, the long copper trombones and twenty-five mighty drums.

We were out on a tour of inspection to take a general survey of the lamaistic temples of Mongolia and Northern China. What we had so far seen had not greatly appealed to us. But here at Boro-tologa, "The Grey Head," we had found what we sought. It was just something in this style that I had in my mind for giving the Christian public in Europe and America a conception of lamaistic temple architecture. Wherever one stood in the principal pagoda of Boro-tologa, the forty-eight brilliantly coloured columns presented a wonderful perspective in the subdued but effective lighting. The light from the entrance door fell across the columns, which stood out against the dark background around the altar. The side walls with their paintings of Buddha and the saints lay similarly in gloom, and the roof disappeared in an enigmatic obscurity. One seemed to feel the presence of an unknown god.

From Boro-tologa our course lies sometimes east-north-east, sometimes east-south-east. We skirt a little lake and enter a valley between hills, the fairest landscape we saw in all our travels in Mongolia. Elms grow there, too sparsely to be called forest. And there are dunes in whose sand a few shy hares have left their tracks. In front of us is seen a little frozen lake, and, not far from its shore, the Swedish mission station of Dojen, with a long house for the missionaries and six yurts for the servants and the nine Mongol children who have been left by their parents in the care of the mission.

The station of Dojen was established by Mr. Skallsjö, who, in 1925, settled in the pretty valley and lived in a yurt. The next year he built the house in which we were now so hospitably received by the two ladies, Miss Blomkvist and

Miss Karlsson, who have been in charge of the station since May, 1929. They belong to the Pentecostal movement, whose management maintains them and supports in all eighteen missionaries in the province of Hopei, the former Chili.

The ladies received us with the greatest hospitality and invited us to coffee and cakes, organ music and singing. They are admirable in their austere devotion to their great vocation, and since they belong to the Pentecostal movement, they are more alien to the world than other missionaries. One could not smoke in their house; smoking is considered a sin. But we failed to understand why nicotine should be more sinful as a means of enjoyment than caffeine. The two women missionaries had suffered many severe vicissitudes. Many times they had been attacked by robbers and plundered of everything of value they possessed. They were indomitable and feared no earthly danger, in the consciousness of the heavenly power that watched over them.

After a simple but well-served supper we climbed into our bunks in the guest-room and once more slept on Swedish ground.

Next morning at 9 we took farewell of the two valiant apostles of the Dojen station and drove back by the way we came through the sandhills and the elms. The ground was now everywhere under snow and it snowed persistently. It is quite still and the sun sometimes breaks through and shines upon the white fields where the snow crystals sparkle like diamonds. Our way winds over undulating country and low hills, now to the south, now to the west or north-west. It is a puzzle to us how Eriksson can find his way in this network of roads and snow-covered hills that are so like one another.

After another look at Boro-tologain-sume, we turn southward by roads on which our wheels slip in the snow. Going up through a valley between high hills, the gradient became too steep and we had to turn. Another pass proved no better. We all turned out and walked. The snow was pretty deep. The wheels spun so that the snow flew up round them, but the cars did not move. Eriksson reconnoitred a byway in his car. He worked himself slowly upwards in the direction of the pass. But suddenly the car stopped and began to roll backwards. The brake was no longer holding, and the car was gathering speed in the direction of a ravine with perpendicular sides. The situation looked desperate. The car must infallibly run down into the ravine and be smashed with Eriksson himself. But Eriksson has come through many perils, and now, too, he was equal to the situation. When he saw where it was carrying him he simply jumped out. The car went on by itself and, just at the edge of the ravine, turned sideways and came to a standstill. It looked as if an unseen driver had turned the steering wheel and saved Eriksson's ancient and worn-out but still serviceable car at the last moment.

After we had got the cars down to more level ground, we met with a Lama and a boy who showed us, by a long detour, to a gently rising lane and a shallow pass with obos or cairns to the divine powers. Not far from thence lies the temple and monastery of Mantaltein-sume.

The snow was now falling thickly. There was a fresh breeze and it was blowing up into a regular blizzard. The whole ground was white and nothing could be seen of the surrounding hills. One gets gradually snowed under in one's seat in the car, sitting muffled in double coats, rugs, caps and baschliks.

The road was hidden under the snow, and how Eriksson could find it was more of a mystery than ever. But he managed splendidly, and at half past four a little house dimly emerged out of the blizzard. We jumped out, shook the snow off us and entered, kindly and hospitably welcomed by a lone woman, Miss Hulda Wiklund.

This young lady, a desert queen, who lived in lonely majesty among the Mongols of the steppe, was a positive revelation to us. For a missionary she was unbelievably free from prejudices, gay, high-spirited and humorous ; her movements were brisk, and she sparkled with kindliness and the joy of living. She flew from one to the other, she changed round the furniture and put the room straight, she turned sofas and ottomans into beds and she brought forth unlimited clean sheets and pillows. Sheets for us, who were accustomed to our simple sleeping-bags! Yes, sheets we should have, and fine ones. And so we were invited into her own room and given coffee the like of which we had never tasted at the hotel in Peking, with cream and milk and mountains of cakes.

"May one smoke here?"

"Yes, smoke your hardest."

One had greater freedom at Naimain-ul than at other mission stations. Smoking was no sin; one might talk of worldly things and declaim the verses of the Swedish bards.

So far as we could see, Miss Wiklund had only a single servant in the house, the sixteen-year-old Topchin, an attractive and roguish Mongol girl, who, dexterous and nimble as a cat, served an excellent dinner of roast mutton and pancakes, and had sole charge of the kitchen department.

Miss Wiklund loved the Mongols and was much beloved by them. She also loved their animals and said herself that she was really a missionary to animals. The support of some society for the protection of animals would not be out of place here. Miss Wiklund is also a patriot, and was unfeignedly glad to meet so many fellow countrymen turning up unexpectedly and unannounced out of the wilderness. After our return to Kalgan we were able easily to fulfil her desire to have a Swedish flag to hoist over the station of Naimain-ul.

But she also had another desire which it was less easy to satisfy. She wanted a whole fortune of money so as to extend her activities in all directions. I believe that even smaller sums sent through the Swedish Legation in Peking to her and to the other Swedish missionaries in "the Grass Country" would be very welcome, and lead many poor and needy Mongols to salvation, ameliorate the hard lot of the missionaries and also bring honour to the Swedish name in the Far East.

When next morning, November the 17th, we resumed our journey to the west and north-west, we had two new travelling companions, Miss Hulda Wiklund and the girl Topchin. They had some business in Gull-chaggan whither we were now returning. It was cold, $-13{\cdot}2^{\circ}$ at

9 o'clock, and it snowed incessantly. We drove over a pass ornamented with three obos and ran down into the valley of Yinding-gol, where we passed a couple of tent villages with the inevitable savage dogs, and where hares were gambolling in the snow-covered grass. It was blowing hard in our faces and the biting wind chilled us to the marrow. But the snow clouds were torn asunder and swept away and the sun came out again. We made a short stay at the temple of Hertein-sume. There is not much to see; the little sanctuary is unpretentious and poor. But, since at midday there were still nearly fourteen degrees of frost, it was pleasant to get out for a while and move about and get into shelter from the penetrating wind.

It was only half an hour's drive from here to Gull-chaggan, where a Mongol double marriage was being celebrated between some of the wards of the station. We were not in time to witness the marriage ceremony itself, but we came in for the banquet and were sumptuously entertained. The brides were afterwards photographed by Dr. Montell.

Gull-chaggan lies about 100 miles west-north-west of the celebrated town of Dolon-nor, one of the places where lamaistic images of gods are manufactured on a large scale. From this town and its surroundings the Swedish missionaries buy the stock of millet and oats they need for the three stations of Gull-chaggan, Hattin-sume and Dojen. They buy about twenty tons for the winter, a provision for forty children at Gull-chaggan, fifteen at Hattin-sume and ten at Dojen. A cart carries 300 kilogrammes and costs about thirty-five Mexican dollars, delivered. About sixty loads are needed. The merchants hang on to their stocks in the first half of the winter so as to be able to raise the price later on.

I must now make a digression from my narrative of travel.

On February the 15th Dr. Hummel received a letter from Joel Eriksson to say that Mr. Skallsjö had been carried off by typhoid fever and that Dr. Ollén was down with it. On the 21st I received a telegram from Larson, who was then at Kalgan: "Ollén dead." A few days later a letter came from Larson saying that he suggested coming with my car to Gull-chaggan so as to bring the bereaved women and children to a safer place. I answered that he must put all work in my service on one side and hasten to aid the unfortunate.

Sister Dagny Hanson relates in a letter that Dr. Ollén was taken ill, clearly with typhoid, on January the 27th, that he had kept up his strength fairly well for the first week, but afterwards he had lain for ten days with a temperature of 40° and in great suffering. On the eleventh day he had died and two days later had been buried. "We are as if stunned with grief and regret." Their colleagues from Hattin-sume had come to Gull-chaggan, but had now gone home, and the bereaved ones were left alone with their grief.

Only three months had passed since we were there. Then Gull-chaggan was full of life; the Christian and medical labour of love was in full swing, Mr. Skallsjö was just about to start for Dolon-nor to fetch winter stores, riders arrived, tied up their horses and rode away again, the sick were brought in for treatment, each had his own task and all rejoiced in their work. We had seen the missionaries at their work and the station in bright wintry weather.

Now I cannot think of Gull-chaggan without seeing it against a background of gloomy, howling snowstorms. I see two women hurrying with hasty steps from one sick bed to the other. They are tired out with night watching, their features are wasted and bear the stamp of anxiety and disquiet. One day it grows still. A Mongol carpenter comes with some boards while two others laboriously dig a grave in the hard-frozen ground. One more day, and the plain unpainted coffin is borne out by Mongols to be lowered into foreign soil. A woman reads the Swedish funeral prayers and psalms, and commits the faithful servant to his Master's keeping. Then follow some more days of hurry. One of the women is prostrate with weeping. She has lost her husband and the support of her children. When the stillness returns it is deeper than before. Next day the carpenter is again at work, a new coffin is put together and a new grave dug in the Mongolian soil. And again the funeral psalms rise through the frozen air, and with submission to the will of God, a brave woman reads, without a tremor in her voice, the words: "The Lord gave and the Lord hath taken away, blessed be the name of the Lord!"

I do not know whether it was she who committed the Christian physician to the grave. Probably it was Joel Eriksson who threw the three shovelfuls of earth over his departed colleague. We know as yet no details of these days of grief and this profound tragedy. We only know that "the comrades from Hattin-sume," that is to say Eriksson and his wife and sister-in-law and the young missionary Martinsson, who had arrived in December, hurried to the assistance and support of their afflicted and so hardly tried friends. But when these left, the two women were alone with the children, of whom there were now four, since another had come into the world a month earlier—and in vain one asks the old question: *Why* should these, the most unselfish and self-sacrificing people on earth, be struck down with so frightful a blow, while we, who think only of ourselves, escape?

While life roared in the abandoned capital like the reflection from an expiring volcano and the echo of a departed greatness, the snowstorms drew, amid the howling of the wolves, their white veils, like tattered palls, about a little Swedish mission station up there on the Mongolian tableland. Within, beside the lamp, sit two women, the last of the brave garrison of the Gull-chaggan fortress of the Swedish Mongolian mission. They feel themselves lost in a sea of dark and unfathomable riddles. But they are not forgotten by their countrymen; help will come one day from Sweden.

In cold, clear winter nights the stars twinkle with incomparable radiance above the lonely grave mounds that conceal the dust of two Swedish martyrs, who fell at their post and died for their faith. Blessed and revered, their memory shall endure.

But we must return to our travels in Mongolia.

On November the 17th, in brilliant afternoon sunshine, we drove to the monastery of Lavajar-sume, which offered nothing of interest except some very well-made brass gods. When about two hours later we reached Hattin-sume we had driven, reckoned from Kuei-hua, 612 miles, or as far as from Paoto to Etsin-gol by the desert road we traversed with 300 camels in 1927.

During the day of rest we spent at the Erikssons', Hummel went through one of the herbaria collected by the versatile missionary, intended for the botanical section of the Swedish Museum of Natural History. Montell purchased a number of ethnographical objects, women's ornaments and images of Buddha.

In clear weather and a biting westerly wind we started on November the 19th, leaving the good Mrs. Eriksson, her sister and her two children and many Mongolian wards to the solitude of the wilderness, and went on to the south-east. After an hour we are on the great caravan road between Kalgan and Urga where, on account of the tension between Russia and China, the traffic is very slight. The local trade is, however, in full swing, and on the stretch on which we kept to the great road we met or passed a number of ox-carts with wool, camel caravans and riders. Several of these still go to Ude on the border of the Mongolian republic, but not beyond it. Here and there one passes wayside villages or a well where the cattle are watered. Twice we met riders who might just as well have been robbers as anything else. The telegraph line follows the road. At the large village of Chapcher, consisting of mud houses and yurts, a couple of camel caravans and a herd of cattle were resting.

We turn westward, pass Hallun-ussu and, soon after 3 o'clock, the monastery of Harring-kerva-sume, or in Chinese Ma Wang-miao. On the way thither we drive through newly cultivated fields which Chinese settlers have bought from the Mongols. The last-named monastery is one of those which have been abandoned and are no longer required, since the Mongolian population has been forced out by the Chinese.

Half an hour farther south we found the lovely old temple of Battumte-sume, where we took the usual general look round before going on to the Canadian mission station at

Gashete where we found hospitality for the night with Mrs. Wynes and Miss Fordham, who had come in for plenty of exciting visits from robbers. The superintendent of the station, Mr. Hindel and his wife, who have lived here for twenty years, were just then expected back after an absence on leave.

On November the 20th we came once more upon the Urga road at the station of Chaggan-chöllo, twelve Swedish miles north of Kalgan. Actually we only crossed the Urga road and then went on to the eastward, now and then passing a village, a Chinese cultivated patch, a small caravan or a couple of ox-carts. The by-road we follow is thoroughly bad, owing to the depth of its ruts. Endless plains extend on every side, and now one sees everywhere marks of the plough of the industrious Chinese. One sees, too, their solid villages of mud houses, sometimes enclosed, as in old times, by walls and dykes as a defence against robbers and barbarians.

The next temple to be an object of our inspection is called Efi-ghalkha. It was in ruins. Vandals and thieves had left their traces in its sacred hall of the gods. Planks and beams had been torn up to be used for fuel, everything of value had disappeared and the wall paintings which either could not be removed or which they had not cared about, were destroyed. Probably the monks themselves when they abandoned the temple had taken with them many of the objects of value. Six bronze gods of three feet or more in height had been left, possibly on account of their weight. Two of them had been mischievously mishandled, but were not badly damaged and could easily be repaired. We determined to get into touch with the owner of Efi-ghalkha and try to acquire the images. The temple is one of those which, owing to the northward penetration of the Chinese cultivators, have come to lie like islands in the newly conquered Chinese territory, now that the nomads have moved northward. It is no longer profitable to the monks to stay in a monastery temple such as Efi-ghalkha. They are surrounded on all sides by Chinese settlers, and the lamaistic community, whose spiritual guides they have been, have deserted the district. They would die of starvation if they stayed. Accordingly they demolish their sanctuary which has perhaps been established for hundreds of years. The carts which now encumber the ruined hall of the gods bear visible witness to the change that has taken place. No divine service is performed here any more. Buddha and the other holy ones have been driven out, and their abode turned into a waggon shed. The owners of a temple thus degraded should ask for nothing better than to sell it. We heard of a temple in this region for which a Chinese trader offered 3,000 Mexican or 1,090 United States dollars, obviously with a view to making his profit out of the materials.

From Efi-ghalkha we went west and south-west to Dabasin-nor, where salt is quarried and sold. We are here about 1,300 metres above sea-level. We then turned south-east to the ruin of an ancient city called Chaggan-balgas or "White City" on account of the discoveries of marble sculptures which were then made and turned to account by the neighbouring Catholic missionaries, who used them and the marble slabs that were recovered for the decoration of their churches. The city had been surrounded by a quadrangular wall, and the road goes through two of its gates.

Our journey continued to the Belgian mission station of Ho-ma-ho, surrounded by a wall. We went up on to the veranda and knocked at the door. A Chinese servant opened it, and we introduced ourselves, handed in our cards and were finally received by Father de Leu, who invited us into his large sitting-room with a table in the middle, a writing-table by a window and several bookcases. He gave us tea and cigars and spoke of the insecurity of the country at the present time. Later he showed us the church, very fine and well kept. The floor, the steps and the balustrading round the altar had been made of marble from the ancient city of Chaggan-balgas. Father de Leu told us that the Catholic missions receive money from home for their churches and for the purchase of land, but afterwards have to be self-supporting. They arrange to let their land to their neighbours, who in return must send their children to the Catholic schools. The parents need not be

Christians. It is supposed to take four generations to make real Catholics out of the neophytes.

Forty miles north of Ho-ma-ho there is another station, called Kung-hueh. When brigandage is rife, Chinese fugitives are allowed to take refuge within the substantial walls of the Catholic stations, where the defence is well organized and sentries are posted. Each refugee has to pay a dollar as well as a separate fee for his cattle and belongings. After an hour's stay with the Father, we set out in the darkness, and three-quarters of an hour brought us to Chang-pe-hsien, a little town with a Canadian mission station managed by Chinese Christians. They received us kindly and hospitably and gave us supper.

November the 21st was the last day of our tour. The temperature fell in the night to − 16·5°, and before 9 o'clock we drove to Davan Jallan-gin-sume, a private temple belonging to one Jellang, chief of one of the post stations on the road to Urga.

In a freezing north-easterly gale we drove south-westward. The strong wind raised the yellow dust and the landscape was hidden in haze. We drove across a frozen watercourse up to the monastery temple of Boro-che-chin-sume, at whose gates two marble lions from the ancient city keep watch. Otherwise there was nothing of interest to be seen. In a full dust storm we passed villages, farms and frozen rivers, and came to the great caravan route to Kalgan. Just after 12 o'clock we were in the pass, 1,465 metres above sea-level, with a temperature of − 13° and an icy wind. Thence the road runs down into the pronounced valley which leads to Kalgan and the Nankou pass. On all the heights on both sides are watch towers, more or less fallen into decay.

The descent is steep. We often have to use our brakes. We pass gardens, villages and ruined walls. The valley widens and grows flatter. There stands a temple surrounded by pine trees. Again and again the road crosses rivers, the ice of which does not always bear, and sometimes we get stuck in the slush. Here and there the landscape is cut up into veritable canyon-corridors, gorges and terraces. At 2.30 we reach the customs and passport station of Kalgan, where we and our baggage and papers are subjected to a thorough examination. And finally we drive through this town, so picturesque in parts, of Kalgan, the Gate of Mongolia. Having driven over the bridge, we arrive at Mr. and Mrs. Larson's hospitable house, now newly built and modern, not simple and Asiatic as when on former occasions I lived under their roof.

XVI

HEADQUARTERS IN KALGAN

WE had thus completed our first tour of inspection among the lamaistic temple monasteries of Inner Mongolia and had taken a preliminary glance at their general character, architecture and decoration and at the numerous different objects which belong to the lamaistic cult. Dr. Gösta Montell, head of the expedition's ethnographical department, had made notes and taken many very successful photographs. We had taken the first steps towards the acquisition of temples, cult objects and ethnographic collections for Stockholm and Chicago, and we stood in the presence of a new stage and new tasks for this, the most eastern contingent of our expedition.

To begin with we were all in need of a few days' rest and warmth by lighted stoves after our cold travels in the land of the Mongols. A better home than Duke Larson's could hardly be imagined. Larson has two houses in Kalgan, one on each side of a seldom-used road, and surrounded by walls furnished with big carriage entries whose massive wooden gates were tended by Chinese porters. In the western house the Larsons themselves lived with the young Miss Dorothy Ruhne from Västmanland whom the Duke had brought out to China with him in the belief that he would be able to open up such a busy trade between Sweden and Mongolia that he would need a private secretary. But these hopes were disappointed, and Miss Ruhne became instead our chief accountant.

The eastern house consisted of a range of three rooms and a bathroom with a veranda facing south, and in this Hummel, Montell and I were living. Alongside of this house was another one of two rooms, where Haslund lived. I had a fine large workroom with windows on the north, east and south sides, an enormous writing table, a sofa, an easy chair, a stove and a cupboard full of lamaistic images of gilt brass. We took our meals with the family, and had to go to them across two yards, through two gates and across the high road. There were breakfast, luncheon, tea and supper. In the evenings the gramophone played Swedish melodies and songs and the expedition's march, "To the End of the Road," and much else. Then, too, Larson used to exhibit the temple paintings and other things he had picked up on our account. We drew up a careful though only preliminary estimate so as to have a clear idea from the start how the amount placed at our disposal by Mr. Vincent Bendix should be expended. So much was allotted to the acquisition or reproduction of two complete temple buildings, a certain sum for their furnishing with cult objects, a second for ethnographic collections, a third for wages and a fourth for transport through China and across the sea. These items would, no doubt, be subject to change as the work proceeded. We based our calculations on a period of six months, but possibly the ethnographical expedition would take considerably longer than we supposed, and so be more costly. Perhaps the cost of carriage might be reduced by concessions on the part of the companies or of particular benefactors. But at least we had a starting-point and an estimate, the limits of which we ought not to overstep until we were on the safe side.

Our young secretary's first task was to enter in a ledger all our expenses during the Mongolian tour, including the purchase of our car, the hire of Eriksson's, the cost of ethnographic objects and other things.

The reading of the *North China Star* brought us once more into touch with the eternally changing Chinese political situation and the civil war on various fronts, as well as with the principal events in the world at large. We received letters and telegrams from home and telegraphed and wrote ourselves. Among the letters was one which aroused our especial interest, from our old friend Mühlenweg who had been with the expedition from the beginning but, like most of the German members, had resigned in 1928. He had now come to Peking at the instance of Luft Hansa to try to find Major Zimmermann, last heard of at our Etsin-gol station. He had been sent orders several months before to return home, but nothing had been heard of him. We shall come to his adventurous Robinsonad later.

In consultation with Montell, I decided that the next journey should be to Jehol, a town which, particularly under the great Manchu emperors, had enjoyed great renown and where magnificent temples, now largely ruinous, had been erected in memory of historic occurrences. In this journey Montell, Haslund and Hummel were to take part. For visiting the province and city of Jehol passports were required which could be obtained from the Swedish Consul Long at Tientsin. On November the 24th I sent Haslund on in advance to the latter city to see to the passports. The next day the others, including Larson, went to Peking to arrange for cars to Jehol and to make certain preparations for the journey.

I myself stayed at Kalgan, where I spent an unforgettable month in unbroken peace and freedom to work. I went over, as usual, for meals with Mrs. Larson and Miss Ruhne, but otherwise was alone in the eastern house, that is to say not quite alone, for the magnificent police dog, Wolf, kept me company, followed me like my shadow across the road, lay on the mat or in an armchair while I worked at night and kept watch on the veranda while I slept.

Thus Kalgan had now become the headquarters of the expedition, and hence I directed all its detachments even to Tashkent and Turkistan, where the antiquary, Dr. Arne, was making his preliminary archæological reconnaissance. It was wonderful how all the threads of the great expedition converged in my hands in Kalgan and how in one way or another I was in touch with all its groups scattered over the continent of Asia. There was only one section to which this did not apply, namely Harry Smitt's botanical journey to the Himalayas, and this for the simple reason that he was not to start until the spring flowers began to sprout in 1931. But I was in communication with all the others. Twice I received letters from Norin and Ambolt in Eastern Turkistan, and I had two telegrams from Professor Yüan in Urumchi. Bergman, Bohlin, Hörner, Bexell and Chên and their caravan leader, Johansen, from whom I had parted on November the 11th, sent me cheering letters by passing trading caravans. From Georg Söderbom in Su-chou I had both letters and telegrams, and now, too, came Mühlenweg who was to try to establish contact with Major Zimmermann.

On November the 27th I received information that our chief meteorologist, Dr. Haude, who had founded all our meteorological stations, had arrived in Kobe and before long would visit me in Kalgan, in accordance with an order I had sent him in Urumchi. Up to December the 25th, or in the course of a month, I wrote eighty-six letters of 332 large quarto pages. A great many of these were to the members of the expedition. I sent several hundred dollars' worth of telegrams. During this time in Kalgan I was without the services of my medical attendant, Dr. Hummel, who is also my secretary, for he was more needed on the journey to Jehol.

As a time of rest my month in Kalgan was, however, somewhat open to question. I began the second half of this book of which the first half was written in Urumchi. I read, took lessons in the Chinese language and thrice a day took meteorological readings. I visited the town's foreign commissioner, Mr. Pan, and twice went to see old Mr. Söderbom of the American Methodist Mission, whose schools, one for fifty-five girls and the other for twenty-six boys, I inspected. Mr. Berubé and Mr. Chang of the Chinese Government Salt Revenue Department called upon me and I returned their visit. I had no other engagements and was delighted to escape wasting valuable time on superfluous dinner invitations.

I learned by telegram from Larson that Haslund lay sick in the German Hospital at Tientsin and thus could not go to Jehol, so that Larson had taken his place and accompanied Montell and Hummel to the old imperial city.

Mühlenweg turned up in Kalgan, well and happy, on the evening of November the 27th, was equipped the next day with sleeping-bag, fur coat, fur cap, arms and provisions, and also took with him the mail for the great caravan under Bergman and Bohlin. I wrote letters to all the members of their group, and by the evening of the 28th Mühlenweg was able to start for Kuei-hua with a view to going on from there by car to Beli-miao and beyond, westward on Bergman's and Bohlin's tracks until he overtook them, and afterwards, by car, continue his search for Zimmermann. He had with him our faithful servant, the Mongol Serat, one of those who were honoured with gold medals for distinguished service.

Even financial questions were dealt with from my solitary headquarters. I received telegraphic information from Ambolt that he and Norin had borrowed 10,000 Mexican dollars from a Chinese merchant in Tientsin, with a branch at Urumchi, to whose head office we should repay the amount. Bohlin's and Bergman's group had only 7,500 Mexican dollars with them, and we later arranged with the post office in Peking for 10,000 to be paid to them on their arrival at Su-chou. We had often made similar transactions between Peking and Urumchi. We paid a certain sum to the post office in Peking and got the same sum from the post office at Urumchi, where we drew the money from Mr. McLorn, by degrees as we needed it. Thus one need not encumber oneself with large sums on the long and unsafe roads.

I have seldom been more astonished than on the evening of December the 4th when I received the following telegram from Kuei-hua-ch'êng: "Arrived O.K. Zimmermann, Mühlenweg." How was it possible for the latter, who left Kalgan on November the 28th, to be back in Kuei-hua on December the 4th, having executed his commission, which I had feared would take a couple of months or more?

Three days later they reached Kalgan and put up with me in the eastern house. The twenty-five months that he had spent at our Etsin-gol station had not affected Major Zimmermann's appearance. For all his forty-nine years he was as resilient and vigorous as a youngster and, with his three Mongols and sixteen camels, had accomplished without difficulty his pilgrimage through the desert. But at the station he had experienced severe vicissitudes and on the first night he was telling me about them till four in the morning. His Robinsonad deserves a chapter to itself.

The headman of his Mongols, Mären, had served him and our expedition with unswerving fidelity and now received from my hands his royal Swedish gold medal. Only one camel had succumbed during the journey of hundreds of miles through the desert. The remainder were taken by Mr. Gustaf Söberbom's assistance to good grazing grounds in the hills.

On December the 6th Montell, Larson and Hummel returned from Jehol, enchanted with the magnificent though ruined temple they had seen. While the two others remained in Peking, Larson came up to Kalgan accompanied by Dr. Haude who had just arrived from Urumchi. And thereupon began new nightly conferences of great importance. For two years and three-quarters Dr. Haude had managed the expedition's meteorological department with great skill and capacity, had trained and instructed our Chinese students and made trustworthy observers of them, had established seven stations and sent up 353 pilot balloons. Our endeavours to gain the consent of Governor-General Chin to Dr. Haude's travelling, in the spring of 1929, across Hami to Kansu, in order to study during the summer in its mountainous tracts the passage of the monsoon over North-Eastern Tibet, had failed, and Dr. Haude had instead been making meteorological observations at Bogdo-ula. By his profound researches he had already reached the point at which he could foretell with almost infallible certainty the outbreak of storms that were on the way from Tien-shan to the desert zone of Inmost Asia. By means of a system of wireless telegraphy the oases and towns in Eastern Turkistan and Kansu would be able to receive warning of approaching storms. But, for the understanding of the circulation of the winds in the interior of the great continent to be as complete as possible, a still more exact knowledge was required of the paths of the monsoons and of the laws governing their movements. This important scientific conquest was denied us by the Governor-General. On this account Dr. Haude had lost a year and must in any event entirely revise his plan of operations. For a clear understanding of his work and his wishes it was necessary that I should meet him personally, and that was the reason

Haude Photo

The Bogdo Lake

[face p. 202

Haude Photo

Glacier Lake on Bogdo-ula, 3,300 metres above sea-level

[*face p.* 203

why I had summoned him all the way to Peking and Kalgan. For in no circumstances did I wish Dr. Haude to discontinue his epoch-making activities in our expedition with a sense of failure to complete his task in a manner satisfactory to himself. If the way from Sinkiang to Kansu was closed to us, Eastern China was able to open for us ways to Kansu from the coast. It sometimes happens that, to gain a great scientific goal, one must sacrifice both time and money. And we were prepared to go a long way rather than let ourselves be deprived of the knowledge of the movement of the monsoons over the mountains of Kansu.

To our request for a further year's leave of absence for Dr. Haude I received an affirmative reply by telegram from Dr. Ficker, the director of the Meteorological Institute of Berlin. I further suggested to Dr. Haude that, so soon as all his meteorological journals had been examined and approved by Dr. Ko Ching-chu, the chief of the Central Meteorological Institute of China, he should pay a hurried visit home for a rest and afterwards return to Peking.

Thence the monsoon expedition was to start and make its way by Ning-hsia to Liang-chou. In this latter town a meteorological station was to be established and staffed by two young Chinese meteorologists trained by Dr. Ko Ching-chu. They, among other things, were daily to send up pilot balloons. Dr. Haude himself, with an assistant and a mobile caravan, was to go up into the mountains and make simultaneous observations at high altitudes. We had a sufficient supply of hydrogen cylinders in Inmost Asia. Ten had been left at Etsin-gol, five had been confiscated at Hami and eight lay at Bachti, since even their importation into Sinkiang had been forbidden.

The planning of Dr. Haude's expedition constituted only one detail in our complicated machinery. There were a thousand things to keep track of, and as usual I had little time left for my own work. After barely three days' stay at my headquarters, Dr. Haude returned on December the 16th to Peking, supplied with letters to our Committee, Professor Fu Liu and Dr. Yüan. My scheme was accepted with the greatest readiness by the Committee, and no obstacle remained in the way of Dr. Haude's expedition.

On December the 22nd he went to Nanking for a conference with Dr. Ko Ching-chu at which all the details of the organization of the expedition were discussed. The station at Liang-chou was to be taken over by China as soon as Dr. Haude had finished his work, and would be permanent. On January the 3rd Dr. Haude started for Germany via Suez. On the 11th Major Zimmermann left Shanghai to settle down for the future in his native land.

On December the 11th I had the pleasure of receiving letters from Bergman and his comrades informing me that all had gone well since we parted and that they were well satisfied with their results. They had met Zimmermann in the desert. He had gone on to Beli-miao and, south of that monastery, had met Mühlenweg, who accordingly returned almost immediately with Zimmermann to Kuei-hua.

In the early part of December the temperature in Kalgan varied between – 15° and – 19°. In the middle of the month we had a heavy fall of snow which put the whole country under a thick white covering. At the same time the temperature became considerably milder. In the night of the 17th it was – 20·4° and exactly the same on the 18th. The days were brilliantly fine. Not a vestige of cloud. The mountains to east and west were dazzlingly white. At night a deathlike silence rested on the neighbourhood and the moon shone upon the glittering snow. It crunched pleasantly underfoot as I walked through the drifts to my meals with Mrs. Larson. As usual I could not take a step without Wolf following me faithfully, as becomes a dog.

In Kalgan I received ill news which grieved me deeply. I always used to take the letters I had written over-night to Mrs. Larson's house at luncheon-time, and a Chinese boy then took them to the post office. Among the letters sent off on December the 21st was one to my friend Joachim von Schröder of Luft Hansa's staff in Berlin. At the beginning of its existence my expedition was in peculiarly intimate relations with Luft Hansa, without whose active and energetic support my plans could probably never have been realized. During the preparations for and the organization of the expedition, I was more closely in touch with von Schröder than with anyone, and afterwards it was with him and with Director Erhard Milch that I corresponded. On December the 21st a letter about Dr. Haude's new plans was despatched to von Schröder. Scarcely an hour after the posting of this letter I received a telegram from Mr. Wilhelm Schmidt, Luft Hansa's representative in Peking, telling me that, on the previous day, von Schröder, one of Germany's foremost aviators, had crashed with his machine in fog outside Berlin on his return flight from Teneriffe. Thus I lost one of my best friends.

Two days before Christmas the Jehol travellers returned, accompanied by a young Dane, Testorf, who wished to see Kalgan.

It was a radiant Christmas Eve on which nothing was lacking. But the host himself, the duke, the friend of the Mongols, as nearly as possible failed to put in an appearance. He disappeared early in the day and had last been seen in the company of some Mongols from the plateau. We waited luncheon till 3 o'clock, but nothing was heard of him. We dipped into the pot in old Swedish fashion, we set to work on pickled herring, caviare and Stilton cheese, we sat down to ham and green peas and were helped by our charming hostess to slices of the most glorious pies baked by her cook. We had drunk our coffee, it had already begun to grow dark and the candles had been lighted on the Christmas tree, when Duke Larson finally appeared. He had a bath and went to bed, as he was feeling poorly. But later in the evening, at 9 o'clock, he was all right again, and when we gathered round the Christmas board under the mighty wreath of spruce boughs, with lighted candles which Hummel and Miss Ruhne had twined, the Duke walked into the room, clad in his famous red Mongol coat and radiant with health and wellbeing. He looked at the splendour of his room, which had been decorated by our doctor as never before. There were bouquets of flowers on all the shelves and cupboards, garlands hung round the walls and over the door, he had arranged escutcheons of Swedish flags surrounded by green wreaths in the hall and lobby, and a bunch of mistletoe swinging under a lamp was a source of danger to Miss Ruhne. Christmas verses were read by Montell and Hummel. They were harmless rather than inspired and contained allusions to gilded temple roofs, glittering images, red Lama robes and high-flown Mongolian ducal titles.

Finally we went back, Hummel, Montell, and I, across the road to my workroom, which, too, had been decked with a Christmas tree. And there we sat down round the crackling stove with a steaming bowl of burnt brandy while we traced the course of the hours and calculated how far they had reached in their Christmas Eve in our homes in the north.

On Christmas Day we had a banquet for the Söderbom family including their son Gustaf, who was almost a member of the staff of the expedition. The good old missionary read the texts of old appropriated to the day, and the gramophone played "Blest be the Happy Day" and "Hosanna." The remains of Christmas Eve's tremendous feast lasted to the end.

On December the 27th Hummel and I got up at half past five, breakfasted with the Larsons and went to the railway station to take the train to Peking. Montell was going to make another motor tour in Mongolia and Larson to remain for some time in Kalgan. The railway journey takes eight hours. It is not particularly agreeable. In our compartment, in which all the steam pipes were frozen, the temperature was — 13°, and we froze in our double coats. Flaring oil lamps dispersed the darkness in our icy cellar. But the sun came up over the eastern hills, and the ice flowers on the window shone as if they had been sprinkled with blood. Then we were not so badly off. By the time we came to the Nankou pass we had only one degree of frost and need freeze no longer. At 4 o'clock the train pulled up at Hsi Chi-mên in Peking, a car carried us to the Hotel Wagons Lits, we got our old well-known rooms, had a bath and were ourselves again.

XVII

WORK AND ADVENTURE BY ETSIN-GOL

IN my book *Across the Gobi Desert* I have described how my column of the great caravan arrived at Etsin-gol on September the 28th, 1927, and how the different groups gradually assembed on the left bank of the river three long days' journey above the point where it flows into the lakes of Gashun-nor and Sogo-nor. Here Dr. Haude established the first fixed meteorological station, as chief of which I appointed Major Zimmermann, with the Chinese student Ma as assistant and the Swedish missionary Georg Söderbom as interpreter and general helper.

On the evening of November the 7th, 1927, we gathered for the last time around an enormous log fire, and there I delivered to Zimmermann, Söderbom and Ma a farewell speech reminding them of the great scientific importance of their continuous meteorological observations at a station which was the only one in a territory as large as the whole of Australia.

We took a cordial farewell of the first fixed station's garrison and their servants, with whom we left behind sixty-five tired or sick camels. Then we mounted our riding camels and moved off through the woods. Once more I turned on my camel and waved a last farewell. Then they and their airy dwellings and the flagstaff with the Swedish flag disappeared from my view. It was like leaving a peaceful and blessed island in the desert sea on which we had spent six unforgettable weeks.

The funds of the expedition were low. The purchase of camels had taken too much of our resources and I was only able to leave an infinitesimal sum with Zimmermann. He had a dozen cases of provisions, and it was arranged that, as soon as we reached Hami, Lieutenant Haslund should at once be sent back to the station with money and mails and at the same time fetch the fifteen camel loads which, for lack of camels, we had been obliged to leave at Etsin-gol.

After we had all gone, the loneliness was felt oppressively by those left behind.

But the three men swore a solemn oath to keep together in loyalty and good fellowship during the long spell of loneliness that awaited them. They set to work at once. To begin with, the yurts were set up in a grove of leafless poplars a short distance from the shore. Zimmermann furnished his yurt with a work-table, a couple of chairs, a bed, a cupboard for aneroids and other sensitive instruments, protected against dust by a curtain, a substantial table for the thermo-hypsometer, a bookshelf, mats on the ground and, under the smoke-plate, a fireplace of clay supporting the stove, which was made of a petrol tin with a pipe composed of jam pots. Ma was content with a somewhat similar arrangement of his yurt, in which he had, among other things, a whole library of Chinese books, both learned and less learned. Söderbom had dug a rectangular cavity in the ground, over which he pitched his tent. In a third yurt was accommodated the kitchen and all its appurtenances, and in this yurt the servants slept.

Presently Mären, the headman of the Mongols, moved with his two subordinates, Sumer and Öljasung, and sixty-one camels to a place thirty li from the station where there was good grazing, and there they set up their tents. Four sick camels were kept at the station, where they were cared for by Söderbom in accordance with the wonderful healing art of the Mongols—they stuffed them with antelope meat and gunpowder, a treatment which is said to have cured them, at least for some time.

Tamtse Lama was Söderbom's special servant, the Chinese, Tung, was cook and Chong Chong general attendant.

Zimmermann and Ma took turns with the daily meteorological observations which amounted to between seventy-five and a hundred. The sun time was taken daily and on a water gauge by the shore the height and temperature of the water were observed. The temperature of the ground was also noted. As a protection against stray camels and horses a fence was put up round the observation shed and the instruments installed in the open. During the winter the thickness of the ice on the river was measured.

Many travellers rode by and always called at the station. Hummel's healing art had been in frequent request during our stay at Etsin-gol, and after his departure Zimmermann succeeded to his practice. People with syphilitic sores, skin diseases, tumours, broken limbs, bad eyes and many other ailments came to the station and were treated according to Hummel's prescriptions. The patients often came back to pay their fees in milk or cheese or other goods. In this way the Major won the confidence of the Torguts dwelling by the river.

Life was by no means tedious ; time passed quickly and the days fled. They felt more and more at home, made friends with a number of Torguts and came to know all their neighbours by name. It was not always any too easy to keep up appearances and avoid betraying how few were the silver dollars still remaining in the treasury. They had no means of buying meat but had to make the best of the tinned stores and simpler Chinese food. The coffee had been rationed from the beginning.

The stern Central Asiatic winter came stealing over Etsin-gol. On the 1st of December a small caravan arrived from the east. From the station the men could be seen trying to get their camels across the ice of the river with a whole skin. But one camel went right through and only its head remained above the ice. Attracted by cries of distress and shrieks our people hurried to the place and found to their delight that it was the long-lost Professor Yüan who had turned up at last. Thus Zimmermann and his companions as it were made contact with the outside world.

The reunion with their old friend and travelling companion was a bright spot in the history of the station. They brought out the best things to be found in the yurt and entertained the returned prodigal with a regular desert feast.

But Yüan was in a hurry and wanted to try to get through

to us at Hami. He therefore only stayed two days. Zimmermann gave him medicine and provisions, and Yüan, who was himself short of money, gave fifty dollars to the Major, who then felt quite wealthy.

Some days after Yüan's departure they got something else to think about. Like a bolt from the blue a courier fell upon the camp, rode up to the Major's tent, dismounted and delivered a letter from the Torgut Prince. It was written in Chinese. Ma read it aloud and Söderbom translated it. Its contents were highly disquieting. The Prince had received orders from the authorities in Su-chou forthwith to expel our people from the territory of the province of Kansu. The tone was imperative, but gave no reason and alleged no cause of complaint. The three men sat in perplexity, looking at one another. What was to be done? Follow our tracks to Hami? The sixty-five camels were not up to it, and besides, there was no money.

A reply was drawn up by Ma: because of the condition of the camels they *could not* leave Etsin-gol; it would mean disaster to the caravan. They requested the authorities of Su-chou to send representatives to the station to negotiate and to assure themselves that the staff of the station, far from having any evil intent, were only pursuing scientific aims.

The reply was sent to the Torgut Prince, who read it and at once sent it on by express to Su-chou, which place the rider, with changes of horses, could reach in eight days.

On December the 16th an official and Government commissioner from Su-chou appeared, to inquire into the circumstances on the spot. He was zealous and in a hurry. All the yurts and their contents were shown, the cases opened and the instruments explained. Since moreover he found no more than a pair of sporting rifles and one as a defence against robbers, he understood that the station staff had no ill intentions. But when finally he came upon the hydrogen cylinders which had been brought for filling the pilot balloons, he became suspicious and could not believe that they had any other than a warlike purpose. They had already heard in Lan-chou about our mighty caravan and were convinced that we formed the advance guard of

Lieberenz Photo

Major Zimmermann and the Student Ma

[*face p.* 210

an army and that the hydrogen cylinders were cannon. After several hours' examination the envoy declared that his orders were to conduct the whole staff to Su-chou and that, if the three gentlemen were unwilling to comply with these orders, the whole station with its goods and its camels must proceed westward towards Hami.

To this Zimmermann answered that he would not, so long as he lived, leave the station which he had received my orders to attend to. He exhibited my written order, which was translated by Ma.

Fresh negotiations followed, and it was agreed that one of the three men should accompany the Chinese to Su-chou. But which should go? Ma at once offered himself because he rightly considered that he would most easily be able to get a hearing from his compatriots. With great determination he promised the two others to do everything to save the station.

Next morning the commissioner departed with his hostage. Ma took most of the station's scanty funds. The Major and Söderbom sat in the former's tent discussing the new situation which had arisen through Ma's leaving the station. Söderbom believed that before long a new commissioner would appear to fetch the remaining two and that the station would be left to take care of itself.

In such circumstances Christmas was celebrated in a mood of depression.

The winter grew severe and the temperature sank to — 28°. But the station was well sheltered from the northwesterly and northerly winds, thanks to the natural barricade of trees and the high dunes overgrown with tamarisks, which broke the force of the wind. On the ice of the river, now hard, the Major and Söderbom skated, having bought skates in Peking, to the amazement and admiration of the Torguts. They arranged contests of speed between riders on the bank and skaters on the river. New Year's Eve came. They brewed a marvellous drink which they called punch. They drank to the past year, to the next and to their comrades far off in the depths of the desert.

January drew to its end, and not a sound was heard from Ma. The two Europeans began to feel uneasy about him.

The treasury was almost empty, and they were daily expecting Haslund to appear, bearing money and mails and news of us. But just at that time half the expedition was being treated rather like prisoners in Urumchi and the other half was in Hami. My request to Governor-General Yang to be allowed to send Haslund to Etsin-gol had been refused and it was thus not in our power to send the station garrison the help that we knew it so sorely needed.

As the winter advanced, the camels too began to come to grief, and several of them died despite all the efforts of Mären and Söderbom to save them.

One day at the end of January a small caravan was heard in the woods to the southward, approaching the yurts. It turned out to be the camels and the leader that Ma had taken with him to Su-chou which had returned after completing their task—but without Ma. The leader brought a letter from Ma, written in English. The Major and Söderbom devoured its contents which were not at all encouraging. In vain had Ma done his utmost to convince the Government at Su-chou of the station's peaceful intentions. He prepared the two Europeans for renewed persecutions, even perhaps forcible measures for their removal. The authorities had decided to send Ma under guard to Lanchou, the capital of the province, there to subject him to a searching examination. In his letter Ma promised his two comrades to do everything to save the station. They could not but admire the energy and prudence Ma had displayed, and they only hoped he would not fall into too great dangers. The young Chinese student was utterly conscientious and trustworthy in the discharge of all his duties. They knew that the fate of the station could not rest in better hands than his. To give him any help was now impossible, and he had asked for none. He was indeed Chinese and was among his own people. He was equipped with winter clothing and ought to be able to borrow money for the journey. He also telegraphed to us in Hami, and Professor Hsü Ping-chang saw to it that a small sum was placed at his disposal through the post office. From the station at Etsin-gol to Su-chou the distance was 210 miles.

From Su-chou to Lan-chou he had twenty-one days' journey.

February was drawing to an end, and the stock of flour was exhausted. Accompanied by five soldiers armed with modern rifles a new Government commissioner arrived at the station on February the 25th. He announced that he had been sent to arrest the two Europeans and convey them to Su-chou. Major Zimmermann answered calmly that he had no authority to desert the station and that, if they used force, he would defend himself and the property that had been entrusted to his charge. The commissioner was amazed and entered upon peace negotiations. When he perceived that he could not move Zimmermann, he said he would be content if Söderbom accompanied him to Su-chou. Söderbom replied that he would come on condition that the commissioner provided them with 150 silver dollars for the purchase of flour for the station. Their treasury was empty because a promised reinforcement had not been heard of from Hami. The amount was borrowed from a rich Torgut, and the Major gave an acknowledgment. The lender did not like it, but had to obey the commissioner. The Torguts in the district, who up to then had been so friendly, now began to be cold and suspicious and could not get it out of their heads that the station staff were spies or other evil folk, since they were treated with so little consideration by the Chinese authorities. Flour was bought and divided between the station and Söderbom. On the morning of the 27th the latter set out with the commissioner. He was treated as a prisoner and five armed riders guarded him. The Major went with them on foot for a couple of kilometres. The ice on a little branch stream broke under Söderbom's camel, which was regarded as a bad sign for the future; everything looked sombre. In a state of depression the Major walked back to the station. He was now alone. The Chinese had picked off the garrison one after another, and he wondered when it would be his turn.

The days went their accustomed way with the constantly recurring meteorological observations. There was a noticeable change after the departure of the commissioner and

Söderbom, namely that vagrant Chinese came much oftener to the station and paid to it and to the Major's occupation an increasingly profound attention. They called themselves merchants, but they had nothing to sell. They poked into everything and wanted explanations of the use of the instruments. The Major understood that he was being shadowed and behaved accordingly. He let them look through his cases and satisfy themselves that they did not contain ammunition, and he never for a moment lost his composure. But when they became too importunate, he let them understand that there was a limit placed on their indiscretion.

It was most of all the gas cylinders that aroused the astonishment and suspicion of these unbidden guests. They were convinced that those bright steel cylinders were cannon. Even an empty gas cylinder that was hanging in a tree and served as a gong, aroused their deep respect and compelled them to long detours. The Torguts, who lived in the woods and did not know what to believe, drew back more and more and decided that it was best to have as little as possible to do with the suspected stranger.

He had, however, one friend, a "gegen" or reincarnate Lama who had his yurt in the woods five kilometres away. He was from Tibet and had lived at Etsin-gol for many years. Soon after the commissioner's departure this Gegen Lama came to Zimmermann's yurt in full canonicals and accompanied by two more monks. The Major had had warning of the visit and made all necessary preparations for a worthy reception. The yurt had been tidied up, tea and pastry were served, and the distinguished prelate stayed a couple of hours. The Major showed him my book *Trans-himalaya*, in which there are many illustrations of Tashi-lunpo and two portraits of Tashi Lama, the Pope of Southern Tibet. He told him of my long stay at the great monastery and of my friendship with Tashi Lama. Gegen Lama touched the book as if it had been a holy thing and carried it reverentially to his forehead and sank into deep thought in the contemplation of the picture of the holy one. The Major was also able to tell him that he had accompanied me once in December, 1926, when I paid my respects to Tashi Lama in Peking, and when we both had the honour to receive gold rings with His Holiness's name upon them.

The result of all this was that Gegen Lama, who was greatly venerated by the Torguts, became a real friend to the Major and to our station. Both the people of the district and the station servants, who, since the Chinese commissioner's inquiries and the intrusion of the spies, had been reserved and suspicious, now changed their attitude and concluded that a man thus honoured by Gegen Lama must be a respectable person, and in this they included his two colleagues.

Yet the espionage of his activities went on all the time. They even established posts on the further bank, and the station itself was kept under observation from close by.

Winter and spring, when the grazing was poor, was the hardest time for the camels. Their number fell to fifty-one head. They ranged widely, seeking better grazing grounds, and Mären and his men had great difficulty in keeping the herd together. In this they were assisted by the friendly Torguts of the region. The new succulent herbage that would save the camels could not be expected before May.

One night a pack of wolves was heard howling on the right bank. They came nearer and crossed over to the left, where the camp lay. The dogs gave the alarm and the station's donkeys began braying. Zimmermann hurried out with his rifle and fired, on which the wolves made off, not, however, until they had worried one of the donkeys.

Then came the spring ice-run; one morning the whole left bank was overflowed, and the flood came right up to the tents. The meteorological observatory became an island to which the Major and his servants made a bridge of tree trunks. Sheets of ice were thrown high up on to the land and lay there long after the water had receded.

In March the days were quite warm, but the nights continued cold. The Major was able to work out of doors in the shade of the poplars. The chief variety he had in his lonely life was provided by the sick, who came in daily on camels and on horseback for medicine and treatment.

On April the 3rd the temperature of the air rose to + 17·5° and on the 5th to + 20°. By the middle of the month it was possible to bathe in water at + 12° to + 14°.

The 1st of April was a great day for the Major. Our Mongols, sent home from Hami, arrived at the station, bringing mail for the three solitaries and 740 silver dollars. Now the camp came to life. The Mongols gave an account of our difficult journey, of the lost camels and of the adversities we encountered on the borders of Sinkiang. When the Major came to hear of all our troubles he became reconciled with his own lot and felt that he had been relatively well off. Bergman's archæological collections, which had been left at the station, were now packed up to be sent south with the Mongols who were returning to Kuei-hua-ch'êng. They also carried letters for Peking.

After they had gone on, loneliness once more descended on the station. Mären's camp was now twenty-five kilometres away, and he only came to the station once a week to fetch provisions and to report on the condition of the camels. On these occasions the Major used to cheer him up and keep up his courage. They drank tea, smoked together and played chess.

April and May passed, and still no tidings came from Ma and Söderbom. Someone from us must surely arrive towards autumn! But Zimmermann could not know that old Yang had forbidden us all communication with the province of Kansu, which was regarded as being in Marshall Fêng Yü-hsiang's sphere of influence.

The energetic Major never suffered from lack of occupation. Now that he no longer had the help of his two colleagues with the meteorological observations, he had to make all the hundred daily readings himself. In the intervals he worked as a farmer. He fenced in a field of thirty by twenty metres and set to with spade and pickaxe, ploughed, brought in leaf mould from the woods and cultivated tomatoes, cucumbers, peas, beans, onions, parsley, maize, radishes, potatoes, melons and gourds as well as ten kinds of flowers.

In May the heat became considerable and, towards the

end of the month, oppressive. On May the 1st the temperature touched 25·4° and on the 31st 38·6°.

One day two wealthy Torguts came to Zimmermann, lamenting the great damage that the wolves were doing to their herds. Some local hunters were called in and got rifles and ammunition from the Major. After four days they returned. Two wolves had been shot and they brought two small cubs in a sack. The neighbours were glad to be rid of a couple of the sheep's most dangerous enemies. An enclosure three metres square and two high was built of stakes and branches for the cubs. There they would be reared on kitchen refuse, hares and milk, and gradually tamed. They grew, became wilder and wilder and longed for the freedom of the woods. They managed to climb up to the top of the enclosure, but did not venture to jump down outside. A couple of puppies were put in with them and the cubs played with them in all amity. But, when the wild beasts took to worrying them, the puppies had to be taken out again. The game was growing too dangerous. In the end they found out how to dig their way out under the enclosure. The Torguts grew anxious, fearing new dangers for their flocks. It was impossible to tie the beasts up; they gnawed through everything. Finally the Major had to shoot them.

A fowl-house was built, which aroused the interest of the birds of prey. But the hens and chickens were well protected, and their winged enemies were shot.

The heat constantly increased and by June was unbearable. The bed of Etsin-gol was dry, and only here and there in the deeper places there were still some pools. One of these was enclosed and the drinking water fetched from it; in another the solitary man bathed in water at a temperature of over 30°. Yet the bath produced a feeling of freshness. The Torguts always went about in boots and thick clothing, the Major in pyjamas or thin white clothes.

Gnats and mosquitoes became troublesome, and big poisonous spiders darted about outside and in the yurt. One had to look out for them. They were caught and put with scorpions and other creeping things in spirit jars. Worst of all were the venomous snakes which, in the hottest weather, positively invaded the camp. Once Zimmermann killed three snakes in his yurt. They also infested the kitchen yurt. The Torguts and the Chinese were afraid of them. The former cauterized the wound after a snake bite with a red-hot iron. When the waiter came into the Major's tent with the tea tray one afternoon and saw a snake there, he was so frightened that he dropped the tray. Every evening before going to bed the Major used to go hunting round the yurt to kill all the pests that had crawled or flown in. But one gets used to everything, and the war against creeping things was always an occupation.

In July the temperature rose to 42·4°. At one time there was a shortage of water, when even the deep pools in the river bed dried up. A well was dug and surrounded by a protecting fence, and the water was always boiled.

Every night the Major made a round of the station to see that no tramps or highwaymen were lying in wait. But so far, peace prevailed at Tsondol, as the district was called by the Torguts, and his relations with the neighbours were now good.

Time went on, but still no news from Ma and Söderbom came through to the Major. But one summer's day—it was already June, as he sat writing in the little park he had laid out in the shade of the poplars—he heard a distant shout that was not Mongolian. He listened. A small caravan was approaching. Already he could hear dry twigs and branches snapping under the camels' pads. Two riders appeared among the trees. It was Ma and Söderbom. Zimmermann and all his servants hurried out to meet them and heartily bid them welcome. For the Major this was the greatest day of rejoicing he had experienced at Etsin-gol. Now they were once more united and the garrison complete. Now his worries were over, now he would have help with the observations and with the care of the station. It was as if a longed for and sorely needed holiday were beginning.

" But tell me, tell me ! "

And Ma and Söderbom told their story, how they had been taken to Lan-chou, thrown into prison and treated as criminals and how they had later suddenly been released and treated as honoured guests, how they had lived in the house of the amiable Dr. Rand, the superintendent of the American hospital, the martyr, who not long after was carried off by typhus. When we in Sinkiang heard of the difficulties of the station garrison, Professor Hsü Ping-chang had telegraphed to the Minister Tsai Yüan-pei at Nanking and begged for his support. He had approached Marshall Fêng Yü-hsiang, who in due course had given orders to the Governor-General at Lan-chou to treat the station and its staff with respect and hospitality, and thereupon the period of our difficulties had finally been closed.

A festal meal was prepared and speeches made, everyone was in good spirits and it was possible once more to look forward to the future with bright hopes. It was certainly strange that no mail had been heard of, but the Major had a sense of liberation and could work undisturbed. New plans were hammered out. Ma made his yurt comfortable and loyally discharged his duties as meteorological observer. Söderbom made a hasty journey to Su-chou to fetch money and mails and to send off the station's letters.

After his return Söderbom got ready for an excursion to Gashun-nor to collect plants and insects in accordance with instructions he had received from Dr. Hummel, a task which he performed in a meritorious manner. A small caravan was fitted out for him for the journey. Only forty-eight camels were left; seventeen had died in barely a year.

The kitchen garden was now beginning to give an agreeable variety to the hermits' monotonous diet. Söderbom and Ma were astonished to see what Zimmermann had accomplished in this way in their absence. Summer drew to an end, and autumn came again. In September my order reached Etsin-gol that eight gas cylinders and a number of other things we had left behind were to be brought by Söderbom to Urumchi by way of Hami.

On October the 17th Söderbom started for Su-chou via Maomo to get himself a passport for this journey. It was long before he was heard of again at Tsondol. Meanwhile the current work continued its regular course and another winter began.

It was not till January the 11th, 1929, that Söderbom reappeared at the station. He reported to the Major that he had been obliged to hire fresh camels in Su-chou, but that he had never got through to Hami, because the frontier of Sinkiang was closed. The gas cylinders and the other baggage had been confiscated by the frontier guard and taken to Hami where they still were. But Söderbom himself had not been allowed to accompany them to the city of melons. Thus Dr. Haude was impeded in his important work of investigating the upper air strata with pilot balloons.

After Söderbom's return they could begin to think of an organized excursion to Gashun-nor, of whose outline, depth and conditions I wanted a map. This journey of investigation was an important item in the instructions I had given the Major.

On their way to the lake they passed the Torgut Prince's yurt and paid a visit to the Prince. His consort, an intelligent young lady, was particularly interested in the Major's woollen gloves which he therefore presented to her—rather imprudently in view of the biting continental cold.

They obtained guides who knew all the tracks and all the wells. Several camels were laden with fuel from the last wood. They travelled along the southern and eastern shores of the lake and then crossed Gashun-nor on the metre-thick ice, not, however, where the lake is widest, because the guide was afraid to go too far out. The Torguts never cross the lake. They are afraid of the ice, whose mysterious appearance and disappearance plays a part in some of their legends. They prefer to make long detours on solid ground.

As at Ngangtse-tso in Tibet, the salt which is released in the process of freezing forms on Gashun-nor a granular deposit on the surface of the ice, thanks to which the camels walk steadily without slipping.

After numerous soundings and measurements of the thickness of the ice, they reached the western shore, where a beach terrace four metres in height was measured, indicating a much greater extension of the lake not so long ago.

On the western bank they divided their caravan in two, for the Mongolian New Year was at hand, and Söderbom must visit the Torgut Prince and offer his good wishes. The Major, on the other hand, turned southwards to Möruin-gol, and followed its bed to a point opposite the station, Tsondol, by Etsin-gol. He made a map of the whole excursion.

Meanwhile Ma had been carrying out the meteorological observations. Afterwards they exchanged parts and Ma travelled with fresh camels to Möruin-gol and Gashun-nor, because he wished to see the country and the lake. A fortnight later he was back and compared his observations with the Major's.

XVIII

MA AND HIS TRAGIC FATE

AFTER Ma's return Zimmermann thought he noticed a change in his mental condition. The young student had become quieter and more reserved than before and often shunned company. But he was always diligent with his meteorological observations, and when the Major took the readings, Ma entered them in the record, and vice versa.

In the intervals Zimmermann devoted himself more and more to his Chinese colleague and began to give him regular lessons in German, which Ma already spoke pretty well. The teacher told him German fairy tales and introduced him to the history, social life and reforms, politics, literature, poetry and philosophy of Germany. In the same way the pupil gave an account of China and its life in the past and the present, and thus they filled their time with instructive occupation.

The money was finished, and Söderbom had to go again to Su-chou to fetch more. Zimmermann thought that the time might have arrived for them all three to leave the station, since their instructions had only provided for their operating it for eighteen months. He therefore contemplated going himself also to Su-chou, but finally decided to stay and let Söderbom arrange by telegram for them to start home on June the 1st at latest.

I had already sent a telegram from Peking in January telling Zimmermann to move the station's equipment into store at Su-chou and himself to come at once to Peking. When no answer came I telegraphed again in April. Many calamitous months elapsed before my January telegram got through. Had it arrived in time there would probably have been no trouble, but one cannot know about that.

At this time a number of Northern Mongols came and settled by Etsin-gol to buy flour, and Söderbom thought they ought to procure flour from Su-chou and help the Mongols. But Ma advised against this. A scientific expedition ought not to concern itself with trade. It seems he was altogether too much upset about this in itself quite trivial matter, and went so far as to write about it in a critical tone to China.

On March the 27th it became evident that there was something wrong with Ma's mental condition. Seeing at the dinner table that his hands were trembling, the Major asked if he was feeling ill and advised him not to upset his heart by smoking too much. When later the Major was going to the observatory, Ma followed him and, with a grave face and voice, begged him to come to his yurt. By the entrance to the yurt the Major found the young student weeping and lamenting:

"I can't live any longer, I must take my life. What will Dr. Hedin think when he gets a letter with a bad report of us?"

The Major tried to calm him with quiet and friendly talk, whereupon Ma answered that he repented of having behaved ill to Zimmermann and Söderbom. The Major said that he had noticed nothing that Ma need repent of, and that if there had been anything it had long ago been forgiven and forgotten. Probably Ma was referring to some letter or another that he had written in a state of agitation to friends in Peking and in which he had used derogatory language about his European comrades.

The next day the postmaster from Maomo arrived on a visit. The Major wished to talk to him with a view to arranging postal connexions between the station and the little town, which was itself in connexion with Su-chou, and thus with the outside world. When the postmaster went into Ma's yurt, the young student rushed to the Major, shouting: "Come at once to my tent, for I can't bear to be alone with him." Zimmermann at once complied and stayed with Ma until the postmaster had gone. Ma seemed languid and without volition all the time.

During the days that followed it happened over and over

again that Ma did not dare to be alone with people, but begged the Major to join them. The sick man used to call out in despair : " When I look in the glass I see a devil. It is I myself who am the devil."

The Major would answer with his imperturbable and winning calm : " You are overstrained, my dear Ma. Speak out and tell me all about it, and you'll soon be fit again. We are good comrades and friends, and you know you can count on me."

Once Ma showed the Major a sheet of paper and said : " I stole this certificate from Söderbom when we were at Lan-chou."

It was a certificate written by Dr. Rand at the time when they were being treated as criminals and imprisoned. Dr. Rand had stated that persons who were members of our great expedition were certainly not criminals.

It appeared that Ma's conscience was reproaching him because he had taken the paper, which was now of no importance. To show the student how little consideration he attached to this paper, the Major burned it. On that the sick man, who really gave the impression of being tormented by devils, calmed down. In his sick brain he built up the most trifling matters into whole mountains of crime. Quite innocent actions destroyed his peace and he bitterly repented words and expressions which had never been ill meant. One day he was inconsolable because he had, so he said, stolen a haddik, or sacrificial fillet, from an obo, and Zimmermann showed him how simply the thing could be arranged by putting the haddik back.

It became more obvious every day that Ma was insane. His illness developed irresistibly, and all the Major's attempts to calm him, to occupy him and to turn his thoughts into other channels were fruitless. In the beginning of April he suggested that Ma should undertake a topographical excursion to fill in some gaps still remaining in their map of Möruin-gol and at the same time to write a description of the terrain. It was a particularly useful piece of work which would have to be done sooner or later. He could be away for two or three weeks, and meanwhile the Major would take the readings from the instruments. He could make his own arrangements about servants and camels, and himself take his provisions from the existing stock.

Among others Ma took with him his own personal servant, Docha. He also took a dog, and he had a pistol for protection. And when everything was ready he disappeared into the forest.

Two days later the dog came back, and the next day Ma himself with his little caravan. The servants said the dog had stolen corn and had been beaten and on that had gone home. To Zimmermann's question why he had come back in such a hurry, Ma answered that it was high water in Möruin-gol so that it was impossible to ford the river. The Major suggested another way, and Ma suspected that he wanted to be rid of him.

" No," answered the Major, " you know very well that I only want what is best for you."

" I can't sleep ; give me a sleeping powder."

" It will be better for you to take regular exercise so that you'll be tired and need sleep."

However he got his powder. It did not help. He constantly complained.

" I am a devil. Everyone stares at me, everyone laughs at me."

Ma entered willingly into the Major's schemes for occupying him. He arranged for him to dig a ditch one hour a day and to build a wooden tower eight metres high from the top of which the force of the wind could be read. They began to fell trees, to set them up, join them together and stay them, and after some days the tower was finished. It was put into use in the middle of April. The occupation had somewhat distracted him, but afterwards he fell back into his brooding and mental anguish. He was afraid of himself and afraid to be alone with anyone but the Major.

One day he wailed : " I shall run away into the desert. I can't stand it here any longer."

His condition grew worse. He was chased by furies that laughed at him and mocked him.

One asks oneself why the young Chinaman suddenly became deranged. Not long before Professor Hsü Ping-chang and I left Etsin-gol with the main caravan, Ma had said to the former that he did not want to stay too long at the station but wished to be relieved by another student. Was it the loneliness and silence of the woods that clouded his mind? It was also said afterwards that he had received letters from home saying that his mother was ill, and that this news upset him. And what could Zimmermann have done to save him? He did everything to free him from his delusions and to force him to turn his attention to things other than himself. If only they could have started together on a long journey—but they could not leave the station entirely without staff, and they were waiting for Söderbom's return with the money.

Zimmermann suggested that with a couple of trustworthy servants he should go home by Su-chou and Ninghsia, and this plan seemed to attract him. But after a few days he fell back into brooding and said continually: "I *must* die. I can't bear it any longer."

The Major spoke again of the plan of his going to Su-chou where he was to meet Söderbom and get 500 dollars for his journey home. The Major wrote a letter to Söderbom to give Ma that amount, and he accepted the letter after he had read it. He decided to go in two days and chose Docha and Öljasung as fellow-travellers.

He seemed very keen on the journey. Next day he said: "I'll start to-day and only travel twenty li; please send any letters that are not yet ready after me by a servant."

Packing and loading were done in a hurry. Finally only an axe was lacking. What did he want with an axe? Well, he would cut wood for camp fires with it. So he got his axe, and started on his fatal journey. He went on foot and had a caravan of six camels. The Major accompanied him a bit of the way. Then he took a last farewell and wished Ma a successful journey. That was on April the 28th.

At 6 p.m. the Major gave orders to a servant to be ready next morning to go with letters to Ma's camp before the latter started. He got there in time. Ma greeted him kindly, took the letters and read one from Zimmermann to himself, encouraging and soothing. He sat down to write an answer which was never finished. It only contained a direction how his letters were to be sent.

Thereupon he sent Öljasung for the camels with the words:

"We shall break camp and go back to Tsondol."

When, half an hour later, Öljasung came back to the camp with the camels, Ma came rushing out of the tent, swinging the axe over his head. Foaming and raving he went for the camel-man. The latter saw that he was out to kill, and made off like an arrow into the woods, with Ma a dozen yards behind him. Öljasung was the better runner, the distance between him and his pursuer increased, and when he ventured to slacken speed and turn round, he saw that the lunatic had stopped and was beginning to slash himself in the most dreadful manner with the axe. Öljasung ran the twenty kilometres into Tsondol and rushed with bare and bleeding feet into the Major's tent, where he breathlessly related what had happened. The Major realized that a frightful disaster had occurred. Öljasung had not seen Docha. Where had he gone? One could only hope he had succeeded in escaping the fury of the madman.

Bandaging materials were got out in haste, and, while Zimmermann was getting his medicine case ready, he told his servants to load up everything else they might need.

Early in the morning they started, a party of six, the Major, Öljasung, the servants Tung and Jankia, a merchant and a hunter. They reached the place. But where was the tent? Yesterday it had certainly stood here among the trees. Ah, here was a black patch. The tent had been burnt.

Zimmermann ordered his party to keep still, so as not to confuse the tracks in the sandy ground. He himself cautiously approached and noted everything. He went to work exactly as a detective would have acted on the scene of a murder.

Docha lay on his face with his head and one arm in the extinguished fire which had been burning in the tent the day before. His clothes were burnt away; he was stark naked, and he was dead.

Ma was lying by a chest, five metres from the tent. He too was dead. He was fully clothed but hatless. On his temples, his wrists and his breast he had inflicted terrible wounds with an axe. He was a horrible sight, covered with his blood. Seven paces from the place where he lay they found the bloodstained axe. Presumably he had thrown it away or dropped it before he fell unconscious by the chest. As much as 100 metres from the tent there were blood traces, and the tracks of his aimless, wandering steps. But in the end he had returned to the tent where, not long before, he had killed Docha.

Fortunately his chests lay outside the tent; otherwise they and several important documents would have been burnt.

In the presence of his five companions the Major put all Ma's letters and papers in a bag, which was sealed and would be taken care of by the servants, whose testimony would without doubt be of importance at a later official inquiry. Ma's money, 135 dollars, was in like manner taken into safe keeping.

Nothing else was disturbed. The two dead men were left lying exactly as they had been found. Docha had an axe wound in the neck that had probably been immediately fatal. It looked as if the young servant from Maomo had been on his knees, occupied in rolling up his master's sleeping-sack on the ground, when, suspecting no evil, he received his death wound. He had fallen with his face and one arm in the dying fire, which had consumed his clothes and probably spread from them to the tent cover, unless the tent had been intentionally burnt by Ma.

Zimmermann's first action was to draw up a preliminary report of the occurrence and send it by courier to the Prince of the Torguts with a request for its forwarding to the authorities at Su-chou. He also sent a very explicit telegram to Professor Hsü Ping-chang and me as well as still more detailed letters to us, all addressed to Urumchi. But at that time we were in Peking, and on May the 13th I started for America. It was thus in Boston and in the month of June that I received the sad news of the young student's illness and death.

The Major entrusted his private letters to Tung and Macha who were allowed to accompany the Torgut Prince's messengers to Maomo, where the father and brother of the murdered Docha lived. The father would not believe the messengers' account of his son's death and made as if to seize their camels till the matter was cleared up. South of Maomo they met Söderbom who was on his way from Su-chou to Tsondol.

Immediately after his return to Tsondol the Major sealed Ma's yurt, and it was only opened in the presence of the Torgut Prince's representative. Thus all the letters and other possessions which the dead man had not troubled to take with him were secured. Among other letters was found that from his home informing him of his mother's illness, and they were inclined to conjecture that anxiety about her health had aggravated his condition. On May the 2nd the two deceased were buried on the scene of the tragedy. The whole of their property was packed in cases which were sealed and were not to be opened until the arrival of the expected Chinese commission of inquiry.

The time which now followed was a very trying one for Zimmermann. Popular feeling was excited and nervous. He was held in suspicion and was believed to be making preparations for flight. Known and unknown people from far and near gathered at Tsondol and the rumour of the murder and suicide spread round the district. Lamas arrived marching in procession and made their noisy music to exorcise the evil spirits and demons that had taken possession of Tsondol. The trombones resounded and the echo of temple drums rumbled in the usually so silent woods, where, a year earlier, we could have no presentiment that this peaceful tract was to be the scene of such bloody deeds. The monks sought from the signs of the heavens and the passage of the winds and clouds to ascertain the purpose of the occult forces, and sat beneath the trees babbling their eternally monotonous prayers and incantations. Zimmermann tried to calm the superstitious people and bade them wait until the officials came from Su-chou. But it was no use; they believed in witchcraft and sorcery, and perhaps the Lamas also found the occasion suitable for making an impression on the superstitious Torguts by engaging in warfare with the adherents of devils and demons.

The meteorological observations went on all the time as if nothing had happened, and the monks very likely thought that the strange Europeans had their own peculiar methods of controlling the evil spirits.

On May the 21st Söderbom came back to Tsondol, bringing Zimmermann's and Ma's mail, including my telegrams of January and April, which contained orders to the Major to return without delay to Peking. I had suggested in the course of my preliminary discussions with the Chinese in December, 1926, that the stations should be handed over to China after at most eighteen months, to be, from that time, permanently carried on by the Chinese. The stipulated time might be regarded as having expired in January, 1929, and accordingly I recalled Zimmermann. Ma would have had to wait until two new students reached Etsin-gol to take over the station and its equipment.

The deceased Docha's two brothers came to Tsondol and persisted in their doubt, and their father's, that Docha was really dead. At last they demanded that the grave should be opened that they might see him and set their minds at rest. It was impossible to refuse them this. When Zimmermann and Söderbom with two servants and some camels were leaving for Su-chou on June the 10th, the two brothers accompanied them to the scene of the tragedy, where the grave was to be opened.

On the 11th they gathered round the grave with spades. Zimmermann feared, because of all the rumours that had lately been in circulation, that the grave had been opened and Docha's body removed, and that his brothers had some secret motive for their demand to see the dead. He was therefore in the greatest anxiety as the spades sank into the ground. But his fears were groundless. The dead man's face appeared; his brothers saw and recognized him and were able to return tranquillized to their father in Maomo.

At Bayin-bogdo, higher up on Etsin-gol where the two arrived on June the 15th, Söderbom heard that 500 soldiers at Su-chou had mutinied and deserted. The situation was therefore perilous. Probably the vagabond troops would come down along the river to plunder, for mutinous and demoralized soldiers in China always become robbers. The two men considered it wisest to stay where they were for a while. They went on collecting plants and insects.

On June the 26th they heard that the mutineers had moved off in the desert towards Hami and that all was quiet at Su-chou. But now they separated. While Söderbom went on to Su-chou, the Major returned to Tsondol, where he arrived on June the 30th.

The station servants were glad to get their master back alive and so much sooner than they expected. They had feared the worst for him in a country where evil rumours were going round and where the feeling was anything but friendly to the two Europeans. And then as ill luck would have it an epidemic of spotted typhus broke out among the Torguts and carried off some fifty persons, which is a very high percentage in a tribe of ninety-five tents with perhaps six or seven inhabitants in each. Feeling accordingly grew more and more unfriendly, for the people believed the station to be the home of sorcery and devildom, and that all recent evils had come from thence.

But they still brought their sick to Zimmermann's yurt, and often enough his life hung by a very slender hair. It only needed that a single louse should convey the infection to him, and his fate was sealed, for among Europeans who contract this disease the percentage of deaths is very nearly a hundred. But he fearlessly busied himself with his patients and never knew how dangerous they were. Once a patient gave him a cap, in gratitude or by way of fee. One of the Major's servants remarked: "That cap comes from a yurt in which five people have died, and it belonged to one of the dead."

They burned it at once.

The meteorological observations were never neglected. Seldom has a series of observations of the ways of wind and weather been taken against the background of a more dramatic chain of occurrences.

In the beginning of August Söderbom came back from Su-chou. Towards the end of the same month the commission arrived, charged with making an official inquiry into the murder at Tsondol.

The commission was led by Mr. Yüan Chêng-hung from Su-chou, and otherwise consisted of an official from Maomo, five soldiers and several other persons. It stirred things up when these settled down at the station; there was life and movement, a coming and going of visitors and messengers. They stayed in the place eight days in all.

The representatives of law and order showed their credentials and at once began their inquiries. Everything was scrupulously noted. When the investigation was finished Mr. Yüan read the document aloud to Söderbom, who translated it for Zimmermann. It was then signed by the two Europeans, and copies of it were to be sent to our Committee in Peking and to the authorities at Ning-hsia and Lan-chou. It was also read aloud to some twenty persons, Torguts and Chinese, at Tsondol. Söderbom made an inventory of Ma's letters and other belongings which were then packed in chests and sealed in the presence of the commission. Docha's father and brothers were present at all these proceedings.

After a brief visit to the Torgut Prince, Mr. Yüan Chêng-hung returned to Su-chou, and Söderbom went with him. Silence and tranquillity once more descended on Tsondol.

During September the Major had a peaceful time. Between the observations he made short tours on horseback and looked after his patients, among whom was the oldest of the Torguts, who was actually cured, to the delight and gratitude of the tribe.

Söderbom returned on October the 3rd. He brought an order from the Government in Su-chou that, if the two gentlemen were both leaving, they should first dismantle the station's instruments in the place. Accordingly the gas cylinders were buried and, at Söderbom's suggestion, the cases of instruments were delivered into the Torgut Prince's charge. The latter received a large pair of binoculars, and haddiks were distributed to many of the station's neighbours and friends. On October the 18th a great farewell banquet was held for the two Europeans. Torgut Gegen himself, a Chief Lama, was there. It began with the frenzied dance which continues until the dancer falls in an almost unconscious trance, foaming at the mouth. He is then dangerous, for he holds bright knives in his hands with which he strikes and slashes around him. When he is at the height of religious frenzy, he can foresee coming events. The feast ended with mutton stew, tea and arrack. Etsin-gol and Tsondol had taken farewell of the mysterious strangers who were now leaving their woods for ever.

Then the Major began packing all the property that was to be carried eastward across the desert to Kuei-hua. On October the 20th everything was ready. Cases, sleeping-bags and tents were corded up ready to be loaded on the backs of their carriers. The camels were brought up and the lading began. In an hour it would all be done and the start made. The hour came to an end, and the caravan began its march.

At the same moment a courier rode in. He came from Su-chou, bringing the telegram I had sent them from Stockholm on August the 16th. It had been a full two months on the way and had been forwarded by the Swedish Legation in Peking. It ran as follows:

> "Thanks letters June fifteenth Zimmermann returns home soonest possible Söderbom remains Su-chou district awaiting my arrival from Peiping late autumn stop hope good camels available thanks you both splendid service greetings. Hedin."

They read the ominous words and looked at one another. The caravan must halt, the camels lie down, the baggage be lowered to the ground again and all the cases opened. All the travelling equipment must be divided into two parts. Everything that I might need on my arrival at Su-chou in the autumn of 1929 was put on one side, and the instrument cases were to be taken to the little town where Söderbom had orders to wait. Accordingly he had to ride back to the Torgut Prince and fetch the instrument cases.

The repacking took three days. The Major must travel alone through the desert, with three Mongols, Mären, Törkhum and Öljasung, and sixteen camels, while twenty-nine camels and two servants stayed with Söderbom.

My plans were afterwards changed, and I did not that

time travel into Inner Asia. It would have been fortunate if that telegram like many of its predecessors had been longer detained. Then Söderbom would have accompanied Zimmermann to Peking, whither we summoned him in vain by new telegrams.

On October the 23rd the Major was ready for the second time. As usual the river crossing was troublesome, and it was not till the 25th that the final start was made from the right bank of Etsin-gol. Söderbom went with him so far, and then they said good-bye. A Lama, who was a firm friend of the Major's, accompanied him, weeping, a long way, and tears glistened in the eyes of many others. They understood now that they had been unjust to him, and that he was an upright and honourable man. For himself, it was not without sadness that he left the place where he had spent more than two years of his life and from which he carried away so tragical a memory.

The road he had to traverse was 950 kilometres long, and he did it in thirty-six days of which two were spent in camp with Bergman, Bohlin, Hörner, Bexell, Johansen and Chên. On the average he marched 26·4 kilometres a day. The first half of the way ran at a distance of from ten to twenty-five kilometres from the Southern border of the Mongolian Republic, where wells were often sought in vain. Not far south of the monastery of Beli-miao, the Major, to his unutterable astonishment and delight, met his fellow-countryman, our old comrade Mühlenweg, who had been sent out to look for him. They went on together to Kuei-hua, where they arrived on December the 4th, and I have already told how, in Kalgan a couple of days later, I had the pleasure of seeing again my old friend the Major and of listening to his description of life by Etsin-gol.

The Major had brought from the station three cases containing a part of Bergman's neolithic collections, a tent, fifteen camel saddles and riding saddles, blankets, baths, tools, cooking apparatus and much besides, which were deposited with Mr. Gustaf Söderbom for future use.

So lamentable an occurrence as a murder and a suicide committed by a Chinese working in intimate connexion with Europeans, may easily, in China, give occasion for mis-

Lieberenz Photo

The Camp by Etsin-gol

[*face p.* 234

understanding and misinterpretation. Fortunately there were witnesses to the fact that no European was present at the place where the act of violence was committed and that its perpetrator acted under an attack of insanity.

It was at all events a relief to me to receive during my stay in Kalgan the following personal letter from the head of the commission of inquiry, Mr. Yüan Chêng-hung, who, after an introduction containing the usual all too amiable Chinese courtesies, continues:

> "I have the honour to inform you that I was some time ago commissioned by the Government of my Province to inquire into the circumstances of the murder of the servant Chao Wan-wu (Docha) employed by Mr. Ma Shê-chien, a member of your scientific mission, and the reason of Mr. Ma's suicide. At that time Hei Ho (the Black River) was so swollen that I was not able to cross it, but so soon as it was somewhat fallen I set out upon my journey. It so happened that, just as I was passing Ting-sin Hsien, the magistrate Huang Wên-chung likewise received instructions from the provincial government of Kansu to make inquiry into the affair in question. Under pressure of urgent official duties, Mr. Huang was unable to travel but charged his immediate subordinate, Wang Chao-chi to accompany me. After we had been five days on the way, we reached Tsung-Tu-lu near Etsin-gol. First we interrogated Mr. Zimmermann and Mr. Söderbom of your mission. Then we isolated the servants and interrogated them one by one. We ascertained the following:
>
> The deceased Mr. Ma was kindly and peaceable in character, conscientious but timid. He had good training as an observer. His relations with Mr. Zimmermann and Mr. Söderbom were entirely friendly and he treated the servants with great gentleness. When we questioned them about the cause of Mr. Ma's suicide, they answered that, before his death, he had received a letter from home, after which he had told those about him that his mother was very ill and that he had felt great anxiety. After that time he became abnormal in his actions and speech and became an entirely different person. When Mr. Zimmermann understood his position, he advised him time after time to return home. Mr. Söderbom had gone two months earlier to Su-chou to buy provisions and had not returned.
>
> Mr. Ma made preparations to depart. He took with him

an axe, and no one troubled about that, since it was needed daily when travelling. Strangely enough, the tragic occurrence happened when the travellers had only gone forty li.

Chao Wan-wu had been Mr. Ma's servant and Ma thought highly of him. The other servants said that no one could have had the heart to commit such a deed, and they were convinced that Mr. Ma did it because his understanding had become clouded on account of his concern for his mother.

Since the case was of great importance, I scrupulously examined all the evidence and tried in various ways to penetrate into the facts. What I found was that the different sources accorded with one another and that there is not the shadow of a doubt concerning the cause of the tragic occurrence.

After the investigation we personally inspected the scientific instruments and the effects which constituted Mr. Ma's personal estate. These, together with an inventory, were given into the charge of a separate mission. A report of the result of our investigations was sent to the provincial government at Ning-hsia and to the Education Office of Kansu, who sent a copy to your mission.

When, on an earlier occasion, I visited Etsin-gol, I made the acquaintance of Mr. Ma. Through conversation with him I found that he was a very trustworthy man, and I observed that he and Mr. Zimmermann and Mr. Söderbom were on very good terms with one another. I deeply lament that, not long after our parting, he went away from us for ever.

Although I have already presented my official report, I am afraid that distance and false reports may give rise to misunderstanding, and hasten therefore to send you a personal letter to let you know the facts.

Yours faithfully,
YÜAN CHÊNG-HUNG."

This noble and chivalrous letter is in truth a valuable document and testifies, at a time when extraterritorial courts are in process of being abolished, that it is not so dangerous to commit oneself to the Chinese administration of justice. Here is a case whose venue lay in the midst of the desert, hundreds of miles from the nearest Europeans, and in which an unjust judge could easily have cast the blame upon the Europeans living in the neighbourhood. Major Zimmermann has himself told me with what scrupulous care Mr. Yüan Chêng-hung proceeded, how astute he was and how equitable in his judicial decision. Mr. Yüan has moreover since that time done us great services. When I telegraphed offering to defray the cost of transporting Ma's body the long distance to his home near Peking, Mr. Yüan replied that the Education Department of Kansu had already assumed reponsibility for that transport. At first Zimmermann and Söderbom had intended to take Ma's coffin with them on one of their camels, and Mären had insisted that, every evening after the coffin had been unloaded, they must not neglect to place a bowl of rice and a pair of chopsticks on its lid and to tie a cock to its side so that the dead should not sleep irrecoverably. The cock would keep him awake by its nightly crowing. However, this original expedient was not put into practice, and since Zimmermann was the only European in his caravan, he was well enough pleased to escape the company of the dead student and the crowing cock.

We of the expedition have often discussed the cause of Ma's insanity, and various opinions have been put forward. It is necessary to distinguish between cause and effect. When it became an obsession with him that he had stolen a haddik from a sacrificial cairn and when his tortured mind constantly returned to this in itself innocent theft, it was not on the ground of the robbery from the cairn that he went out of his mind, but rather his distress about the theft was a symptom of an abnormality already existing in his brain. And just as little could he have become deranged owing to the letter from his home with the news of his mother's illness. His distress at having written something derogatory of his companions was a symptom too.

The prevalent opinion was that he could not endure the loneliness of the silent woods, with boundless desert spaces all around, and it was thought that to him as a Chinese the presence of the two Europeans did not constitute real companionship. I do not altogether believe in this theory. There were two Chinese servants at the station and merchants of the same race were often passing through. Moreover, Ma was for long periods travelling to Su-chou and Lan-chou and came into contact with many different kinds of people.

I do not believe that the quietness by Etsin-gol affected Ma in the slightest degree. It is possible that he would equally have been ill if he had stayed at home. Very likely he had the germ of his illness in him already when he started from China proper.

He first became noticeably ill in March, and during April his condition became rapidly worse. Towards the end he even said that he must die. His madness also took the form of an irresistible necessity to kill someone, and the young Docha happened to be his victim. Ma was ill, irresponsible. During the last days his distracted thoughts seem to have pointed to the Major. Once, in the middle of the day, when the Major was sitting writing in his tent, he heard two shots which pierced the tent cover. His first impulse was to rush out and see whether Ma meant mischief. But he realized that it was wisest to feign indifference. When, soon after, Ma came into the tent, the Major accordingly went on writing. After a little while he turned slowly and asked : " Did you hit a bird ? I heard you shooting." The Major's apparent calm reacted this time on the sick man, who, if Zimmermann had shown a sign of suspicion or fear, would probably on this occasion have become violent. One night, when the Major was lying awake with a feeling of insecurity, he heard Ma come stealthily out of his tent and quietly approach his own. The sick man tried as soundlessly as possible to open the flap and creep in. But when the Major coughed to show that he was awake, the footsteps retreated. Had he succeeded in his purpose the drama would have been even more tragic. For in that case one would have had good reason to expect a struggle ending with the death of both parties, and there would have been no witnesses, for all the servants were asleep. One lucky thing among so much ill luck was that the madness of Ma did not reach its climax until after he had left the station, and that there was at least one eyewitness of his suicide. He had just begun a letter to the Major when the demons got such a power over his soul that he was no longer able to resist them. The paper, which was found on one of his boxes, was bloodstained, and yet he had a short time before given orders to return to the station and to Zimmermann. His decision did not reach fulfilment, his understanding was clouded and he did his deed.

To such a melancholy end came our first fixed station in Innermost Asia. Long before we had a suspicion of Ma's illness, Dr. Haude, our Chinese friends and I had decided to remove it, on its transfer to Chinese hands, to Su-chou, whence weather reports could be sent to Nanking—if ever the telegraph line were got into order. From the moment when the Major left Etsin-gol, the responsibility for the future of the meteorological station's management was taken over by Dr. Ko Ching-chu at Nanking. I have no doubt that after a brief interruption it will be re-established at Su-chou and put to all the practical and scientific uses we had in view for it.

A collection was made among our committee for Ma's parents, to which, after my return to Peking, I made a contribution on behalf of the expedition. The dead servant's father also received a gift of money. It was no more than a simple demonstration of sympathy—the dead could not be brought back by money, and the wind sighs sadly through the woods where in hard and faithful labour they spent the last two years of their lives.

XIX

A SWEDE'S ADVENTURES IN THE FOOTSTEPS OF MARCO POLO.

WE have heard Major Zimmermann relate the story of his Robinsonad by Etsin-gol where for two years he conducted the meteorological station. In his saga appears from time to time the figure of a young Swede, Georg Söderbom.

This Söderbom joined our expedition in the summer of 1927. He is the son of a missionary in Kalgan whom I have known for many years. When he entered our service Georg was not yet twenty-three years old. He was a head taller than anyone else in our band, strong as a bear, good-humoured, happy and unpretentious, and spoke Chinese like a native, for he was born in Kalgan and had only, as a child, spent one year in Sweden. His Chinese was thus much better than his Swedish.

He assisted the Major with the observations. One day in the beginning of December, 1927, a rider from the Prince of the Torguts arrived at the station with orders from the authorities in Su-chou that, owing to the then prevailing state of war, the station staff was not permitted to remain and carry on its strange activities, but must depart westward.

Gloomy forebodings seized our people. Not long after there came to Tsondol a commissioner from Su-chou, Wu Chên-yüan, together with one Tsêng Fu-kuan and a small force of police. Wu was a very haughty and distinguished gentleman, who had been in Russia. He clearly had a certain respect for the mysterious visitors who had descended on the woods, for before he ventured to approach the station, he sent a couple of merchants to spy out the strength of the garrison and to ascertain how many rifles and pistols it had.

Courteously and urbanely Wu informed them that it was known in Su-chou that the station had quite other purposes than scientific research, and that its staff must therefore go on to Hami.

After protracted altercation it was decided that the student Ma should go with Wu and the police to Su-chou to explain our intentions.

Then Söderbom went to Möruin-gol to shoot birds for the Museum's collections. It was just at the time of year when the camels are rutting and are savage, and now a wild bull camel from the desert had joined the herd of its tame kinsfolk and accompanied them every evening to the tethering-place. The wild one was a tyrant who attacked all human beings within range, and no one dared come near him. In the end he was shot.

Once a wild camel calf came to the station at Tsondol and became intimate with our tame ones, of which there were sixty-five head in all. At watering-time he drank with them from a hole in the river ice. Söderbom tried to catch him, but he then dashed away out into the desert to the westward.

The Torgut Tubut Tsanggai once caught two wild camels, one of which died, while the other grew up, became big and strong and fierce, kicked, jumped and danced, but was subdued and tamed, and was ultimately sold to a rich Mongol at Alashan. A wild camel was found at Noyin-bogdo, which was subdued and offered for sale at a hundred taels. The Torgut Prince, too, had a double-humped captive from the desert, which, however, partly retained its own habits. In the winter he strayed back to his relations in Gobi, and in the summer he concluded an alliance with the tame ones by Etsin-gol. But one day he went to the desert and never came back.

The wild camels which again and again appear by Etsin-gol, are evidently less shy than the herds I have so often seen in the desert south of Kuruk-tagh or where the Keriya Darya ends in Takla-makan.

At the station all stores except tinned goods were coming to an end. Then another commission of inquiry arrived, consisting of Chao-Fu-lu, Chief of Police at Maomo, the clerk, Pai, and four constables. Chao too sent spies in advance to ascertain the strength of the garrison. And now the Torgut Prince was also summoned and his two chief men, Chaherektsi and Jundung Mären. A little town of tents grew up around the station, swarming with Mongols and Chinese, horses and camels.

The inexorable demand was now put forward that the Major and Söderbom should also travel to Su-chou and, after a lively palaver, the latter protested that they could not leave the station with its valuable instruments and equipment to take care of itself and that moreover they had neither money nor flour. They got a loan of 150 Mexican dollars from the Torgut Prince, flour was bought, and Söderbom went off with Chao by Maomo to Su-chou. There the chief of police, Chao Fu-lu, received orders from the Civil Governor to guard Söderbom strictly, and he was housed in a wretched inn. We had sent money by postal order to Su-chou and on the Civil Governor's guarantee Söderbom obtained a sum, most of which he sent, with provisions, to the Major.

Uneasy about the fate of the station and its staff, especially after Ma had been sent to Lan-chou, the capital of Kansu, Söderbom demanded to have speech with the Civil Governor. Since the latter refused to receive him, Söderbom lay in wait for him in the street, and was then informed that he too was to be sent to Lan-chou to undergo interrogation and to explain what the station staff was really about. Söderbom protested, but was all the more harshly treated by various magistrates. Only the Mayor, Chiao Ting-yüan, was kindly and assured him that all would go well. "Put irons on my hands and feet," roared Söderbom, "I will not go voluntarily." Thereupon he wrote two telegrams, one to the Swedish Legation in Peking and the other to me, to the effect that he had been arrested and imprisoned in Su-chou. The telegrams were confiscated in the yamên, where it was said that he was *not* arrested, but must explain our intentions. "Of course I am arrested since I am not free to return to Tsondol. I am outlawed here, since I am even denied the right to appeal to the protection of the Swedish Legation."

However that might be, the stiff-necked Swede had to submit and sit in a large two-wheeled prison cart which he shared with two police constables, his warders. As if that had not been enough, he was also escorted by an officer, Fan Tuei-chêng, and a troop of soldiers who were at the same time commissioned to drive a hundred horses to Lan-chou. The dangerous Swede had thus a guard of thirty men with him. But Fan was civil and they soon became the best of friends. He invited Söderbom to ride and told him to choose for himself whichever horse he wanted. He chose a lively and restive stallion from Tibet and rode, while Fan preferred to sleep in the cart.

At each " hsien " or borough the cart, horses and police were changed. At Gao-tai he put up with a kindly Catholic missionary, the German, Götsch, with whom he left 150 dollars so as to be able to draw a like amount from the German bishop at Lan-chou. At Kan-chou, seven days' journey from Su-chou, he met with Father Lois, equally hospitable and friendly. At the Protestant mission there were only Chinese evangelists. At Shandon he got two new police guards, armed with enormous blunderbusses, " because the road was swarming with robbers." But the police had no cartridges.

After a further seven days from Kan-chou the motley cavalcade reached Liang-chou, where Söderbom got house-room with Father Klein and another missionary. He also visited Mr. and Mrs. Belcher of the China Inland Mission, in whose hospitable house I stayed for two weeks in 1896, and where I spent a Christmas. They were now delighted to meet a Swede who belonged to my new expedition and sent me the most cordial greetings. By the time the message reached me, nearly two years later, Mr. and Mrs. Belcher had died of typhus.

Liang-chou was looking dreadful after the earthquake of May the 24th, 1927. A torrent from the mountains had done its part. Pretty well everything between Liang-chou and Ko-lang-hien had been levelled with the ground. In the latter town 3,000 people had perished. On the other hand Lung-ko-fu, only four li away, had not felt the earthquake. Immense masses of rock had been hurled down from the mountains, and in a small village forty out of its sixty inhabitants had been killed.

Over the pass of Tsa-ko-yu they reached Ping-fan. The last relay stage before Lan-chou was Hsiao-lao-chi. From thence Söderbom, Fan and four soldiers rode into Lan-chou where they arrived at 7 p.m.

Söderbom went straight to the yamên to report his arrival and to inquire after the student, Ma, and spoke to Fu Kuan-chang, the chief of staff, while Fan showed the stranger's papers and passport from Su-chou. The Governor was not up, and no one knew where Ma was. One of the military guard conducted him to another part of the yamên and into a room where an authoritative gentleman took his seat at a table covered with red cloth.

" Excellent," thought Söderbom, " this looks like being the great interrogation." He was quite right. The magistrate asked how he could prove that he belonged to the expedition when this was not stated on his passport, which was from Shanghai and only entitled him to *travel* in China.

He was taken out, undressed and searched to the skin. He was only allowed to keep on his shirt and drawers. Then he was taken to a hole full of Mohammedan prisoners sitting on two kangs. Two of them had been flogged, and it stank of rotten meat in there.

The Swedish prisoner's head was going round, he was frozen, hungry, tired, and felt sick. He asked to speak to the chief of the military police who had held the inquiry, and when he came, Söderbom asked what crime he had committed and why he was thrown into prison. The other answered : " Certainly you are innocent. You will soon be able to go to an inn and get something to eat."

" Now the play is over," thought Söderbom. Not a bit of it ! He was taken out into the yard, where he recovered his clothes and money. Fifteen police, armed with Mauser pistols and " cheese-cutters," large broad-bladed knives, formed a circle round him. In a harsh tone the captain of the troop ordered him to march, and thus he was conducted through the streets of Lan-chou, jeered at by all the people and accompanied by yelling crowds, who were going to see how the foreign devil was executed.

"That's it," thought Söderbom, "they are taking me out to the North Gate of the City where all the criminals are beheaded." But to show himself unmoved he lit a cigarette.

All traffic was stopped. In shops and doorways people sat enjoying the unwonted entertainment. The following grew. At last they stopped before a tall house, the police prison of the city. Here he was hustled through several doors and passages into a cavity beside a small yard, where they took from him his money and other belongings. In five other holes by the yard sat four Mongols, a Buriat and two Chinese. One had been sitting there for thirteen years, and looked apathetic. Three of the Mongols had come from Manchuria with a living Buddha on the way to Kumbum. They had had a Mongolian escort and had bought uniforms for it. But these happened to be of Chang Tso-lin's cut—so their wearers were from the enemy camp and were imprisoned. And there they had now been sitting for three months.

Surrounded by police, Söderbom sat wondering. Then the spirit moved him and he began to pour out on them the worst terms of abuse the Chinese language possesses—and that is no small matter. A warder brought a dish of "mien-t'iao-tzŭ," coarse, thick noodle.

"Eat!" ordered the Chief of Police.

"I don't eat dog's food," answered Söderbom.

"Eat!" the order was repeated.

"I only eat on Sundays," answered Söderbom.

In a milder tone the man said:

"You are our guest. You must eat."

"I don't eat your food, only foreign."

The Mongols were choking with laughter. The Chief of Police went away.

All the "criminals" were brought out into the yard which was some few square metres in size. The Buriat whispered to Söderbom that he recommended Moscow; they arranged things better there than at Lan-chou. From the next yard, where other prisoners were kept, a half-smoked cigarette came flying over the wall, evidently thrown by someone who was afraid of being caught. The Buriat seized it and let it go round the party, but when it came to Söderbom's turn there was nothing left but paper.

The prison doors were shut at 2 o'clock. Fine food was now set before the Swede, jelly-fish and shark's fins from the Eastern Sea and other dainties. The Chief of Police came in again and tried to persuade him to eat.

"No! I am no criminal. I don't eat in a prison. If I die of hunger there will be a row in Peking, and you'll get hell."

He asked for writing-paper and got it. He wrote in English and German to the missionaries in the town, but the letters were confiscated. In a letter to the Governor-General he asked to be told why he had been thrown into prison. This was taken charge of by the Chief of Police, who did not wish to take any responsibility and who was afraid, since there was no document establishing Söderbom's criminality.

The prison was horrible, dark, small, musty and full of bugs and lice. His travelling companion, Fan, came to visit the prisoner, did everything he could to get him released and told the Chief of Police it was a shame to treat a foreigner so badly.

When the Governor was apprised of the matter, he at once gave orders that Söderbom should be released and taken to Ma. The latter had for two months been living in a room at police headquarters and had been well treated, but was only allowed to go out once a week to have a bath.

Ma was aware that telegrams had come from Tsai Yüan-pei, and that the Governor of Lan-chou had exchanged telegrams with Marshal Fêng Yü-hsiang concerning our station and stating that the latter enjoyed the full protection of the Marshal.

In Lan-chou, too, they soon found a real friend in the American, Dr. Rand, who was in charge of the China Inland Mission's hospital in the city. They lived with him for twenty days and enjoyed the very greatest hospitality. Dr. Rand was delighted to be able to be of use to our expedition and undertook full responsibility with the authorities for Söderbom's and Ma's integrity.

At last there was no obstacle in the way of their return to Su-chou, where they were hailed as conquering heroes and were entertained at several banquets, with much wine and many speeches. They went on by cart to Maomo, where the new Mayor received them honourably. By the middle of June, 1928, they were back at Tsondol, where they found the Major and his servants in the best of health and spirits. Everyone was delighted by their return. No one had known what had happened to them.

A little later Söderbom went to Gashun-nor under instructions from Hummel to collect plants, birds and insects.

His next trip was to Su-chou to draw money from the post office. Then back to Tsondol to get ready the camel caravan which was to carry six hydrogen cylinders to Hami for Dr. Haude. The Military Governor of Su-chou, Cho Se-ling, provided passports and other necessary documents. But the cylinders were confiscated at Hami and are still waiting there to this day. On his way back to Tsondol he had the magistrate, Yüan Chêng-hung, with him.

In January, 1929, Zimmermann and Söderbom made a journey to Gashun-nor, whose ice was two feet thick and whose depth only amounted to two metres.

During the whole time Söderbom was the station's flying column and the Major's courier. He had to wait upon the Torgut Prince on all solemn anniversaries, to ride to Su-chou to fetch money and flour, and to post or collect letters. He remained in Su-chou during March and April, waiting for money and telegrams from me. On the way back to Tsondol he met the Major's cook, Tung, near Maomo and received from him the sad news of Ma's death.

Söderbom found the Major in a state of great dejection after this frightful occurrence, and the Torgut Prince charged him to console the Major—everyone knew that only Ma's illness was to blame for the misfortune.

Yet again Söderbom went to Su-chou, this time to request an official inquiry into the circumstances of Ma's death. Mr. Yüan Chêng-hung was appointed to lead this commission, the result of which has already been related.

The next mission of the young Swede was to buy flour at Maomo, where he was also to have a coffin made for the conveyance of Ma's remains to his native land.

At this time there was a band of six robbers on the road to Maomo, on the other side of the river, where they had plundered Jingpen and several other villages. A cunning Mohammedan had played a clever trick on the bandits. He visited their camp and asked to be allowed to join them. He served up a story to them that he had stolen a big consignment of opium, which had been taken from him not far from their camp. He got the loan of a refractory horse on which he pranced around. It was strong and a stayer, but would go much better under the constraining influence of a proper load. The robbers loaded it with several sacks containing silver and opium, and on the top of the load the Mohammedan mounted to make a little trial trip. But he never came back. He got no good out of plundering the robber band, for by Etsin-gol he was himself taken by the Torguts and lost his stolen property.

Afterwards the robbers crossed the river and set their course for Maomo. Sixty soldiers were sent out against them. Then the robbers retreated and moved down Etsin-gol. But the soldiers held their triumphal march through Maomo as if they had returned from a great victory.

Before long the robber band returned and began plundering in the outskirts of Maomo. Söderbom happened to have his camp in a hollow at the side of the road along which they marched. Luckily they did not see him.

In Maomo he gathered information and offered to take part in the pursuit of the band. He got an officer and twenty-nine police and was appointed leader of the force.

Now it was war to the knife. Towards five in the evening Söderbom marched with his troop to the village of Chi Ko-tung, which was said to be occupied by the robbers. Five li from the village Söderbom and his force dismounted and crawled on on their bellies, so as to steal a march on the band. A scout reported that the robbers had sentries out. The police officer fired three shots. At that moment reinforcements arrived from Maomo. These supposed that it was the robbers who had fired and replied with a volley. However, the situation was explained, and the whole party marched into the village, there to learn that the robber band had departed three hours earlier.

The bandits were now on their way to another village. Thither Söderbom steered his course, taking with him only the mounted contingent of his force, which now consisted of eighty men. He intended to surround the village. The band had just fixed its attention on a rich man's premises. The Swedish hero rode into the village with five Chinese, dismounted at a distance of 150 metres from the enemy and opened fire. His first shot got a robber's horse, another robber dismounted voluntarily and a third was thrown out of the saddle. Then the enemy took to flight and plunged head over heels into the river with a view to crossing and making a stand on the other side. But Söderbom hurried after two of them, caught them up and fired a shot which deprived one bandit of his nose. On that all six fled into the desert, and then the pursuit began. Three of the bandits were caught and secured by the Chinese. A fourth threw away his rifle and lay down on the river bank shamming dead. On the cry: "Give him a bullet!" he stood up and was taken prisoner. A fifth man ran towards the hills, throwing off his clothes so as to be better able to run, and was taken. The sixth, without a nose, fled to Kao-tai, where he was recognized and shot.

The campaign against the robbers had occupied two days and a night. After the victory they marched back to the village, where a feast was held and they were regaled on meat, rice and melons. The captured robbers stood with their hands tied behind their backs and ropes round their necks. Orders for their execution came from Maomo, and they were shot one after the other.

At the division of the spoil the most cowardly grabbed the most. Then they marched to Maomo. Almost the whole population had assembled outside the little town with the old and the new Mayors among them. The victors rode two and two on horses and camels. Outside the town gate they dismounted to hear an address of welcome and to drink wine. To the sound of music the triumphal march continued to the old yamên, where the feast of victory was held with revelry and rejoicing and where a theatrical troupe gave a performance.

The next day representatives of the authorities came to Söderbom to pay their respects and to give him his share of the spoils. He declined, however, to accept anything but an official document from the Mayor, adorned with a stamp, which was presented to him.

This distinguished certificate of courage, which certainly strengthened the expedition's reputation in Kansu, is worded as follows :

> " Since upon the fifteenth day of the ninth month of the eighteenth year of the Republic robbers had occasioned disturbances, they were pursued for their destruction by a force of police. It was so ordained that the member of the scientific expedition to the North-west Provinces, the Swede, Mr. Söderbom (Shêng Yui-hêng), who was passing through our town, fell in with the police force by the way. He expressed his desire to join with the police force to help in exterminating the robbers. But, since the stranger from abroad who comes hither on his travels must be protected, we sought to turn him from his purpose. But Mr. Söderbom said that robbers were people whom everyone must slay, and he insisted on taking part in their pursuit. The next day they came to the village of Shuang-chu-tsun and cut down several robbers. His bravery and his rage in battle were a spur to the courage of our men. So we devote these words to him in token that we shall never forget Mr. Söderbom.
>
> " The circuit magistrate (hsien-chang) of Ting-hsien, HUANG WAN-CHUNG."
>
> *Stamp.*
>
> *Eighteenth year ninth month nineteenth day.*

After his exploits at Maomo, Söderbom went with the coffin to Ma's grave, where he had the unpleasant duty of exhuming the body. His servants would not come anywhere near the grave. He had to do everything himself. It stank so that he came near to fainting. There was little more than a skeleton left of the dead man. He wrapped him in oilcloth and red stuff and laid him in the coffin. No-one would touch it and he had to load it and unload it every day himself.

After Major Zimmermann had returned through the desert to Kalgan, where he stayed with me a couple of days, Söderbom remained three weeks at Tsondol to deal with those of our belongings which were to be left at Tsondol, where they might be needed for the new enterprise, such as the ten hydrogen cylinders and all the equipment of the meteorological station as well as four Mongol yurts. He also made pack saddles for the camels he himself was to use for the journey to Kuei-hua.

Afterwards he had to ride a last time to Su-chou to fetch a lot of our things and camels which were there. During this visit he was taken ill and was tormented by the most frightful rheumatic pains, which was not surprising, since he had been lying out without a tent in the middle of winter. He had no drugs with him except the quack medicines of the country, and his journey back to Tsondol was a road of torment. When at last he arrived there he lay up till long after Christmas before starting on the long journey of thirty-seven days across the desert to Kuei-hua. When he returned to us in Peking on March the 20th he looked like a man of eighty and had great difficulty in walking.

But he soon recovered and is now completely restored. The reader who has the patience to follow our fortunes will soon renew his acquaintance on our joint journey to Jehol.

In the course of his travels Söderbom has collected a fine herbarium, sixty-five birds from Etsin-gol and numerous insects and has followed the routes over which Marco Polo travelled six hundred and fifty-seven years ago. It was Hummel who directed his education, and it is seldom that a teacher has so grateful a disciple. He enjoys the greatest popularity in our fellowship for his happy, tranquil and companionable nature, as well as for his diligence, his ability and his reckless courage.

XX

NORIN'S RESEARCHES

WHEN in October, 1926, I went up to the Geochronological Institute to ask my old friend, Professor Gerard De Geer, if he could spare his disciple, Dr. Erik Norin, and let him take part in the great expedition in Asia, I received the answer:

" He is certainly occupied with other work at present, but he is the man for great enterprises. Ask him. You will find him in the library."

Within half an hour he had accepted permanent employment in my service. I knew he was a coming man. Now three years have passed, and he is one of the veterans of our peripatetic Swedish University. By a series of pioneer discoveries he has illuminated the hitherto obscure story of the geological formation of innermost Asia. Gashun-nor, the Gobi Desert, Eastern Tien Shan, Kuruk-tagh, Lop Nor are a few of the principal stages in his course during the first year's work.

Norin was no novice in Asia when we set out together from Paoto on May the 20th, 1927. He had made several fruitful journeys in Shansi and had accomplished two expeditions in Kashmir and Ladakh where, among other things, he had corrected in essential particulars the English conception of the origin of the Himalayas. He thus began our journey with sure step and confident demeanour, and he knew from the first day what he wanted. I have seldom seen a man approach his work with such enthusiasm. When he talks about his plans and his experiments it grows light around him as though electric sparks were flying round. He understands the art of managing men. After three years he has still the same little company of Chinese in his caravan as when we set out. He is strict but just.

They love him. All admire him for his determination, his iron will, his love of the earth and his untiring industry. He also understands how to look after his camels, to spare them and to see that they get sufficient fodder. In a word, Erik Norin is a born explorer. I was lucky to get him as a colleague. He has solved many of the great problems that I was unable to solve when I travelled in Sinkiang forty and again thirty years ago. And thus these conquests too have fallen to Swedish exploration.

I have neither the capacity nor the time, nor does the purpose of this book allow me to communicate even a fraction of the contents of the reports and letters that Norin sent me during the course of three years. The geological, palæontological, stratigraphical and topographical investigations are of interest only to experts. It is equally impossible to give a cursory description of his travels and his results. Among other things I have heard nothing of him for months, for half a year. The postal service is not good in the desert. I can only offer a few samples of a more generally intelligible character.

First of all I ought to mention that on the way between Beli-miao and Shande-miao Norin drew a topographical and geological map in twenty-four sheets to a scale of 1 : 50,000. The plane-table work was based upon Major Heyder's simultaneously carried out and very servicable triangulation and Mr. Dettmann's astronomical latitudes and wireless telegraphic longitudes. From Shande-miao to Sebistei Norin produced a map to a scale of 1 : 100,000.

At the same time he studied the desert problem with particular regard to the distribution of the sand-dunes. He found that the occurrence of sand deserts depends upon the presence or absence of suitable sandstone formations in the region and on climatic conditions favourable to the disintegration of these sandstones.

His preliminary investigation of the Gashun-nor basin showed the presence of widespread lacustrine sediments and ancient coast lines. These sediments have been deposited in the depression at an early stage of the quaternary period.

As we approached the eastern spurs of the Tien Shan

mountain system he investigated the latter's relation to the adjacent country. Tien Shan's puckered mountain ranges die away towards the east, and, in the eastern prolongation of the system's axis, the surface of the earth has been broken up along vast longitudinal lines of dislocation which extend even to Gashun-nor.

In the earlier volume of this account of our travels, *Across the Gobi Desert*, I have described the great hydrographic changes which had taken place at Lop Nor since my last visit in 1900 and 1901. On old Chinese maps the lake of Lop Nor lay in the eastern extension of the River Tarim, which flows directly to the east. The Russian, General N. M. Prjevalsky, found on his notable journey of 1876–7, that the terminal lake of the Tarim lay a geographical degree south of the place allotted to it on the Chinese maps and that the Tarim's lowest reach turned off to the south-east and south of the lake. The German geographer, Baron von Richthofen, famous for his epoch-making travels in China, then produced evidence that the Tarim had changed its course, that the northern Chinese lake had dried up and that Prjevalsky's lake was a new formation.

During my travels in the Lop Desert in 1900 and 1901, I was able by taking the levels to show the existence of a depression in the northern part of the desert in just the region where the Chinese maps showed a lake which they called Lop Nor or Pu-chang-hai. I have dealt exhaustively with this problem in volume II of my book *Scientific Results of a Journey in Central Asia*, 1899–1902, in which I expressed the conjecture that the Lower Tarim periodically changed its course and swung between north and south like a pendulum. At the time of my visit the northern depression was dry but there were dead, dried-up stems of trees on its shores, and I discovered there the ruins of the ancient town of Lou-lan which, according to manuscripts found on the spot, flourished about A.D. 270. In the neighbourhood of this town the lowest, eastward flowing, reach of the Tarim debouched sixteen or seventeen hundred years ago. Its existence at one point had been confirmed by Colonel Koslov in 1892. In the year 1900 I drew a map of the dried-up river-bed which is called by the East Turks of the district Kuruk-darya or "the dry river." In the book referred to above I said in 1905, ". . . it is not too daring to say that, at some time, the river *must* go back to Kuruk-darya. . . . It is only a question of time for the country round Kara-koshun (Prjevalsky's Lop Nor) to become so filled up with alluvial sediment that the river will be compelled to return to its northern bed."

In *Across the Gobi Desert* I have related that the natives of Turfan told me in February, 1928, that the river had in 1921 actually returned to Kuruk-darya. Since I ardently desired the solution of the fascinating problem, I sent Norin, after our arrival at Urumchi, to map the re-arisen river and the ancient lake, now, after sixteen centuries, once more filled with water. I only wish my friend and teacher, von Richthofen, had lived to see the confirmation of the correctness of his theories.

With a caravan of two drivers, one cook, one coolie and fifteen camels, Norin, on April the 11th, 1928, left the little village of Singer in Kuruk-tagh. Not far from Toghrak-bulak he saw, at a distance of 7·5 kilometres, the re-arisen river winding like a blue ribbon over a boundless white clay desert. Three days later he crossed the low ridge of gravel that slopes from the foot of the mountains towards the lacustrine sediment of the Lop Nor basin. The verge consists of an imposing terraced shore line. Between this and the river he found marsh, small lakes and a luxuriant growth of reeds. In 1900 I had not seen a living blade by Kuruk-darya. Since 1921 vegetation had reawakened to life under the influence of the new-come water. The camels revelled in the succulent pasturage. Even tamarisks had taken root, but not a single poplar sapling was seen. In the third century, however, forests had grown upon the banks of the river. They died when Kuruk-darya dried up. They will assuredly come back if the water continues long enough to flow in the northern bed.

Wild pig, hares, antelopes and wolves had wandered back into the desert. Duck, wild geese, cranes, storks and other birds were there in multitudes.

Norin followed the river 220 kilometres to the eastward to a point north-north-east of Lou-lan. He says in a report: "The river is flowing in Kuruk-darya's bed, and its course is, in the main, the same as on Dr. Hedin's map. It is a great river, from 100 to 150 metres wide, several metres deep and has a current speed of about one second metre. At this time of year the water was very muddy, a brown clay soup."

Four miles east of the well of Yaka-yardang-bulak the river forms several large shallow lakes in the former desert. Further on, the river divides into arms and forms a delta where it passes to the north of Lou-lan. Two miles north-north-east of Lou-lan flowed one arm, fifty metres wide and with a current of half a metre. The water was clear and drinkable. Great bodies of water also reach out into the desert east of Lou-lan. Half-way between Altmish-bulak and Lou-lan, where in 1900 and 1901 I found the most hopeless drought, Norin's progress was now hindered by marsh and lakes. The district can only be mapped in winter when all these new waters are frozen.

In the western part of the course, reeds predominate, in the eastern, tamarisk. In the longitude of Lou-lan the vegetation becomes sparse and soon ceases, a result of the water's progressive expansion. Norin says in conclusion: "I have succeeded in showing that the new river follows, on the whole, the old bed of Kuruk-darya and that a considerable part of its waters flows on in several branches to the north of Lou-lan and discharges into the Lop Nor basin."

Norin also devoted his attention to the former shore lines which follow the southern foot of Kuruk-tagh. They open wide perspectives for new researches and throw light upon the chronology of the later quaternary period. He has mapped one such erosion terrace all the way to the tract north-north-east of Lou-lan. At some period this constituted the boundary of the old Lop Nor. In its western part the lake has been quite deep and the force of the waves considerable. To the eastward, this lake, which Norin calls Lake Tarim, had passed into marsh.

Simultaneously with, or soon after, the existence of Lake Tarim the whole basin had been subjected to movements of the earth's crust. The western part of the area has been

Ambolt Photo

Abd-ur-Rahim with his family and friends

[*face p.* 256

raised in relation to the eastern. Thus the old shore line sinks towards the east.

Lake Tarim was fresh, and jardang sediment was found in its basin. The diversiform land elevation resulted in the water masses of Lake Tarim being thrown over to the easternmost part of the basin to form the fresh-water lake of Great Lop Nor. An older formation of lacustrine sediment he calls the Meza series.

Later in the spring the heat became unbearable. It was only possible to work out of doors in the early morning and late evening. On May the 20th, 1928, he was in Shindi, and during June and July he devoted himself to the orography, tectonics and geology of Kuruk-tagh. As guide he had my old servant of 1900, Abd-ur-Rahim.

Tectonically this mountain system is a ramification of Tien Shan and has in the main undergone the same development. Here also he observed fine-grained straticulate clay-sandstone of ten metres in thickness, an annually stratified sediment, in all ways corresponding with normal glacial annually stratified clay-sand, and in which the thickness of the strata varies from three to five centimetres. He made a copious collection of geological and palæontological material, discovered plant fossils of the permo-carboniferous age and found clear evidence of permo-carboniferous ice submergence in these tracts. In the beginning of the autumn he went to Bogdo-ula, to return later to Kuruk-tagh and the Lop Desert. In spite of his full programme of work, he made meteorological observations thrice daily, drew maps, made notes and took photographs.

On my return to Urumchi on October the 4th, 1928, I found Norin at headquarters. But a week later he was on the march again. On November the 1st he writes from Shindi in Kuruk-tagh that Bergman has come to his camp and is "full of enthusiasm for the tasks that lie before us. This meeting with Bergman was the pleasantest thing that has happened to me for a long time. It is good to have someone to talk to—and an expert at that."

Norin had been snowed up on the pass of Pu-chêng-tzŭ and had lost some of his donkeys, but was relieved by his servant Ottehong, who arrived with camels.

"Abd-ur-Rahim thanks you heartily for the silver watch, which greatly delighted him. He is eager to meet you, and make his acknowledgments."

He further expresses his delight with Bergman's maps of Northern Tibet, in districts in which I had not been.

> "Bergman is now playing the gramophone, dear old records which we have already heard a thousand times in these months which will soon amount to two glorious years. I shall never forget these old tunes. When, one day, I go home and grow old, I shall play them again, and they will awaken countless memories of these wonderful years in your expedition."

On November the 19th he wrote a letter to my home in Stockholm in which, among other things, he says:

> "Yardang-bulak, that is a name which quite certainly is familiar to you all. I expect it sticks in the memory from proof-reading in earlier years. For Sven it has certainly many a time loomed large as the name of a metropolis, when he was wandering in the waterless desert which stretches southward hereabouts and melts into the haze on the horizon. The conditions now are quite different from what they were then. All the mighty waters of the Tarim are rolling forward through the field of vision, and Yardang-bulak with its salt water and salt-encrusted reeds is a doomed place, only visited because our work has led us hither. Bergman and I have combined archæology and quaternary geology along the shores of the former Tarim lake, and Bergman hopes to find here traces of a settlement in the ice age. His work is difficult, for much has happened since the ice covered Kunlun. The violent alternations of temperature between day and night have had the effect, in the course of eight thousand years, of macadamizing all loose stones and possible stone implements. There is nothing now for him to go by but splinters and some lucky find or other.
>
> "Bergman is returning in a couple of days to Urumchi. His field of labour is Lop Nor, but he cannot go there just now, since troops have been pouring into the district for several weeks. They fear disturbances there during the winter. I myself am forced into the mountains, but that matters the less in that I have work everywhere where there is anything to map, and particularly in Kuruk-tagh. I cannot help admiring the amazing organization the Chinese have succeeded in establish-

ing, despite the smallness of their numbers and the immense uninhabited spaces. This very evening a man has come from Yü-li-hsien (Konche on the map) with a beautifully written letter from the magistrate, which I do not understand and which, for the matter of that, interests me very little; but the fellow has ridden his one horse, day and night, about 200 kilometres—I assume—and followed our trail to this place. The man's name is Abd-ur-Rahim—not, I fancy, unknown. He is one of Sven's old men.

"Of the fate of Sven and Ambolt you know more than I. Ambolt has become a myth to me. I have been hearing about him for more than a year, and I have been expecting him for six months. Now I say there is no such animal. It is a terrible pity, for his work is of extraordinarily great importance to me. I expect a great deal from co-operation with him.

"I am counting on being able to finish the tasks entrusted to me during this season. They are the quaternary history of the Tarim basin and the geology of Kuruk-tagh. This disturbance down at Lop Nor necessarily comes to an end with the spring, when the waters thaw out and the floods cut off communications with the East. Till then I must keep away from the great highways and make my way into the mountains. In the course of my map-work during the summer I have acquired a pretty good knowledge of the locality, so that there is no occasion to be uneasy about my safety. But I cannot send letters either home or to Urumchi.

"The climate is ideal here now; cold at night, but by day just right for the camels not to take hurt. During the summer I always had to march by night, which was a great hindrance to map-work.

"Thanks to Sven, my equipment is now first class, both as regards instruments and tent gear. He sent me one of his Primus stoves and a Primus lamp which are just the thing to keep the tent warm. Some days ago I met Dr. Haude, who was on his way from Charkhlik."

From Yigde-bulak Norin writes, on November the 23rd, about the stream of couriers that was sent out by the higher powers to keep track of him, and relates that the inhabitants of Kuruk-tagh and the neighbourhood were forbidden to sell him camels. He speaks of his map-work and of his co-operation with Bergman where archæology and quaternary geology touched on one another. "Judging by the little I have seen of Charchak or the mountain range to the west of Yardang-bulak, it is a geological detail of very great interest. It is clay limestone and a series of continental clay and sand deposits of, I guess, the Jurassic age and is likely to contain vegetable fossils." He has seen a lot of fragments, but has not yet had time to assemble them.

He speaks of his plans and aims, and troubles himself little about the prohibition from Urumchi since it makes no difference which region is thrown open to him.

> "Kuruk-tagh and Lop Nor will do very well for the present. It is not so little that has already been accomplished. I have a substantial framework and the thing now is to fill it out to a complete whole. But I long for Ambolt. I dare not think how he will one day come to hate me, when he finds out how much of his valuable time I take up, but he has only himself to blame for choosing a field of work so intimately bound up with mine."

The next letter is from Sharazak-tala, Camp 185, by Bagrash-köl, and is written on November the 9th. He is immensely delighted with the post we had sent him from Urumchi by the courier Haid Ahun. And he is now on his way to the south-east corner of Lake Bagrash, which I once visited at its western side and which Roborovsky mapped—how accurately will appear when Norin has finished his map.

From the middle of the southern shore he means to strike southward through the sandy desert to the foot of the mountains, where he will stay for a while. It is full winter and everything is under snow. In the daytime the temperature does not rise above − 15° and at night it falls to − 20°. But he has a splendid stove that he got from Bergman, and he sometimes sits up till 10 o'clock merely to enjoy the delightful warmth.

The camels are in good fettle, and the grazing is holding out. The district to which he is going is almost unknown even to hunters; not even the much travelled Abd-ur-Rahim has been there. The neighbourhood is uninhabited. Only to the north, east and west of the lake there are Mongols. Of his field of work at the northern foot of

Kuruk-tagh and by the southern shore of Bagrash-köl he says: "This is a fascinating field of work in which every step is a new bit of country. I guess that I am the first European to come here. Geologically and orographically this vast mountain mass is a problem of the first rank."

The map sheets cover an area of about 2,000 square kilometres, not counting the Lop sheets to the scale of 1 : 100,000. But it is cold working outside, and he often has to thaw out his fingers by a fire. He has been working at high pressure, fearing to be recalled one fine day by couriers from the authorities. When he feels safe he will allow himself a day's rest.

Three days later, at Camp 188, he has reached the south-east corner of Bagrash-köl. The district is empty of people. He has seen only one yurt. He has still flour for two months, and Abd-ur-Rahim shoots as many antelopes as are required.

> "This trip promises to be very enjoyable. On the way here I crossed a shore line six kilometres south of the present edge of the lake and at a level fifteen metres above it. The dune belt lies within this shore line and is here half a kilometre wide. The dunes seem to originate from stratified lake sediment as in the Tarim basin."

The lake was frozen, and when the ice cracked it was heard at a range of two miles, sounding like far-off camel bells. The ice is said to reach the thickness of a metre and the natives walk across the lake from shore to shore.

After Norin had completed his work at Bagrash-köl he returned to Urumchi, where he arrived on February the 25th, 1929, in the belief that the new members of the expedition sent out by the Academy of Science, Hörner and Bexell, Dr. Bohlin, appointed by me in Peking, and our archæologist, Folke Bergman, who had been home on leave, would already have arrived there. Nothing, however, had been heard of them. On the other hand he at last met Dr. Nils Ambolt, who was afterwards to become his faithful companion, but who was not yet fully recovered from his severe illness.

During his stay in Urumchi he went, accompanied by

Ambolt and Haslund, to visit the Governor, "who was extremely amiable and asked us to come again on a subsequent day and let him see a part of our collections." This they did. Norin and Dr. Yüan showed a number of their fossils, while Haslund reproduced Mongolian songs on the phonograph.

> "We had a very pleasant time," he says. "The Governor-General showed us a collection of very interesting old bronzes which are said to have been found in the Turfan district and, according to Yüan, probably are of the period of the Han dynasty. When we left he begged me to come again. Later in the day I received a pass for outward journey and return, good for four months."

At the end of March Norin went to Chuguchak, and finding nothing had been heard of the others there either, he availed himself of my earlier offer of leave and travelled home. We met in Berlin at the end of April, together with Bergman, Hörner and Bexell, who were on their way to Sinkiang. With the two latter he discussed the great geological problems, especially with regard to the aims of Professors Gerard De Geer and Halle in quaternary geology and palæobotany.

Norin stayed three weeks in Stockholm. Under the direction of Professors Rubin and Carlheim-Gyllensköld he acquainted himself with the most modern methods of basic mensuration with "Invar tape." From the Institut Guillaume in Paris he procured one of these lines, seventy-two metres in length, which was later of incalculable assistance to him, owing to its freedom from variation under changes of temperature.

He also devoured the literature concerning the permo-carboniferous ice age in America, Africa, India and Australia and obtained valuable points of comparison with the ice age formations of the same period found by him in Kuruk-tagh. To the geological congress assembled in the summer in South Africa, which had this very problem on its programme, he sent a communication about his discoveries.

On May the 27th the return journey to Sinkiang began. He took with him from the firm of Wichmann Brothers a

Wild theodolite of the smaller type, furnished with electric lighting and optical plummet, and fitted for triangulation.

At Novo-Sibirsk he fell in with Dr. Bohlin and the young geodesist Chên, who was to be Ambolt's assistant. The German Consul, Captain Grosskopf, gave them the very greatest help and hospitality such as several of the members of the expedition, both before and after, have had the privilege of enjoying.

In the middle of June, Norin, Bohlin and Chên were at Bachti, where Bergman, Hörner and Bexell had been held up because the frontier authorities had refused them permission to enter Sinkiang. All Norin's representations were unavailing. No-one was to enter the province. Norin, who was leader of the expedition during my journey to America, then decided to send the three geologists to Peking, whence they were later to proceed through Gobi to Gashun-nor. This rearrangement of the programme was, however, so considerable and so costly that Norin telegraphically requested my sanction, which I of course gave.

The exploration of the Gashun-nor basin had been from the beginning one of our most vital aims. Geologically regarded, it greatly resembles the Lop Nor depression, and now that Hörner was taking Gashun-nor in hand, Norin would obtain particularly valuable material for comparison with his field of labour at Lop Nor. Bohlin, Hörner, Bexell and Chên accordingly started immediately for Peking.

Norin and Bergman, who should also have gone to Peking, were obliged to wait at Bachti because large consignments of travelling equipment from Stockholm and Peking had not yet arrived. This postponement was a piece of luck, for on the evening before their departure for the north, a telegram from the Governor-General arrived through the Russian Consul at Chuguchak to the effect that all the new members were permitted to cross the frontier and proceed to Urumchi. This was at the end of July, 1929. At that time the others had already arrived in Peking. Norin and Bergman consulted; should the new members be recalled from Peking? "No," says Norin in his report, "I considered that the new geologists had far richer fields of labour out there than in Sinkiang, and, above all, greater freedom of movement." Accordingly no change was made, and Bergman travelled to Peking to assume the leadership of the new great Gobi expedition. Norin went to Urumchi. If difficulties met him there, he intended, in accordance with our earlier decision, to transfer headquarters to Western Kansu.

> "In Urumchi it appeared, however, that our situation was unexpectedly favourable. Ambolt and I were kindly received by the Governor-General and at once received our passports for the work in Kuruk-tagh, Turfan and other districts. The Lop Nor district was, however, closed to us on the ground that new movements of troops were there in progress."

The caravan was immediately fitted out. The camels, which had been grazing all the summer in the mountain meadows of Tien Shan, were fat and strong. On September the 10th they started off to Ulan-bei, forty li (twelve miles) south-east of Urumchi. They had forty-two camels and ten donkeys. The young Russian, Vorotnikov, who had been trained by Dr. Haude and Dr. Hummel, was their meteorologist, and the Tatar, Sabitov, was Ambolt's assistant and interpreter. For the rest the party consisted of two cooks, two understrappers and five camel-men. Special guides were engaged from time to time.

Three days later they started for Camp No. 3, on the south bank of Lake Ainak-köl, not far west of the great road to Turfan. Here Ambolt carried out a complete fixed-point-determination, took magnetic and pendulum observations, and soundings of the lake, while Norin made a plane-table map of the northern edge of the mountain chain of Dchirgös-tau and the lake basin. They worked here for several days with Dr. Yüan and gave him fixed points for his map-work in Tien Shan.

Later they steered their course by unknown ways through Dchirgös-tau to the Turfan depression, Kumush and Shorbulak in the western part of the great ventless basin which divides Chol-tagh from Kuruk-tagh south of Turfan. Shorbulak was their second main station and starting-point for triangulation. The usual labours were carried out. From

Shor-bulak and the well of Arpishme-bulak 25 or 30 miles away they explored this remarkable ventless basin which has a length of over 90 miles and is a tectonic subsidence of the same kind as the Turfan depression, although less deep. In the middle of it are large salt marshes surrounded by immense reed-beds. Round its edge the subsoil water comes to the surface in the form of springs.

> "At Arpishme-bulak there are marine limestones and salt-water sediments of the carboniferous (probably subcarboniferous) period. Here I have made a vertical section through the sediment complex to a depth of about 500 metres. No less than six fossil-bearing strata were met with and very rich collections were made. These localities are my richest hitherto.
>
> "From Arpishme-bulak we went on to Pu-chêng-tzŭ where we made a stay of a few days to develop our photographs. Thence we travelled to Mo-chia-hutuk, where we still are and where we have been working since December the 16th. It is the fourth of our greater stations with astronomical fixed-point-determination and magnetic and pendulum observations carried out by Ambolt. I have completed my map-work of last year and connected up with the triangulation network from Shor-bulak."

From 7 a.m. to 9 p.m. Vorotnikov carried out hourly meteorological observations which were of great importance for the altitude figures. The meteorological station stayed behind at each camp until the new camp had been pitched, so that a series of corresponding barometric readings was obtained. A mercurial barometer was smashed beyond Shor-bulak. For the rest they had one aneroid (Bohne), six Paulin aneroids, which Norin praises very highly, and four hypsometers.

During the autumn Norin produced 300 kilometres of route-mapping and 1,100 square kilometres of plane-table maps. He had also an opportunity of completing his section through the permo-carboniferous glacial deposits, and their age was fixed by abundant finds of fossils. The photographic material is as ample as it is interesting, and the colour plates, too, are successful.

At the end of his last report which is dated from the camp at Mochia-hutuk, Kuruk-tagh, January the 2nd, 1930, Norin says that he and Ambolt intend either to work along the southern edge of the Tarim basin between Keriya and Khotan or to stay yet another three months in Kuruk-tagh. If the former alternative is denied them they go to Kansu, where they have great plans and problems.

> "It has not appeared clearly enough in my reports," he says finally, "what extremely valuable assistance has been afforded me by Ambolt, above all in map-work and in triangulation. The basic mensuration has always been carried out by us together and also the calculation of the triangular network. He has always been ready to assist me with advice and action. So intimate and harmonious a co-operation as ours must surely be a rarity."

In one of his more detailed letters Norin relates that, when Dr. Haude, after a task well done, travelled home by Peking, Dr. Yüan and Norin had determined to maintain the meteorological stations, which, however, owing to internal political causes, underwent a certain change. Bogdo-ula and Charkhlik were dismantled, and in place of them new stations were established at Keriya, Turfan and Shindi. Urumchi was maintained as before.

In the late summer of 1929, when Carlson was obliged to go home on the ground of ill health, and it often happened that none of the members of the expedition was in residence at Urumchi, Norin and Dr. Yüan installed the Anglo-Russian veterinary surgeon, Dr. Etches, as superintendent at headquarters. Dr. Etches attends to the mails, sends couriers to the members in the field and negotiates on their behalf with the authorities. From time to time he sends me reports.

It is now long since I heard from Norin and Ambolt. I know through letters and telegrams from Dr. Yüan that they got permission to work for three more months in Kuruk-tagh. Whither they go afterwards I know not. I always feel most tranquil when I do not hear a sound from them. For then they are in the field and working undisturbed. But thus much I know, that it will be said of their results, when once these become available to science, that they are the most original and epoch-making in their sphere that have ever been attained in the interior of the greatest continent. I need only mention the determination of the gravity in the Turfan depression, which lies 300 metres below the level of the ocean and, next to the Dead Sea, is the deepest subsidence on earth. Geology, palæontology and geophysics will make vast new acquisitions. The astronomical determinations of locality, the triangulation and the accurate observations of elevation give to Norin's masterly maps an authority hitherto unknown in Central Asia.

One can understand with what eagerness I open the letters that reach me at long intervals from Norin and Ambolt. Every day that they work in the silent deserts and mountains brings to science an enlargement of territory and confers lustre and honour upon their country.

XXI

AMBOLT'S DIARY

THE young astronomer from Lund, Professor Charlier's pupil, Dr. Nils P. Ambolt, was in all respects well equipped when he joined our expedition. He was provided with the highest testimonials from competent men and had been studying for a year under Professor Kohlschütter at the Geodetic Institute at Potsdam. Ambolt and I met for the first time in Berlin in June, 1928, and in August of the same year we went together to Sinkiang. At Chuguchak he was struck down by a severe illness, as I have already related. It was not until the New Year of 1929 that he was able to begin his astronomical and geodetic observations at Urumchi and only in the spring that he set out for researches in other regions. Having paid his farewell visit to the Governor-General and got his passport for Turfan, he left headquarters on April the 4th, 1929, accompanied by the mechanic Carlson, the Tatar Sabitov, the cook Nikolai and two Chinese servants. They all rode, while the baggage was carried on two "arbas," or two-wheeled carts.

On the very first day he was put to the test of a nine hours' ride in a gale, but none the less drew his sketch map of the route, which led by Tsai-wu-po and the town of Daban-ch'êng to the large and ancient oasis of Turfan, known to fame through the explorations of von le Coq and Grünwedel. He found the scenery wonderful, the verdure tropically luxuriant, the scent of flowers and fruit intoxicating, but the heat already oppressive. He is feeling ten years younger and rejoices to have left the chicaneries and intrigue infested atmosphere of Urumchi behind him. Our friend Mussel Bai receives him kindly. He sends his cards to the Governor and other mandarins, the Mayor visits him—he has had orders to keep his eye on the unknown guest, and, to disarm him, Ambolt shows him all his baggage, chest after chest. The old man is tranquillized and asks him to dinner. He has a little daughter who is ill. "If we succeed in curing the child we shall be all right."

In a letter home he bursts out: "If you only knew how happy I am. In this place there are many who want to examine my equipment. Only now everything is going well."

The apparatus is unpacked, the pendulum stand is set up and on the evening of the ninth he hears the time signals. He receives visits from the English missionary, the postmaster, the military governor and, for the second time, from the Mayor, who cannot marvel enough at the queer instruments he sees. He works for twenty-four hours at a stretch. Sometimes the time signals give trouble; he supposes it is a question of climate and is uneasy about the result. The accumulators are charged—it is Carlson and Nikolai who run the little generator. He tries in vain to master the wireless and feels paralysed. Pity that, so as not to upset the authorities, one has to do without running a proper lead to an aerial!

By the 17th he is happy again, for now he has succeeded, and Carlson, with the help of all the Chinese servants, has got the accumulator fully charged. It is stiff work at a temperature of 30°. The pendulum observations and magnetic determinations are continued. Sometimes his work is impeded by storms. Then he collects snakes, scorpions and lizards. The signals are working again. One night he intercepts Bordeaux and then works for twenty-four hours. At Kosh-dung, too, complete series are made. He executes a map measuring his distances with the arba wheel. Both Nauen and Bordeaux are heard but faintly. There has to be dead silence round him when he is listening.

He goes for walks round Turfan to extend his map. In the town he takes photographs. The Aksakal or village elder, Abdul Kadir, puts in an appearance to spy and is so kindly received that he is disconcerted. The Mayor, the postmaster and the commandant are his guests at a dinner, and when he finally leaves Turfan he feels he is leaving many friends behind there. He thinks better of the Chinese than of the East Turks.

On May the 10th he left Turfan.

" On the way we encountered a sandstorm of a loathsome kind. It was one of the worst I have yet been through. We stuck it till 4 in the morning in that lashing, chilling misery. One's eyes did not enjoy it ; one could scrape heaps of sand out of them." At a bend he believed himself to be in shelter and got up, but got such a buffet from the storm that he fell. The plane-table was upset. His sun helmet took to flight.

" The Chinese, Wu, started off to retrieve it. But it was labour in vain. He came back exhausted and out of breath and in despair, and said he had lost face. I consoled him by saying I valued his good intentions more than the helmet.

" He had tucked me up in his fur coat and was freezing himself, poor fellow. Our three boys deserve a chapter to themselves. Sabitov, headman, groom and interpreter, is the least sympathetic. But he is efficient at his job, understands how to bargain and saves his higher wages many times over. Between times he can be abominably lazy and negligent. I have several times been in a red-hot rage with him. But he still sticks it out. Number two is Wu (Chinese for five—so we call him Five) and is an intelligent, cheerful, industrious and capable youngster. He knows how to make himself generally useful and to help in every way. Especially in the astronomical work he is of great use to me. After a couple of times, he knows just what to do. The level to be lit up, the book brought out, the scales read and so on. It is a blessing to have such a boy. Number three, Nikolai, the cook, is a sedate and sober person who thinks everything is fine. He attends to his job and does not say much, but always has a humorous glint in his eye. He generally counts the wheel revolutions when we are mapping, and he does it conscientiously. This boy is also as strong as a bear and, for this reason, a desirable companion. When we left Urumchi we were warned not to be too easy with our people. Everyone said we must keep a tight hand on the servants. On this trip we have treated them as friends, with nothing but good results, and we hope this may continue. I believe that Norin does the same and that he is wise. Of course it would not do with everyone, but it does with our boys. Their mutual relations are, however, warlike. Sabitov is a Tatar, and the other two are Chinese. They try to score off one another in every way."

They stopped at Kindik to repair what had been damaged in the night's storm. They went on in a gale, and now had a taste of their first hardships. Hat number two flew away and his student's cap was brought out. The carts reached the night camp; the horses were tired out and must rest. The poor beasts had had two frightful days in the storm.

"One often sees mirages at various distances. On the way to Turfan we thought we saw a lake in front of us and supposed it to be the water of the depression. But after a while it completely disappeared. On the way here we saw a poplar wood, but that too was the same optical illusion.

"At the next station we ate a highly seasoned dinner with a soldier. When he was showing us his rifle it appeared that he was using a blank cartridge full of opium."

For the sake of the map Ambolt now took another road to Daban-cheng. It was "awfully jolly. To my delight I am in a position to correct an error in Stieler's map."

On May the 16th they are back in Urumchi after a successful journey to the Turfan depression. Haslund had started for home the day before, but Haude was at headquarters waiting for a passport for the journey to Bogdo-ula. Then followed the usual tiresome round of social engagements. One morning he wakes up with a splitting headache and fever. Doctors Pedeschenko and Eichtmayr are called in and diagnose typhus. He gets a Russian nurse. In a couple of weeks he is on his feet, but must go slow with work.

Bergman sent word from Bachti that he and his companions had been refused permission to enter Sinkiang. Time after time Ambolt writes to the Governor-General and begs him to sanction their journey. On May the 29th comes the answer:

"By its strange activities the expedition is giving rise on all hands to rumours and unrest, which render it difficult to maintain the peace in the province. Moreover, information concerning the extension has not yet arrived. Thus it is not convenient for Mr. Bergman's party to come here, and when Dr. Hedin arrives later, he will be stopped in the same manner."

Ambolt therefore sent a courier to Dr. Yüan who was usually able to clear up difficult situations.

One day the Prince of the Torguts came on a visit and invited Ambolt to his yurt in the mountains to recover his strength. Mr. McLorn, the Scottish postmaster, tells them that Hummel and I have gone to America on account of my health, and they are uneasy about my fate and that of the expedition.

The staff of the Russian consulate-general showed our people the same kindness as before and helped with the conveyance of their letters. Yüan acted promptly. He dropped all his work and hurried to headquarters by forced marches. There he was received with open arms. He was enraptured about his latest discoveries. He had found remains of dinosaurs in twenty-two places and, in a prehistoric grave, two painted earthenware pots, and human skeletons so fragile that they fell into dust at a touch. The grave had clearly been plundered at some time.

A communication came from the Far East that the government of Nanking had appointed Professor Yüan Inspector of Mines in Sinkiang, an honour which, however, he thought would only render his work in the province more difficult. In answer to the Governor-General's statement that he had not received orders from Nanking, Yüan suggested that they should request the Governor-General to have a telegram sent to the Nanking Government in these terms: "Your telegram not received here. Please send duplicate." The telegram had, however, been sent on March the 13th, when I was in Nanking, and now it was the 8th of June! Haslund wrote from Chuguchak that the Governor of that place had said: "The whole expedition shall leave this province, both Chinese and foreigners. Our people do not wish to see you here any longer." In actual fact the expedition was very popular, partly because we treated everyone kindly, and partly because many got employment through us. A couple of days later the Foreign Commissioner, Chên, called. He told them that instructions had at last arrived from Nanking concerning us, and he believed, therefore, that everything would arrange itself. But when nothing was done and no attention paid to the wishes of our people, Yüan wrote a strongly worded letter to the Governor-General. Presumably as a result of this, the Chief of Police appeared that evening at our house. After four days our people received the Governor-General's answer to this effect: "I have entered with interest into your views and understand that they are concerned with science. I am also willing to help you. But I have not yet had any communication from Nanking and cannot, therefore, give any definite answer. Pray excuse me." Then our telegram was despatched to the Government at Nanking: "Please send copies; no orders received here."

On July the 3rd Yüan visited the Governor-General, who was extremely friendly. "It looks like clearing up. The Governor-General has nothing against us or Professor Yüan, but protests that if Professor Hsü Ping-chang wishes to come back he will be refused permission to do so. Yüan was asked to write a memorandum about those who are waiting at Bachti and expects, and we hope, they will then be allowed to enter."

And so it happened; but the permission came too late. They had already gone to Peking.

"Masses of people are running round here now trying to nose out our affairs. They are conscious, however, of our good relations in the East and wish as far as possible to keep on good terms with us. No imagination can conceive a worse bed of intrigue than Urumchi. One lives in a daily atmosphere of spies, tale-bearing, suspicion and gossip."

On June the 10th the English Colonel Schomberg arrived from India and stayed till July the 4th. "He intends to provide England with a new Afghanistan in Sinkiang," said the Chinese. When, in the spring of 1928, I had asked Governor-General Yang for an aviation permit, and he had refused, Colonel Schomberg was also in Urumchi. Unfortunately I did not meet him. But Ambolt met him, got books, plates and developing materials from him and found him a particularly pleasant and amiable man. He certainly got clear and straightforward answers from Ambolt to his indirect questions, that neither he nor any of the members of the expedition were the bearers of any political secrets. But the Colonel himself was a famous power in the secret service of India. Of course it was a pure accident that our difficulties, both in 1928 and 1929, coincided with the Colonel's visits to Urumchi.

At this time Carlson was taken ill with dysentery and heart spasms and asked Ambolt to greet his wife and children " if anything should happen." Dr. Pedeschenko looked after him with never failing care, and he had an equally vigilant Russian nurse. " The expedition is out of luck just now, it seems. But perhaps the stars will soon change," Ambolt wrote in his diary.

On July the 6th he notes:

" To-day some headmen came in from Turfan and told one of our boys that when we left Turfan we had let the wind loose. It had blown for six days, so that the town was turned upside down. They had reported this outrageous proceeding of ours to the Governor and hoped we would be duly punished. We seem in truth to possess miraculous powers! To-morrow is the anniversary of Yang's death, and there is to be a solemn celebration. Yüan advises us against taking part. It might easily happen that the populace would be egged on by someone to make things unpleasant for us. Although we had nothing to do with Fan's crime, one never knows what an excited mob may be up to. There was no-one in Urumchi who more deeply lamented the former Governor-General's death than we."

On the 8th he writes:

" A secretary, who made a rather disagreeable impression, came to our home and inquired about the newly arrived gentlemen. He explained that they were afraid of Hedin. Previously we had heard that it was Hsü Ping-chang they feared. The secretary told us that a telegram had come from Nanking. Presumably our people are now at Chuguchak. He tried to get us to give a written undertaking to submit to the Governor-General's orders. That was of course impossible. He wished in any event to know our settled routes of travel. So we telegraphed to Norin asking him to enlighten us as to the new members' plans and, if possible, to hasten hither himself.

"In the evening Yüan's collector, Pai, came and was in despair over all the devilry that was going on to get him and his comrades away from their work. Pai had therefore come incognito to Urumchi to get instructions from Yüan. The boy is a very good sport. He has dug out a lot of fossil fish of different kinds and has moreover found a new dinosaurus bed. He led the soldiers who were sent to find out about his work a long detour up the mountains and down the mountains and in the end chipped off and gave them a few plant fossils. They had gone back with these to the Governor and had written a report on the affair."

On July the 22nd the temperature rose to 36·2°. Yüan went off to Bogdo-ula, after having first asked the Governor-General's permission for Major Zimmermann, who was still at Etsin-gol, to travel home by way of Urumchi. This request was refused on the ground of the "prevailing disturbances." In actual fact complete calm prevailed in all Sinkiang. Thanks to the wise government of Marshal Yang, Sinkiang had remained throughout the civil war the most peaceful province in China.

"Every morning a couple of beggars come to our yard singing and merry. They are said to be from the beggar school at Turfan. In this institution the young are taught the tricks of the trade, and if nature has not provided them with suitable deformities, the want is made good at the school. An arm is removed, a foot turned back to front and such like. Ghastly! Wealthy gentlemen, 'bajer,' as they are called, take the beggars into their service, simply buy them and earn money with them. Charming!"

July the 30th. "Our garden is magnificent now. It is full of brilliant flowers. There are tall hollyhocks and sunflowers, mallows, nasturtiums and a mass of others. When I go home one day I shall take seeds of various sorts with me."

In the beginning of August the temperature rose to 38° and remained between 26° and 29° at night.

On August the 1st a telegram came saying that Norin had left Chuguchak for Urumchi, and on the 10th he came,

"bringing instruments and thousands of other jolly things. It was a pleasure to see him here again, full of energy and new plans. One can't expect many such cheery days. Carlson beamed and declared that I did too. Norin also was radiant. The new Wild theodolite was admired. The mercurial barometer was all right. The Paulin altimeter, gramophone records, typewriter tape, camera shutter, etc., etc. And yet he had only half the baggage with him. One of the best things was a wireless licence."

During the days that followed, magnetic observations and time determinations were made. All the instruments were overhauled and, where necessary, repaired. Since all our staff, Swedish and Chinese, were soon to leave headquarters, it was decided to invite Dr. Etches to take over the charge of headquarters and the guardianship of our interests, and this he kindly undertook.

From the Russian Consulate it was learned that visés for Chinese and aliens were no longer given, but that exception could be made for members of the expedition.

Yüan exchanged visits with the Foreign Commissioner, Chên. He has learnt that the expenditure on the army is ten times as great as before and reaches a very considerable amount.

Carlson's nurse Botvina was sent home, " having spread comfort and happiness around her the whole time." In her place appeared the Mongolian Princess, Palta de Torgut.

McLorn is a genuine friend to them, comes often to visit them and always brings wine and other good things. All transfers of money are dealt with through the post office. Mr. Ting, who also is a post office official, and his charming wife are among the expedition's particular friends.

The time has now come to make a start. Pendulums, chronometers and theodolites are carefully packed for transfer on donkeys. Haude put the meteorological equipment in order and, after the students Li and Chao arrived from the meteorological station of Charkhlik, which had now been abandoned in favour of Keriya, the instruments could be further completed. The wireless set which had been taken charge of at the yamên, was not released, but there was another, and the time signals from Nauen were intercepted. Ambolt is consumed with longing to get away, as he hopes, " to destinies and adventures such as it is seldom given to man to experience in this world." Finally the customs examination took place and the passports came.

On the 8th Norin started with a part of the baggage. "Everything seems to be all right between the august ones and us. They bid Hedin welcome back and, according to Burkhan, are keeping a car in readiness at Chuguchak on his account. The air is clearing."

The next day Ambolt followed with five laden donkeys. He had thirty-two cases with him, Norin eighteen. They needed forty camels. At Olabei they made their first camp together. They enjoyed it to the full, and even their servants were glad to be on the road. When Ambolt asked Norin's cook if he was enjoying it, he answered: "Yes, this is the only proper life." They have also two nice dogs, Dangidang and Tien Shan. They put together the excellent collapsible boat and went for a sail on a little lake by the camp. Their first day in the field on this expedition was more than successful. The camp was so near Urumchi that visitors came to call. Then Dr. Haude with letters and Mr. and Mrs. Ting with "yüeh-ping," or moon-cakes, which are eaten all over China on the fifteenth day of the eighth month.

On September the 14th they went on to Aidin-köl, the southern shore of which they followed. Ambolt took soundings in the lake, which was only three metres deep. Besides all the usual labours they also measured the angles to the peaks of Bogdo-ula and began the triangulation. The "station building" and meteorological shed are erected, negatives developed, Nauen is heard clearly, and the boys are set to run the generator so that the accumulators may be well charged—"it is a divine life. The days are warm and at night the temperature falls to + 3° and + 4° and it is glorious in the yurt.

"Fresh air and lovely in every way. We swagger about in our student caps and bubble with excitement. Scarcely any privations to speak of."

Sometimes he can have five hours' sleep to fifty-four working hours. "It is a pleasure to be able to state that the yurt with its inner tent serves for the pendulum."

During the night a temperature-constant to a hundredth part of a degree prevails, and the yurt is as good as a room. They make a base measurement with Invar-tape both for their own work and for determining the temperature-expansion coefficient of Yüan's measuring tape.

"Only one thing is tiresome, September the 29th. Erik (Norin) came upon Lao Chang lying and smoking opium. The boy has been splendid. But up in the glen he was taken ill. Pains in the stomach. That is the usual consequence when a smoker does not get his opium. We cannot very well keep him. He might become prostrate and delay us. Annoying! He was one of our best servants. This kind of thing makes one miserable. To-day after dinner Erik and I went for a little row on the lake. On our way back we saw a sandstorm approaching at furious speed. We had to pull all we knew to get in. The wind velocity jumped up to eighteen second-metres.

"Have made a tip-top astronomical programme. If it only gets to being carried out it will be fine. This point is on the whole first class. Erik's map is a pleasure to the eye, and when he gets his geological observations entered it will certainly be something out of the common. Where is Hedin now? We are frightfully anxious about letters. Presumably a courier is coming the day after to-morrow. I am sitting waiting for the wireless signals which come at 12 o'clock. Everything seems to be all right now.

"Erik and I are inspired by the same interest in the work. It is an uncommon bit of luck to have interests which run so close together without, on that account, competing with each other. And at the same time one learns a lot of things which are both useful and amusing. We made a graph of the variations of wind force extending over an hour and showing wave-like variations from six to fifteen second-metres. Thrilling but rather trying."

On October the 2nd Norin assists with the fixed-point-determination.

"It was even more delightful than I had expected to work with him as helper. It would be fine if I could train Vorotnikov as assistant.

"October the 4th. In the evening we had thought of making an azimuth determination of the base line, but it persisted in going altogether wrong. It was dark when we set out, and Erik walked into the thick of it. He had the ill luck to go straight towards one of the steep precipitous ravines. He stepped right into the air and fell headlong with the Wild theodolite in his hand. My heart came into my mouth. The least bit more of a drop and he might have broken his neck. As it was he got off with a hole in his breeches and a scratch on the knee. And, wonder of wonders, it looks as if the instrument has escaped damage!"

On the 5th Vorotnikov arrived after having gone through the usual difficulties in getting his passport. A few days later they go over a pass about 2,000 metres above sea level. Ambolt has never been at so great a height before. One camel succumbs and six are ill. Magnetic and astronomical determinations are made at Kichik-agis-bashi.

Storm at the rate of 22·5 second-metres. It is necessary to load the animals carefully, for they may be blown over, which would be dangerous to the pendulums. One of the tents ripped.

Kuruk-tagh is in sight.

"It looks as though we shall succeed in doing great things together. And I am glad to see our field of labour at closer range. Shall try to make a magnetic chart which should be interesting. So by degrees there will come to be a pretty good monograph on these mountains. With Erik's splendid topography and geology as groundwork, gravity and magnetism, and with the subsoil water levels inserted, the whole thing is going to be something superfine. We are also planning a sheet to the scale of 1 : 500,000 of the whole route which may be very interesting. To-day we are going towards the lower tracts in one part of the Turfan depression, and it will be blazing hot."

On October the 12th, at the camp at Shor-bulak, Norin

"found many remarkable geological features, and his map is really splendid. Yesterday another camel died. Tragic!

"Here we are almost three hundred metres above sea level. Vorotnikov assisted me splendidly with the work yesterday and last night. He is a great acquisition and a nice boy to have to do with, practical, methodical and cheerful. I have every reason to be satisfied. Our camp, No. 8, Katlik, is a big place with much grass. We are pretty nearly at sea level."

On the 13th they are at an absolute elevation of — 7 metres, that is to say 7 metres below sea level. The temperature is 15° at 10 a.m. They continue their scientific work at Bar-bulak and Su-bashi.

Then their course lies upward again, and on the 15th they are once more 1,100 metres above sea level. "Our work here is going to be first class; I see that now. We have really every reason to be thankful to have been put in a position to do all this." Of his latitudes he says that they are very exact. "That makes our work all the more valuable. I estimate the margin of error of our still only approximate determinations at between 0·1 and 0·2 kilometres and expect soon to have it down to 0·05 to 0·08, and one can hardly ask for more. Norin's map accords precisely with the fixed-point-determinations."

On the way to Shor-bulak they took turns with the measuring wheel. "Here is a great station with work of all kinds." The instruments are again unpacked and mounted. It is beginning to grow cold. At night the washing water freezes. At midday it is roasting hot. A first-rate fixed-point-determination is made. The wireless is working brilliantly. Vorotnikov is excellent, willing, capable and energetic.

Again and again he glories in the co-operation with Norin.

> "Not only practically but also in theoretical respects I increase my efficiency in all sorts of ways, and the geological lessons are a joy. I already look at the country with quite different eyes and now have quite other qualifications for my own job. We intend to make a trigonometric connexion all through our field of work here. It is fortunate that we get very exact elevations for we can thus make better use of the meteorological material. Here we have now a regular little town around us, a first-rate camp among the tamarisks. The grazing is good, and so is the water. Of antelopes we have only seen the tracks here. Ottehong has caught a young eagle. All goes well. The chief ought to come and see us here."

On the 20th Sabitov and Ottehong are sent to Qara

Shahr to buy camels. Colour-plates are developed and are successful. On an off day the observations are worked out. "The signals come through finely, and now I carry on all night. Every pendulum value I enter in the journal is a new joy. It has been a great success keeping the temperature constant."

The distillation apparatus for the thermohypsometer was set up. "Erik toils all day and every day at his map and is pleased with it. He correctly conjures forth the contours of the landscape. He has become an enthusiast for astronomical fixed-point-determination. His Wild theodolite is the very thing for rapid determinations, at least of longitude and azimuth."

Vorotnikov is studying Neymayer's textbook and is much interested. He is only twenty-four. "He looks after the meteorology in our expedition and seconds me in every possible way. He is an excellent lad, of good moral character, with a highly developed sense of exactitude, order and neatness. Moreover he is very clever with his hands." Ambolt cannot sufficiently praise the young Russian, who had served under both Hummel and Haude.

On the 29th a courier comes in from Urumchi. Rapture! "On such a day one feels really happy." They have got two new radiation thermometers and a wind-gauge. "Our equipment grows better and better. How glad I shall be on the day when I hold the new large Wild theodolite in my hands. Oh, it is so jolly here! And on a day when the post comes in one is as happy as a child. Erik has made a tip-top map here, and I a first-rate station. Hurrah!"

On November the 1st the courier is sent back with twenty letters. In the evening the gramophone is set going. "It is quite unbelievable how nationalistic one becomes out here. One loves regimental marches and that sort of thing passionately."

Next morning the mercurial barometer gets a fatal shock. On the 6th they do not forget the anniversary of the death and victory of Gustavus Adolphus; *moriens triumphavit*. On the evening of the 8th, magnetic declination and azimuth with Polaris. And on that a new pendulation is begun. At Arpishme-bulak, on the 12th, they have salt water. They try to repair the mercurial barometer and work at it for eight hours. Sabitov comes in with fifteen new camels. During the following days new base measurements and pendulum series.

November the 18th.

> "Parents' wedding day. Flew the large flag. Erik found a splendid fossil bed, corals and bivalves. He says it is his best day in 1929. I carried on with the accumulators, made a determination of the variation of the magnetic declination, distilled water, made up my mind as to the great part played by the solar parallax in the magnetic measurements and attended to a lot of repairs. The tool-box was in full use. The wireless apparatus has already provided much enlightenment. If only the valves hold out! I shall soon have to renew a lot of my equipment. Turfan has taken it out of all the gear. In the evening a toast to Mother and Father, Norin, Alma and the Chief. We really had cause to be happy. A packet of newspapers was produced as a prize."

A few days later Norin discovers five new lots of fossils and an ancient ruin. Ambolt too found a fossil bed. They are also busy with photographic mensuration and take a couple of dozen plates. The map grows. They now have ten and twelve degrees of frost at night, and on the 26th the first snow falls. At $-15°$ they are glad of a fire. A magnetic observation becomes difficult when the fingers freeze fast to the instrument. They have to go in and warm their hands at the fire after each series. Vorotnikov always stays behind at the old camp and takes observations by which the elevation values are increased by twenty-five to fifty per cent. They have fifty camels and march in double caravans. At Suksuk-bulak the grazing is good. At Tunkusluk, "the region of wild pig," they have twenty-five degrees of frost inside the tent on the morning of December the 2nd and eighteen after the fire was lighted.

On December the 7th they march to Pu-chêng-tzŭ and meet Abd-ur-Rahim. Here they live in the house of Kerim Bai and can resume the development of their plates. Then they go on to Yettim-bulak and Ran-köl and, by separate roads, to Shindi, where they get a splendid room in Abd-ur-Rahim's house and are regaled with mutton, eggs, partridges, melons and milk. The work follows its usual course, and Ambolt gets brilliant fixed-point-determinations.

And then it was Christmas again. Ambolt made burnt almonds and baked sweetmeats according to recipes he had from his sister Anna. He made branched candlesticks and a Christmas tree out of poplar twigs. The family portraits were set out. But the work went on as usual. Among the Christmas presents were cigarettes, notebooks, mittens and other useful articles. Vorotnikov got a field-glass, Sabitov a silver watch. The latter presented a goose, the former a compass and a whistle. The Christmas table was spread with smoked sturgeon, pickled herring, sardines and hardbread, and there were soup, goose, mushroom omelet and cake. The gramophone played Christmas tunes, and the four men danced round the Christmas tree. Abd-ur-Rahim's room was decorated as never before. On the morning of Christmas Day the gramophone sang the Christmas hymn.

That is as much of Ambolt's diary as has come into my hands.

But he has also sent me his annual report for 1929. This is altogether too scientific to be of interest except to experts. Two points only may be quoted from his pendulum observations. He succeeded in reducing the combined oscillation of the tripod and pillar to a normal amount or about *fifty ten-millionths of a second.* "For determinations of time I used completely modern, one may really say hyper-modern dispositions of apparatus according to suggestions made to me by the gentlemen at the Geodetic Institute of Potsdam." He fixed three stations in the Turfan depression, Turfan, Kosh-dung and Su-bashi. "With Norin's arrival an immensely more effective work begins, rendered possible by common interests and, especially for me, by his great geological and topographical knowledge." The gravity was determined at Ainak-köl, Shor-bulak and Arpishme-bulak. The magnetic declinations have been ascertained at practically all camps. Moreover, the routes wherever possible were fixed by azimuths and determinations of polar elevation.

The network of pendulum stations which is now complete embraces three great geological formations, the Turfan depression, the Daban-chêng depression and the extended Shormak depression from Shor-bulak eastward to Arpishme-bulak and beyond. They are three similar phases in development in different longitudes. These stations are certainly very interesting from both the geodetic and the geological points of view. The Turfan depression has indeed from of old been a desired goal of everyone occupied with pendulum determinations, and the other two depressions are not likely to be far behind in interest, particularly regarded in connexion with the first. To get the elevations as exactly determined as possible is a problem of the greatest importance as well for topographical as for geological work, and for the solution of this problem this part of our expedition had at its disposal a complete meteorological station installed for us by Dr. Haude.

It would occupy too much space to give here extracts from Ambolt's private letters to me. They are full of sparkling life and the joy of living. Occasionally he is not quite pleased when instruments give trouble or when something is completely smashed. He complains that the Chinese students have left their meteorological station, and it is a poor consolation to him that we hope to get a fresh supply of students before long. But everything moves slowly in China, and it takes time to get trained observers from China proper to Central Asia.

He sends me at Stockholm a list of wants, of twenty-five items—this in the last letter I have received dated from Mo-chia-hutuk, January the 3rd, 1930. It concerns chronometers, Invar pendulums, whose sensitiveness to variations of temperature is a fraction of that of those he has been using hitherto, and other instruments representing thousands of crowns in value, but absolutely necessary for the highest degree of accuracy in the observations. It is not easy to get them out to Central Asia. But we know that in Consul Grosskopf at Novo-Sibirsk we have an untiring friend, and he has promised to help us this time too.

He tells me in the letter that he has got yet another main station determined at Mo-chia-hutuk. The astronomical fixed-point-determination he has carried out there is the best of all. He concludes with the words:

> "I cannot lay down any definite results of my work; they are all dependent upon factors which can only be determined at home and must be calculated by long-continued work at the writing table. Preliminary calculations have, however, shown that the agreement between topographical and astronomical work is remarkable and, when the definitive values are available, looks like being brilliant. In all my astronomical determinations I have had invaluable help from Norin. I hope the results that have been gained will be of use to him and thus give him some equivalent for what he has done for me."

On January the 20th Ambolt writes:

> "Erik has now gone a bit up into the mountains to connect up the network we have laid down here with his former observations around Bagrash-köl on Qara Shahr. We are anxiously awaiting a letter from Urumchi to settle the extension of our passports. We have only permission to work here till February the first, but hope there will be no difficulty about the extension."

And with that I must for this time leave the young astronomer, just thirty years old this 1st of April, to the stars of night and the measured oscillations of the Invar pendulum. He is a credit to our expedition and we are fortunate to have him on our staff. I am convinced that the work which he is now carrying out so conscientiously and with such enthusiasm will make his name famous throughout the scientific world, and that his results, when they have been worked out, will be referred to in all geodetic, geophysical and geological text-books. For he is the first to carry out such delicate researches in tracts which in these respects are the most interesting on earth. It is in Asia that we find the deepest depressions in the earth's firm crust, as also the highest mountains and the mightiest uplands. There we find the greatest deserts and the most extensive depressions, compared by Arrhenius to the conditions on the surface of Mars.

When such a man as Dr. Nils Ambolt requisitions new instruments so delicate that they must be sent to him by special messenger and so costly as to make a serious hole in the expedition's funds, I simply cannot refuse to send him both instruments and messengers, in the conviction that if our means do not suffice to carry his work to a glorious conclusion, then our country, or individual Swedes, will give us all the support required.

XXII

BERGMAN'S ARCHÆOLOGICAL RESEARCHES

DURING the spring, summer and autumn of 1928 Folke Bergman and our Danish member, Lieutenant Henning Haslund, have undertaken a fruitful and satisfactory journey of 1,800 miles. Like Norin they had their headquarters at Shindi in Kuruk-tagh, and their route led thence by Tikenlik and Charkhlik, then up in the border mountains of Northern Tibet to my former headquarters at Temirlik (1900) and on to the source of Cherchen-darya, Cherchen and Charkhlik. Here Haslund fell sick and was obliged hurriedly to seek out Hummel at Urumchi, while Bergman betook himself to Miran, a place situated to the south of Lake Kara-koshun, discovered by Prjevalsky in 1877 and visited by me in 1896, and now dried up.

Bergman made a map of the whole route, which received very high commendation from the expert Norin. In several places he made neolithic and historical discoveries, but he is not himself satisfied with this part of his results. I suspect, however, that it may be of a certain interest to know that the southern portion of the Lop Nor basin was only to a small extent visited and inhabited by the people of the stone age. In Tibet their traces are probably completely wanting. By negative observation one may define their wanderings and dwelling places. However, during the greater part of his journey, Bergman obtained abundant results even in archæology.

Meanwhile, Haslund carried out 135 anthropometric measurements of Mongols, Lopliks, East Turks and Tibetans. During the six months they were out together they kept diaries, took 300 photographs and made respectable progress in the East Turki language.

Here follow some extracts from a letter of Bergman's

dated from Miran Kona-shahr or " the old town by Miran," September the 6th, to the 10th.

" It was not with a very easy mind that I parted from Haslund, seeing that he was a sick man and had to make the long ride with practically no outfit. I need not say that he left an immense void behind him. All through our long journey he has been an ideal companion. He has managed the caravan like an artist. Of the twenty starved, worn-out camels that left Turfan I have now sixteen well-fed powerful animals with me. The four which have made the whole journey are now at Charkhlik and are to be taken up to Shindi by one of my men so soon as the grass begins to lose its food value from the frost. Thus they too will get a thorough rest and be able to put on a bit of flesh.

" There was really nothing to take me up into the mountains, and my conscience was in fact reproaching me with having run away from the heat in my proper field of labour. It was therefore a real relief to me to receive your letter urging me to set my course up among the mountains. Of course I have never been idle. My days have been constantly filled with work, but I have accomplished nothing positive in the way of archæology during the mountain tour.

" It was not until we reached Cherchen that a digging site at last turned up, and at that town I raked together a whole lot of things from the Kona-shahr. I even succeeded in coming across my first painted burial urn from the stone age, but alas it was not by excavation but by purchase. It is of an extraordinarily elegant shape and the painting is finer than on those formerly found in China and is possibly unique in pattern. In spite of prolonged and persistent search, the place where it was discovered could not, however, be found again.

" In the Kona-shahr of Vash-shari, as here in Miran, I have also picked up a mass of things from historical times, of more or less value. My present plan is to make my way by Merdek to the district of Korla-Kara-shahr where I am certain to get a great deal.

" At the ruins at Miran I was visited by a number of the people of the district headed by the 'aksakal,' the village elder. Among them was your old servant Tokhta Ahun, formerly settled at Abdul, but, after that place had to be abandoned, at Miranbo. He was a grey-haired man with gentle smiling, kindly eyes. He asked whether you were not coming back here. He is not the first of your old men we have met with. It is always pleasant to meet them, for it is like falling in with old acquaintances."

Owing to pains in the neck Bergman rode back to Charkhlik where Haude was then living. On the way, the camels broke out in revolt and threw off their loads, a sign that they were really feeling fit. Haude was expecting new balloons which we had sent from Urumchi, and everything at the station was in the best of order. The student Li was up at the mountain station.

After that there was an interval of six weeks before the next letter came, dated Shindi, November the 1st.

"The day before yesterday I burst into Norin's camp and gave him a regular shock. He was not in fact expecting me. It was quite a chance encounter, for he had only arrived there an hour earlier. I need not say that it was awfully jolly to see him again. That evening was the most festive occasion in my whole journey, for it was then that I discovered that all my drudgery up in Tibet had not been entirely in vain. In my moments of gloom I had in fact thought so, and was annoyed and dissatisfied with myself for having travelled so far, taken with me a lot of valuable camels to no purpose, and put you to the expense of my many servants, all without making any but the most infinitesimal archæological finds. Norin was also delighted with my study of the drying-up process in the lower Tarim, which indeed is on the wrong side, so to speak, of the new river.

"It is now becoming colossally interesting to explore with Norin the shore line round his quaternary lake. In a day or two we are going to share the investigation of some of the graves he has found in the mountains here, and I shall also examine the rock carvings here, hitherto unique of their kind.

"On the way here from Korla, where I mapped a new crossing from Konche-darya over Suget-bulak (where you once were), and up to Norin's road across the mountains, I made a most valuable discovery. I found in the Suget-bulak valley the ruins of a fortress which have never been seen by a white man. A skull from a grave close by may possibly furnish an answer to the question what people built the pretty substantial stone building, and a couple of small bronze objects may well, in due time, throw light upon the important chronological question.

"All these different finds, taken together, show that the mountains here possess a hitherto unsuspected interest for an archæologist, and it will be my task during the next campaign to solve the problems involved. But I hope to be able now to make a preliminary survey as well as to get some more definite indications than those which my present calculations of probability afford. Thus much I can say with certainty: the newly discovered fortress marks a hitherto unknown ancient main road.

"The investigation of the stone-age finds in the ancient shore line comes then as a conclusion of this season's work. I have a feeling that this is going to be the climax of this year's efforts.

"Yes, here we sit, Norin and I, in the big tent that we have not lived in together for nine months. We are having a delightful time, in a degree of comfort which seems fabulous to me. A lamp which lights up the whole tent and a fine stove. That kind of lamp from B. A. Hjorth & Co. was really a find on which I congratulate you."

On the work which he has so far carried out in 1927 and 1928, Bergman has sent me a report of which I give the following brief extracts.

On the way from Beli-miao to Shande-miao in Mongolia he discovered and investigated 103 sites with remains of stone-age settlements. In all 11,807 objects were found of which 1,674 were from the most productive places. Six of the sites were mapped on a large scale. Most of them are situated in the intervening space between mountain and steppe, beside rivers and wells. The district is rich in graves of pre-lamaistic times, marked above ground by rectangular or circular cromlechs, often beautifully built. The upright stones are reminiscent of the Nordic menhirs. Two stones were furnished with incised human faces. A couple of the graves that were excavated produced no finds.

Near Shande-miao a fortress-like building was discovered which, from ceramics found there, is judged to belong to the time of the Han dynasty.

On the way from Shande-miao to Etsin-gol, Bergman discovered nineteen prehistoric dwelling-places with altogether 5,984 objects of which 1,959 were found in the richest places. The prehistoric remains are to be found

Ferry across the Konche-darya opposite Yü-li-hsien

Bergman Photo

[*face p.* 290

Bergman Photo

Pools in the Tarim by Camp 233

[*face p.* 291

near the rare water places and especially in the basalt regions where material was available for making tools. That the harvest has been more meagre than in the first part of the journey is due to the less favourable natural conditions which prevailed in ancient times also.

The way from Etsin-gol to the boundary of Sinkiang yielded only seven stone-age dwelling-places and 742 objects. Here he was traversing completely sterile desert. Remains from historic times were entirely wanting.

The prehistoric buildings thus became less frequent towards the west and finally ceased.

> "The material found consisted for the most part of the usual small tools of flint, quartz, chalcedony and similar kinds of stone. One type common to practically all localities is that of the small thin chips that were used as knife edges. Otherwise there are cores, scrapers, 'coup-de-points,' arrowheads and spearheads, axes and axe-like tools of greenstone. As finely polished as implements only roughly cut can be, too, although not to the same extent as the flints mentioned above. A few handmills of granite have also been met with. The ceramics, when they occur, are nearly always unornamented and of pretty coarse stuff. In exceptional places ornamented fragments of pottery were found, and, still more rarely, some painting. The peoples who supported the civilization of polychromatic ceramics and who were settled and agricultural did not have the same chance to exist in Mongolia with its relatively poor soil and inadequate water supply as on the alluvial soils round the great rivers of the south in what are now the agricultural districts. Most of the relics discovered may be taken as vestiges of a nomadic population who moved from one place to another according to the incidence of adequate grazing. This also explains the absence of definite successive deposits on these sites.
>
> "The fairly uniform types of relics of antiquity are allied to those encountered by the Andrews expedition of 1925 in Northern Mongolia and also to those occurring in Kansu and Honan.
>
> "An insignificant number of small bronzes belonging to the Scythio-Siberian civilization has also been met with."

On the way from the eastern boundary of Sinkiang to Urumchi they had no chance to work freely, and consequently Bergman found only 155 objects at two places, almost exclusively painted pottery fragments.

In the Lop Nor region he was not able to work much owing to the heat, but made nevertheless a number of very interesting collections from historic excavation sites.

Eight sites belonging to prehistoric times were discovered and investigated. . . . The richest lay by Singer in Kuruk-tagh, where 829 objects were gathered. . . . In all 1,510 objects were found. Six sites are dwelling-places, and two others burial-places, with painted ceramics. The material found in the dwelling-places follows in part the Mongolian types, but there are small divergencies in certain details.

The painted ceramics belong to the same family as those familiar from Kansu and Honan, although the complete urn acquired at Cherchen in particular shows a form differing from those hitherto known and also a dissimilar arrangement of the pattern. This urn, which according to report was found in Cherchen's "Kona-shahr," is of particularly great importance, since it is the first complete painted stone-age earthenware vessel from Sinkiang.

The excavations at Cherchen, Vash-shari and Miran were visited and Bergman also discovered inconsiderable vestiges of an older settlement in a previously overlooked spot in the Charkhlik oasis.

> "At all these places investigations were carried out which produced finds of pottery fragments, shuttles, wooden combs, pearls, articles of bronze and stone, bits of glass and suchlike things. In the very extensive Kona-shahr of Charkhlik the excavation of several graves was undertaken, of which two contained complete earthenware vessels. At Miran, also, graves containing well-preserved skeletons were excavated, covered with hollowed-out tree-trunks. The only object of antiquity met with was an earring of bronze. One complete skeleton was taken and the skulls from the other graves. A couple of skulls were taken from two Mohammedan graves at Ying-pên on Kuruk-darya and a piece of paper with Turkish script from one of them. From this place comes a fine bronze mirror. . . ."

In Kuruk-tagh Bergman, as already mentioned, discovered a ruined fortress as well as graves and bronze objects.

> "Immediately south of Shindi was discovered a very extensive and interesting rock-carving with hundreds of beasts and human figures. It has been produced during different, probably pretty widely separated times. The most recent part may be taken to be of no considerable antiquity. I cannot yet say anything definitely as to the antiquity of its oldest part."

When, on December the 17th, 1928, Bergman left Urumchi to travel with Hsü Ping-chang, Hummel and me to Novo-Sibirsk and thence alone to Stockholm, he had laid the foundation of a very comprehensive study of the stone age in Central Asia. In the districts in which he worked he had been the first of his profession. He had collected over 18,000 objects from nearly 150 sites, and of several of these he had made sketch maps to a scale of 1 : 1,000 and 1 : 5,000. From the distribution and frequency of the sites he had drawn the conclusion that the climate has not altered in any essential degree during four or five thousand years. In North-Eastern Tibet he executed a map of about 300 sheets.

I had given Bergman a couple of months leave in Stockholm, a time which he employed in a way profitable to his coming work in the field. On April the 8th he left Stockholm and joined Hörner, Bexell and Norin in Berlin. On the 20th Bergman, Hörner and Bexell went on, after making large purchases of instruments from Agfa and Fuess, to Moscow, where Lundberg, the Secretary of Legation, was of invaluable assistance to them.

At Semipalatinsk they felt themselves rather at a loss at the Customs, but ultimately found a young Austrian ex-prisoner of war, who helped them. They also met the Swedish engineer, Rollin, and our old friend, the railway engineer, Hartstein, who put them under the protection of the Geographical Society. No motor-cars were to be had. But they were invited to make the journey to Sergiopol in a goods van in which, on the evening of April the 29th, they stowed themselves and their 1,400 kilogrammes of baggage. Their hope of being soon coupled to a goods train was, however, disappointed. For three whole days and nights they were shunted in the van over every conceivable track, and were only left stationary during the May Day celebrations when the new bridge over the Irtish was being inaugurated. " The Geographical Society evidently means to give us a thorough knowledge of the topography of the goods yard." The German doctor attached to the railway telegraphed to Sergiopol, and when they arrived there on May the 4th, they found a lorry at their disposal.

Owing to the wretched state of the road, it took them three days to get to Bachti. The consul at Chuguchak at once came to their aid. They were held up at the Chinese frontier. No one, not even Chinese, was let through without direct permission from Urumchi. The Mongol Princess Palta de Torgut had also been detained three days at the frontier. " The next day we all went on to Chuguchak and put up with our friend Hochriekov. Governor Li had been dismissed, probably on the ground of his friendliness to us." They paid visits to his successor, the Foreign Commissioner and the Mayor. The reply from Urumchi was expected within three days.

> " On the third day a bus came driving into the yard. In it sat the Foreign Commissioner. The Governor-General's reply had not yet arrived, but the Governor of Chuguchak had heard through people from Urumchi that our expedition was in the habit of digging up old family graves and committing other malpractices, which annoyed the people and made them ill-disposed towards us. In such circumstances the Governor dared no longer take the responsibility for allowing us to remain in Chuguchak, but must request us to return to the frontier where everything should be arranged for us as soon as possible. In three or four days everything would doubtless be cleared up and we would then be welcome to return. The whole situation was so ludicrous that we roared with laughter. However we had to submit. They had orders from the Governor-General."

Having obtained new stamps on their passports from the friendly Consul, they drove back to the frontier.

> " At the Chinese custom-house we were witnesses of a ghastly tragedy just enacted. At the end of the little street

lay the body of a man. He was a Russian from Urumchi and had evidently been shot.

"The Chinese at Chuguchak professed to know nothing about the concessions you had obtained in Peking and Nanking. The time specified in our contract had come to an end, and until fresh instructions were received we could not travel in Sinkiang. It is clearly a subterfuge."

As I have already related, the Nanking Government's categorical telegraphic orders as to our complete freedom to travel and work in Sinkiang had been despatched on March the 13th.

Meanwhile, they had to wait at Bachti. On June the 12th they had a telegram from Norin and Bohlin who were then at Semipalatinsk. When they arrived the great campaign for entering Sinkiang would begin. "If we do not succeed, I am very keen on going to Ordos and certain districts of Inner Mongolia in which we were the first summer, districts which may give me much more easily accessible results than Sinkiang, but of course I do not give up that province without an effort."

Bergman's next letter was written at Semipalatinsk on July the 23rd. He is on his way to Vladivostok. One can understand that his patience had been sorely tried.

We may pass over the next three months. I have already described our meeting at Beli-miao in the beginning of November, 1929. On November the 11th we said farewell and watched the great caravan winding westward into the Gobi Desert.

Since then I have again and again had the pleasure of receiving letters from Bergman, usually conveyed to Kuei-hua-ch'êng by passing caravans. The first is from Camp No. 8, Ulan-bulak, and written on November the 23rd. They have already had a temperature of — 28·4°. He thanks me for having come to see them off.

"Another thing I have to thank you for is Johansen. He is a find, and is especially invaluable to me, because now I do not have to think about the servants and animals, but can devote all my time to my own work. So far everything in the caravan has gone with admirable precision. The camels have not so much as attempted to make trouble and everything else has functioned satisfactorily."

He gives an account of the work of the other members and tells of one of " these Chinese walls which have begun more and more to capture my interest."

After a couple of days they met Major Zimmermann, who was " touchingly kind and friendly," and gave them all he could spare of his provisions as well as a son of our favourite dog Hami, " the very picture of his father."

The Major brought with him their collections up to that time and several letters.

Bergman had found " a whole lot of neolithic sites," and carries out the meteorological observations, assisted by Bohlin.

After they had left the valley of Chogungtai-gol behind them, the caravan is divided into two groups. A trading caravan brings a letter of November the 28th from Haileotai-gol, Camp No. 12. Bohlin, Hörner and Bexell travel in one group, the rest in another.

> " To-day I visited one of my old diggings about fifteen li east of this place, which I found in 1927. It yielded rich and fine results then, but to-day I ascertained that the deposit was considerably more extensive, and in three hours I and my young collector gathered at least a thousand flint implements, many of which are extraordinarily fine. I have not yet had time to sort them, so great heaps of flints are lying round me."

On their next division Hörner and Bergman are to form the flying column. They work on parallel lines exactly as we did in 1927, and they have an excellent framework in Norin's masterly maps. He only complains of the shortness of the winter days and of the frozen ground.

" Once more I want to thank you for Johansen, the splendid Dane, who relieves me of all drudgery with the caravan. Mr. Chên is an uncommonly considerate and pleasant travelling companion, who does all he can to be useful. We really had great luck in getting him."

Teben-tologoi, Camp No. 15, December the 13th. He has just, in a letter from me, had the sad news of the death of his little son.

At Haileotai-gol the marks of our tents were still clearly visible on the ground, although two and a half years have passed with all their storms, their rain and their snow. The geologists have just returned from an "extraordinarily successful excursion to the Huang Ho. They also brought me a lot of jolly finds from ten stone-age dwelling-places as well as fragments of pottery from a watch tower on a remarkable Chinese wall—God knows how many such there are!"

He made an excursion with Bohlin northward to some interesting basalt rocks by two small lakes, where there were masses of stone articles. At Camp No. 15 Bexell discovers a bed of plant fossils. Bergman's own collections increase "at an alarming rate, for I scarcely get time to catalogue and pack them, and they are also becoming very heavy now that I have begun to find many much larger implements. At present almost summer weather prevails, and the night temperature does not fall below − 15°." Bohlin's maps are a delight to the eye. All the three rivers, Chogungtai-gol, Haileotai-gol and Honger-gol, flow separately into the Huang Ho without previously uniting as had been supposed. They are still within the drainage area of the Pacific Ocean.

Man-huei-t'ang, January the 8th, 1930. The place is a Belgian mission station. They had had snowstorms and frightful cold in the middle of December. They all kept on getting frost-bitten. Hörner froze two fingers of his right hand, which incapacitated him for work right up to the New Year. The snow was a great hindrance to all field work. They celebrated their desert Christmas together, after which Bohlin and Bexell made an excursion to the north and joined Johansen and Chên at Khara-tologoi. On December the 30th Bergman and Hörner travelled towards the south-east, past Lang-shan by a new route to Hoyer-bogdo. On January the 6th they reached the mission station, which lies fifteen or twenty li to the south of the northern dry bed of the Huang Ho. It was 850 metres above sea level. There too snow was lying. On the night of January the 6th the temperature dropped to − 40·9°, "which is something of a record." They are right in the middle of a bandit district, but have had no trouble except with the Mongolian soldiers guarding the Lang-shan line. "Hörner was shot at and pursued the other day." He had the luck to get clear, but the bullets whistled round his ears.

Hörner found plant fossils, and Bergman a tombstone with incised figures of animals, "an extraordinarily important find."

All instruments, watches, photographic apparatus and fountain pens suffer from the cold. Bohlin has a thermometer that goes down to − 80°, and Bergman hopes that will suffice. "For the rest, we are getting along splendidly. Hörner's fingers, though crooked and unsightly, are well on the way to recovery, and I do not think he will lose the use of them."

To everyone's grief the new dog, Hami, has run away.

On January the 23rd a cheery letter came from Khara-tologoi, brought by a passing caravan. On the way back from Man-huei, Hörner has another serious adventure. He was set upon by insolent Mongol soldiers, shot at and robbed of all his things, "which, however, our excellent Mongol cook later succeeded in recovering." Their excursion lasted three weeks and was very successful in spite of the snow. Among other things Bergman found a fine rock carving. At Shande-miao, which they reached on January the 17th, they heard that Bohlin and Bexell were still at work north-east of Khara-tologoi and that Johansen had found a great quantity of stone implements there. Hörner then went back to the dangerous Lang-shan to explore a little drained lake in a gorge, while Bergman travelled eastward.

> "The fossils Bohlin found north of Dalain-obo are probably something unique, for he does not even know himself what kind of animal they are. The tent here is full of parcels of bones, teeth and masses of large bones of one and the same kind. The locality seems to be inexhaustible. I have occupation for some time with the sites Johansen found. The material looks very interesting and is unlike all I have hitherto. There is a palæolithic feeling in the air."

The letter concludes with the words: "We are feeling splendid and kicking up our heels over our fine discoveries."

From Tebeh, Camp No. 23, I received a long letter of February the 12th and 14th. It deals chiefly with questions of organization and new plans. "Dondur-gun, the Mongol Prince, seems to have nothing against the excavations. Several of his officials have ridden past without forbidding us to root in the earth. We have not once been requested to clear out of the province, as happened to both Norin and Yüan last time."

Bohlin has found such masses of fossils that they have decided to send Johansen back to Beli-miao with seven fully-laden camels so as not to have to drag these heavy weights with them to the west. Bergman considers that it will pay to run a car to and fro between Kuei-hua and the excavation site.

> "Bohlin and Bexell as well as Chang deserve special recognition for their work here and at Ulan Chönch, for scarcely ever have similar excavations been carried out under more adverse weather conditions. The Mongolian winter is, as you know, not to be played with, and to lie out day after day chiselling fragile fossils out of frozen sandstone, in the severest cold, is really admirable. There is nothing wrong with the camels, though they have of course begun to lose a lot of their fat. We have lost two dogs but have got a most entrancing cat instead."

The last letter which has this moment (May the 2nd) reached me from Bergman, is written at Camp No. 40, Otakhoi (see *Across the Gobi Desert*, p. 159), on March the 22nd. The first transport column from Sinkiang conveying a part of the expedition's collections in ninety cases and led by the collector Chin, arrived that day at Camp No. 40. Bergman sent a letter by Chin.

> "We are well, we have come successfully through the severe winter and we are now rejoicing in summer warmth and in the fact that each of us in his department is daily making new and valuable observations. Bohlin, Bexell and I have been here by the mighty triple peak since the 7th, while Hörner, Chên and the main caravan are at Olon-toroi. We three have plenty to do here for as long as we can hold out in this barren desert tract, and Hörner is glad to have this time for the study of the drift sand. We have already had one regular sandstorm since

we came here, and to-day the dust is flying again, driving through the tent cover and covering everything within it horribly. Johansen may be here any time now, and when he comes, we start for Etsin-gol. I do not now much believe in our chance of seeing you in Su-chou, but we can always get letters from you, and even that will be very pleasant.

"Bohlin is writing about his finds here. I myself have been so overwhelmed with flint implements in this district that soon I shall not know what to do with them. This is perhaps the most interesting and most productive territory I have been in.

"I would have liked to keep Chin, but he is responsible for all the great collections and for their safe arrival at Kuei-hua.

"This letter is only to let you know we are alive, but you may be confident that our work goes forward, even if we ourselves do not get very far west. We have nothing to complain of and our spirits are splendid."

I am not an archæologist, but I nevertheless believe myself able to predict that Folke Bergman's researches among the vestiges of the people of the stone age in Inner Asia are going to carry one of the most gigantic and important problems of archæology a long step forward. His inflexible energy, his imperturbable calm, his substantial knowledge and his wonderful patience when obstacles arise in his way, are qualities which should carry him forward all the way to the great goal.

XXIII

HAUDE'S METEOROLOGICAL OBSERVATIONS

SINCE meteorology is one of the most important of our expedition's spheres of activity, I will now give some extracts from the report of our German meteorologist, Dr. Waldemar Haude, upon the work so far accomplished.

He says that the groundwork of these observations consists in the hourly readings from 7 a.m. to 9 p.m. and in the more exhaustive observations at 7, 2 and 9.

At the hourly observations only the direction and force of the wind, the variations in visibility and the frequency, form, height and direction of movements of clouds are recorded. At 7, 2 and 9 these observations are amplified by records of temperature, atmospheric pressure, humidity and precipitation.

On these lines Dr. Haude began his programme at Paoto on March the 30th, 1927, and has constantly carried it out until the autumn of 1929, both while travelling and in the permanent camps in which he has resided. In the latter, self-registering apparatus was immediately installed.

In addition to the routine observations, all climatic changes were, of course, noted, such as the beginning or cessation of rain, snowfall, storms and the like, as well as data on the general condition of vegetation.

The constantly recurring hourly observations amount to not less than a hundred daily.

These labours are also carried out at the permanent stations.

The station by Etsin-gol was established on October the 1st, 1927, that at Urumchi on January the 22nd, 1928, that at Charkhlik on June the 22nd, 1928, and that at Kucha on June the 30th in the same year.

In support of the lowland or valley observations a fixed

station was established on July the 1st, 1928, at Bogdo-ula, 2,600 metres above sea level, after observations had already been carried out there during the months of February, March and April.

Owing to shortage of water, the mountain station at Charkhlik had to content itself with an elevation of 1,600 metres above sea level, and this one was established on July the 18th, 1928. From the 2nd to the 30th of October observations were, however, also made at an elevation of 3,100 metres above sea level, where the temperature of the water of the River Ilve-chimen was noted every two hours, as well as the ground temperature. This station will, in Haude's opinion, furnish us with important material for comparison with the records of the expeditions formerly located at Temirlik, and particularly mine of the year 1890.

The station staff at Kucha also established a mountain station of which I have not yet received full particulars.

All these stations work in accordance with the same main programme.

For the completion of the observations some sixty inquiries have been made from the natives about the weather during the past year. The Swedish missionaries in Kashgar have also supplied valuable information.

Investigations have besides been undertaken of the structure and origin of the storms, and of radiation and the temperature of the ground.

The observations at the stations were carried out by the three capable Peking students, Li, Liu and Ma, of whom Dr. Haude speaks highly, and by five Sinkiang students appointed and trained by Dr. Haude.

For the investigation of the upper air currents balloon observations have been carried out since June, 1927. In 1928 these unfortunately had to be discontinued, because the authorities of Sinkiang forbade the importation of the gas cylinders we had left by Etsin-gol.

Still there have so far been 353 ascents, in which the balloons reached a mean height of from six to seven thousand metres and a maximum of 21,200 metres above the surface of the ground.

As an explanatory appendix to the observations, a series

Haude Photo

Cloud forms above Tien-shan in the neighbourhood of Bogdo-ula

[*face p.* 302

Haude Photo

Dr Haude's tent on Bogdo-ula, 2,500 metres above sea-level

[*face p.* 303

of good photographs have been taken of various cloud formations.

Dr. Haude summarizes some of the most important results in the survey which follows.

Urumchi, to the north of the Tien Shan range, is our observation point for the polar currents which invade Central Asia through the gateway of Dzungaria. Since Urumchi lies about 500 metres higher than the surrounding country, the ebb and flow of the cold atmospheric sea moves frequently back and forth over the town and its environs and thus produces violent and rapid variations of temperature. The mountain station at Bogdo-ula registers such of the cold waves as are powerful enough to force their way over the mountain passes and reach Turkistan proper. Since the prevailing north-westerly air currents are compelled to mount the northern slopes of Tien Shan, the rainfall, and with it the vegetation on these slopes, is very copious. The conditions on the southern side of the system and even on the southern slopes of its northern chain are sharply contrasted with this. In a belt from three to four hundred metres in width along the northern crest the prevalance of cloud is much greater than further north over the plains of Dzungaria. On the south side the amount of cloud is much less considerable. The familiar extremely violent storms on the south side are occasioned by the great contrasts in temperature between the north and south sides, which in their turn are due to the deficiency of cloud and the consequent unrestrained summer insolation and to the absence of cold air flowing to the south side. These storms, which are of "föhn"[1] character, arise when, in consequence of increased cloudiness and of snow on the north side, cold air flows over the mountains. The storms on the south side are dreaded for their violence. In certain parts they hold up all traffic for days, even that by carts.

At the station at Charkhlik we were able to collect valuable data as to the structure and origin of sand and dust storms. We could also observe that Eastern Turkistan is by no means so completely cut off from the weather

[1] föhn—south wind in Switzerland.

disturbances by the protecting wall of mountains but that invasions of cold air from the north-east, probably through the Dzungarian gate of entrance, can take place and bring rain and low-lying cloud. A series of balloon releases carried out here gave valuable indications of the stratification of the winds in respect of direction and force, which may later be of great importance for practical purposes. The sending up of these balloons will also certainly furnish valuable information concerning the altitude of the stratosphere over the continental masses of Central Asia. The work with the pilot balloons suffered great injury from the intense summer heat (+ 42°), which destroyed a large number of the rubber balloons, and was also hindered by the fact that the air was mostly thick with floating dust.

The mountain station of Kucha encountered the same difficulties at its inception as that of Charkhlik. It was not till the end of September that they succeeded in getting it into order. Together with the two other stations, north of Tien Shan and south of the desert belt, it will enable Dr. Haude to convey a clear meteorologico-climatic picture of the whole of that territory.

The observations by Etsin-gol were not interrupted for a single hour between October the 1st, 1927, and October the 20th, 1929, and this in spite of the great political difficulties its staff had to contend with. Dr. Haude expects that these series of observations will be of the greatest value in determining the climatic conditions in the midst of the Gobi Desert and will also afford a not less valuable contribution to the consideration of the range of the various monsoon currents and of the influence exercised in these regions by the penetration into them of the polar air currents. They are expected to allow of inferences concerning the conditions and causation of the violent storms which annually visit Eastern Asia.

Dr. Haude records with gratitude and satisfaction that the mission stations in Kansu, as a result of our circular letter to them and to their bishop at Lan-chou, have shown themselves exceedingly willing to extend and support our work by ocular observations and to answer the questionnaires that have been sent to them. These contributions facilitate the correlation, during the storm and monsoon seasons, of the Central Asiatic stations' observations with the material derived from Eastern Asia and enable him by this means to trace the mutual interactions.

So much for Dr. Haude's latest report. I know that his keen faculty of observation and his marvellous versatility and profound knowledge of the physical sciences put him in a position to explore many other meteorological problems which concern the whole northern hemisphere, and I can guarantee that the extraordinarily abundant material which he is gathering from Inmost Asia will be regarded for all time as fundamental and epoch-making.

After the death of the learned and wise Marshal Yang, Dr. Haude, like the other members of the expedition, had to work under difficulties. The shining steel cylinders in which the hydrogen was stored were mistaken for cannon, and the balloons were presumably supposed to be connected with some secret signalling system. The sending of them up was therefore absolutely forbidden, in spite of the Nanking Government's specific order that they were to be permitted. Ten of the heavy and costly gas cylinders had been left at the Etsin-gol station to be fetched later, six had been confiscated at Hami and eight on the frontier at Chuguchak. We had been uselessly encumbered with them for hundreds of miles, and they never had a chance to fulfil their mission in the service of science. I had rather not speak of what they cost in money, transport and labour, nor of the injury caused by the prohibition to Dr. Haude's systematic investigation of the air currents at great heights above the earth.

It had been Haude's wish and intention to travel, in the spring of 1929, by Turfan, Hami, An-si and Su-chou to the border mountains of North-Eastern Tibet, there to study the paths of the monsoons. The way lay open within the territory of China proper, but the Governor-General of Sinkiang forbade his journey under the pretext that the eastern border district of Sinkiang was a war zone and that disturbances were to be expected there. In actual fact the most profound peace prevailed in the silent, sterile deserts. Haude accordingly devoted most of the year 1929 to observations in Sinkiang. Since I wished to consult with him about the contemplated monsoon journey and since it was expedient for his future work in China to establish relations with Dr. Ko Ching-chu, the head of the Central Meteorological Institute in Nanking, I summoned him at the close of the year to Peking. We had our conference at Kalgan in the middle of December. Thence he travelled to Nanking, and afterwards to Germany for a brief visit to Berlin, before betaking himself to the mountains south-east of Liang-chou. Under normal conditions he would have been able to reach his field of labour rapidly by car. But in the New Year all traffic ceased in those districts, which were instead overrun with bands of brigands. I therefore telegraphed to him that his journey must be deferred till 1931. Meanwhile, he would work in Berlin and would there have the opportunity to prepare himself and his expedition much more thoroughly. His plan is to have a station at Liang-chou, where balloons will be sent up daily by an assistant and two Chinese students, while he himself works simultaneously in the highlands. His work in North-Eastern Tibet will form a natural and necessary conclusion to the year-long observations that he and his assistants have been carrying out at the fixed stations ever since 1927.

When Dr. Haude has finished his work and rounded it off into a complete whole, and then has revised, edited and illustrated with maps and diagrams his immense material, he will be in a position to give to meteorological science an unprecedentedly comprehensive contribution to the knowledge of the movements of the air masses and the law-governed relations of the other meteorological elements over the earth's greatest continent, and thereby to solve many problems that concern the whole northern hemisphere and indeed the entire planet.

Meteorologists in all lands may expect from Dr. Haude's faithful, accurate and substantial labours epoch-making discoveries from the world of the weather and the winds.

XXIV

PROFESSOR P. L. YÜAN'S REPORTS

THE first detailed narrative of travel that our Chinese comrade, the professor of geology, P. L. Yüan, sent to me is dated from Guchen, May the 28th, 1928. It concerns the road from Hana-gol, Camp No. 8, to Hami. The departure from Hana-gol took place on July the 4th, 1927. He had with him nine men and nineteen camels. After I parted from Yüan's column, which went to the southward of mine, I did not see him again till six months later in Hami. Route maps of the whole road were made, geological investigations conducted and plant fossils found. The archæological excavation sites numbered fifty-six and the objects collected over 20,000, almost all neolithic. The most productive site was at Getshik with 6,991 finds. Ceramics also occurred among them.

On the journey through Dondur-gun he had a Mongolian escort and was in general well treated, after he had promised not to shoot any wild animals in the neighbourhood of the sacred obos, a promise that was the easier to keep that his column had no firearms. At Durbandjin he fell in, for one evening, with Norin's column, in which were also Bergman, Heyder, von Massenbach, Söderbom and Ting.

In order to avoid the road I had chosen, he decided to steer southward through Ala-shan with Chên-fan as his objective, where he wished to locate a couple of ancient towns of which he had heard in 1923. On the way there he found vestiges of an ancient watch tower and a number of relics of antiquity. He considers the place of such importance as to demand a later visit. On October the 13th he reached Chên-fan and, on excavating in the same district that he had visited in 1923, found skeletons, pots and bronzes.

The long journey to Etsin-gol was begun through the sand desert of Badai Giron Elisun. When his fellow-travellers, Chan, Kung and Pai, saw the high sterile dunes, they became nervous and hesitated to accompany him. Chan reminded him of my experiences in Takla-makan in 1895 and said that he had no fancy for going through similar perils. But after Yüan had succeeded in getting hold of a guide resident in the district, a seventy-year-old Lama from Eastern Jehol, who brought along his wife, three children, his sheep and his camels, the three realized that it was not so perilous as all that and agreed to risk it.

The dunes rose to heights of 100 and 200 metres. And the guide even had names for several of them, which showed that they were tolerably stationary. It would have been impossible to find their way without a guide. The year before, a party of seven men had gone astray and died of thirst by a well, the water of which they had not had the strength to bring up from the depth.

It took Yüan's column eleven days to cross the sand desert, and during this journey they passed only two wells. Only one camel was lost. By the second well they found eleven ceramic fragments of the neolithic period. On November the 12th they reached the well of Hara-makan-huduk, where the guide had his headquarters.

For six days they sought in vain for Khara-Khoto, and went on to Etsin-gol without having seen the ancient town. By the river they met two travellers who told them that two gentlemen, who had bought a couple of yurts, were living in the Tsondol district and possessed sixty camels.

On November the 23rd their new guide caught sight of the poplars and dunes of Tsondol, but they were not able to cross the river. They could now see Zimmermann's camp, and the meteorological shed, whose pyramidal roof shone red in the setting sun. Yüan says: [1] "We shouted to this far-out station of a gigantic endeavour hardly equalled to by any previous undertaking of the same kind." Mären, the Mongol, was the first they caught sight of. Next morning they went across on the ice and met Zim-

[1] Yüan writes in English.

mermann, Söderbom and Ma, whom they had not seen for five months.

We heard afterwards in a letter from Zimmermann how friendly and hearty this meeting was, and what a pleasant time the garrison had with their guests. At this time Zimmermann was almost penniless, and he cannot sufficiently praise the generosity of Yüan, who, although he himself had no more than he needed, gave a considerable part of his store to the station people.

Then the caravan continued its way westward through the desert. Once they were four days without water, another time three. With the Chinese at one water place they found a note from Hempel's, Haude's, Dettmann's, von Kaul's and Li's column. "The first column of Dr. Sven Hedin's expedition passed here November 9th."

By Etsin-gol they had bought four new camels and flour for forty days, and had engaged a guide. The desert was fearfully empty. They met only two caravans and passed three. But they found no further trace of our earlier columns.

By the time they reached a place called Er-kund, nine of their camels were still alive. They hired fresh camels from the friendly inhabitants of the place.

Yüan concludes by describing his pleasure in our meeting at Hami on January the 23rd, when he had "the charm of the adventure behind him and had had an experience which many a man in the world might have envied him."

In a new report which Yüan handed to me shortly before my departure from Urumchi on December the 17th, 1928, he describes his discovery of dinosauri and begins with the words:

> "Fully to understand the palæontological importance of the discovery and its relation to the geological background, an exhaustive discussion will be necessary. This must, however, be deferred until I have studied all the Asiatic literature on the subject and particularly that which concerns Tien Shan. And here in Sinkiang one has not access to that literature."

In passing he mentions the brothers Grum-Grschimailo, Klementz, Mertzbacher, Gröber, Prjevalsky and Carruthers as predecessors in these tracts. Bogdanovich, Pevtsov, Roborovsky, Obrutscheff and Huntington touched upon Eastern Tien Shan, though they had not been in Urumchi.

Gröber, whose maps of 1907 and 1908 he had with him, he thought highly of. In April, 1928, Yüan explored Gröber's territory and admired his accuracy and penetration.

In May he investigated several iron and coal mines to the south-east of Santai. Of the fossil finds belonging to the series which he calls shui-hsi-kao he concludes that they were of the jurassic system. Further east he believes himself to have found plant fossils of the permo-carboniferous period.

During the summer he carried out archæological excavations at Santai, Ginsa, Guchen and Mo-li-ho as well as excavating some ruins at Besh-balik. A considerable area was triangulated. He wants to obtain a basis for a detailed geological map of this alluvial belt belonging to the so-called Angara series.

On August the 27th, when measuring angles from a hill of pleistocene gravel twenty li south of Santai, he caught sight of very well-defined red strata in the valley of Chao-kao-kuo. He realized at once that important discoveries might be made. But it was not until September the 11th that, on the crest of a red hill, he found small pieces of the metatarsus of a dinosaurus. He continued digging for fourteen days, and by the end of that time he had found in several different places in the valley fragments of thirty full-grown dinosauri, three young ones and one egg. His methodical work had thus been crowned with complete success and he rightly lays stress on the importance of the discovery. This reptile is the forefather of all the later dinosauri in Asia, and Yüan gives him the name of Tien Shan-saurus.

> "Tien Shan has a very long geological history. Deposits have been carried thither from land and sea, volcanic masses have been forced up, mighty movements of the earth's crust have followed—crumpling and dislocations of these mountain masses, which finally by the process of denudation have been levelled to a peneplain—all this can be read from the mountains as from the pages of a book of history."

By following the fossil-bearing chalk stones 320 li to the eastward he has been able to show that a displacement has occurred in the middle of the carboniferous age and that the sea then was full of life. Finally he described the geological structure of the mountains as well as the displacements of the sea and the elevations of the land which have taken place among the foothills on the northern side of Tien Shan. In a diagram he exhibits a clear view of the stratigraphy. The dinosauri occur in the upper parts of the lower jurassic strata. They indicate changes in climate and land formations in contrast with the over and underlying strata, which are lacustrine or marine beds.

I need not say what delight it awoke in us at headquarters when the news of Yüan's important discovery came. He was hailed as a conqueror on his return in the late autumn, and my only complaint was that my immediate departure for Peking prevented me from paying a visit to the site. Yüan arranged a little exhibition of the fossil fragments he had brought thence, and this was also visited by the high mandarins of the province.

After my arrival in Peking I had the pleasure of reading in a Swedish newspaper Professor Stensiö's pronouncement on the great importance of the find, and hastened to communicate this in a letter to Yüan.

But I hope the French newspaper which came under my eye is alone in its misconception, when it regales its readers with the following notice:

> "Sven Hedin announces that Professor Yüan, a geologist who is taking part in the expedition in the district of Urumchi, has found thirty living full-grown dinosauri. . . . It is the first time that anyone has discovered living specimens of these animals which are supposed to belong to the jurassic period, that is to say an age many million years ago."

During the year 1929 I again and again received letters and telegrams from Professor Yüan, mostly concerning the current work and finances of the station, the movements of the various members and the negotiations with the authorities. One of these letters was despatched from

Urumchi on September the 10th, 1929. He says among other things:

"This is probably the only opportunity I shall have for several months of writing to you without being censored, for Mr. Carlson, on his way home, will be my messenger.

"On the whole, the members of the expedition who are still in Sinkiang are able to go on with their work. But, since you left, every member has met with more or less opposition. It is probably fortunate for Mr. Bergman and his companions that they are beginning their work in Mongolia instead. On the other hand Drs. Norin and Ambolt have now full liberty to work for three months in Kuruk-tagh. As to their further researches we must consult later. The best concession we have secured from the Governor here is that he will welcome you back to Sinkiang and to your enterprise in the Tarim basin.

"I am now engaged in preparing to send home to Peking all our Chinese members who have been working here these three years. At the time when you return here I shall perhaps still be in Urumchi or its neighbourhood to welcome you.

"I may say that the few members who have been here during your absence have many times had difficulty in defeating the capricious attempts of the local officials to drive us out. But they have succeeded in closing up around you. I only hope that when we next meet we shall be able to say we conquered in the end.

"I have still work to do in the geology of Tien Shan, and hope to be able to finish it after two months of uninterrupted activity. This year my work has many times been interrupted by my journeys to and fro between Urumchi and the field. But you may rest assured that some important discoveries have still been made. This year, twenty-five kilometres from Urumchi, I stumbled upon a marine carboniferous bed full of fossils, so that Dr. Grabau can now find work on them to fill four or five volumes. Three complete skeletons of dinosaurus have now been prepared. There are besides about forty more individual specimens. I can no longer call them Tien Shan-saurus, for too many genera and species have been found. The best preserved skulls differ from last year's finds.

"I have written to your sister and Professor Halle and am delighted to hear from them that your friends are so well satisfied with my work. I am going to get Professor Halle to identify several plant fossils.

"There is much else that I would like to write about, but

Mr. Carlson is just getting into his car, and I must give him the letters. With the heartiest greetings and wishing you a fortunate journey back here."

The last we have heard here in Peking of Yüan's plans is that, having been appointed professor of geography at Tsing-hua College, and therefore recalled hither, he has asked and obtained yet six months' leave because he wishes to extend his journey of exploration to Altai. The work he has already performed in geology, palæontology, archæology and topography is signally meritorious and is an honour to modern scientific research in China.

The extremely able students, trained by Dr. Haude, Li and Liu, had returned to Urumchi in the spring of 1930, and their desire to go to Berlin, there to continue their studies for two years, had been granted. The National University of Peking provided the means, but only enough for one student. Far on in the spring I learned, however, that they had both gone to Berlin and had there met Dr. Haude, Major Hempel, Mr. Dettmann and Mr. Burkhan.

Of the archæologist Huang and the palæontologist Ting, Dr. Grabau's pupils, I have only heard that they are at Urumchi awaiting the opportunity to travel home.

The collector Chin has very admirably conducted the first caravan of collections from Urumchi to Kuei-hua, and his colleague Pai still remains at the disposal of Dr. Yüan.

Our co-operation with representatives of Chinese research has turned out particularly fortunately and well. For my own part, after these experiences, I shall not wish to undertake a journey into the interior of China without the company of at least one Chinese fellow worker. Such an one is besides a great help in all negotiations with the local authorities. Without Yüan's calm, wise diplomacy our people would have been worn down in Urumchi in 1929.

Finally I wish to emphasize that China intends to continue and complete the work we have begun by the establishment of meteorological stations. For practical and political reasons there is likely to be an interruption after we have finished with the observations. But I hope and believe that in quieter times the work will be resumed and carried on for the future.

XXV

DR. HUMMEL'S PRELIMINARY REPORT

IN addition to his special function as guardian of the health of our peripatetic University, Dr. David Hummel has also devoted assiduous attention to botany, zoology and anthropometry.

He wrote here in Peking, in the spring of 1929, a succinct report, and I now let him speak for himself.

BOTANY

"During the two months' stay by Huchertu-gol on the Southern Mongolian steppe in June and July, 1927, the collection of a Mongolian herbarium was begun. It should give a very good picture of the flora of the grass steppe in spring and early summer. Further to the west appears low bush steppe of several different types, and in the region of Shandemiao the flora of the sand desert was first met with. A few solitary elms in the river ravines constitute the only tree vegetation in the grass steppe region, in the sand-dunes there is often a rich æruginous green shrub growth of saksaul. It was strange to see reeds of as much as five metres in height crowning the yellow sand-dunes of the desert in the same way that they encircle our own blue lakes, and in the hollows between the dunes the reed fights its way into the desert and often extends further into it than all other vegetation—just as with us it fights its way furthest in the contest with the water.

"In the Goizo valley east of Etsin-gol we met for the first time with Populus diversifolia. It grew in large groves on dry reed beds, old giant trees only, for the caravan traffic is brisk, and the camels take care that no young offsets get a chance to develop. 'Bird Phoenix Island,' which Dr. Hedin has described so graphically, seems doomed to destruction.

"In the valley and delta of Etsin-gol an abundant vegetation flourishes. In many places poplar, tamarisk and whitebeam form regular primeval forest. At the time of our arrival at the end of September the flowering of herbaceous plants was for the most part over, but Söderbom who, throughout the summer of 1927, took part with enthusiasm in the work of botanical and zoological collection, was later able to assemble a fairly complete herbarium of the plant world of Etsin-gol.[1]

"A typical salt-marsh flora was met with round the alkaline lakes of Gashun-nor and Sogo-nor.

"In the Gashun-nor tract we encountered Gobi in earnest—low, sterile mountain chains, alternated with blackish-grey macadam and gravel wastes on which a starveling scrub and bush vegetation struggles for existence. Except for some poplar oases round the wells in the valleys of Koko-timurtun-ula, the stony desert stretches westward unbroken right up to the foot of Tien Shan, nearly 600 kilometres to the west of Gashun-nor.

"During the spring and summer of 1928 I remained at Urumchi and on the Bogdo-ula spur of Tien Shan to the east of that town. While the southern side of the 'Mountains of Heaven' is to a great extent waterless and desert, the alpine valleys of their northern slopes are often clothed with woods of deciduous trees and pines, the meadows provide excellent grazing and along the foot of the range there extends a belt of green oases and fertile cultivated lands. Urumchi is such an irrigation oasis, with poplar, elm and willow vegetation, lying about 950 metres above sea level along the southern bank of a mighty river-bed, which usually carries only a small rivulet in its deepest channel. The town is surrounded by hills and steppes with grass and artemisia vegetation.

"In the lower valleys of the Bogdo massif (1,000 to 1,500 metres above sea level) there are elm groves and copses with very rich meadow vegetation. Poplar, aspen and sallow first appear in the wild state at about 1,400 metres and cease at about 1,900 metres. On the northern and eastern slopes the spruce forest vegetation is abundant; on the southern and western slopes forest is lacking or is grey and dry at the root—conditions of life must have grown worse in recent times. Above 1,400 and 1,500 metres the wood and meadow flora becomes rich and luxuriant, and at a height of 2,500 to 2,800

---

[1] On his return to Peking in March, 1900, Georg Söderbom brought with him important collections of preserved plants and animals.—S. H.

metres a splendid alpine flora flourishes which exhibits many points of contact with ours in the north.

"In the spruce forests on the slopes of Bogdo-ula I met, for the first time during the journey, with mosses and ferns, and at 1,500 to 2,500 metres a very abundant growth of fungi —Psalliota, Agaricus, Lactarius, Russula, Lycoperdon, Clavaria, Hydnum, Morchella and others. Black and red currant bushes are plentiful in the woods, and large flowered clematis climbs everywhere high up on the spruce trunks and lights up the greenery with cascades of white stars. In the meadows yellow and white roses bloom so profusely that one can hardly see any green between the flowers, and large white pinks give out an intoxicating fragrance. At the bottom of the yard-deep many-coloured carpet of the meadow, red strawberries peep out among the stones.

"Above 2,700 metres one finds the high alpine flora. The upper limit of vegetation lies at about 3,500 metres.

"The summer up on Bogdo-ula is brief. The wild tulips certainly gleam red at the end of April, but in the middle of June I was still having snow. In the beginning of July vegetation is at its height; in August the meadows are already beginning to turn brown, and in the middle of September the snow again begins to fall. In the high-lying valleys, above 2,500 metres, it even snows in the middle of summer.

"From our meteorological station near the top of the sacred mountain of Fu Shu Shan (2,700 metres), one looks over meadows and woods down into the valley where the dragon-decked gables of the Taoist monastery rise out of the verdure about the blue waters of Haitze. 'The little sea' is declared to be bottomless, but I succeeded in limiting its depth to the still respectable figure of 95·5 metres. Beyond the lake to the south-east the fells mount wing-like, and high above them the triple-toothed, glacier-covered chain of Bogdo-ula rises 5,400 metres above the level of the sea. To north and west one looks out over the low brown-grey foothills, over the green oases at the mountain's foot and over Dzungaria's yellow desert sea. Beyond, in the infinite distance, the Altai mountains melt with the desert into space.

"I hope my herbarium has secured a fairly representative delineation of the plant world of Bogdo-ula and of the steppe and oasis vegetation on the northern side of Tien Shan.

"Folke Bergman, during his travels in 1928, made a fine botanical collection from the district around Tarim and Charkhlik and from the high alpine area of Kunlun."

Hummel Photo

Anemone Silvestris on Bogdo-ula

[face p. 316

[face p. 90

Doctor Hummel on Bogdo-ula

[face p. 317

ZOOLOGY

"In Zoology our collecting work has been confined to insects, fishes and reptiles.

"On the steppes round Huchertu-gol the insect fauna was very abundant in the early summer—particularly in grasshoppers, but further west, where sand desert and stony wastes predominate, there was less to be had.

"Of snakes we only met with six species, among them a viper which appears to be widely distributed in Mongolia.

"The 'Allegoi-horhoi,' feared by all Mongols—the desert snake, which 'lacks tail' and which paralyses its human victim at first sight, and whose bite is said to be infallibly fatal—we never succeeded in getting hold of. It is everywhere, the Mongols say—but it seems always to be in some other place than just where one happens to be. Andrews' expedition also sought for it in vain. It seems to belong to the same family as the great sea-serpent at home at Värtan.

"A few species of fishes and frogs were found in the scanty watercourses of Mongolia—no abundance was indeed to be expected in those arid tracts. Sand lizards of various kinds were, on the other hand, common. Georg Söderbom took part successfully in the work of zoological collection and, while at the Etsin-gol station, even extended it to include birds.

"During 1928 the collection of insects was continued at Urumchi and in the Bogdo-ula neighbourhood. Masses of grasshoppers swarm upon the steppe, and magnificent white Parnassus butterflies flutter about the alpine meadows.

"A viper and a large grey watersnake were the only reptiles we could discover in these tracts.

"In Haitze, the mountain lake three kilometres long which lies 1,800 metres above sea level on Bogdo-ula, there are oddly enough no fish, but a small crustacean in great multitudes."

ANTHROPOMETRY

"During the journey through Inner Mongolia in the summer of 1927 some sixty anthropometric measurements and blood-group determinations were made upon Mongols. The plan for the anthropometric work during the expedition had been arranged by Dr. P. Stevenson of the Peking Union Medical College, who also supplied the equipment of instruments and devoted much time and trouble to training us in the method of work.

"Dr. T. Rietz of Östersund had urged me to make anthropological blood-group determinations during the expedition and had equipped me with a small practical travelling laboratory.

"Unfortunately the anthropological work met with great difficulties by reason of the Mongols' superstition and shyness of strangers. Many refused to let themselves be measured, others trembled with fright during the examination and fainted before it was completed. Photography and blood testing were suspected of being diabolical arts of sorcery, and a common view was that the examination had to do with selection for military service. In the monastery of Shande-miao, where at first we were pestered with swarms of inquisitive young Lamas and where I succeeded in making a dozen measurements, after a couple of days the ruling Lamas forbade the monastery people to come near our tent. After our departure they gave out that all who had let themselves be examined had been poisoned and were doomed to death within a hundred days. It is just as well that I never went back to the monastery—my reception by the death-doomed would have been none too friendly.

"Even our own caravan Mongols, with whom we were on the best of terms during our nine months' journey, steadily refused to let me measure them, and our caravan leader, Duke Larson, declared that I had ruined the whole expedition's reputation and prestige among the Mongols by my anthropometric magic arts.

"At Möruin-gol in the Etsin-gol delta we left the last yurt in Mongolian territory—then our way lay through desolate stony deserts and scrub-covered steppes right to the borders of Sinkiang.

"Owing to political difficulties no anthropometric work could be done during the journey through Sinkiang to the provincial capital, Urumchi. After permission for it had been obtained in March, 1928, the work was resumed, but, owing to other work and journeys, I myself had no opportunity of making more than some seventy measurements of Altai Kirghiz, East Turks and Tatars. No blood-group determinations could be made, for the test serum I had taken with me on the journey had been ruined by the heat in Gobi, and it proved impossible to obtain fresh serum before the late autumn of 1928, just as I was leaving Sinkiang.

"The principal anthropometric work was carried out in Sinkiang during the summer and autumn of 1926 by Haslund-

Christensen, who in the course of his journey took 170 measurements of East Turks, Lopliks, Dede Mongols, Torguts and Tibetans. His work among the Qara Shahr Mongols during the autumn of 1928 was unfortunately interrupted after only a few days owing to the new Governor-General's suspicions. The Mongols in Sinkiang are not nearly so shy and suspicious as their kinsmen living on the desolate Mongolian steppes. The Mohammedan population of Sinkiang showed no particular antipathy to the anthropometric work."

It goes without saying that Hummel, during his stay among Mongols, East Turks and Chinese, also directed his attention to the diseases prevalent among different peoples and in different climates. Of his observations in his own special department he will in due time give valuable particulars.

Hummel's reports, like those of the others, are very brief and entirely preliminary. To his detailed report, which cannot be written till later, will be attached climatic data and a route map.

The expedition's doctor and my medical attendant shared all my fate in the year 1929 and was thereby hindered in his botanical, zoological and anthropological work. But on March the 22nd, 1930, he was ready to start. He was to lead a botanical expedition to the Choni valley in Kansu on the Tibet border. As assistant he had the young German, Manfred Bökenkamp, from Tientsin, who had distinguished himself in adventurous journeys in Mongolia and was immediately willing to leave his employment in order to accompany Hummel. The Swedish missionary Halldorf was just about to return with his wife to his station in the Choni district, and Hummel arranged to travel with them. Our Chinese friends in Peking proposed that Hummel should take the young student Hao Chang-shêng with him. The day before their departure Mr. Halldorf received a letter from the English missionary, Simpson, of Min-chou, that he was arriving at Chung-ching with his wife and three children on April the 15th to see doctor and dentist and for other business, and would be returning in a couple of weeks to Min-chou. The Simpsons had their own junk on the River Kialing from Pao-ning to Chung-king and would make use of it on the return journey to Pao-ning, proceeding thence by mules. He said the road was tolerably free from bandits. Hummel's group would probably join up with these missionaries too. Mr. Simpson had been living up there on the borders of Tibet for nearly forty years.

In ordinary circumstances Hummel would naturally have taken the motor road from Si-an-fu to Lan-chou by which the distance can be covered in ten days. But I have already mentioned that this part of the country is in the hands of bandits and that all traffic is at a standstill. The road through Ordos and Ning-hsia is equally impossible. Captain Point, Citroën's representative out here, attempted it in February, but was so hard pressed by large bands of brigands that he had to turn back.

Hummel had thus no choice but to make the long detour by Shanghai, where Consul-General Lilliehöök was of great assistance to him, and up the Yangtze Kiang past Nanking, Hankou, Ichang and Chung-king. He left Ichang on April the 10th and on the 14th telegraphed from Chung-king. It is a quite complicated business arranging the transfer of money in these uncertain times, but our friends Mr. Nixon and Mr. Greenfield of the postal service here have helped us out. I pay in the required sum here and they send telegraphic authorization for its withdrawal at Chung-king, Min-chou and Lan-chou.

When Hummel left Peking on March the 22nd, he was very well equipped in all respects. Besides his collector's outfit, he had a complete meteorological station and a Paulin's altimeter as well as a very good photographic equipment. His passport, arms permit and other official documents were in the best of order. I had written to my old friend the Pope of Tashi-lunpo, Tashi Lama, who was now staying at Mukden, begging him to give Hummel a letter of recommendation to the border Prince at Choni, and Hummel had gone to Mukden to deliver my letter in person. A day later he had received an exceedingly friendly and valuable letter from the Grand Lama with his official seal.

Haude Photo

Head Monastery by the Bogdo Lake

[*face p.* 320

I am not free from a certain anxiety, as I sit alone in Peking and all my young investigators are out in the field in different parts of Asia. But from time to time good and reassuring news comes from them. Those are my days of rejoicing. My warmest good wishes go with Dr. Hummel. The botanists of the Academy of Science, Professors Samuelsson and Fries, Dr. Hulthén and others have bestowed the highest encomiums on his plant collections from Sinkiang, and Professor Yngve Sjöstedt has expressed satisfaction with his collections of insects. I am confident that he will also bring from the highlands of the Tibetan border abundant and well-preserved specimens of the flora of those regions.

XXVI

LIEUTENANT HASLUND'S REPORT

THE oldest of the veterans in my expedition was F. A. Larson, the Duke of Mongolia, for I came to know him at Paoto and Kalgan in the winter and spring of 1897; later he had been engaged as caravan leader, having telegraphed his acceptance in October, 1926. The next in seniority was Major Eduard Zimmermann who was my travelling companion on the journey out to Peking in November of the same year. The third was the young Danish lieutenant, Henning Haslund-Christensen, who, after seven years of adventure in Mongolia and service with the British American Tobacco Company in China, was appointed, on Larson's recommendation, as his second-in-command in the conduct of our caravans.

He entered our service in the spring of 1927, and conducted caravans for Norin and Bergman and for Hempel and Haude on the road by Etsin-gol to Hami. As a caravan leader he proved to be unsurpassable and, by his care of the camels, reduced the mortality among them to a minimum. He never neglected the golden rule of the Chinese caravan leaders to take concentrated food in the form of beans to keep the animals in good condition in the sterile desert tracts. In the spring, summer and autumn of 1928 he was Folke Bergman's caravan leader in the Lop country and Northern Tibet, and during that time carried out anthropometrical investigations of great value. During the last phase of his service in our brotherhood he devoted himself to the Torguts, a Mongol race living not far from Qara Shahr, and I gladly approved his suggestion of trying to acquire a temple yurt of the kind which the princes take with them on long journeys.

When for urgent private reasons Haslund left us in the beginning of February, 1930, he delivered a brief report of his dealings with the Torgut prince, Seng-chen Gegen Khan and of the acquisition of a complete temple yurt. I let him speak for himself.

"My first visit to Seng-chen Gegen Khan took place in October, 1928, and I went there because the territory of that Torgut ruler lies isolated in the midst of the magnificent and wild Zuldus mountains. The Mongolian name Zuldus signifies that the wild and fertile river valleys that one there meets with high up among the mountains lie higher than hundreds of peaks in the neighbourhood, hence the Mongols are wont to say that one can sit up there and gaze down upon countless mountain tops standing below the river valleys.

"The Torguts love Zuldus and are convinced, perhaps justly, that they dwell in the loveliest land on earth. Their songs, both old and new, tell of all the beauty that daily meets a Torgut's eyes. The melodies accord with the changing moods of nature-worshippers, and the tales of the hunters gathered round the evening camp-fire extol the bounding flight of the mountain goat and the wild sheep towards the snow-clad peaks, and the stern life and death encounters of man and bear in the dim loneliness of the pine forests.

"In June, July and August the broad river valleys in the midst of the hundreds of mountain peaks are a Mongolian Utopia. Millions of fat-tailed sheep, hundreds of thousands of horses and countless herds of horned cattle wallow there in a sea of the lushest grass, and on the mountain slopes the shepherds sit among fragrant colour-drenched blossoms, absorbing all this loveliness of which the notes of their primitive flutes have so much to tell.

"A century and a half ago these vigorous and hardy people came from Edil-tsaer or Volga, where much blood had flowed in the war against the Bashkirs, Russians and Kirghiz, but then the great Obish[1] Khan led them back to their former home in the ancient Öret Khanate, the present Sinkiang, thousands of marches nearer to the holy Potala at Lhasa, and therefore a so much more blessed tract than that in which they had lived surrounded by white sorcerers over whom their lamaistic gods and saints had had no power.

"My first stay among the Qara Shahr Torguts only extended to six weeks, which I employed in taking phonographic records of their songs and in carrying out anthropometric measure-

[1] In literature referred to as Oubacha.

ments of the inhabitants. The former part of my work was very simple, because the Torguts themselves and their Khan took a great interest in it. The Khan sent out riders to the various camps to bring in the best singers, women and men, to the palace, Öreget.[1] By day the various pieces of music and songs were tried and in the evenings the result was given on my wax cylinders.

"Their enthusiasm was boundless when they heard their own performances come back from the little tin funnel of the phonograph, and the applause was often so vigorous that the saddle horses tied up outside the door broke loose and galloped madly round inside the wall that surrounded the residency.

"A Mongol smiles when he is pleased, and he almost always is. If he sees a fine feat of horsemanship or a successful shot from rifle or bow, he gives vent to his approval with lively shouts and vociferous applause; but if a couple of Mongols are really enjoying themselves, the noise of it can be heard afar off. They roll and writhe on the ground, they slap their thighs, and tears of joy stream down their cheeks. My little dilapidated phonograph had the greatest success among the Torguts, and the fame of the man with the box that could talk spread far and wide.

"The other part of my work was considerably more difficult. The Mongol has an inborn abhorrence of letting himself be touched, and when one opens one's case with the many nickel-plated instruments required for accurate anthropometric measurements, he draws back politely but firmly to make room for the next.

"However, after the Khan had held a review of his body-guard, I succeeded in interesting him in the stature of some of the soldiers, and since he knew that they were famous as the best and most imposing in Turkistan, he saw nothing against the foreigner assuring himself of the fact. When the six weeks were at an end, I had thus attained my object and was able to return to the expedition's headquarters at Urumchi with my results safely stowed on my packhorses.

"The Khan's last words to me at parting were that I must come back and tell him about my people and learn to know his Torguts, and on my way home I made up my mind to return to Öreget, the Khan's winter residence, as soon as circumstances permitted.

"What chiefly interested me in these Torguts was that they still constituted a Mongol tribe with all its old traditions in

[1] By the Turkomans called "Khotan Simbel."

being, and that here a powerful and beloved Prince held sway over the only one remaining of the five Mongolian Khanates.

"In December an officer and four soldiers came to the expedition's headquarters at Urumchi to invite me on the Khan's behalf to Öreget. They brought horses for my baggage and a Mongolian guide to conduct me across the mountains by a way known only to the Torguts.

"We did not make a start until the middle of January, not the best time of year for travelling over the many passes one has to cross to reach Qara Shahr. Besides the guide, Shageder, a powerful young Torgut of the Khan's bodyguard, I had also an elderly, very well read and widely travelled Lama, Tön Geling, in my company. Tön Geling was the uncle of the young Mongrolda Noyen, chief of the Hoshut Mongols and second in command in the Khan's army.

"The further we penetrated into the mountains the deeper lay the snow. Twice it happened that the pass we were to cross was so sheeted with ice that it was impossible for our horses to get through, and we had to return to our last night's camp and look for another way.

"On the seventh day we found ourselves, with our ten heavily laden horses, at a place where only mountain sheep and rock goats and perhaps bold hunters on foot had penetrated before us. A snowstorm came on, and the horses were unloaded to save their failing strength for a last attempt when the weather should improve.

"Old Tön Geling sat hunched up in his great wolf-skin coat, telling his beads, and Shageder, of whom it was said that he knew Zuldus like his own tent and who had been sent by his ruler to lead the stranger to Öreget, went out alone and in distress into the snowstorm to seek the way to Tekhe'en-darban, the mighty pass which forms the parting of the waters between north and south.

"Next morning the snowstorm ceased, and the sunrise flooded the landscape, lately so chill and harsh, with splendour. And the sun brought us, too, a little warmth. The horses, recovering their courage, shook off the snow from their backs and began to paw the snow on the ground to find something to eat. Tön Geling pointed joyfully to the southward, where, behind a row of mountain chains, shimmering like pearls in their mantling of snow, the mighty peak of Tekhe'en-darban stood up against the azure January sky. And then Shageder came back, happy and hopeful, for he had found fresh human tracks leading in the direction of Tekhe'en-darban, the pass that forms a difficult entrance to the country of the Qara Shahr Torguts.

" And while the sun brought beauty to the landscape and fresh courage to the hearts of man and beast, a very precarious ascent began. The tracks in the snow, leading in the right direction, encouraged us, for they showed us that a man had gone before us, and where he could go there we surely could follow. We were grateful to our unknown guide and admired the hard fight he had put up alone against the angry elements. His tracks were deep and sometimes half buried in snow, which showed that he had performed the difficult ascent while the snowstorm was still raging.

" The nearer we came to the top of the pass, the more eagerly we pressed forward, the Torguts to gaze out once more over the familiar mountains of their native land, and I inspired by the glorious feeling one has when, after an arduous climb, one at last reaches the top and looks out over a landscape never seen before. When the setting sun threw its last rays in red and gold over the snow-clad mountain battlements, we reached the head of the pass.

" On the last stretch we had not had our unknown forerunner's tracks as a guide. Where the trail ceased the body of a man lay half snowed over in a crouching position. As we passed by, the Mongols muttered prayers, to incline Yama, the powerful god of death, to forbearance. Tön Geling stayed for a moment to lay bare the breast and belly of the corpse so as to attract the vagrant wolves to the spot, and turned up the face so that the dull, cold eyes should draw the birds of heaven to the body. For when the dead has fulfilled his last service, that of sustaining life, his soul is set free and wins the right to pass into a new life that is born at the same moment.

" A glorious view greeted us from the top of the pass. Far off to the northward the three majestic peaks of Bogdo-ula rose against the sky. The sight of that mountain, which we had not seen since the day we left headquarters, made us forget all the difficulties and all the hardships we had gone through since that day.

" And the Mongols turned their gaze southward over the mountains out into the infinite void where, far across boundless deserts and high plateaus beyond the range of vision, the Dalai Lama sits enthroned at Budul Ole or Potala.

" The sun sank and clouds rose from the depths. Soon only the peak on which we stood was bathed in sunlight, and below us darkness brooded over all. But the sun went down, and we too were wrapped in gloom.

"During the descent one clear star after another was lighted, and the stillness of the frosty winter night was broken only by the long-drawn howling of the wolves.

"When the moon rose we pitched our camp. Early next morning Mongrolda Noyen arrived with some of his soldiers. They brought fodder for the horses, fuel and a fresh horse for me. As the road was now considerably better, I left the caravan and rode forward with Mongrolda Noyen, at whose camp we arrived in the evening. Later on in the evening Tön Geling also came in, and we sat talking far into the night. We enjoyed being in comfort again, stretched ourselves out on bearskins and sipped our tea while the pipe passed from mouth to mouth. We agreed that it was good to be there.

"Escorted by Mongrolda Noyen and a squadron of his cavalry, I went on next day to Öreget, where we arrived at sunset.

"There, quarters were assigned to me in the building in which the Khan himself lives. My servants were informed that they were released from all work so long as I remained there, and in their place I was given servants from the Khan's staff.

"All the houses in the residency were built in Western style, with large comfortable rooms hung with Chinese silk embroideries, while the furniture was in part imported from Russia. The Khan's dwelling-house consisted of two storeys and faced south.

"On the east side of the house a racecourse had been laid out, to which the best trotters were brought, and, from a long balcony-like projection built out in front of his work-room, his Highness watched the races every morning. During recent years the Khan had been at great pains to train good pacers, and he was, with good reason, proud of the result. The competing horses were decked with bells and red plumes, and from the moment the signal to start was given it was as though a roll of drums were thundering along the track. So soon as a horse broke into a gallop he was disqualified. The Khan knew all about every one of the competing horses, from which herd he came and by what stallion he was sired.

"In the same house as the Khan were living also the seventeen-year-old daughter, Shire Noyen, and the fifteen-year-old son, Bichigen Khan, of Seng-chen Gegen's elder brother, the former Khan. A twenty-one-year-old daughter of the same deceased Khan is married to my friend already mentioned,

Mongrolda Noyen. Since Seng-chen Gegen, in his capacity of 'hutuktu,' cannot marry, the great silver seal, which is the token of the Khanate and which was given by the Emperor Chien Lung to the reigning Torgut Khan in October, 1776, passes to Bichigen Khan after his uncle's death.

"The residency is surrounded by a ten-foot wall with a great gateway to the south. A military guard is mounted in front of the palace entrance and at the gate in the wall. Above the gate there is a watch tower, from which buglers announce the approach of those having errands to the Khan.

"Outside this gate seven large, handsomely decorated temple yurts have been erected, in which the chief gods and saints of lamaism are represented, and here prayers are offered daily by the learned and eminent Lamas of the Torguts. Here also resorted two of the highly esteemed astrologers of the Torguts. Each day the Lamas receive from the Khan his instructions as to which prayers they should read, and if he intends to begin a new work or is in doubt about some person or some enterprise, he asks the astrologers for counsel.

"A Russian army surgeon, who was forced to flee his country during the revolution, has settled here, and the Khan has built a hospital which he controls.

"All the people under the Khan's dominion are more or less prosperous and give the impression of being well contented. Nor do they ever speak of him without raising their hands in reverence to their foreheads.

"When Seng-chen Gegen's elder brother died nine years ago, his son was only four years old, and Seng-chen, who for many years had spent his time in pilgrimages to the holy places of Buddhism, was summoned home in haste from Tibet. The Torguts themselves say that from that day began a splendid time for them. The herds of horses and cattle multiplied and throve and the conditions of life among the population improved. Their only anxiety was that so few children were born, but even in that respect an improvement has been noticeable during recent years.

"On my visits to the Lamas in the monasteries scattered among the mountains and during my many sojourns in the Torguts' tents, and from conversations with hunters round the camp fire, I have found with pleasure that here still lives a population of whom all, without exception, fear their God, love their country and honour and revere their ruler, a ruler who recognizes his responsibilities and governs his country to the universal contentment of his subjects.

"It was in December, 1927, that I first came into contact with the Torguts and their chief, Seng-chen Gegen, but it was not until a year later, when I was travelling among them in their own district of Qara Shahr, that they confided in me that they had already observed in Hami that our air-horse was strong and active, since we made our way swiftly and without mishap through the desert. And now, fortunately for me, a series of events occurred which, in the Torgut's eyes, were of good omen, and which therefore all turned to my advantage and facilitated my work.

"Tön Geling—Tön indicates that the Lama in question is of princely birth—an uncle of the Prince of the Hoshut Mongols, had given me a prayer-flag on which an air-horse is painted, bearing the sacred jewel and prayers in Tibetan script, which would bring me fortune in my travels, if I let it wave over my tent. Learned Lamas can interpret many things by studying the movements of such a prayer-flag in the wind, which may be of either good or evil omen.

"On the way we met seven Torgut hunters who were going to Kum-darya to try their luck at hunting wild pig. We drank tea together in my camp, and one of the Torguts, who was something of a scholar, studied the flag with great care. I heard later that in the first week at Kum-darya they had killed forty-three wild pig and that the good result was clearly due to their having camped with me under my strong air-horse.

"During my travels in the Zuldus mountains the wind had been so obliging as regularly to direct the flag in such a manner as the Lamas could interpret as friendship with the princely family and approximation to it. I had no suspicion of any of these things until long afterwards, but the Torguts who were watching the stranger with alert attention so as to decide whether he was friend or enemy, let nothing escape them. And the result was that I was conducted to the Khan's residency, Öreget, to stay there as the guest of the princely family.

"During my visit to Beli-miao in 1927, the hutuktu of that place, Yolros Lama, had declared that, on our journey to the west, I should make friends with two hutuktus. I had met a Tubet hutuktu at Shande-miao, and we had exchanged gifts of friendship. My Mongols had related all this to the Torgut soldiers at Hami, and when a stranger arrives in a new Mongolian territory everything that is known about him goes round with the speed of lightning.

"This time I arrived at Öreget shortly before the Mongolian

New Year. Among the Torguts the ancient custom is still held sacred, that the first fifteen days of the New Year are devoted to feasting at the houses of the fifteen persons of highest standing, and only selected guests are invited. Since I had the luck to be counted among these, I was introduced by the Khan himself in fifteen days to everyone worth knowing in that part of the world.

"The series of feasts began with Seng-chen Gegen's. The road from his palace to the residency, where the day's banquet took place, was laid with straw, and at the appointed time all the guests met outside the Khan's main entrance, where a detachment of the bodyguard was drawn up. When Seng-chen appeared—each day in a new magnificent costume—all bowed, and slowly and with ceremony the procession moved off. On our arrival at the host's house we were cordially received by him at the outer door and took our places in strict order of rank. All except myself knew where they were to sit, and there were no empty bowings of politeness or attempts to depreciate their rank such as are customary at Chinese dinners.

"On the first day of the new year a deputation of five Chinese officials arrived with presents from the Tao-t'ai in Qara Shahr. These were not bidden to the banquet, but were served after we had finished, which was not so very early.

"The first part of the dinner consisted of the finest Chinese dishes served on Chinese silver plate, and Chinese and Mongolian spirits drunk from cups of jade. Since none of the Mongols was particularly clever at eating with chopsticks, a cordial and fraternal mood was soon induced by the Khan's decree that anyone who bungled with his chopsticks must empty his beaker to the bottom. Some of the guests seemed to be driven by this into making mistakes with the hateful chopsticks, but perhaps it was only that their thirst was greater than their hunger.

"Seng-chen Gegen himself and all hutuktus drank only tea, but they were not greatly displeased to see their worldly brethren sink deeper and deeper under the table. On the contrary, Seng-chen explained to me with pride that those who were really thirsty were true Mongols, and he was certainly right.

"Now all the Chinese small dishes were carried away, and the Mongols sat expectant. The fine silken robes were unbuttoned at the neck or taken off altogether, the peacock-feathered hats were flung to servants, the Chinese chopsticks thrown scornfully aside and the long silver-mounted knives drawn from the belt, and in all faces one could read that now they were going to eat.

"Then the doors were opened, and in came dishes of steaming boiled mutton. The pieces were handed round, chewed and gnawed, and sublime enthusiasm prevailed among the Mongols. After the first onslaught was over they began again to empty the beakers. Laughter and song alternated with merry tales. Now and then a Mongol disappeared to mount his horse with halloos and yells and career over the steppe, to dream for a moment that he was following Chingis Khan on one of his victorious marches.

"In spite of the genial mood which towards the end grew pretty wild, respect and reverence were observed towards the great; and I never saw anything which even a sober man could not enjoy and heartily laugh at. And to me, the stranger of other race and religion, they showed always the greatest hospitality.

"The temple yurts which stand to the south of Seng-chen Gegen's palace had aroused my interest on my first visit to Qara Shahr, and my ardent desire was to acquire such a one for the expedition's collection.

"Temple yurts are nowadays very rare in Mongolia, but their great interest arises from the fact that they constitute the primitive form of god-houses before the Mongols, under the influence of immigrant Tibetan hutuktus, began to build temples of wood and masonry.

"During my stay at Urumchi in December, 1928, I described the tent yurts to the chief of the expedition, and it was decided that I should try to buy one of them.

"A sum was placed at my disposal, and I carried a letter from the chief, written in Mongolian style, in which Seng-chen was requested to give support to my work at Qara Shahr. Nothing was said in the letter about temple yurts, only that I wished to buy ethnographical objects.

"When I met Seng-chen in January, 1929, and delivered the letter, he was very well pleased by the chief's greetings. We sat talking the whole evening, and I had to tell him all about the expedition and its aims, and a great deal about Dr. Hedin's earlier travels in Tibet. An illustration which I found in the *Weekly Journal*, showing him on a visit to Tashi Lama, greatly appealed to him. He promised to give orders to one of his servants or secretaries to help me in my work and suggested that I should next day tell this man what I desired to buy.

"I answered that what I wished to buy should be copied

by a silversmith on the spot, and that I would take the original and leave the copy by way of payment, and this seemed to content him.

" Some time now passed in the study of the interior of the temple yurts and in making notes of the names and uses of their contents. In the evenings I always called on Seng-chen, and we conversed on miscellaneous topics. I showed him all the illustrations in a number of papers I had brought with me, and these gave occasion for many questions on his part. He was especially attracted by pictures of soldiers and horses, kings and princes.

" He was much interested to hear about the King to whose country the members of the expedition belonged, and, since my knowledge of King Gustav's life and history was extremely limited, my Swedish newspapers came in very usefully, for they contained a large number of photographs of His Majesty in uniform and plain clothes, distributing the prizes at sports competitions, in his car, out shooting and so on.

" Riders and couriers from the different Torgut princes under the Khan's dominion came and went daily, and delegates from the distant Mongol princes and Tibetan hutuktus resided in Öreget to transact political or religious business.

" I had brought in my baggage a set of telephone apparatus which had been given to Dr. Hedin by L. M. Ericsson, and this I installed between the Khan's work-room and the ' tuslarchi's '[1] yamên. Seng-chen was pleased and proud, and grateful for this present, but the tuslarchi, on the other hand, was less enraptured by being brought into so intimate and easy connexion with his ruler.

" When guests visited the Khan, the newly acquired treasure had somehow to be displayed. The guests were informed that Seng-chen would cause the tuslarchi to walk into the room at a given moment without having sent anyone to fetch him. A ring of the bell, a couple of words into the mouthpiece—and the venerable official came hurrying in through the door.

" In contrast with Seng-chen, who daily became more and more eager to introduce Western invention and knowledge, the tuslarchi was an avowed opponent of innovation.

" One day, when the telephone bell had been ringing unusually often, he came to me and declared that talking machines and suchlike things might be all very well for Westerners, but were not suited to Mongols.

[1] 1st minister.

Lieberenz Photo

Mongol Yurt

[*face p.* 332

"A rider came in one day from Urumchi with mails for Norin and me. Seng-chen sent out scouts to look for Norin. After a couple of days they came back and reported that Norin's caravan was moving along the banks of Bagrash-köl and might be expected to arrive before long in Qara Shahr. Seng-chen supplied me and my servant with fresh horses, and, as I hoped to be able to reach Norin's camp in the course of the following night, I took no sleeping-sack or other baggage with me.

"I met Norin, delivered his mail and returned to Öreget. On the way I made a fire to guide my servant who had gone astray with a camel. Towards evening I fell asleep and only awoke in the night to find that the fire had caught my fur coat and had burnt away or charred a third part of it.

"I was prepared for my burnt coat causing remark, but that some Lamas should seize it and show it to Seng-chen astonished me a little, and I was even more surprised to see with what eagerness every detail was studied.

"It appeared later that the Lamas had arrived at the conclusion, from the study of the burnt coat, that Seng-chen and I were foreordained 'axa-due,' which, among the Mongols, signifies much the same as foster-brothers. After many religious ceremonies had been performed and various mystic formulæ recited, the brotherhood was established, with the important result that my good standing among the Torguts was absolutely assured.

"During my stay at Öreget I had made up my mind that the magnificent temple yurt which always accompanied Seng-chen on his travels and which was the dwelling of Shara Gegen, the most eminent of the Torgut's divines, was the best suited for an ethnographic collection, and I therefore asked Lobsong Geling to sound the Khan as to his attitude to the affair.

"The next evening Lobsong and I were summoned to the Khan's house and, contrary to custom, all his servants and guards were ordered to leave the room.

"We were together all night, and Seng-chen related many interesting episodes and occurrences of his youth in Lhasa, Tashi-lunpo and other of the holy places of Buddhism. He told us about his predecessor, the elder Seng-chen Gegen, and his friendly relations with Englishmen, from whom he received many and costly gifts which were the occasion of hatred and envy on the part of Dalai Lama and finally led to the murder of Seng-chen Gegen.

"To escape further persecution Seng-chen Hutuktu had been

reborn at Olon Chogorso Hagorchin Toredolok and incarnated in the powerful body of the Torgut Khan's second son, whom even Dalai Lama must beware of injuring.

"He told us of the British military expedition to Lhasa, of the flight of Panchen Bogdo and of many other things.

"Finally Seng-chen Gegen Khan informed me that the whole temple yurt would be handed over as a gift from him to the King of Sweden. He gave me detailed instructions as to how the whole affair was to be arranged and spoke of the sentiments of friendship that it was his duty, as the incarnation of the Seng-chen godhead, to display to Westerners.

"It was decided that I should return next day to Urumchi by Qara Shahr and Toksum, and that the collections should be transported by the Khan's own people.

"In the morning all the officials were assembled in front of the palace, and there Seng-chen presented to me a magnificent horse as a parting gift.

"After a cordial farewell I set out and arrived at Urumchi after six days' riding.

"Some days later the Khan's people arrived and made ceremonious delivery of the whole collection, and thereupon erected and decked the temple yurt in the expedition's courtyard.

"For several days Lamas conducted divine service in the yurt, and a multitude of Mongols living in the Urumchi district came to show their veneration for the images of the gods.

"During the summer of 1929 the temple yurt was erected in Stockholm and on the 8th of September it was ceremoniously handed over to H.M. King Gustav the 5th.

"As a token of thankfulness the Seng-chen Gegen was made Commander of the Swedish Vasa Order by the King."

XXVII

BOHLIN, HÖRNER AND BEXELL

IT is usually Folke Bergman who is the spokesman of the many-headed Gobi expedition in his reports to me, and I have thus only received shorter communications from its remaining three new members. But I cannot refrain from giving a few extracts from their letters. To Hörner and Bexell the ways of Asia were a new experience. Bohlin had already spent a couple of years at Chou Kou-tien near Peking, where he played an important part in the discovery of " Sinanthropus pekinensis," the representative of the human race who inhabited that region perhaps a million years ago.

His first brief letter is from Camp No. 8, November the 24th, 1929. So far he has only had occasion to occupy himself with geology and topography.

> " In an hour we go westward again. Now we are sitting at a farewell breakfast with Zimmermann. We have made a number of profitable exchanges with that traveller. For a box of geological specimens which he is taking east, we have got instruments, medicines and even provisions, including three large sausages which he has been saving up for two years by Etsin-gol."

He writes from Taben-tologoi on December the 13th describing various phases of life in the caravan.

During an excursion with Hörner he has cleared up the complex hydrography of the region and come back with such quantities of specimens that the camel's burdens were dangerously heavy.

On December the 15th he has had fifteen degrees of frost at 8 a.m. and snow, which geologists and archæologists fear most of all. " Here to-day I visited an excavation which yesterday shone red and fair. To-day it was regularly sugared over, and I had to tramp round in the snow between the red patches which still remained exposed."

Tebeh, February the 2nd, 1930. At a sedimentary pillar thirty metres high, an erosion residuum, they found an abundant deposit of fossils. They stayed there a whole month and excavated—

> " some thirty finds of which, however, only three are likely to be anything like complete skeletons.
>
> " Whether there are whole skulls I do not know. All the finds were revealed by crumbled fragments, among which fragments of skull and teeth almost always appeared, which suggests that this important part is as a rule wholly or partly destroyed ; the fragments may be of great importance, but are unlikely to admit of combination into any whole."

For several reasons the fossils have to be taken out in larger or smaller blocks, and so Bohlin's knowledge of them is still " pretty imperfect."

" All the finds originate from the same species (to judge by the teeth). It is a saurian of about the size of a donkey, and I have a feeling that it is something new to science, but I do not venture to say so yet. The specimens must, when opportunity offers, be sent to Beli-miao and Kuei-hua."

He says that this and other fossil-bearing places would be worth a special expedition extending over years, and with many workers.

On February the 13th he describes how the bone fragments have been bandaged with flour-paste and sack-cloth, and gives detailed instructions how they should be handled after arrival in Peking, so as not to suffer injury. The weather and the time of year have been very unsuitable for the work.

> " And then we have found fossils that we have not had enough strength of character to leave untouched, so as to hurry westward. When it is a question of huge dinosaurus bones, we must get them off with the consignment to Beli-miao. What we have got out are a couple of big extremity bones, unhappily incomplete, a tooth, ribs and an interesting carapace. Bexell made the first find."

He speaks of a place where there are "fossil insects and mussels, a couple of fine bits of fossil cykad stem with leaf impressions, fossil vertebrates and others."

He speaks with enthusiasm of his Chinese collector, Chang. "He has proved a pearl. He has done exemplary work without haste and without carelessness, even though the thermometer stood at $-24°$ at 2 o'clock, and there was a strong wind blowing. That is an achievement, and the man deserves a reward for it."

He praises equally warmly the Dane, Johansen, who has been of invaluable assistance to them even in the scientific work.

"Bexell sends greetings. He has had a very difficult excavation and is engaged in plastering one of his large bones. It is 3 o'clock, there are not many hours left before we start, and by then the bones must be ready and packed."

On St. Lucia's Day Nils Hörner is infinitely grateful for the longed-for mail and all the good news it brought from his home. "It is glorious out here and mighty interesting! The quaternary has been almost entirely wiped out by erosion and one seeks in vain for quaternary remains. But what does it matter when there are so many other interesting and promising things here, and, besides, the prospect is good of finding the quaternary elsewhere."

He tells many notable things of the tertiary and quarternary deposits by the dry bed of the Huang Ho and encloses coloured sections in his letter. The tectonic history of the area attracts him irresistibly, and he prepares me for "very good results."

One observes in Hörner's letters that he enters heart and soul into the great and intricate problems that he is engaged in solving. To his personal adventures, frostbitten fingers and being shot at by soldiers, he gives only the merest passing mention. He has sent me his whole geological diary for safe keeping, and it strikes me as being full of matter and substantial.

As lately as March the 22nd, 1930, Bexell writes from Otakhoi and gives an account of the finds that have been made since Khara-tologoi. They have passed a number of rich fossil beds.

"All these places were for the moment only examined as to their geological formation, and in the circumstances we could not of course make any very large collection of fossils, but such a collection would quite certainly be of the greatest significance both from the stratigraphical and the palæontological points of view, since certain marine deposits in this region may be said to be hitherto unknown and even unexpected.

"The results hitherto have been good, and everything else has gone well and under the best conditions, and we all hope that headquarters and the other members of the expedition have been and are enjoying the same advantages."

It is delightful to lead an expedition in which every member of the staff is a first-class man in his own line. Thus much can be said already, that the three new members, Bohlin, Hörner and Bexell, are going to bring home magnificent results from their labours. And yet they are still only at the beginning of their campaign.

The young Chinese geodesist, Chên, who is travelling with them, describes in a letter his impressions and his study, in leisure hours, of my book *My Life as an Explorer*. And he ends with the words: "All members in the expedition are very kind to me, and so I feel as comfortable as at home."

In the foregoing pages I have given a very brief survey of my young comrades' field-work. They themselves shall develop their observations and arrange their collections one day, in the fulness of time, when the campaign is finished.

Of the topographical work and the mapping of different routes I have for obvious reasons given no account at all, although that particular activity occupies so distinguished a place among our results. Here indeed it is a question of pure geographical exploration and of the delineation of parts of the earth's surface which before were very imperfectly known. Of the regions of the Gobi Desert which we traversed there are no trustworthy maps. Those which existed before, and which we had with us, proved in many districts untrustworthy or inadequate. By Dettmann's astronomical observations during 1927 several of our routes have been assigned their true geographical positions. Norin's road from Huchertu-gol to Shande-miao in the same year was admirably triangulated by Major Heyder.

One of our aims has been, by means of new maps, to ascertain and study the changes which take place in certain regions, for example the movements of rivers and lakes and the distribution of drift sand. As regards hydrography my thirty-year-old maps of the Tarim delta and the Lop Nor lakes are totally antiquated. But they have their historical value and afford us a possibility of observing the laws governing the variations of watercourses.

The maps Norin produced on his long journeys through Asia are models, not least because he has included the geological features in them. To an old map-draughtsman it is a veritable delight to behold Norin's large noble map sheets with their beautiful workmanship, their amplitude of detail and their coloured indications of geological formation. Norin's cartographic work is among the expedition's finest and most valuable results. And it has gained immensely in value since he began his fruitful co-operation with Dr. Nils Ambolt.

I have already mentioned Bergman's admirable route-map in 300 sheets, of the summer of 1927. Major Hempel also drew a map of the southern column's road from Etsin-gol to Hami which clearly bears the stamp of great accuracy. Of Professor Yüan's map work I have only had the opportunity of seeing a number of sheets of the district east of Etsin-gol, and they betray the trained topographer of keen powers of observation. The topographer Chan, who no longer belongs to the expedition, has mapped various stretches of the road by which Yüan's column travelled, as well as the southern spur of Tien Shan in the district of Kucha. What I have seen of it appears to be very sound, and the drawing masterly. The student Li, who afterwards became chief of our meteorological station at Kucha, has on various occasions drawn maps which redound to his honour. Even Major Zimmermann and Mr. Söderbom have contributed to our topographical material.

I myself drew a map of the middle column's route, which,

however, only takes in the road itself and its immediate surroundings.

After the expedition's work is finished it becomes the task of the expert to enter and combine the various columns' maps upon large sheets and as far as possible to bring them into accord with one another. This work of collation could not be left in safer hands than those of Dr. Erik Norin.

XXVIII

THE DISCOVERY OF NEW LOP NOR[1] BY NILS G. HÖRNER

THE last camp was No. 118; this is No. 61. This means that I have come some way on the return journey eastward from Lop Nor and am now once more on the old familiar route of the outward journey. This is the place of the Christmas camp, and it has turned out that I have celebrated Easter here too. Came back here on April the 2nd, here to the nearest water we had found east of the dry, hard, lumpy salt-crust of the former greater Lop Nor. Left here on the morning of the day after Christmas, 1930, and returned on Holy Thursday, 1931. On Easter Eve we had a feast of joy and thanksgiving. With improvised cloth on an improvised table, bright lights and Easter decorations. And then the banquet. Afterwards coffee by a blazing Easter fire close to the camp. After the recent Spartan life of the desert crossing, with strict rationing of food and water and fuel, this Easter celebration was mighty festive, refreshing and pleasant. All happy, and with good reason.

I believe we have, broadly speaking, accomplished our task successfully.

The task was this: Go to Lop Nor eastward through the desert without coming into contact with the authorities of Sinkiang. Map the whole of new Lop Nor, including those parts of it which lie nearest to Kara-koshun, but do *not* go to Kara-koshun, where there would be a risk of meeting people from Miran or Charkhlik. Take note of

[1] Since the previous chapter was written for the Swedish edition of this book, an important record has come from Dr. Nils G. Hörner about the Lop Nor problem. It is a continuation of the last chapter of the book *Across the Gobi Desert*, and it is the solution of the problem.

the river ramifications east of Lou-lan and ascertain whether there are any river ramifications south-west of Lou-lan. Without archæological obligations, still keep your eyes open for finds *en route*. Do *not* make any exploration of the terraces at the foot of Kuruk-tagh, because this task belongs to Norin's programme. If possible get out again without having been in any settlement in Eastern Turkistan.

Fortunately, considerate comrades had, before my return to Su-chou in October, taken care of the provision of suitable camels, and when I made the plan for the Lop Nor journey, it was an advantage to be able to consult with the comrades on various points. I got much good advice. Johansen's suggestion that instead of Mongol felt pack-saddles such as we had used hitherto I should get Chinese pack-saddles stuffed with hay, proved very well considered and sound.

The plan for the Lop Nor journey was something like this: The main part of the equipment from Su-chou. Flour, camel-beans, meat, a little green stuff, etc., from Tun-huang. Thence also meat supplies in the form of live sheep as far as possible. At Tun-huang I would hire an auxiliary caravan to take provisions out to the depot I intended to establish immediately to the east of the former greater Lop Nor's dry salt-bed. The hired caravan would afterwards accompany me a bit further, as far as the owner would allow it to go (two days' march beyond the last grazing), and thus ease the expedition's own camels at the start. I intended to take a part of the provision of ice blocks from where the caravan road crosses the lower Sulo-ho at Toghrak-bulak, and the rest would be taken at Bash-toghrak and other water-places along the caravan road between the lower Sulo-ho and the great salt-crust. We would go with a sufficient supply of ice over to the north side of ancient Lop Nor's great eastern bay at the foot of the westernmost spurs of Pei-shan. Stein's map shows grazing there, and I would try to dig a well as far as possible to the west. If the well proved satisfactory in quality and quantity of water and in position, the depot would be established there. If the conditions were sufficiently favourable I would try to get some more sheep to the depot, so as to have meat for the return journey. My extra man would take charge of the depot during our absence for at most three months. If we found no suitable water-place, the depot would be established at the terminal point of Pei-han in the barren desert and left to take care of itself, and we would have to put up with a diet of flour on the return journey.

The plan has held good, apart from the fact that our water supply had to be taken in somewhat otherwise than we had intended. As you know from the letters at Christmas-time, we found a suitable depot with water and grazing, and sent a man back with the returning hired caravan. Our man was commissioned to send off and collect letters and to find out whether my traps, which should have gone with the last consignment from you to Folke Bergman, had yet reached Tun-huang, which however they had not. Then he was to buy two camel loads of flour and eight live sheep, hire two camels with one man, bring out the flour and the sheep at once to the depot, send back the hired camels, and himself wait for us at the depot, looking after the sheep meanwhile. He was to reckon that we should be away from the depot three months, but in case we might return earlier, he was to hurry over the Tun-huang journey and be back at the depot as soon as possible. It could not be very pleasant to be left alone by a little newly dug well in the desolate desert, without means of transport, especially for a mountain Tibetan with no desert experience. But the man had come on this journey at his own urgent request, which had finally overcome my great misgivings. He had been our guide at Nan-shan last autumn (good) and promised to do anything if only he got employment for the winter's desert journey too. Now he got a rotten job. Did not grumble, though he was mighty scared the water would give out in the well (needless apprehension). It reassured him somewhat that he had a spade. When we started out on the Lop salt-crust, and he saw us disappear over the horizon on the great "salt sea," he was afraid we would never come back, but fortunately he still carried on with his job. He told us afterwards that he thought of trying to load up enough flour and other indispensable articles and to take them back with him to Tun-huang, if we had not appeared a month or two after the appointed time. To be on the safe side I had, however, written to Birger Bohlin asking him to send and fetch the man at the end of May, if we had not been heard of before that. A sketch map and description of the road was enclosed in the letter to Birger Bohlin. So there was scarcely any risk for the marooned man, but I do not wonder he found his job unpleasant. I have described the journey up to the time when we parted with the auxiliary caravan, in the letters then sent. I certainly thought then that the going over the salt-crust was rather like that over a rough-ploughed and then frozen or dried-up field, but I soon came to look at it otherwise. Some hours after I sent off the letter by the returning caravan we got into an unpleasant terrain in a jumble of hard salt-blocks, sharp edged in parts. Very difficult for the camels. The encampment in the field of salt-blocks that evening was quite fantastic.

During this memorable pilgrimage over salt and "yardang" country not much was written in my geological diary. Instead, I entered notes of the journey itself, impressions and so on. Since I am now short of time, paper and ink, I refer you to diary for 26.12.30 to 8.1.31 (Part VII, pp. 17–34). It is in the bundle of diary pages I send at the same time as my letter. The journey undeniably had its hardships, but it was, above all, interesting. Enormously! If only you can, without too much difficulty, interpret my illegible crowsfeet, you, as the great desert traveller and pioneer in these regions, will share with interest the experiences of our desert crossing. Thanks to the detour round the large open salt-water lake our journey was indeed longer than we counted on. We came very near the utmost limit of what could be done on our resources. We thought our water supply, in the form of snow, was large at the start, and we economized strictly from the beginning. (Such luxuries as washing, shaving and tooth-brushing were, as a matter of course, strictly forbidden during the fourteen days the desert journey lasted. One exception: a little, little drop of water for the cooks' hands before the preparation of food, as well as a little water for possible wound treatment.) When we reached the Tarim (water-bearing Kuruk-darya) our water supply was finished. Through the salt desert we had, of course, also to be sparing of the fuel supply: only what was absolutely necessary for cooking. Nothing extra for warming ourselves. Well yes, after the cooking Mr. Chên used to have a part of the kitchen embers brought into our tent on a dish. Very beneficial to the fair copying of the day's route, to be able to warm our fingers. Fortunately no cold to speak of. Evening and morning temperature often round — 10° C. During the whole journey, too, the morning and evening temperature fell only once to — 20° C. (Lucky it was not cold.) My fingers, that were frost-bitten last year, go on strike altogether when it is cold, and my nose freezes again far too easily. During the crossing, went a little footsore now and then, and there were other petty casualties. But everyone had enough to eat and drink and, in spite of minor defects, was in fairly good condition. The camels on the contrary in a bad way. The soles of their feet were badly worn by the hard, sharp salt-blocks and wet salt-slush. Bloody tracks. Not a drop of water had they had to drink from December the 25th, Christmas Day, till January the 8th, fourteen days. And practically speaking no grazing either during the whole time; a few reeds a day's march from the Christmas camp and a little scanty shrub grazing by the "River of Disappointment," otherwise nothing. Fed on a limited quantity of beans of which scarcely a day's ration remained when we reached the Tarim. Banche and his assistants had their work cut out to keep the camels in any sort of condition; "breakdown" seemed imminent several times and at the end of the journey it was all too plain that they could not hold out much longer. How Banche, sacrificing his own rest, stayed up doctoring the camels, "soled" them, physicked them, rearranged the loads and used the hay from the pack-saddles for fodder, by degrees, as they grew lighter through the shrinking of the supplies. How Banche managed so that all the camels came through, though most of them looked pitiful. For one thing the belly ropes had not been re-tightened, and as they hung dangling, they emphasized in, to say the least, a striking manner the brutes' almost ghastly loss of flesh during the fourteen days. The endurance of camels is astounding—sometimes. Their delicacy is equally astounding at other times.

On December the 28th we found in the barren desert an apparently dying tame camel (marked ⊏.) When we came, it got up with obvious difficulty. Close by lay a very immature camel fœtus, frozen stiff. The "dying" camel, which had its nose-pin in place, but not a sign of a saddlemark, was the most emaciated beast I ever saw. The camel was left to its fate, and we went on. But it came stumbling after and soon enough recovered its power of walking. I had certainly said that we would leave the poor beast in peace, but when it followed of its own accord, my men, after a while, put a cord on its nose-pin and fastened the cord to the end of the last string—and since the camel was anyhow out in hopelessly barren desert, it might as well have a chance to get out. But it had no appetite and would not even take beans. However moribund it seemed to be when we found it, it went fasting all the way to the Tarim. There it gave in, lay down in passive apathy while our camels feasted on the reeds and water of the Tarim and made up for their time of fasting. A month later one of my men had an errand to the place where the sick camel had given in. It had come round, had grazed and drunk a little, and was taken over to our camp on an island in the Tarim delta. If it lives, it seems it will have to stay in solitude upon its island with abundant grazing and unlimited fresh water until another winter makes ice-bridges for it. When the caravan left the island, the stray followed for a bit, but was scared and turned back when it saw one of our camels go down through the ice.

Well, to return to our journey. On January the 8th we had thus successfully reached the Tarim delta, but scarcely a beginning even had been made of the mapping of Lop Nor. The chief part remained; how much it was impossible to know, but it was important to lose no time. A couple of days' halt for rest, repairs, washing—I had not a clean stitch when we reached the Tarim, and not a whole stocking—and the completion of notes and maps; then we would start again. But the most cursory glance at the camels was enough to convince me that Banche was right; impossible to travel with these camels in two or three days, even if they found grazing and water on our march. The best camels needed at least a week to feed up and get thoroughly rested. Most of them ought to have about a month if only to give their sore feet time to heal.

The camels, yes, they give one a lot to think about. Quite uncertain whether they can manage the necessary additional journeys in the Lop Nor district and then take us back to Tun-huang. And the fodder question. The beans which were to have lasted back to the depot, where we left the bean supply for the return journey from the depot to Tun-huang—the beans are already used up, down to a bare day's ration. Shall we procure fodder and possibly some fresh camels from Tikenlik or Singer or perhaps some other place? It seems almost necessary, but I will avoid it if possible. First and foremost I do not want to announce our presence in the country of Sinkiang. Further, none of my men is familiar with the country, no-one knows our roads. In the event of a tour to Tikenlik or Singer I must go with it myself. First the delay here (Camp H 75) with only a slight reconnaissance, then a journey to Tikenlik or Singer through territory which Norin has already dealt with; no, it costs too much time; we *must* try to find a way out. We might take reeds as camel fodder instead of beans. But we have nothing to cut the reeds with. Certainly I had once procured two sickles, to be on the safe side, but they had gone by mistake with one of the other caravans. We can gather reeds by hand, though it is a slow process, Banche declares, and agrees that somehow we must find a way out. Well, the ten days' immediate rest for the camels can be arranged all right. I shall reconnoitre as much as can be reached from this camp meanwhile, just find out about the river ramifications and go to Lou-lan. So I thought! But I was held up with a vengeance. On January the 11th I got strictly localized but very severe pain in the right calf, that is to say only a small spot was affected; nothing was to be seen. Supposed it was some sort of passing muscular cramp after the march. Soon could not stand on the leg: Lang and Li had to help me. Soon be over, I thought, but must go to bed. Little bit of fever. Comes of the muscular cramp, I assumed. But next day a little worse, and no better the day after. Could not help myself at all. Yes, that was a good one! I found nothing that suited in *Advice and Instructions in Hygiene and Care of the Sick for Vessels in Coastal and Baltic Voyages*. This is the only medical work I possess—thanks to it all the same—I got it from Folke Bergman. Since, in contrast with the many-sided Birger Bohlin I have no knowledge of such things, there was nothing to prevent me imagining the worst I had heard tell of about leg complaints other than fractures and blood poisoning, for even I could see it was not that. Wonder what sciatica feels like or what are the symptoms of thrombosis. It could not be varicose veins. But what about rheumatism? Or gout? Certainly my attempts at diagnosis disclose an ignorance remarkable even in a layman. But how long would it be before I was fit again? Here we are, the work begun, the sequel within reach. Is this ailment to make a fiasco of the whole enterprise? Think about what remains to be done in the time at our disposal—the time is limited both by climate and by the stock of provisions. Feel uneasy. Very.

My falling ill occasioned a general lassitude in the whole camp. The only thing that went on as usual was the grazing of the camels. After three days Banche was commissioned to ride thirty li to the south-east, find out about the ruins of Lou-lan and then discover the easiest possible way there for the caravan. I discussed the situation with Mr. Chên and asked if he would map the river ramifications in the neighbourhood of the camp and up to the foot of the mountains. He fully understood the awkwardness of my position, and answered something like this: "Don't you worry. Stay quietly in bed, rest and recover. The mapping must be done and I will do my best." And, like the modest and considerate man he is, he added: "Of course it won't be the same as if you did it yourself, but I will do my very best. You just rest, and don't worry." Said it, went and did splendidly. As usual.

Banche came back surprisingly soon. Yes, he had found the ruins. Strangely forked branches of the river had forced him to the south instead of the south-east, but in any case he had found a ruin. I discovered later that this was ruin L.B. on Stein's map. But it was possibly thirteen li away, nothing like thirty. And south of the camp, not south-east. If it was not due south it was possibly a shade west of south. It could never be the right one, so Banche was sent out again the following day. Was to ride, whatever detours might be necessary, to a point thirty li south-east of the camp, find out about the ruins there, find a practicable way through the yardangs and ascertain how near the river came to the ruins, and also get such information as he could about the river. Was given two days for the job. Took sleeping fur and small food bag, and went off. Came back on January the 16th in the evening. Had found Lou-lan and had a good deal of information about the river and the grazing, which, however, did not reach the immediate neighbourhood of Lou-lan.

Meanwhile Mr. Chên had mapped the area close round the camp, and I was decidedly better. Could get about a little on crutches, but not bear any weight to speak of on the leg. Had two handles on the cyclometer, and these served for making into crutches. Had a pitiable effect, and the too obvious commiseration of the servants was frightfully annoying. I determined in any event to make a start on the 17th with Lou-lan as my objective. They made me a bed on a big camel; I was helped up and tucked in, and made a pleasant little journey up and down, down and up through the wind-eroded pits of the yardang country, after we had crossed and circumnavigated fantastically branched curves. Flooded yardang country like Lake Mälar or the Skärgård in miniature. Neither trees nor rocks. Mr. Chên mapped the route. The transport travelled slowly. The caravan wound forward in extraordinary curves.

We only reached Lou-lan on January the 18th. Sent two men at once with the camels and most of the baggage to the grazing-ground by the river, only keeping what was necessary. We were to be fetched with the requisite number of camels on January the 20th. Mr. Chên made an astronomical fixed-point-determination, with the special object of obtaining a standard point in relation to his previously ascertained longitudes. My wretched leg prevented my making a sight-seeing trip in the famous town of Lou-lan. I fixed a Swedish flag uncommonly firmly to a flagstaff we had brought. Both nailed and sewed it tight. The flag was to be flown on the highest tower of Lou-lan. I prepared two documents to accompany the flag. The first document I engrossed in red and black Chinese ink and thought it looked fine. Mr. Chên was delighted with the flag flying and the documentary addition when he had taken in the wording, which, duly signed, was as follows: " In honour of Dr. Sven Hedin, Lou-lan's discoverer and first explorer, his men hoist this flag here. Lou-lan, January the 19th, 1931. Nils G. Hörner. Parker C. Chên."

The other " document " contained only the information:

> " Dr. Erik Norin of the Sven Hedin Expedition studied part of the ancient Lop lakes in connexion with his extensive geological and topographical survey of Kuruk-tagh, 1928–30. We are surveying geologically and topographically other parts of the Lop region, especially the new rivers and lakes, during the winter, 1930–31, hoping to return from here to continue our previous work in other lake basins. Lou-lan, January the 19th, 1931. Nils G. Hörner, Parker C. Chên."[1]

Mr. Chên and I attached our visiting cards, he writing under his name: " Member of Dr. Sven Hedin's Expedition." The " documents " and the cards were carefully rolled, and placed in a substantial brass thermometer case, whose proper occupant (minimum thermometer) had unfortunately come to grief. The case was closed with its

[1] These " documents " were written in English.

well-fitting cover, and the joint was caulked with leucoplast. Then Lang climbed up on to the highest tower, planted the flagstaff there and stayed it with iron wire—strong stays which, however, were scarcely visible from below. The document cylinder at the foot of the flagstaff, half buried, half projecting. There is not likely to be anything left of the flag after a spring's desert storms have raged over Lou-lan. The staff ought to last some years, thin as it is. But the "documents." If no traveller takes the trouble to remove it before that time, some archæologist two thousand years hence may find the paper well preserved (despite its poor quality) and will try to interpret the strange script. When the flag and the "documents" were installed on January the 19th, I was fit enough to be out and to photograph the incident.

The journey from Lou-lan to Camp No. 79 by the Tarim had also to be made in my bedding on camel-back, but I was clearly well on the way to recovery. By January the 22nd I could walk a very little and could sit in the saddle. Slow reconnaissance ride with Banche as attendant. Serious obstacle that the river arms great and small had long stretches of open water. Some seemed not to be frozen at all. January the 23rd, I had a try to walk with a stick and reconnoitre to N.N.E. from Camp 79. The river crossings troublesome. At one place I had to drag myself over precariously thin and precariously bending ice.

By January the 24th I was sufficiently recovered to undertake, with Banche, Lang and five camels, a long reconnoitring expedition for the mapping of the western shore of Lop Nor, south of the river-mouths. Reckoned our absence at a week or at most ten days. Mr. Chên, who had the main body of the camels and equipment and two men, would meanwhile be mapping in the Tarim delta. The distribution was made so that I took the salt lake for my share, and Mr. Chên the river ramifications. I, however, was to deal with the flooded area east of Camp 79. The first day's march through dry yardang country and flooded yardang country was very troublesome with my ailment, and the second day it was a tough job examining certain deposits and measuring up vertical elevations and taking samples—

and as far as time permitted seeing something of the remains of new L.M. 1, and L.M. 3 close by Camp 91. The remains occurred, for the most part inconsiderably, in the mesas of the river, especially where these are somewhat detached. There was no march on the second day. Only to have one small tent and to live with the caravan men was pleasant in some ways, but the cooking, simple though it was, filled the tent with smoke, and the smoke filled my eyes with tears when I was trying to draw maps and make notes. Depended on wind conditions; tried, sometimes successfully enough, sometimes with difficulty. When I had no writing work it was pleasant by the open fire with the caravan men's company.

On January the 26th and the following day we continued our little reconnaissance patrol. Had little trouble with the leg as I went on, so it was luckily some chance harmless ailment, though it was troublesome enough so long as it lasted. We went through the discharge area of the many-branched Tarim, bays and promontories and "yardang skerries," river channels and little expansions here and there, only some hundreds of metres, at most some kilometres, straight across till the yardang islands begin again. Abundant reeds in the "yardang skerries" where sometimes the islands, sometimes the water, occupies the greater part of the surface. Here and there larger dry yardang areas between the channels. We passed Stein's "Castrum Le," immediately contiguous with a large detached ice surface (probably an extension of an arm of the river). Also small pools in the wind pits beside the walls. The surface of the ground on which the walls rest is about four metres above the present water level. That is to say the ground level of the time of Lou-lan lies about four metres above the present surface of Lop Nor. Visibility was, annoyingly enough, very poor, so one could see little of the surroundings; much dust had been deposited on the reeds when the "buran," which was only a moderate wind this time, was followed by calm. One got thoroughly powdered with the fine dust when one walked through the close standing reeds. Progress was slow. Glare ice, which was always too slippery for the camels to cross without difficulty. My two caravan men took soil from the yardang islands in their greatcoats and "sanded" the footways for the camels. Here and there open water obstructed us; in other places the ice was weak. A man might perhaps get over dry or with a slight risk of getting into the water, but the camels had to make a detour.

Then we came from the fresh water and its reeds up on to a small area a couple of metres higher, or rather more, covered with salt crust, and soon to a sterile bay of salt Lop Nor. The water was not, however, nearly so salt as in the southernmost and easternmost parts of the lake which we visited on the outward journey. Here the fresh water of the Tarim flowed into salt Lop Nor, and in front of the river-mouth the salt content of the water was far from saturation-point. Probably the islands and aits, with narrow and shallow passages between, prevent the free exchange between the great lake basin's concentrated salt solution and the brackish water here. Some aits appeared dimly, but the flying dust destroyed visibility, so that it was impossible to get a general view. The water in front of the river mouths was covered with ice when I was there on January the 27th. The ice too weak for camels. Accordingly the islands had to be reconnoitred on foot, but the ice broke, so the attempt had to be abandoned. Here and there shallow sounds connecting the fresh-water with the salt-water lakes, in other places regular river channels, very obstructive, since they were for the most part open and impassable—curved, winding, branched. Having to follow the windings and ramifications up stream through yardang country to find a practicable ice bridge was a tedious business and the devil for route mapping, especially as the light was too bad to make any checking observations. After we had got well over the river branches and sounds, the route mapping went at full speed with no obstacles. In the tract near the river-mouths, quite distinct shore lines and small beaches. Somewhat further off new Lop Nor had overflowed a salt-crust region with very marked ridges and blocks. At the edge of the flooding the salt-ridges and salt-blocks had been left unaffected, the hollows between them had been submerged and, on the evaporation of the water, had got a clean, white, fresh salt crust (later somewhat soiled with dust). The old northern salt-ridges stick up like small islands above the new salt crust after the water has withdrawn a good way. Here and in the continuation southward the salt-water lake is edged with a belt of salt-marsh of varying width, covered for the most part by a thin, new salt crust—or film. This belt divides the water from the dry salt crust. Here the white or faintly yellowish (cream-coloured) new salt surface passes beyond the range of vision (which in any event is very soon the case with a very flat surface. The most extensive observations did not exceed five kilometres). Beaches in miniature, spume wreaths, small drifted shrub branches, ripples, etc., mark the edge of the new salt against the old salt crust.

Just as during the outward march at the New Year, it was impossible to find any bearing points for route mapping. Banche had to be our bearing point, to ride on in advance until he on his trotting camel appeared like a little exclamation mark in the distance, to turn his camel broadside on and stop. I take compass bearings and hurry along with my cyclometer wheel to Banche in as straight a line as I can. When I get there, Banche rides on at the trot again to be the sighting point for the next bearing, and I have to wait quietly till Banche and the camel come broadside on again. It is quite a strain, marching thus turn about, to keep up the same average speed as Lang, who trudges along more slowly but untiringly with his little string of transport camels.

When we make our evening camp it is growing dusk. Late attempts to penetrate with lanterns, or excursions over new salt crust, and tramp to find out where the present fortuitous shore goes. Ascertained in another direction that the difference in height between the prevailing chance height of the water and high water level did not reach half a metre. That a fall in the water level of less than half a metre should displace the shore line as much as five kilometres shows the flatness of the area.

On January the 30th we again came to the "River of Disappointment," and got direct connexion with the mapping of the outward journey (point passed January the 3rd). This time the "river" was no disappointment. We knew beforehand that it was only one of the salt-water drowned river channels—and in the actual "debouchment area" there was no mistaking it even at the first glance—profuse salt deposit and no masking overblown sand as further up.

After this mapping had been joined on to that of the outward journey and some further shore investigations dealt with, we again crossed a region of dry salt crust towards the west-north-west, considerably further north than on the journey out. Then a camp on the salt-block ground for the night of January the 31st to February the 1st.

In the border territory between the salt crust and the yardang country, observations of the ancient changes in greater Lop Nor. We had thought of examining the depression (probably old lake basin) which you found when taking levels in 1891, of studying the nature of the sediment, etc., but the condition of the camels made it necessary to make for water and pasture. It is probable, however, that there were small salt-water lakes when the river branches of the Lou-lan time also flowed in this direction. One finds lakes, or at least temporary lakelets among the obvious river deposits of the yardang country. In the small crossing towards the north-east, which we now made through a piece of yardang country, there was a good opportunity to study the nature of the sediment: the delta deposits left by the very variable river branches before these reached their final discharge basin, the salt lake. In passing, a quantity of small archæological pickings was found, mostly neolithic small implements, sundry scrapers, etc., as well as several stone axes (neolithic). Also some objects of later date. Moreover, a lot of hewn logs, all of which were left from some house, probably of the Lan-lou period.

On February the 2nd we camped again on the western edge of the salt crust, and had not far to go to grazing and water. Had wished to make a number of further studies here, but Banche explained the absolute necessity of bringing the camels as soon and as easily as possible to grazing and water. Certainly they had this time only been without these necessaries for seven days, but it was clearly too much for their powers. Banche had said before the start that, though he had chosen the best camels, they had not sufficiently recovered for a journey like this, and their condition deteriorated all too obviously day by day, thus confirming Banche's misgivings. The reeds we had brought with us were clearly not nourishing enough. As much as possible of the hay from the pack-saddles had been sacrificed as camel fodder, and the weakest of them were forcibly fed in the evenings with the same sort of " dumpling gruel " or " dough soup " that we had ourselves. It was fun to see Banche with difficulty holding the refractory camels' mouths open. The boiler stood alongside, and Lang rammed the big ladle full of food into the camel's mouth and emptied it as far down as he could. The ladle banged audibly on the walls of the mouth ; the camel was ungracious and tried to spit. Did so every time. I could not help reflecting that it was our food-ladle and that we were short of water. so that washing up was a bit perfunctory—a thing that can also happen when there is abundance of water.

On February the 3rd in the morning Banche was very eager that we should get away as quickly as possible. When we were ready to start it was still dark, and we had to wait an hour for the dawn on account of the mapping. Sandstorm and headwind, cold and unpleasant, the camels ill-disposed, do not want to go. One lies down time after time and refuses to go on, though it is travelling unladen. Banche has all kinds of trouble to get it along. He succeeds in getting the wretched camel into a little shelter where the driving sand is not quite so troublesome. The camel is allowed to rest for a while. A pack-saddle is rifled, our last bread is pressed upon the beast, and Banche's patience overcomes the submissive camel's resistance. Fortunately we quite soon reached fresh water and a patch of reeds. Camped immediately and loosed the camels to graze. But, as ill luck would have it, the most exhausted camel goes through weak ice. Shallow water, half a metre, bottom soft, but not impossible. The camel gave in at once, lay down, humps and sundry other things stuck up. Neck bent back, head resting on the ice. The camel awaited death and did not trouble itself to try to come up on to dry land. Four hours we worked on him. Broke away the ice so that the brute should be able to come ashore easily. There were not many metres between the camel and the land, but close to the land was thick ice frozen to the bottom, and it was a laborious business getting the ice away with the tools we had. Tried by hook or crook to get the camel to get up, but it remained passive. Held its head up, though, and looked at us. Badly off for salvage tackle. However, my men had brought along as fuel a piece of a small joist they had found remaining from some house in what is now desert. The joist was too short for a lever, but still we tried, pushed the joist in under the camel, and then Lang and I lifted, while Banche pulled on the nose rope and encouraged it. This was clearly too much for the camel. It got up. But did not trouble itself to go ashore, in spite of Banche's leading. When there was no longer anything supporting it underneath, the camel lay down again, for all Banche's shouts of encouragement. After a moment or two it was lying there as before. I tried to get the joist across from ice-edge to ice-edge under the camel to prevent it from sinking down. But the joist was too short and too weak. When the camel's weight came on it it gave way. But we had succeeded in throwing under it a rope we had lying ready. We tried to haul, we hitched camels on in front and made them toil and pull. We tried by every means to get the camel to get up once again so as then to lay it down where the ice was strong enough and thence, with the help of the other camels, to haul it ashore. Nothing was any use. It was clear that the camel must be given up as lost. Cold and strong wind. The water froze in the camel's wool. If only I had had a rifle with me, but I had not even a pistol. Lop Nor is a very peaceful "war-zone," so one can safely leave weapons behind at the main camp when one goes reconnoitring. For once in a way a firearm would surely have come into use if I had had one. But now, instead, we went on toiling at hopeless attempts at rescue, in slush and icy wind. After four hours the camel began definitely to expire. Wet through with the splashing, sweating and frozen at the same time, we stayed up the tent better against the wind, made a fire and dried our clothes. No-one wanted to eat. Banche looked as if he had lost a dear friend, and Lang, who is usually happy at the worst of times, was anything but content. The camels, which to begin with had been too much taken up with their grazing to give more than a passing glance at their unhappy comrade, seemed anxious and stayed close beside the tent instead of by the reeds. Next morning the lost camel was dead and stiff and firmly frozen in the ice. The back and humps stood up as in a normal lying camel, but the head hung down, partly frozen into the ice.

I now employed two days in mapping the southern border of the flooded area between salt Lop Nor and the Lou-lan tract. Flooded yardang country, lakes and wide reed beds. To a great extent the distribution of the water was determined by ancient river-beds. The water has certainly now penetrated into old dry river furrows and forms elongated curves, but this on a very limited scale. More important is the function of the old river-beds as ramparts which check the further extension of the flood. Principally by reason of their greater resistance to wind erosion, the old river-beds—or, more accurately, the old river-banks—have remained as elevated ridges several metres above the level of the surroundings. One can easily distinguish the different types and different "generations" of former rivers, and perhaps the attempts at a more comprehensive reconstruction might lead to an illuminating map. In this tract between Lou-lan and the mouths of Kuruk-darya is clearly seen a circumstance which I have observed in other quarters and which Stein has already pointed out. There have at some time been two distinctly separated periods of water transmission in the "Kuruk-darya system," divided by a long period when, as in the last river diversion many years ago, the water went other ways. The water transmission period in "Kuruk-darya," which next preceded the present, is recent. Kuruk-darya is of course an inappropriate name now that a great river actually flows there. The two "generations" of water transmission with intervening wind-erosion are confirmed among other things in the following manner. Yardangs, scattered or in small groups, raise themselves above shallow wind-eroded

" low surface " with remnants of abundant brushwood where later wind erosion has not yet had time to tear up the ground—(there are also many remains of bushes on the high yardangs). After a period of wind erosion from which the higher yardangs remained standing as evidence of the erosion, there followed a new " wet " period—that is to say locally wet, while the Tarim again flowed in the northern channel. Probably some sedimentation between the older yardangs. On the low surface between the yardangs an abundant brushwood then grew up, and then the river again left the northern channel, probably for the last time previous to the present flow. After the land was left dry, the wind erosion has slightly and irregularly eaten into the scrub country. It is pretty certain that both the erosion periods are post-Lou-lan. Similar phenomena are widespread in the lower " Kuruk-darya " region (among others " castrum L.E."). In the lowest " Kuruk-darya " tract there are a number of old tamarisk stumps with life still in them. In fact there are old tamarisks close to a newly flooded region, which as a whole seem as dry and dead as anything can be, but from whose apparently dried-up stems fresh young shoots are springing out.

Let us return to my reconnaissance of February the 4th and 5th. These days were devoted to the mapping of the southern border of the region flooded by fresh water and to the study of the sediment. Also excursion to Stein's " Mesa L.C." near Lou-lan, to look at these outermost of the preserved mesa stratifications. Unfortunately the work had to be hurried because we were short of food. On February the 5th we had not a scrap of food left of any kind except tea and a little sugar, and without food one soon gets out of form. So it was a matter of marching to camping-place 79 in the faint hope that Mr. Chên would still be there with the main camp. We got there at nightfall, mighty peckish. No camp. Mr. Chên, reasonably enough, had moved, so as to have his sphere of labour nearer to hand. But, like the kind and considerate man he is, he had foreseen our probable shortness of provisions—though he could not know that we had been obliged to divide our own food with the camels. He had had a little cairn of shrub branches built on a yardang hill close to the camping-place and had hung up an empty butter jar to attract attention. And under the branches a sack containing flour and a little bread. Also a gay and friendly letter expressing his hope of soon seeing us safe and sound, reunited at the main camp. Information as to its position. Marvellous how reviving food is when one has been living on short rations for a while and has fasted altogether on the last day. Now there was joy and contentment again. Banche crooned, Lang laughed, and even the mishap with the camel seemed forgotten. Oddly, here were three men travelling and getting on splendidly together: a Swede, a Mongol and a Tibetan. The Swede understood neither Mongolian nor Tibetan, the Mongol neither Swedish nor Tibetan, the Tibetan neither Swedish nor Mongolian. And none of us understood a word of the Turki language that is spoken in this country, Eastern Turkistan, where we are travelling. But things go splendidly for all that. The Tibetan speaks Chinese like his native tongue, the Mongol speaks very fair Chinese and knows a couple of dozen English words. The Swede, that is to say I, knows perhaps a couple of dozen Chinese words besides the numerals. But certain words are extremely serviceable, for example one which sounds something like " dongchi " and seems more or less to correspond with the Swedish slang collective " grunkor."[1] Is used with success for all sorts of things, cameras and cooking utensils, field-glasses and bedding, drills, spades, tent fittings, saddles and ropes. For its completion the word only needs an easily made indication in the wonderfully effective sign-language. There cannot indeed be any more profound interchange of thought, but this did not prevent us understanding one another perfectly. As for Turki, we have no need for it, seeing that we never meet any of the natives of the country.

In any case it was pleasant to meet Mr. Chên again on February the 6th, after nearly two weeks' absence from the main camp. Pleasant to be able to converse freely again, and, besides, the varied cuisine of the main camp was welcome. And, when the meat gives out, a fairly good cook

[1] Gadgets (Tung-hsi).

can accomplish a whole lot with flour and rice and fat, a few raisins, dried fruits and dried milk, and a little jam. There can be multifarious and varied meals, but Mr. Chên and I have to help in thinking out how they are to be prepared. The cook knows, alas ! nothing without instructions, but if the instructions are sound, he turns out the meal admirably. Pity neither Mr. Chên nor I know anything at all about cooking, but, as it is, it has gone splendidly, and the diet has been varied and good. Some tins of sardines have provided an extra relish from time to time, and so long as the soup cubes lasted they were a welcome addition. During the reconnoitring expeditions I have lived with the servants, shared their tent and their victuals : "dough-soup" and perpetually dough-soup. It is prepared with admirable efficiency. Immediately after making camp the fire is lighted and the pot is put on with ice, snow or water, whichever is available. As soon as the water boils the tea-pot is filled, and the rest of the water goes to the dough-soup. While waiting for the water to boil one kneads flour and water into a dough, rolls it out and cuts it into strips. When the water boils and enough has been taken out for the tea, a man sits on either side of the pot and divides the strips of dough by hand into small pieces about the size of biscuits and throws the pieces one by one into the pot. It is done with vast energy and precision. When the dough strips have been thrown in the dish is ready. Possibly a pinch of salt goes in too. If one has meat one puts the cubes of flesh into the water before the throwing in of the dough begins. Then the dish is pretty good, but how people can stand eating nothing but dough-soup, without meat, day after day, for a couple of months, without complaint and without comment, I do not understand. But my caravan crew put up with this diet after the meat came to an end in the beginning of February. (On our reconnaissance it had already failed in January.) The "garrison" can in no way be blamed that the food then becomes in such a degree monotonous and plain. We had with us a quantity of lard and quite a lot of sugar too, so that there should be enough for all. But they did not care about either sugar or lard, at least not as far as I could see. Nor did they bake bread for themselves. Dough-soup and tea, that was their diet, and the men concerned found it quite in order. I got thoroughly sick of the food in the weeks I was out on reconnaissance, though I always took a little stock of bread with me at the start. The main camp's varied menu, with three or four sorts of pancake, boiled flour dishes, baked flour dishes, fried flour dishes and puddings of both flour and rice and little else to ring the changes on, was magnificent after dough-soup.

From February the 7th to the 15th I stayed at the main camp at camping-place 91. The first two days for notes and maps of the reconnaissance just finished. Then mapping round the camp. Investigation of mesa sediment, sectional measurement, specimen taking, etc. During three of these days Mr. Chên made an excursion with two men and two camels for measuring the volume of water and mapping. I had promised my men that they should be together and have a holiday on the Chinese New Year's Day, and they had stated that this would correspond this year with February the 15th in our calendar. On the evening of the 14th they began to doubt if they had given the right day and came to ask how it was (as if I should know). Yes, that is right, I answered, for I could not wait any longer. Gave them five dollars and a packet of cigarettes each and some dried fruit and caramels. February the 15th was celebrated in our camp as the Chinese New Year, while I chopped and dug mesa sediment without helpers. When I saw the moon again some days later, I understood that we had anticipated the Chinese New Year by a couple of days, but we all kept our countenances.

It was high time for me to go. Had a lot more investigations to make in the Lou-lan district, and the spring was on its way. Necessary to hurry to get across the river while the ice still bore. Mr. Chên had begun a little triangulation that I had asked him to do, but I told him if necessary to discontinue everything and take the main caravan over to the tract north of the northernmost arm of the river while the ice still bore. We must in no circumstances take any risk with our main caravan now. If there were any serious trouble with the main caravan, we were as good as caught in a rat-trap. If we delayed a little too long, we were shut up on an island. Felt a little uneasy when I found on February the 16th the ice broken up, and open water at a place where we had taken the caravan across on sound ice on February 6th—the same place where I had slid across over too weak ice on January the 23rd. A short season indeed ; only for a couple of weeks round the turn of the month January to February had the passage been frozen.

After a lot of search we found a place where the ice bore and went on. During the following days a number of supplementary studies were made of the yardang sediment, and then the levelling from new Lop Nor (from the fresh-water lake certainly, but the difference in level between this and the salt-water lake is so slight that in this connexion it can be left out of the reckoning) to Lou-lan. Partly I wanted to ascertain the relative elevations in the yardang landscape of the lake and the river, partly I hoped to be able to join up with your great levelling southward from Lou-lan, of 1901. Uncertain whether the junction would succeed, since I did not know from what point in Lou-lan the 1901 levelling had started. (Unfortunately had not Sven Hedin's works with me, except *My Life as an Explorer* and *Im Herzen von Asien, erster Band*. Wish I had the other part and also a lot of information from *Scientific Results* at hand.) Well, my levelling broke down in any case. Began one morning in calm, fine weather, and the first part of the levelling is certainly successful. Then it began to blow, not particularly hard, but more than a telescope will stand without shaking. The later part of the levelling leaves much to be desired in point of precision. Ought to have done it again, but with the knowledge of the rivers and the river arms we *must* cross, I could not sacrifice a day to renewed levelling, especially since the day which might have come into question was windy, so that we would have had to delay further, waiting for calm weather. In the great yardang country between the lake and Lou-lan the depressions lie in many places below the level of the present lake, but the higher lying parts—particularly the ancient river-beds—have kept out the water. According to my levelling, the natural ground level on which the great stupan (tower) at Lou-lan rests is eight metres above the lake level. (The wind cavities immediately around the tower are more or less at the lake level and a few of them even below it.) The ground in the central room of the house where you found the manuscript (the room excavated) 7·8 metres. The floor in the west room 8·1. Natural ground level by the remains of the "city wall" 6·9. The remains of the wall reach a height of fully two metres. The ground level at the palisade close to the wall 5·9. The upper end of the palisade 6·1. This palisade thrown down, probably for mapping or levelling by some of Lou-lan's modern explorers, Sven Hedin or Stein? I have further points in Lou-lan levelled, so it is conceivable that it will succeed in according with your levelling in 1901. But, as I said, my levelling needs checking. Lou-lan was obviously built on somewhat uneven ground. The manuscript house (yamên?) and a number of other large buildings lay on a little rise, by a whole-fossil river-bed from a much earlier phase and certainly not to be identified with the river-bed of Lou-lan's inhabitants. The near-by rivers of the Lou-lan period outside the town are indeed to a great extent blown into large dry wind cavities. The simpler small cabins, of which ruins still remain, lie partly at a lower level than the manuscript house, as you know better than I. Wish I had had both Hedin's and Stein's publications about Lou-lan. I had neither *Scientific Results* nor *Serindia*. Presumably both Hedin and Stein are aware of the late period bushes in the wind cavities of Lou-lan. The bushes have probably still " latent life, though they hardly budded last year, perhaps for several years. But also the finest twigs, yes, even dry leaves (needle tamarisk) are still in place. If one breaks the very finest twigs, one sees a slight greenish tinge in the fracture. For that matter similar bushes observed in other places in the Lop Desert. In *Innermost Asia* Stein mentions some isolated living tamarisks in desert otherwise without life.

In connexion with the levelling of Lou-lan it may be mentioned that the ruins of a potter's workshop close in to the fresh-water channel lie seven metres above the present water level. The workshop ruin (only the bottom of the oven and thousands on thousands of pottery fragments remain) lies now on the top of a yardang surrounded by wind cavities—a memorial of the activity of the wind erosion since the place was abandoned by the people and the water.

On February the 21st I passed camping-place 79 again on my way to reunite my little group with the main caravan. At a distance it looked like a beacon erected with old dry tree-trunks. My men were glad to see this greeting from the main caravan, but I was almost alarmed. What in all the world! It should have gone north and across all the river arms and ought to have been in safety on the north side by this time. It should not have come in this direction at all. The signal here is a bad sign. The caravan has evidently not been able to get across. Since they have raised the beacon here they have in any event succeeded in getting back to firm ground from the island. But has it been done without mishap? At the "beacon" found a note from Mr. Chên saying that he had been almost all day on February the 18th trying to get across the river to the north with the caravan, but had not found bearing ice anywhere. Therefore he had come back to firm ground in the south. Had had two accidents on the ice. The worst was that the camel carrying the instrument-case managed to go through the ice and went partly into the water. Masen had readily and quickly unloaded the pretty heavy instrument case and got it into safety, and then the camel too had been got out. Now the main caravan had gone westward to make the crossing of the better frozen single river north of Camp 75, where we first reached the Tarim. We might well lose three or four days by the detour, but what of that if only we got across without disaster. Certainly, if the main caravan had still found strong ice north of Camp 75, we ought not in any event to lose any time. Set our course at once westward in multifarious curves in the tortuous wind-furrows and cavities between yardangs. Reached the river at noon on February the 22nd and got over without difficulty. But I agree with Banche; "river to-day not good, to-morrow much not good." Glad we did not delay longer. On February the 22nd the river was already partly open, big holes and swirling current. Still, strong enough ice bridges to get over easily and without risk. But it did not look pleasant. Doubtful if it would have done a couple of days later.

On February the 23rd we caught up with Mr. Chên and the main caravan. They had camped half a kilometre from the place where I said I reckoned to cross to the northernmost river bank on the assumption that I was able to cross the river branches without detour. Mr. Chên had never been in the place before, and I had only supplied directions from Camp 91, no signs for identifying the place. Had only mentioned it in passing without wishing to limit Mr. Chên's freedom of movement by an agreed meeting-place. To be on the safe side he had nevertheless now camped here, and after the detour and without cross bearings it was certainly well done of him to find the very place I meant.

At my request Mr. Chên had during the winter measured the volume of water, partly in the unbranched river north of Camp 75, partly in various branches. The most northerly remained. Mr. Chên had not found anywhere, so late in the year, ice bridges from which to measure the open water. While the camels were being loaded for our departure from Camp H 97, we found, however, a suitable place, and just as the caravan was about to march, I gave the order to halt and camp again so as to make use of probably the last chance of measuring the water volume. Anyone who has seen how much labour is involved in breaking camp and loading a caravan will understand that this was not precisely a pleasing order. But not a sound or a look of discontent! Good humouredly, carefully and well as usual, our men pitched camp again and put our tent in order. Mr. Chên measured the current—an inconsiderable volume of water there. The year's first flight of migrant birds passed over the camp. Spring!

From Camp 97 we continued westward along the northern fresh-water channels, mostly through mesa country, which displayed interesting morphology and tectonics. When one day I passed a ruin by the bank and found it newly excavated—a ruin which is not on the map in Stein's *Innermost Asia*—it started me thinking. What if the Stein expedition has been mapping Lop Nor this winter here too, though we have not seen a trace of it! The excavation seemed to have occurred recently. Was it the Hedin expedition's Chinese archæologist, or was it Stein come back? The camping-place by the ruin appeared pretty fresh. I asked the caravan men about the age of the camel droppings: something like a couple of years, and at a time of year when there was green pasture. On that the thing was clear. When, on a later occasion, I again passed the ruin and looked round a little more, I found an empty, frayed tube of a Kodak film packet. The label remained—size 2¼×3¼ No. one Emull. No. O.H. Expires July, 1929. This ruin by the bank—the position of which Mr. Chên later determined astronomically—cannot have been a town. There are now many obvious remnants of a large house (the timbers in part still standing) and a smaller, more substantial building. There have probably been more.

Let us continue our journey. Mr. Chên and the main caravan stayed, as usual, by the pasture and water. He was to try to deal with as much as he could get at of the lower delta region and the mesas, but there was open water in the way almost everywhere. I went on eastward with a small "reconnoitring patrol" for the mapping of the most northerly and north-easterly parts of Lop Nor. The mapping would be continued to a point where we first reached the lake, on the outward march, at the end of December. Many islands in salt Lop Nor's most northerly part. Partly narrow serpentinized branched sounds and creeks: old river arms from an earlier phase, now salt water. By Lop Nor's north-eastern shore traces of older lake shore with higher water level.

On March the 2nd we reached our old camping-place No. 66 of the outward march, and thus had gone round Lop Nor. The water was now rising. The rim of marsh land between the dry crust and the lake was narrower at Camp 66 than on the outward march. From 66 we turned north again. Had a chance to see something more of the effect of the rising water. Now no longer depositing salt as in winter, but dissolving it. In their turn small streams were actually running in from the lake to the surrounding new salt crust (probably deposited the previous year); the stream is divided into a multitude of branches, which seem to come to a dead end; the little stream looks as if it were devoured by the ground, but little by little the ground is broken and the stream penetrates further. A restricted shore phenomenon, of course, but amusing to watch and should do well as a film shown at many times the speed of the photography.

By March the 3rd our water supply was as nearly as possible finished. We had had mostly ice, and a good deal of it had run away in the heat. The little reserve cask, in spite of packing, had not held tight and so now we had a water famine. And I wanted to make a little excursion to the north-east for ancient shore studies. Banchė and Lang were willing to do without water (and without food as well) for a day, to give me opportunity for the desired studies.

On March the 4th and 5th we went a bit thirsty and hungry, and I studied old "gypsum faces," salt crusts, salt incrustation on mesa remains ("white dragon hills"), shore lines, etc. The human being can stand surprisingly little on an empty belly. This small restriction of food and drink had already set the ground swaying and stars dancing in front of me in broad daylight on March the 5th. A couple of minutes' rest, and it was all right again, and no more trouble. But that Sven Hedin was able to push on to the blessed pool of Khotan-darya on his calamitous march, that I find a miracle. Now that I have tried ever so little how it feels to go empty and dry in the desert, when there is not a vestige of risk, I can understand his feelings.

Finished the shore-line examination at dusk on March the 5th. Fortunately I had the map, with distances, in memory, and Polaris could be dimly seen between the clouds. The desert unusually level and easy going here. We set our course for the nearest creek where we could hope for water fit to use. Night march after a laborious day. But what will one not do if one is hungry and thirsty, and food and drink are calling? I have seldom anything against brick tea, when I have no Lipton's at hand, but this time brick tea was glorious. And even dough-soup tasted good.

On March the 6th, when the spring had already made its entry into Lop Nor, it was sufficiently frozen for me to be able to go out to some of the nearest islands in northern Lop Nor and amplify the map a little. At the New Year the salt lake of Lop Nor was still for the most part open, and in the end of January I had tried to get out to some islands, but the ice had not borne. But on March the 6th, when the fresh-water streams and sounds of the delta were irrevocably open for the year, I could at last get out to some (and those few and near) islands in salt Lop Nor. This is how it happens : the salt lake was still for the most part ice-bound. The spring flood had begun in the Tarim, if on a modest scale, and considerable quantities of fresh water were discharged into Lop Nor. The slight ice covering was enough to prevent the wind from stirring the water of the lake, the lighter fresh water spread out like a thin layer over the heavier salt water. The winter's heavy ice covering was lifted and was mostly detached from the land, then in the beginning of March came a few cold days and nights, the fresh or only slightly salt surface water in the channel between the ice covering and the land froze up, and even the ice covering itself seems to have grown stronger than it was during the winter.

The greater number of the islands was unapproachable ; open water and too weak ice. Mankind needs a number of things to get along. It had been splendid to reach water the evening before and get food and tea. But fuel hardly sufficed for breakfast next morning, and after it there was not a scrap left. When I came back in the evening to Camp 105, the question once more was whether we could travel in the darkness and get what we needed—this time fuel. Here the ground was worse. But we would try. Was quite certain I could find my way in the dark back to Camp 99, and the camel droppings there must have got dry since we left. Kept the line exactly. Found the camping-place, and after we had waited for the moon to rise, we were able to pick up argal enough.

On March the 7th continued the march back. At the ruin mentioned earlier found a communication from Mr. Chên. He had not been able to cross the river branches anywhere, and had thus not been able to map the debouchments of the delta. On account of cloud and moonlight he had deferred the astronomical fixed-point-determinations we had discussed, and had instead gone back to Camp 98 to make a plane-table map of an interesting mesa region, a task I had suggested as an alternative if he should be unable to cross the stream and map the delta. We got back to Camp 98 in the evening and found everything in order. A camel had fallen through the ice while grazing, one of our best. There was clear water without ice in one place, and when they failed to get the camel up otherwise, Li went resolutely into the water up to his armpits, took the camel by the nose rope as though it had been on land, and the two walked, with no more ado, round and up on to dry land, and so all was well.

On March the 8th we moved our tent and baggage over to Camp 106, so as to be in the region for special mapping. Grazing there is poor, so the camel camp has to stay at Camp 98. Preparations for return journey eastward are in full swing, the caravan men have brought in several camel loads of reeds for fodder, the water casks are filled and closed, the pack-saddles seen to, tent and other outfit repaired and put into as good shape as possible. Mr. Chên has finished the little plane-table map and made the astronomical fixed-point-determination at the ruin. I put in the geological features on the plane-table map and made a section. Found, by way of exception, some vertebrate fossils, a few bones only, of a larger animal in the later sediment. Probably of no great importance, but we dug out all we found. The fossil was sticking out a little from a yardang wall, but otherwise we had to dig away 2·4 metres of heavy yardang sediment to get at it. Had only one man available for the purpose and scanty time.

Then the question was how to find anything to pack these fragile—some extremely fragile—things in. No cotton wool. No camels' wool, no paper left. Better lack bread than brains—Lang picked up gypsum crystals, a whole sackful, from the ground. "Burned" them in the embers and pounded the burnt gypsum to powder—not easy with the unsuitable tools we had. Then we plastered as best we could. A worn-out ragged shirt and other garments past use served as wrappers. Certainly we did the plastering altogether wrong, but we did what we could. The plaster was not nearly half dry when we had to pack the treasure. It was absolutely necessary to start. Our somewhat restricted flour ration was enough till we got to the depot, if we hurried and all went well. In the course of my mapping tour to north-east Lop Nor, I had seen enough to be certain that a direct return march by the shortest way across the salt crust to the depot presented no very great difficulty, apart from a couple of days over the salt crust which here seemed not too bad. It was necessary that the main caravan should go very gently back to the depot at the Christmas camp. Now that almost the whole stage was familiar it ought to get through well. Most of the camels had had a long rest with good grazing and we were taking quantities of reeds. One difficulty was the heat. The camels must, however, go without water for at least six marches. Banche was confident that they would be all right; perhaps we should lose a couple of camels on the journey, but certainly they would get through. This of course applies to the camels. For my own part I was very anxious to make a considerable detour, and map the northern shores of ancient Lop Nor and see as much as possible of the filling in of the basin. Asked Mr. Chên if he could and would undertake with two men to take sixteen camels and the greater part of the outfit back by the shortest way to the Christmas camp and the depot. He got the necessary maps and such information as I was able to give. As usual he was immediately and gladly ready to do anything for the common good.

On March the 17th in the afternoon we left Camp 106, Mr. Chên, with Masen and Li and sixteen camels, going eastward, I with Banche and Lang and six camels on the northern detour via the two easternmost salt springs at the foot of Kuruk-tagh, Yetim-bulak and Kaurük-bulak (though there was no hope at all of finding drinkable water there), thence to follow the ancient shore. Both at Yetim-bulak and Kaurük-bulak the water level lay considerably below the ground level, so that it was only after one had made a little hollow in the wet ground that one got free water, and this even thirsty camels refused to drink. At the easternmost spring, Kaurük-bulak, traces were seen of a quite recent encampment, footsteps of men and a few tame camels. Probably the two Mongols we met on December the 19th. Obviously people have sometimes travelled and still occasionally travel north of ancient Lop Nor. Small cairns in several places. At one place we passed the skeleton of a horse, half a day's march further east a little fuel left behind. Recollected what Stein relates about a Chinese merchant who, probably in November 1913 (or 1915 ?) was treacherously plundered and abandoned on the desert road south of ancient Lop Nor by the men who had undertaken to bring him to Tun-huang. The thieves had got away by the northern road round greater Lop Nor with their booty, including a horse. Perhaps it was that horse whose last small load of fuel was dropped half a day's march before the horse itself succumbed, a day's march from Kaurük-bulak. It may be that the thieves got clear for all that, provided they found ice at Kaurük-bulak and afterwards found wells all the way. How their food supply lasted is another question. In spite of their nearness to Kaurük-bulak (if it was their horse) the thieves may very well have perished in the desert.

We continued our journey along the ancient shore as far as possible, but cut across the headlands and bays sometimes, to shorten the way. We started before dawn, rested a while in the middle of the day on account of the heat and went on again till dark. Had a couple of unpleasantly hot days, especially March the 22nd, and the camels began to be seriously exhausted. I had trouble with one knee. Managed to slip on a steep bit of salt ground in the special map area by Camp 106 some days before the start. Only a trifling bruise on the knee, but it was annoyingly obstinate.

March the 24th we had a violent sandstorm. Happened to be in a tract with quantities of dust-fine sand and a little coarser stuff with it, and our course lay obliquely to the wind. Since we were very short of water and a long way from the well at the Christmas camp, we tried to press forward against the sandstorm. Dr. Hedin knows better than anyone else what a regular desert storm is like, when the "sand" is dust-fine and abundant. Sand in eyes, nose, mouth—one can scarcely breathe. And, unless one's goggles hold tight, one can hardly use the twenty-five to fifty metres' visibility there is. It is not easy to keep one's direction by compass and pace one's distance. And we must all keep close so as not to get lost. After some time Banche reported that the camels could go no further in that weather. Nor could I. So we had to make a forced camp. By toil and persistence we at last got up the one tent we had—fortunately a small one. Knocked the tent pegs firmly into the salt crust and laid salt-blocks on them. The tent cover would not stand the wind pressure. We succeeded in getting some empty sacks over the windward side of the tent. Lashed the tent about with ropes and stayed the whole, in raging sandstorm. The tent split and sand drifts were piled at the foot of the tent, grew up higher along the sides, pressed them down and burst the fabric. Stopped up the tent from the inside with what gear we had, chiefly reed-sacks, so that there was scarcely room for ourselves. Built a "breakwater" of salt-blocks to windward of the tent. A quantity of flying sand piled into the lea of the "breakwater" without reaching the tent. Our situation was none too pleasant. Uncertain whether the tent would hold, and the driving sand outside seemed to be chokingly thick. Our camels were failing, our water supply almost finished, and at best three long days' march still to the depot. The flour would last some days.

The sandstorm was rather less violent in the afternoon, and we made a start. The continuance of the march was almost as poor going as before camping. But in the evening it was considerably calmer, and the evening camp was made easily enough. The storm died away. The following day it was ideal weather—good visibility, cool and lovely. The march went splendidly. We came on Mr. Chên's tracks—that is to say those of the main caravan. Thank heaven! Then Mr. Chên was safe. Had been a little uneasy lest he had been detained for some reason and not got across the salt crust before the storm. Perhaps he reached the depot in time; in any case he cannot very well have gone astray in the sandstorm. An hour later we were on the trail of the outward journey.

The following morning, March the 26th, the camels managed noiselessly to break loose while we were eating breakfast. Evidently meant to run on in advance along the trail to the depot and water. Banche had great difficulty in catching them again. Then loading and start. After a while we met a man from the depot with water, flour and meat in abundance. Sent to meet us by Mr. Chên according to arrangement. It was Nachiring the Tibetan. And he had with him the mail he had got in Tun-huang in January. I camped at once for the night and read my letters. Among them some clippings about the Andrée celebrations. Read them. And came to see the proportions of my Lop Nor journey. Insignificant! Thought before there had been some difficulties. But travelling under such favourable conditions in a country so well known before. Childsplay and bagatelle when I think of Andrée and his men.

March the 26th, Camp 116. I also had a letter from Mr. Chên by Nachiring, written before the severe sandstorm of the 24th. The main caravan had evidently got in to the depot in good time to get the camp in order before the storm; as soon as the camp was pitched and the camels had drunk and fed a little, Mr. Chên had sent a man, as arranged, with necessaries to meet me. Everything in order at the depot. Stores in good condition and the six sheep marvellously fat. (The reason appeared soon enough: Nachiring had been feeding the sheep on camel beans and had thus used up a third part of the stock so badly needed for the coming return journey to Tun-huang.) The main thing anyhow was that the stores were in good condition, including the flour and the sheep Nachiring had brought out from Tun-huang. Good thing my emergency instructions had not needed to be followed. It might well have happened that for some reason Nachiring had not been able to come back to the depot with the additional supplies from Tun-huang. In that event we would certainly have found a whole lot of miscellaneous stores at the depot, but neither flour nor meat, and the rice was practically at an end. (When we arranged the depot last Christmas we found that we had underestimated the flour consumption when we laid in provisions. Took, therefore, the whole supply with us to Lop Nor, including all that was to have been left at the depot, and Nachiring was, as I have said, to fetch the depot flour on his journey back.) When I parted from the main caravan by the Tarim on March the 17th, I had said that, in the event of Nachiring's flour and sheep, contrary to expectation, not being there, they were to slaughter a camel. We should in that event had to eat camel meat, though the idea was repellant. And they would have had to try eating camel-beans. Fortunately these extreme measures did not prove necessary; all was as it should be; the stores were adequate. On the other hand the report on Mr. Chên's camels was less satisfactory. The greater part in a bad way.

As soon as we made camp again after meeting Nachiring on March the 26th, I sent Banche and Nachiring back with the camels to water, pasture and rest at the depot. I stayed with Lang out in the barren desert for five days. Studies of the terraces of the shore line at the foot of Pei-shan. Fossil hunt—with negative result. Then we were fetched with camels.

On April the 2nd I returned to the depot, and am remaining there. All possible equipment needs to be repaired. Of our three tents only Mr. Chên's and mine are in any sort of condition. Only some fragments remain of the kitchen tent after the sandstorm, the greater part having been blown away. The caravan men's tent, which Lang and I had, could be put right again. Every kind of handicraft is going on here all day long. The tents, except the hopeless kitchen tent, have been pretty well mended. Pack-saddles, boxes, shoes and clothes are being repaired. I am collating maps and drawing up reports, after which the courier will ride to Tun-huang on our best camel, hire a horse there and continue his journey to Anhsi. Send off telegrams and letters. Then, if possible, find out whether Bohlin or Bexell is in the neighbourhood, then fetch my mail from Tun-huang and meet us somewhat westward of Khara-nor. He ought easily to ride from here to Anhsi in fourteen days, perhaps in nine or ten.

On March the 27th we unexpectedly met a human being

again, for the first time since December the 19th. Same man as then, a Qara Shahr Mongol in the Prince's service. Is riding between Qara Shahr and Tun-huang via Kuruk-tagh and ancient Greater Lop Nor, not along the river. Only one or two Mongols can get through now. The road closed. The only authorized way of entrance to Sinkiang from China proper is via Hami. All others closed. Violation punished by confiscation of beasts and baggage. Military guards in all quarters, including the districts north of Lop. The Mongol seems rather astonished that we should have been able to travel unmolested. But the way along the river is not used at all. The Mongol, who seems well informed and trustworthy, asserts that positively *only* the Konche-darya flows northward. The Tarim unchanged southward. He says further that the Konche-darya has flowed in that direction for about two hundred years.

P.S.—April the 6th, 6 a.m. Ink finished. My courier is ready to start, and I cannot delay any longer. Report and small jobs have taken up too much time. I have promised the comrades to let them hear of me in April, and time presses. Some of them are perhaps beginning to be uneasy in the Tun-huang district. The courier *must* go, though only the letters to Dr. Hedin and to De Geer are ready, a brief summary of the journey to Miss Hedin half written and letters home begun.

INDEX

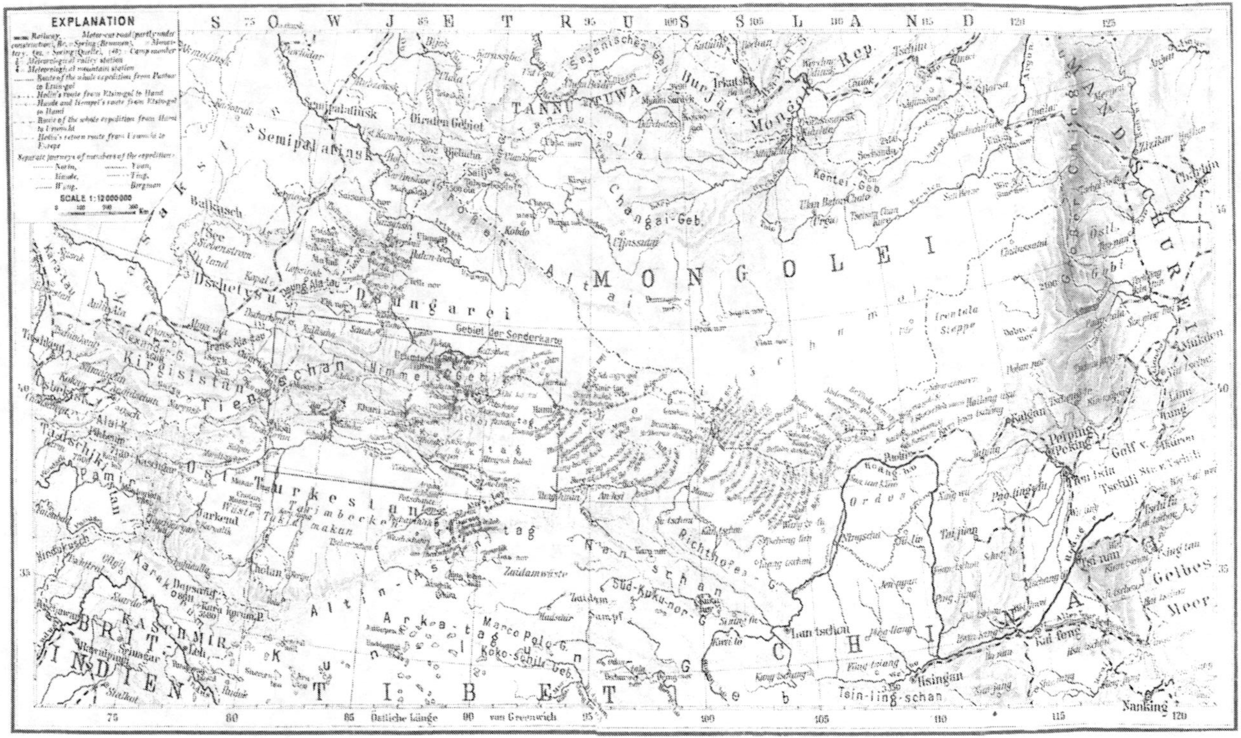
EXPLANATION
SCALE 1:12000000
S O W J E T R U S S L A N D
M O N G O L E I
T I B E T
C H I N A
M A N D S C H U R E I
Semipalatinsk
Balkasch
Dschetysu
Dsungarei
Gebiet der Sonderkarte
Kirgisistan
Tien-schan
Ost Turkestan
Pamir
KASCHMIR
BRIT.-INDIEN
TANNU TUWA
Changai-Geb.
Kentei-Geb.
Altin-tag
Zaidamwüste
Arka-tag
Marco Polo-G.
Koko-schile Geb.
Süd-Kuku-nor-G.
Richthofen-G.
Nan-schan
Ordos
Tsin-ling-schan
Peiping (Peking)
Kalgan
Mukden
Charbin
Gelbes Meer
Golf v. Tschili
Nanking
Östliche Länge von Greenwich